# PONTYPRIDD TROLLEYBUSES

## David R.H. Bowler

## Cover caption

The Pontypridd UDC coat of arms as used on the Council's trolleybuses throughout the lifetime of the system.

## Frontispiece

1930 English Electric SD6WTB trolleybus, fleet number 1, passes the 'Maltsters' public house on the east side of Victoria Bridge, Pontypridd, in this colourful interpretation by transport artist George (Sid) Cooper. Reproduced by kind permission of his son, David Cooper. Additional transport paintings by G.S. Cooper are available on www.cooperline.com

As a result of the Local Government England and Wales Act 1894, Pontypridd Urban District Council was formed that same year to replace the Pontypridd Local Board of Health and take on additional responsibilities in the parish of Pontypridd, Glamorgan. The Urban District Council ceased to exist on 31 March 1974, and was merged with part of the Caerphilly Urban District and the Rural Districts of Llantrisant and Llantwit Fardre and part of Cowbridge to form Taff Ely District Council. Taff Ely District Council and Cynon Valley District Council were amalgamated in 1996 to form the unitary authority Rhondda Cynon Taff County Borough Council.

This book is in no way to be considered as an official publication of Rhondda Cynon Taff County Borough Council.

A smartly turned out No. 10 pulls out to overtake a utility bodied motorbus still in matt grey livery and PUDC 1931 Bristol B motorbus 7 with Eastwood & Kenning B32D bodywork loading for Trehafod in Taff Street at the junction with Mill Street. (Cy Yandell collection)

Publication no. 101
Published in 2014 by Adam Gordon Books
ISBN 978-1-874422-97-6

Text © David R.H. Bowler
Maps and line illustrations © as credited
Photographs © as credited

Printed by Henry Ling Limited, at the Dorset Press, Dorchester DT1 1HD
Design and production by Trevor Preece (trevor@trpub.net) and Henry Ling Limited

# FOREWORD

Anyone arriving at Pontypridd Station or travelling through the town on the main Cardiff-Merthyr road from the 1930s to the mid 1950s could not fail to notice the Council's blue and white electric trolleybuses. They provided a fast and furious service through Taff Street all the way from the Albion Colliery at Cilfynydd to John Street in Treforest. I used them many times and they have a firm place in my youthful memories of Cilfynydd and 'Ponty'.

David Bowler, who lives in the valleys far away from Wales, has put a tremendous amount of time and effort into accurately recording an important aspect of Pontypridd as it was, now more than fifty years ago.

I'm very pleased to see yet another part of Pontypridd's history committed to paper.

*Stuart Burrows OBE, D. Mus.*
*Cardiff, February 2014*

*Stuart Burrows was born in William Street, Cilfynydd, birthplace of fellow opera star Sir Geraint Evans, politician Lord Merlyn Rees, and Welsh rugby international Glyn Davies, only a few yards from the trolleybus route, the terminus and of course their traffic objective the Albion Colliery. Initially a teacher, Stuart Burrows' talents as a tenor led to him joining the Welsh National Opera in the early 1960s followed by a long singing career in opera houses around the world. He enjoyed a 25-year association with the Royal Opera House Covent Garden, and his own BBC television series in the 1970s and 1980s. His uncle was Harold Ludlow, who joined Pontypridd UDC Transport Department in 1932 as a conductor and was appointed its General Manager in February 1958.*

# CONTENTS

# AUTHOR'S ACKNOWLEDGEMENTS

Although this is not the first record of a British trolleybus system that I have attempted, my research into Pontypridd's electric buses has brought with it a number of special challenges. Since the last trolleybus ran on 31 January 1957 the Urban District Council, which was responsible for the transport undertaking, has been abolished and amalgamated into Rhondda Cynon Taff County Borough, and the erstwhile Transport Department itself has ceased to exist, with no logical successor. Furthermore simple arithmetic shows that any former employee from the trolleybus era must now be at least 73 years of age, whilst any member of the public with meaningful memories of seeing Pontypridd's trolleybuses in operation is probably in their late 60s! Personal recollections are thus somewhat rare.

The foundations of this book are thus the historical documents covering the tramway and trolleybus era cared for by the efficient and helpful team at the Glamorgan Records Office in Cardiff, which is entrusted with the safekeeping of the erstwhile Pontypridd UDC archives. I am grateful to all the Records Office staff for their friendly assistance during my visits, but would particularly like to thank Laura Russell and Richard Morgan who went out of their way to help me on a number of occasions.

In the late 1960s the British Trolleybus Society approached all former and extant trolleybus operators and enquired if they had any trolleybus related archive material that they might wish to entrust to the society for posterity. A single positive response was received; that from Pontypridd UDC, and I have been able to sift through a hoard of internal memos and notes referring to the minutiae of almost half a century of the Transport Department's daily activities.

During the course of my investigations, I have received tremendous support from two gentlemen with a particular interest in the erstwhile Pontypridd system, although neither of them was professionally involved in public transport. In alphabetical order, Peter Smith, a trolleybus enthusiast who has spent his entire life in Cardiff, just a few miles from Pontypridd, and who is currently working on a long-term project to chronicle that city's former trolleybus system. Cy Yandell has had an interest in everything involving the former Pontypridd UDC Transport Department and the town in general throughout his life. His childhood and youthful memories of the trolleybuses and the characters, many friends and relations, that ran the service, has filled many gaps in my research and brought a number of recollections to life. To these two gentlemen I extend my most sincere thanks.

Hywel Matthews responsible for Local Studies at Pontypridd Library also warrants a special mention. He has made a huge effort to identify and forward me relevant information, and put me in contact with those who could help fill the gaps. The team at Pontypridd Museum have also been most helpful.

I am particularly grateful to those former Transport Department employees and their widely-scattered relations who have responded to my calls for assistance. These include Jessica Evans, George Glaves, Dr Alun Hughes, Bernard Stogden, Dr Shirley Ward, and Mrs J.M. Watkins (daughter of George Glaves).

Help has also been forthcoming from a number of other members of the trolleybus enthusiast fraternity, often in respect of very specific points or uncertainties, namely: David Beilby, Ashley Bruce, Geoff Burrows, John Carter, David Cooper, Roger Funnell, Philip Groves, Robert Hall, Dave Hall, David Harvey, Allen Janes, David Janes, Bernard Jefford, Martin Jenkins, Stephen Lockwood, Geoff Lumb, Roy Marshall, Alan Oxley, Colin Page, Bob Rowe, Phil Sposito, Chris Taylor, Hugh Taylor, Malcolm Wells, Francis Whitehead and John Whitehead. My sincere apologies to anybody I may have omitted.

I am both pleased and honoured that Dr Stuart Burrows, a leading light on the operatic scene, who originates from Cilfynydd, generously agreed to write the Foreword to my book, and I extend to him and his relations my thanks for permitting me to use information and photographs from their family records.

---

## Pontypridd UDC Transport 1905-1974

Remember the Trams
With their clanging bells
From Treforest to Ponty
And then on to Cil
The Driver with his coat
Huddled up to his neck
From the wind and the rain
Or a leak from Top Deck

The draughty old Oil Bus
Was rough for the crew
And the worst one for driving
Was old Twenty Two
No heaters no doors
They were cold to the touch
You'd be jerked off your feet
As they let up the clutch

From Ponty to the Coedcae,
To Porth and then back
Full of coal black colliers
With Tommy Box and Jack
As we pushed through them all
With our Bell-punch and Rack
By the and of the shift
We were almost as black

The Trolleys came
With their silent glide
They were easy to drive
And they gave a good ride
But suddenly the arms
Would go flying in the Air
The power lines were down
There'd be sparks everywhere

The little old Mess Room
Was always a joke
With the old fashioned fire place
Piled up with coke
If some-one came in
And gave it a poke
You'd be drinking your tea
Through a mouthful of smoke

Those were the days
When your friends were all true
There was always someone
Ready to help you.
To swop shifts or change rest-days
Or holding the fort
In those hard happy days
With old Ponty Transport

*Viv Roberts*

# INTRODUCTION

[...page v ... the second sentence of the 4  paragraph should read "It was one of just two trolleybus operators in the UK to receive vehicle loans from more than one operator (Kingston upon Hull and Portsmouth) during the Second World War."[The other operator was Newcastle upon Tyne Corporation Transport which had trolleybus loans from Bournemouth and Brighton.]

n 1963 a comment in the occasional series of articles on buses in the erstwhile *Meccano Magazine* attracted my attention to possibly the first-ever book produced with the trolleybus enthusiast in mind. *Trolleybus Trails* compiled by James Joyce was a brief survey of British trolleybus systems past and present. The chapter headed "Ireland, Wales, Scotland" contained less than a page about Pontypridd, but was accompanied by a photograph taken by Bob Mack of a double-deck trolleybus heading south along Cilfynydd Road. I was impressed by the attractive mountainous background, unaware that the site of the Albion Colliery was only a few hundred yards away, and resolved to visit the town one day and seek the remains of the trolleybus system.

That single photograph was the catalyst to this attempt to produce a detailed record of the diminutive, one route trolleybus system that served Pontypridd from 1930 until 1957. My first attempt to visit the town was thwarted by the A470 by-pass, and I finally only made it almost half a century after the last trolleybus had run. And what an attractive little town, full of character, it proved to be!

Pontypridd operated trolleybuses on but a single 3.3-mile-long route although there were ambitious plans for expansion. Nonetheless much of interest was packed into this tiny system.

Pontypridd UDC was one of just three Urban District Councils in the UK to run trolleybuses in its own right — the other two were Aberdare and Ramsbottom — and the last to operate such vehicles (Eston UDC operated the Tees-side Railless Traction Board jointly with Middlesbrough Corporation). It was the sole trolleybus operator in the UK to receive vehicle loans from more than one operator (Kingston upon Hull and Portsmouth) during the Second World War. Turning to operational matters, not only was Pontypridd unusual in running mainly single-deck trolleybuses until after the War, but it was one of just two undertakings to own vehicles manufactured by the Bristol company. Traction power during most of the system's lifetime was, foresightedly, generated by burning the town's refuse! Pontypridd was the last user of trolley wheel current collectors on trolleybuses, and no less than 15 out of a total of 17 trolleybuses operated were sold for further use by other undertakings.

In the early 1930s Pontypridd UDC firmly intended to convert its final tram route to trolleybus operation with the aim of connecting up with a network of new routes foreseen to replace the 21 miles of tramways operated by the Rhondda Tramways Co., Ltd. Alas, these intentions, together with repeated plans for an extension to Rhydyfelin and possibly the Treforest Industrial Estate and Nantgarw, never became reality. Thus we are left to ponder on what might have been if Pontypridd had become the hub of an interurban trolleybus network in the Valleys of South Wales.

Today parts of *'Ponty'* have been amputated from the rest of the town by the afore-mentioned by-pass, the local council has been abolished and amalgamated into Rhondda Cynon Taff, and the erstwhile Transport Department has disappeared entirely. As in much of the UK, political ideology has seen urban transport entrusted to a mixture of national giants and minor firms, both of whom are only interested in profit maximisation rather than in providing an all-day, all-week, quality public service.

As slowly but surely the population of Britain belatedly begins to realise that the internal combustion engine and the private car not only create gridlock traffic congestion, but are also destroying the very environment that makes life possible on "spaceship earth", could there be a new future for electric public transport in Wales and Britain as in so many other countries?

*David R.H. Bowler*
*Pfungen, Switzerland*
*February 2014*

## Terms and expressions

For the benefit of non-enthusiasts the more obscure terms used in connection with trolleybuses, and in particular the trolleybus overhead line installations, are explained:

**Arc shute**
A method of *arc* suppression that extinguishes *arcs* by channeling them into chambers above the contacts.

**Bracket arm:**
A tubular steel support bolted to the upper section of the *traction pole* at right angles and projecting over the road, from which to suspend the *trolley wire* as an alternative to a *span wire*. Usually employed where the length of *span wire* between traction poles would be unduly long, or along straight stretches on narrow roads to reduce the number of traction poles.

**Converter:**
Rotating electromechanical device, like a motor or a generator, used to convert alternating current (AC) into direct current (DC).

**Composite (body):**
In this form of bodywork, the main framework constructed from hardwood, reinforced as necessary with steel flitches, supports and brackets, and panelled in metal.

**Curve segment:**
A special curved fitting replacing several separate *pull-offs* in the *running wire,* which gave a smoother passage for the *trolleyheads* on sharp curves.

**Drop light:**
A type of opening side window employed in the main side bays of the lower and upper saloons of bus bodies whereby the entire pane of glass dropped downwards into a recess within the side panels below.

**Frog:**
The overhead line equipment equating to railway points where one pair of running wires left or joined another, known as facing frogs where the lines diverged, or trailing frogs where the lines converged. Facing frogs were operated either by hand (the conductor leaving the vehicle and pulling an operating handle, connected by cable to the frog mechanism, on an adjacent *traction pole*) or automatically by the trolleyheads of a trolleybus energising a solenoid through a contact fitted to the overhead line a short distance before the frog. All facing frogs in Pontypridd were hand-operated. Trailing frogs were spring loaded.

**Half-drop:**
A type of opening side window employed in the main side bays of the lower and upper saloons of bus bodies whereby the window was divided horizontally into two, the upper pane of glass dropped downwards outside the fixed lower pane.

**Hanger:**
The attachment which, by use of soldering or a mechanical grip, also known as an "ear", and a porcelain insulator, supported the *trolley wire* beneath a b*racket arm* or *span wire.*

**Line-light:**
A lamp on the driver's cab dashboard that glowed continually when the traction power supply was available. The lamp would accordingly cease to glow briefly when the trolleybus passed beneath insulators in the overhead wiring that interrupted the power supply but go out and stay out in the case of a dewirement.

**Metal framed (body):**
In this form of bodywork, a steel or aluminium frame was built with timber packers and wooden inserts to accept the many screws needed to hold the interior finishers and exterior panels. Also referred to as an "all metal" body.

**Pull-off:**
A *span wire* or wires providing additional support or securing a correct alignment of the trolley wires on bends under the correct tension, creating a curve consisting of a series of short straight sections.

**Quarter light:**
A separate, roughly triangular, side window situated between the driver's cab door or main cab side window(s) and the front pillar.

**Railless:**
See *trolleybus.*

**Rectifier:**
A device for converting alternating current (AC) into direct current (DC).

**Reversing triangle:**
An arrangement in the overhead line to enable vehicles to turn by means of a three-point reversing procedure into and out of a side turning.

| | |
|---|---|
| Rosette: | An anchor fitting, rag-bolted (an iron pin with barbs on its shanks to retain it in place) or otherwise fixed to the face of a building, used instead of a *traction pole*. To which a *span wire* or wires were attached. |
| Route: | The way or series of roads and streets between two points. |
| Running wire: | See *trolley wire*. |
| Section insulator: | An overhead line assembly containing a short length of non-conductive material of the same profile as the *trolley wire* to break the route up into electrically isolated half-mile sections as required by law in the United Kingdom. |
| Service: | The timetabled frequency of vehicles identified by a service number along a stipulated route. |
| Span wire: | The load-bearing wire erected across the width of the roadway (usually between opposite or diagonally opposite *traction poles*, but sometimes anchored to buildings by a wall *rosette*) from which the trolley wires were suspended. |
| Spreadover: | A working day made up of several inconsecutive periods of duty covering only the busy traffic periods. |
| Trackless: | See *trolleybus*. |
| Traction pole: | A steel tubular pole used to support bracket arms, gantries and span wires, usually about 31ft long, set 6ft into the ground at the roadside at a 5° rake away from the road (to compensate for the weight supported) and embedded in concrete. There were four grades of pole – light, medium, heavy and extra heavy, varying in girth and used according to the weight and/or strain they were expected to carry. |
| Trolleybase: | The point at which the *trolleypoles* were attached to the roof or a roof-mounted gantry of the vehicle. The trolleybase enabled the *trolleypoles* to move laterally and vertically, whilst large inclined springs, latterly more or |

| | |
|---|---|
| | less parallel to the *trolleypoles*, provided the tension necessary to keep the under-running wheel in contact with running wires. |
| Trolleybooms: | See *trolleypoles*. |
| Trolleybus: | A public passenger transport vehicle with rubber tyres which travels along ordinary roads and is powered by electricity that is collected from a pair of conductor wires hung above the road by means of under-running wheels or skids attached to sprung *trolleypoles*. Contrary to a tramcar, a trolleybus does not require tracks laid in the road surface and was accordingly known initially as a *railless* or *trackless*. |
| Trolleyhead: | The retention and swivel device at the extreme end of each *trolleypole* which held the under-running current collecting wheel. |
| Trolleypoles: | The roof mounted tubular booms which, by means of a sprung base permitting lateral and vertical movement, kept the under-running wheel in contact with the running wires in order to draw current to propel the vehicle. |
| Trolley vehicle: | The official term used in legislative documents for a *trolleybus*. |
| Trolley wire: | The conductor wire along which the under-running wheels ran. The pair of wires was kept laterally apart and suspended about 20ft above the surface of the road. The wire nearest the centre of the road had positive polarity, and that nearest the edge of the road had negative polarity. |
| Twin line hanger: | A spacer assembly designed to clamp the two *trolley wires* the correct distance apart (generally 2ft) when supported by *bracket arms* or *span wire*. The *trolley wire* itself was held by "ears" bolted to and insulated from the hanger assembly. |
| Turning circle: | An arrangement in the overhead line to turn vehicles back along the route by means of a U-turn. |

# Abbreviations

The following abbreviations are used in the text:

| | |
|---|---|
| AA | Anti-Attrition Metal Co. Ltd. |
| AC | Alternating Current |
| ADR | Alexandra (Newport and South Wales) Docks & Railway |
| AEC | Associated Equipment Company |
| AEU | Amalgamated Engineering Union |
| ARP | Air Raid Precautions |
| ATC | Air Training Corps |
| BET | The British Electric Traction Co. Ltd. |
| BoT | Board of Trade |
| BR | Barry Railway |
| BS | British Standard |
| BTC | British Transport Commission |
| BTCC | Bristol Tramways and Carriage Co. Ltd. |
| BTH | British Thomson-Houston |
| CR | Cardiff Railway |
| DC | Direct Current |
| E&TD | Electricity and Tramways Department |
| EE | English Electric Co. Ltd. |
| ETC | Electricity and Tramways Committee |
| ETU | Electrical Trades Union |
| f.s.s. | Feet per second per second |
| FP | Feeder Pillar |
| GPO | General Post Office |
| GWR | Great Western Railway |
| hp | horse power |
| LPTB | London Passenger Transport Board |
| MCCW | Metropolitan-Cammell Carriage, Wagon and Finance Company |
| MoS | Ministry of Supply |
| MoT | Ministry of Transport (known as the Ministry of War Transport between 1939 and 1946, and the Ministry of Transport and Civil Aviation between 1946 and 1959) |
| MoWT | Ministry of War Transport |
| MP | Member of Parliament |
| MPTA | Municipal Passenger Transport Association |
| NFVT | National Federation of Vehicle Trades |
| NJIC | National Joint Industrial Council |
| OAP | Old Age Pensioner |
| pa | per annum |
| PAYE | Pay As You Enter |
| PCNR | Pontypridd, Caerphilly & Newport Railway |
| PRVT | Pontypridd and Rhondda Valley Tramway Company |
| PSV | Public Service Vehicle |
| PUDC | Pontypridd Urban District Council |
| PUDCT | Pontypridd Urban District Council Transport |
| RT | Rhondda Tramways Co. Ltd. |
| RTC | Regional Traffic Commissioner |
| SWALEB | South Wales Electricity Board |
| TGWU | Transport and General Workers Union |
| TVR | Taff Vale Railway |
| UDC | Urban District Council |
| UK | United Kingdom |
| VE | Victory in Europe |
| VJ | Victory in Japan |

At various points in the text use has been made of a standard code (which will be familiar to enthusiasts) when referring to the type of body and seating capacity of a particular type of trolleybus. The code usually consists of two figures separated by an oblique stroke to indicate, respectively the upper and lower-deck seating capacity. Letters are prefixed to indicate body type and suffixed to indicate doorway positions. The elements of this code used in connection with Pontypridd's trolleybuses are as follows:

| | | |
|---|---|---|
| Prefix letter(s): | B | Single-deck bus |
| | H | Highbridge double-deck layout i.e. with centre as opposed to side gangway in upper saloon. |
| | U | Utility |
| Figures: | | Indicate the number of seats in the upper and lower saloons respectively. |
| Suffix letter(s): | C | Centre doorway position. |
| | R | Rear doorway with open platform. |

For example, Karrier Ws 8-9 (GNT301-302) were UH30/26R, i.e. utility highbridge bodywork with 30 seats upstairs, 26 seats downstairs and a single rear doorway with open platform.

## Conversion Factors: Units and Currency

During the period in which the trolleybuses operated, Britain used Imperial units of measure and pre-decimal currency. These traditional units are used throughout this book as no useful purpose would be served in providing conversions in the text. The following table will be of use to readers wishing to convert any figures quoted to metric units and decimal currency.

| | |
|---|---|
| Length: | 1 inch (in.) = 25.4 centimetres (cm)<br>1 foot (ft) = 12 inches = 30.5 centimetres (cm)<br>1 yard (yd) = 3 feet = 91.4 centimetres<br>1 chain = 22 yards = 20.1 metres (mt)<br>1 furlong = 10 chains = 22 yards = 201 metres<br>1 mile = 8 furlongs = 1.6 kilometres (km) |
| Area: | 1 acre = 4,840 square yards = 4,046.86 square metres |
| Weight: | 1 quarter (qtr) = 127 kilogrammes (kg)<br>1 hundredweight (cwt) = 4 quarters = 50.8 kg<br>1 imperial ton = 20 hundredweights (cwt) = 1.02 metric tonnes |
| Currency: | 1 penny (d) = 2.4 pence (p)<br>1 shilling (s) = 12d = 5 pence (p)<br>1 pound (£) = 20 shillings (s) = 240d = 100p |

# THE WILD WEST

*The town of Pontypridd grew up in the steeply-sided valleys in a natural amphitheatre around the confluence of the River Rhondda and the River Taff (which flow south-eastwards to the Bristol Channel) some 12 miles northwest of Cardiff, the capital and largest city of Wales. The birth and expansion of the town is inextricably linked to the mineral wealth of the area.*

Pontypridd lies towards the eastern end of an elongated carboniferous sedimentary basin which makes up the South Wales Coalfield, extending almost 90 miles from Pontypool in the east to St. Bride's Bay in the west. Geological folding and faulting since the sediments were laid down has brought many important coal seams closer to the surface where they are relatively easy to reach. The Pontypridd area was particularly known for steam coals. The surface geology is typified by another sedimentary rock, the blue-grey Pennant Sandstones, much used in local building construction, including the characteristic terraces of miners' houses, and which around Pontypridd rise to bleak uplands up to 1,200 ft above sea level between the steep-sided valleys.

In the midst of this sparsely populated area containing little but scattered farms, the River Taff was sufficiently shallow some 600 yards north of its confluence with the River Rhondda as to offer a ford. There were a number of attempts to replace the ford with a wooden bridge and a settlement sprung up, known in Welsh as *Pont-yr-Hen-dy-Pridd ("bridge of the old earthen house")* named after the workmen's hut nearby. It is this name, albeit shortened and anglicised, that survives today. A more permanent structure, the longest single-arch stone bridge in Europe at that time, was constructed across the river in 1756 and stands to this day. The hamlet that grew on both sides of the river became known, appropriately, as Newbridge.

About 13 miles to the north at Merthyr Tydfil, the presence of iron ore in the coal measures with limestone nearby led to the birth in the mid 18th century of an infant iron industry. Once it became possible to move quantities of raw material and finished products more easily, the surrounding mineral wealth was to ensure the growth of a substantial local iron and steel industry of world-renown, and the catalyst for the industrial revolution throughout the Valleys.

In an effort to supply markets further afield and reduce the cost of transport of their products, a group of Merthyr ironmasters financed construction of a canal to the sea. Work on the Glamorganshire Canal between Merthyr Tydfil and Cardiff started in 1790, the southern portion between Abercynon and Cardiff through Pontypridd being completed in 1794, and the remaining 9 miles to Merthyr in 1798.

In 1790 Dr Richard Griffiths discovered coal to the west of Newbridge in Gyfeillion and collieries soon followed in Cilfynydd, Graig, Hopkinstown and Trehafod to fuel, literally, the industrial growth that followed completion of the northern portion of the Glamorganshire Canal enabling the easy supply of raw materials from the Cynon and Merthyr Valleys.

At the end of the century the Taff Vale Ironworks were set up to the south at Treforest. In 1818 the Newbridge Chain Cable and Anchor Works, later known as Brown, Lenox & Co., was founded alongside the canal in Ynysangharad. The firm was a major supplier to the Royal Navy and bridge builders, becoming the largest single employer in Pontypridd.

The Glamorganshire Canal's success soon led to congestion north of Abercynon. To provide some relief a horse-drawn tramroad paralleling the canal between Abercynon and Merthyr opened in 1802. In 1809 a ¾-mile tramway, the course of which was subsequently renamed Broadway, opened from Dr Griffiths' Trehafod coal pit to Treforest, where it connected with the mile long Doctor's Canal which in turn joined the Glamorganshire Canal in 1813. Empty wagons on the tramway carried people home from the Treforest and Pontypridd markets at 3d fare.

In 1835 the owners of the Dowlais and the Plymouth Iron Works, in Merthyr, asked I.K. Brunel to estimate the cost of a railway to Cardiff and Bute Docks to ease transport and reduce costs. Based on the £190,649 estimate Parliamentary approval was sought; Royal Assent to the foundation of the Taff Vale Railway Company (TVR) being given on 21 June 1836. Construction started immediately with the Cardiff – Newbridge – Abercynon section opening on 9 October 1840 and the remaining portion to Merthyr on 12 April 1841. It was constructed to 4ft 8½in. gauge and followed the valley of the River Taff with an impressive skew stone arch viaduct spanning the River Rhondda and Mill Street just to the north of today's Pontypridd Station. That same year Newbridge became a junction when a line running northwestwards was opened through Porth to Dinas in the Rhondda. Thereafter the TVR expanded its network to the north and northwest of Newbridge along the valleys of the Afon Cynon, Nant Clydach, Afon Rhondda Fawr and Rhondda Fach serving a growing number of collieries. The railway enabled this part of the South Wales Coalfield to become the world's single most important coal exporting area and by 1850 the TVR was carrying 600,000 tons of coal pa and paying a 6% dividend.

Even then Newbridge was still a village consisting of little more than one long street extending from the bridge over the River Taff to the railway station, with a few houses at the beginnings of Mill Street (leading northwest towards the Rhondda) and along the tramroad which ran through the present Sardis Road across the top of the Tumble towards Treforest. In 1857 a new three arch road bridge across the River Taff, the Victoria Bridge, was opened next to the original stone bridge which now became known as the Old Bridge. This made the name of Newbridge inaccurate and it was decided to revert to an anglicised version of the Welsh name: Pontypridd.

The importance of coal to urban development and population growth throughout South Wales cannot be overestimated. The dependency of world industry and transport on steam coal ensured that extracts from the surrounding area, known for their high calorific value, were in great demand. Mining began in earnest in the mid-1800s and the population rose dramatically as migrants, eager to secure a regular job, arrived from all over Britain to meet the insatiable demand for labour. Between 1891 and 1901 Pontypridd's population rose from 13,000 to 20,000.

Between 1855 and 1913 the annual output of the South Wales Coalfield rose from 8.5 million tons to a peak of some 57 million tons, or a fifth of the UK's entire output, provided by 620 coal mines employing 232,000 men. Pontypridd became totally dependent on the coal industry, and was thus economically exposed when the coalfield went into decline in the first decade of the 20th century as the more accessible seams were depleted. The major local collieries were: Albion, Bertie, Hafod, Cilfynnd, Dinas Isha, Penygraig, Great Western, Hafod, Maritime, & Newbridge Rhondda. Although the levels of extraction recovered after the First World War, economic hardship struck the coalfield and continued irregularly thereafter. Output gradually fell to 45 million tons in 1930, 35 million in 1939 and 20 million in 1945, increasing to some 25 million tons by 1957 when it once again began to fall.

Coal and coke exports from Cardiff and Penarth rose from 2,886,000 tons in 1874 to 7,774,828 tons in 1882 but railway and dock congestion meant that mines had to regularly cease production. Pontypridd was the focal point for the TVR's coal traffic destined for the coast, handling as many as 250 trains daily. In order to cope with this volume of traffic the line south of Pontypridd was subsequently quadrupled. The TVR also operated passenger trains from the beginning. In due course services between Cardiff and Merthyr, Treherbert and Swansea ran via Pontypridd which became renowned for having the world's longest station platform ($\frac{1}{3}$ mile).

The Glamorganshire Canal's fortunes declined once the TVR opened whilst mining subsidence led to leakages from the upper section. Frustrated by the railway's stranglehold on moving coal from the Rhondda, the Marquis of Bute, who owned Cardiff Docks, purchased both the Aberdare and Glamorganshire Canals in 1883 with the intention of replacing them with a railway. The section of the Glamorganshire Canal between Abercynon and Cilfynydd closed in 1915 and that between Cilfynydd and Cardiff in 1942.

Also in 1883 a group of Rhondda coal owners, headed by Ocean Collieries, applied for powers to build a dock at Barry, south-west of Cardiff, with railway access to the coalfields but the application was defeated by TVR objections. A renewed attempt succeeded in 1884. The 19-mile long, heavily engineered Barry Railway (BR) ran from Barry to Cadoxton Junction, 5 miles southwest of Cardiff, and then followed the west side of the River Taff valley with stations at Treforest High Level, Pontypridd Graig and Trehafod, where there was a junction with the TVR. It opened in February 1889 and the docks in July. As the BR undercut the TVR by up to 43% the port was immediately successful: in 1890-2 nearly one third as much coal passed through it as through Cardiff and by 1914 Barry was handling more than Cardiff and Penarth put together.

In July 1884 the Alexandra (Newport and South Wales) Docks & Railway opened a line (the Pontypridd, Caerphilly & Newport Railway (PCNR)) between Caerphilly, which they reached over the Brecon & Merthyr Railway, and Pontypridd joining the TVR just south of Pontypridd Station. In 1887 passenger services started and halts in and around Pontypridd were progressively opened at Glyntaff, Treforest, Dynea and Upper Boat on the east side of the River Taff.

By May 1891 the Cardiff Railway (CR) extension from Heath Junction to the north of Cardiff on the Rhymney Railway's Cardiff – Caerphilly line, through Whitchurch to Tongwynlais and then along the east side of the River Taff as far as Rhydyfelin, was complete. A skew bridge across the river gave access to a junction with the TVR just south of Treforest Low Level. Although the junction had been laid, the TVR purchased a strip of land to the east of their line claiming that they were intending to build sidings there which, despite court cases, forestalled CR access to Pontypridd and the TVR mainline thereby cutting out further competition.

The TVR line to Abercynon, Aberdare and Merthyr, ran on the opposite side of the Taff Valley. to Cilfynydd. When the Albion Colliery was sunk there in 1884, it was necessary to build a new branch line which left the main line just north of Coedpenmaen, crossed the River Taff over an iron viaduct and then ran alongside the Glamorganshire Canal to the colliery. Passenger services to Cilfynydd began in June 1900 ceasing on 12 September 1932.

Following the 1922 amalgamations, all the railways in and around Pontypridd became the responsibility of the Great Western Railway (GWR). In 1930 a short connection was laid between the Barry Railway at Tonteg Junction and the TVR at Treforest Junction with passenger trains diverted into Pontypridd TVR Station. The former BR between Tonteg Junction and Trehafod was subsequently closed in two stages: Tonteg-Pwllgwaun in 1951 and Pwllgwaun-Trehafod in 1956.

Road communications played no part in the area's economic development; links to neighbouring valleys and towns being limited to the Merthyr – Cardiff turnpike built in 1767 or the mountain ridgeways used by packhorses carrying wares in panniers. There was not even a road from Newbridge into the Rhondda. Only in the second half of the 19th century were uncoordinated efforts made by individual colliery owners to construct or improve roads close to their collieries. whilst no agreement could be reached on proposals for a 50ft wide road between Pontypridd and Porth with a similarly wide network extending up the Rhondda Fach and Rhondda Fawr. There was also an almost total absence of transport links between the Valleys until the 1920s, many of the lateral routes being cul-de-sacs.

Despite its early reputation as the main settlement in an unruly and explosively growing "Coal Klondyke" or "Wild West", the 19th century left Pontypridd with both culture and attractive buildings. St Catherine's Church with its fine spire was built in 1868, the Town Hall and Market Buildings in 1885, the Public Library and the Town Hall Theatre in 1890, and in 1905 the Municipal Building with its fine Council Chamber. Many of the old buildings in Pontypridd are decorated with fine stonework and constructed from locally quarried distinctive blue pennant granite-hard stone.

During the period under review the town of Pontypridd was administered by an Urban District Council in the County of Glamorgan; this UDC was the municipal passenger transport and trolleybus operator. The Pontypridd UDC Transport Department ceased to exist in name in 1974 following local government changes but operations continued albeit somewhat rationalised as Taff Ely Borough Council Transport Department. As a result of the 1985 Transport Act which effectively abolished municipal transport an 'arms-length' limited company, Taff-Ely Transport Ltd., was formed on 28 October 1986. Aggressive unrestrained competition led to the company's insolvency and it was acquired by National Welsh on 5 September 1988. Taff Ely District Council and Cynon Valley District Council were amalgamated in 1996 to form today's unitary authority Rhondda Cynon Taff County Borough Council.

# THE TRAMWAY ERA

*The first steps to providing a regular public service for passengers along the streets of Pontypridd were taken in 1882 when the Pontypridd and Rhondda Valley Tramway Company (PRVT) was founded. The company planned to operate a tramway between Treherbert, at the northwest extremity of the Rhondda Valley (Rhondda Fawr), running south-eastwards through Treorchy, Tonypandy and Porth, to the Bridge Street end of Taff Street, Pontypridd.*

The Pontypridd and Rhondda Valleys Tramways Order, 1882 stipulated that the track gauge for the 12 miles 30 chain line was not to exceed 3ft 6in. although there were no restrictions as to the type of motive power that could be used. There was a requirement to provide cheap workmen's fares and operate at least two trips each morning and evening.

Although a 3ft 6in. gauge single track with passing loop line was constructed between Porth Square and the north end of Taff Street, Pontypridd, the low railway bridge on the TVR Rhondda line across Rhondda Road prevented horse trams continuing beyond this point into the town. The company was undersubscribed and in October 1887 the Welsh tramway *entrepreneur* Solomon Andrews agreed to operate the line for three years. An opening ceremony took place on 26 March 1888 and services commenced the next day. By July 1888 there were 15 journeys a day and 22 by the beginning of 1889.

In 1889 the company was fined for not keeping the track in good repair. During 1890 the company ceased operating, and a "receiver, manager and liquidator" were appointed. Until the financial situation could be sorted out Andrews continued to run the line, retaining the fares but paying all revenue in excess of 8½d per mile to the liquidator. The concern was put up for auction but did not reach its reserve price. On 18 August 1891 one of Solomon Andrews' companies, the South Wales Property, Machinery and Carriage Co. bought the line.

On 24 June 1898 the British Electric Traction Company (BET) purchased the tramway as a going concern for £12,000. In May 1899 the BET informed Pontypridd UDC of their plans to electrify the line and extend it through the town to Cilfynydd. The UDC agreed to support the plans subject to the BET's commitment to widen certain streets, lay a substantial track foundation and road surface, and use electricity from the UDC generating station. Owing to objections from the TVR, whose Coedpenmaen branch from Pont Shon Norton Junction through Cilfynydd to Ynysydwr Junction would be paralleled by the tramway extension, from Glamorgan County Council, Rhondda District Council, Pontypridd Waterworks and the Glamorgan Canal Co., amongst others, the December 1900 application to the Board of Trade (BoT) for a Provisional Order was refused.

In February 1902 horse tram services were reduced to the statutory two workmen's cars each morning and evening due to the death of most of the equine motive power, and the BET offered to sell the PRVT to the Pontypridd and Rhondda UDCs. The councils, however, preferred to wait as, under the provisions of the 1870 Tramways Act, a local authority could compulsorily purchase privately-owned tramways in its area after 21 years and

thereafter every seven years. The first statutory right to buy the PRVT was in August 1903 by which time it is understood that services had ceased completely.

The PRVT initially asked for £15,000, to include all machinery, rolling stock etc.; however, by September 1903 they were prepared to accept £12,100 to be divided equally between the two UDCs. The General Manager of Leeds Corporation Tramways, John Hamilton, was engaged by Pontypridd UDC to value that part of the PRVT in their area. He suggested £2,842 which was deemed unacceptable by the company. The UDC increased their offer to £4,644, then to £5,000 and finally to £5,500 which was accepted and the sale completed on 31 October 1904.

In October 1900, Pontypridd UDC's consulting electrical engineer recommended that powers to operate municipal electric tramways should be sought to prevent private enterprise making similar moves. Should the UDC subsequently decide not to construct and/or operate its own system, they would be in a good position to negotiate a lease with any suitable company. Although the population at that time was only about 36,000, the council boldly *"Resolved unanimously that application be made to the Board of Trade on or before 22 December 1900 for a provisional order under the Tramways Act 1870 to authorise the Pontypridd Urban District Council to construct and work tramways within the Urban District of Pontypridd in the County of Glamorgan"*, and a public notice appeared of the council's intentions to construct 3ft 6in. gauge electric tramways along the following routes:

1.    Under the east side of the Taff Vale Bridge, Rhondda Road, Mill Street, Taff Street, Victoria Bridge, Coedpenmaen Road, Pontshonnorton Road and Cilfynydd Road to Cilfynydd (Albion Colliery Road).

1a.   Double track loop around Market Street.

2.    High Street, Union Street, Rickard Street, Wood Road, Park Street.

2a.   Single track loop along Station Street.

3.    Tramroad, Fothergill Street, Park Street (where there would be a junction with Route 2).

4.    Ynysangharad Street, Pentrebach Road, Cardiff Road, Castle Street, Park Street (where there would be a junction with Route 2).

4a.   Single line loop from Coedpenmaen Road to Ynysangharad Street.

4b.   Cardiff Road, Tramroad (where there would be a junction with Route 3).

The BoT granted a Provisional Order in April 1901 but excluded the Mill Street and Taff Street portions of Route 1, due to frontager's opposition, and Route 2, due to the gradients in Rickard Street and Wood Road, and the Tramroad portion of Route 3. The Parliamentary Bill confirming the Provisional Order was passed and received Royal Assent on 17 August 1901 as the Pontypridd Urban District Council Tramways Order 1901.

This did not provide a coherent, contiguous route through the town, not least due to the private ownership of Market Street and the Tramroad. Agreement was reached with the Market Company that on their request trams would not run along Market Street during the hours of the twice weekly market, whilst the Tramroad owner was prepared to lease the UDC a strip of land for 30 years at £200 pa, provided that there was no interference with the working of the Tramroad. Based on this, in August 1902 the Pontypridd Urban District Council Tramways Order 1902 authorised a number of additional routes but still not the Mill Street line:

1.  Taff Street with single track loop around Market Street,
2.  An end-on connection from the above, along the Tramroad to the previously authorised track in Park Street,
3.  From Pentrebach Road, over the Glamorganshire Canal to Cemetery Road, terminating at a new depot in Gas Works Road,
4.  A connection from Pentrebach Road, across the River Taff over the Machine Bridge to a junction with the Tramroad.

Despite the objections of Mill Street traders the third attempt to gain electric tramway access to Rhondda Road and Porth succeeded. Several properties in Mill Street between the junction with Taff Street and High Street, and the TVR Rhondda

One of Pontypridd's first double-deck trams, uncanopied open-top No. 8 built in 1904 by Brush and mounted on J.G. Brill Co. 22E maximum traction bogie trucks is seen in Market Street, Pontypridd, going north to Cilfynydd via the Market Square. Trams going south to Treforest traversed Taff Street, which runs parallel to Market Street. Trams could only use Market Street on days other than the twice weekly market (held on Wednesday and Saturday). The majority of the buildings remain today, including that shown here housing Hepworths on the corner of Church Street and the impressive block with the deep awnings beyond. This coloured sepia print features the Pontypridd UDC arms in the right-hand corner. (Postcard without publisher's details: David Bowler collection)

line viaduct, had to be purchased for road widening purposes; however, the greatest problem remained the narrow roadway beneath the railway at the Colliers Arms. As the TVR opposed every effort to widen the road, the council built a new road carried on a viaduct over the banks of the River Taff passing beneath a different arch of the railway viaduct providing greater clearance. The Pontypridd Urban District Council Act 1903 received Royal Assent on 21 July 1903.

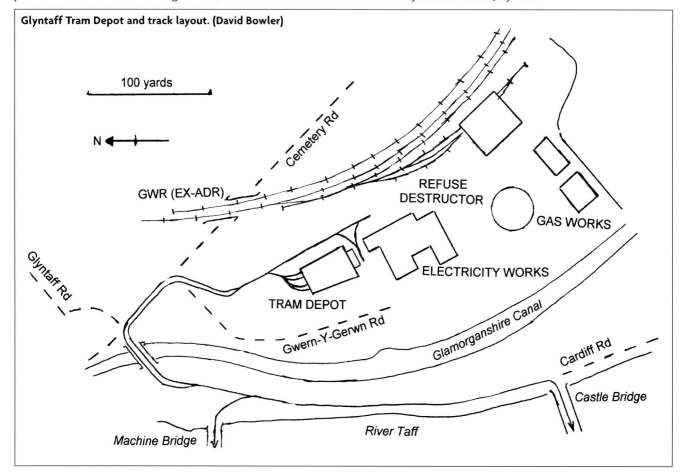

**Glyntaff Tram Depot and track layout. (David Bowler)**

Short top-covered car 31 built by Brush in 1920 is seen in Pontypridd Road, Porth, ready for departure back to Mill Street, Pontypridd. The tram carries an advertisement for Thomas & Evans, a firm which owned a sizable number of grocery shops located throughout South Wales, and who had their headquarters and production facilities in Porth. Thomas & Evans also owned the Corona brand of soft drinks that were well-known throughout the UK during the tram and trolleybus era. (David Bowler collection [photographer's name not recorded])

In January 1903 Pontypridd UDC formed an Electricity and Tramways Committee to co-ordinate and direct progress on the construction of the tramway and a generating station for both traction and other purposes. Work commenced in July 1903 and in November 1904 John Teasdel was appointed Electrical Engineer and Tramways Manager.

Pontypridd's first electric tram route opened on 6 March 1905. It ran between the south end of Park Street (John Street), Treforest, just to the north of the TVR railway bridge, and Cilfynydd, Albion Colliery, by way of Park Street, Fothergill Street, the private road then known as the Tramroad (renamed Broadway in 1921), High Street, Taff Street, Victoria Bridge, Bridge Street, Corn Stores Hill, Coedpenmaen Road and Cilfynydd Road. The route was 3 miles 560 yards long and subject to sharp curves, a number of steep hills and narrow streets. Just to the south of Treforest Station (TVR) a depot access line branched off the route, followed Forest Road, crossed Castle Inn Bridge over the River Taff and then ascended the steep, curving Cemetery Road, crossing the Glamorganshire Canal on its way, to reach a two-bay, four track, depot. This was located next to the new power generating station fuelled by a waste destructor, adjoining the UDC gas works. The tramway cost about £60,000 to build and the generating station for traction, power and lighting purposes a further £55,000. The initial 9 minute service was reduced to 10 minutes from 26 February 1906. The tramways proved popular and in the first year of operation some 1,865,924 passengers were carried, earning £8,845 but which due to loan charges unfortunately generated a loss of £601.

Construction of the second route between Mill Street and the Rhondda UDC boundary was delayed by disagreements with the contractors about the materials used and the quality of work. The double track 1 mile 1,562 yards line commenced at a junction turning north into Taff Street then along Mill Street, Rhondda Road, Hopkinstown Road and Cyfeillon Road to the boundary at the 'Trehafod Hotel'. Services commenced on 4 April 1907 and a small depot for four tramcars was built at Trehafod.

The tramway infrastructure suffered considerably from the difficult terrain, mining subsidence and minimal maintenance during World War 1. The Ministry of Transport (MoT), as successors to the Board of Trade, authorised a loan of £20,500 in 1925, repayable over fifteen years, to enable much of the life-expired track to be replaced. This mortgage would prove a substantial burden for the tramways and subsequently the replacement trolleybuses for much of their existence. The majority of the tram track and its foundations between Taff House and the top of Corn Stores Hill, and the Trehafod route along the River Rhondda were replaced.

In 1920 powers were obtained for a further tram route from Machine Bridge (on the Glyntaff Depot access line) along Cardiff Road and part of the course of the filled-in Doctor's Canal to Upper Boat. Although the powers were renewed with a Light Railway Order for about one mile of the route between Machine Bridge and a point near the Rhydyfelin housing estate in September 1927, no work was done.

The post-World War 1 recession and industrial strife saw monthly passenger figures plummet from 485,000 ordinary and 185,000 workmen in March 1921 to around 291,000 and 16,000 by May 1926. Workmen's figures never reached 100,000 a month again during the life of the tramways. In an effort to cut costs, services were thinned out and fares reduced. The situation was exacerbated by the introduction of cheap day return fares between GWR stations in the Pontypridd area in November 1925 at rates far below the comparable tram fares (although the service was less frequent). On the positive side, Sunday tram services started on 7 February 1926 and proved extremely popular.

Although the Rhondda Tramways Co. Ltd. (RT), lessees of the Rhondda UDC tramways, had been operating up to the Pontypridd UDC boundary at Trehafod since 11 July 1908, a through running agreement was only negotiated in December 1918. Commencing on 14 July 1919 Pontypridd UDC operated a service between Mill Street, Pontypridd and Porth every 7½ minutes whilst the RT ran cars between Maerdy and Mill Street, Pontypridd via Ferndale, Tylorstown and Porth every 30 minutes. After several years of bickering between the two parties about mileages run, Sunday services and congestion at Mill Street terminus, the Maerdy service ceased in December 1927. However, joint operation of the Porth service continued until 30 August 1931 and the final abandonment of Pontypridd UDC's tramways. Trehafod depot closed with the introduction of through running. The building was dismantled in 1920 and re-erected at the rear of Glyntaff depot to accommodate additional cars.

No. 5, one of the single-deck combination trams built by Brush in 1904 and mounted on Brill 22E maximum-traction bogie trucks, heads south along Taff Street just south of the junction with Market Street. The impressive bank building on the right with five arched recesses and surmounted by two gabled cornices has been the local branch of Barclays for at least the last 60 years. (David Bowler collection)

Over the period 1904-1920 the Pontypridd UDC Tramways acquired the following cars:

1-6    Single-deck combination cars built in 1904 by the Brush Electrical Engineering Co. Ltd., Loughborough, for 32 passengers and mounted on J.G. Brill Co. 22E bogie trucks.

7-12   Double-deck uncanopied open-top cars built in 1904 by the Brush Electrical Engineering Co. Ltd., Loughborough, for 46 passengers and mounted on J.G. Brill Co. 22E bogie trucks.

13-20  Double-deck canopied open-top cars built in 1907 by the Brush Electrical Engineering Co. Ltd., Loughborough, and mounted on Mountain & Gibson Ltd., Bury, type 4 bogie trucks.

21-26  Double-deck canopied open-top cars built in 1908 by United Electric Car Co. Ltd., Preston, and mounted on Mountain & Gibson Ltd., Bury, type 4 bogie trucks.

27-31  Short top-covered cars built in 1920 by the Brush Electrical Engineering Co. Ltd., Loughborough, and mounted on J.G. Brill Co. 22E bogie trucks.

Not all cars were in service in their original state at any one time. The single-deck cars were irregularly used after 1910 whilst the double-deck fleet benefited from an improvements programme which continued until 1930. Cars 7-12 were rebuilt with extended canopies in 1914 increasing their seating capacity from 46 to 54 and received low height short top covers, i.e. not covering the canopies and staircases, giving just 5ft 5½in. headroom to clear the PCNR railway bridge, in 1921-23. Between 1921 and 1930 cars 13-22 were thoroughly rebuilt.

In June 1927 Pontypridd Council's Legal & Parliamentary Committee learned that Cardiff Corporation under their 1920 Act had applied to run omnibuses on certain routes outside their area, including the County Main Road from Upper Boat to Machine Bridge, Treforest, and thence along Broadway to Station Square, Pontypridd. Cardiff Corporation Transport was about to acquire Tresilian Motors Ltd. and County Motors Ltd. subject to Pontypridd UDC consent and the necessary licences being granted. The increasing motor bus competition in the area led Mr Teasdel to urge the UDC to obtain motor bus powers in co-operation with neighbouring authorities. It was accordingly resolved that Pontypridd would support Cardiff's application subject to that city supporting Pontypridd's application for operating powers and agreeing later to a jointly operated Pontypridd-Cardiff service.

In early September 1927 Mr Teasdel pointed out that the industrial recession and motor bus competition were seriously affecting receipts. Although he could not see where further economies could be made without jeopardising efficiency or safety, the Electricity Subcommittee asked him to look for more savings.

In response to those who suggested scrapping the trams he replied:

*"If the Council decided to close down this year, there would be a liability of some £10,145 to be met for some years to come, the rates would lose nearly £1,000 a year, and the Highways would have to maintain those portions of the road which the Tramways Department unfairly bears for other vehicles, our competitors included, a cost which I should say is not less than £1,500 a year. This again would be thrown on the rates. There are the £1,400 paid to other Departments and also other items that would cause other Departmental costs to go up, so that the total cost to the town would be nearer £14,000 pa. What we want are as many passengers as possible, and as much mileage; hence the reason I should like to see the Rhydyfelin extension carried out.*

*Buses? Yes, by all means! The Council should have obtained the necessary powers years ago, as they might act as feeders to your cars. I hope I may yet live to see the day when the Council will possess their own buses and run in conjunction with the Cardiff Corporation".*

By November 1927 he reported that he could not withdraw a single car on the Treforest – Cilfynydd route but that the salaries of senior traffic staff could be cut. Together with a reduction in the cost of traction power to 1.4d per unit, saving c. £321 pa, a total of £876 could be economised if all the recommendations were implemented. The financial situation was compounded by losses on the through running agreement with the Rhondda Tramways Co. and specifically the Pontypridd – Maerdy service operated entirely by the Company. Pontypridd's Tramways Department was now 1,424 miles in arrears. (Contrary to the through-running agreement, Pontypridd was now "owed" 1,424 miles by the Rhondda Tramways, i.e. they had had to operate 1,424 miles that should have been run by the RTC.)

As a result of Pontypridd's pressure this service ceased in December 1927 but did little to solve the situation. Joint operation of the Pontypridd – Porth service continued despite Mr Teasdel's efforts to break this service at the Trehafod boundary.

By 1928 the fleet was made up of the following tramcars:

1 Double-deck open-top car originally built in 1904 as a single-deck combination car by Brush mounted on Brill 22E bogie trucks.

2 Snowplough car originally built in 1904 as a single-deck combination car by Brush mounted on Brill 22E bogie trucks.

4 Permanent way car originally built in 1904 as a single-deck combination car by Brush mounted on Brill 22E bogie trucks.

7-12 Double-deck canopied cars with short top covers originally built in 1904 as uncanopied open-top by Brush mounted on Brill 22E bogie trucks.

13-20 Double-deck canopied cars with short top covers originally built in 1907 as canopied open-top by Brush mounted on Mountain & Gibson type 4 bogie trucks.

21-24 Double-deck canopied cars with short top covers originally built in 1908 as canopied open-top by United Electric Car Co. Ltd. mounted on Mountain & Gibson type 4 bogie trucks.

27-31 Double-deck canopied cars with short top-covers built in 1920 by Brush mounted on Brill 22E bogie trucks.

The local topography, sharp curves and continual mining subsidence resulted in high track maintenance costs and daily punishment for the ageing rolling stock. By 1928 total tramway capital expenditure had reached £135,577 or £15,728 per mile (compared to an average of £10,916 per mile for 27 similar undertakings) and the undertaking remaining in debt until 1940. Revenue exceeded operating expenses every year except 1926 but was not always sufficient to cover interest charges and repayment of capital when support was required from the general rate fund. Operating costs per car mile for May 1928 were 16.922d, excluding loan charges, compared to receipts of 15.27d or just 13.70d on the Treforest – Cilfynydd route.

On 12 June 1928 the Legal & Parliamentary Committee recommended that a Bill be promoted in the next session of Parliament seeking powers to run motor buses within and outside the urban area. This was approved by the Council and referred to their parliamentary agents (Messrs Sharpe, Pritchard & Co.) on 12 September 1928. That same day the Electricity and Tramways Committee discussed continuing tramway losses and a further fall in receipts, and formed a Subcommittee to consider possible solutions. The Tramways Engineer, Surveyor and Treasurer were instructed to report to the Committee on the financial effects of tramway abandonment:

*"and in particular to submit an Estimate (a) of the Cost of the Removal of the Tramways Permanent Way, and the Restoration of the Roadway and (b) of the additional burden which would be placed upon the rates in view of the fact that the Tramways Undertaking would not then bear any portion of the cost of road maintenance and (c) the total amount of loan charges outstanding particularly in respect of the construction of the Tramways and the dates on which such several loan charges will be completely discharged".*

Their report was presented at the Electricity and Tramways Committee meeting of 10 July 1928 and recorded in the following Saturday's *Pontypridd Observer* under the headline *"Abandonment of Pontypridd Trams, an Impossible Financial Proposition"*. In respect of the Cilfynydd-Treforest route, the Surveyor estimated that the cost of removing the tram track and reinstating the road surface would be £19,027, less a £4,655 MoT grant. Removal of 380 traction poles and recovery of some 12 miles of trolley wire, less the cost of the work, would result in a credit of £250. As the underground feeder cables were buried in concrete and tar their recovery would cost more than their value. There was no market for the tramcar bodies or their equipment – breaking them up would cost £1,120.

Whichever mode of transport replaced the trams a considerable loan would be required, but to calculate the future annual loan charges, accurate estimates of the likely costs and revenues in the ensuing 10 years were needed. Past experience was the only guide yet the undertaking's annual loss, after covering all costs, interest and capital repayment, since 1921 had fluctuated between £1,191 and £10,671, the latter figure admittedly in 1926-27, the year of the coal strike. Mr Teasdel felt that the average deficiency 1921-28 to meet the full loan charges of £3,369 should be increased to £5,000 to allow for any further fall in the undertaking's results. Allowing for the cost of road reinstatement, and the loss of road maintenance charges and rates paid by the Tramways Department, he estimated that the total direct cost to the UDC of tramway abandonment would be £9,969 pa for 10 years.

Should the tramways be abandoned without any replacement there would additionally be a number of indirect costs. The tramways had 138 employees whose combined income of £20,000 pa would no longer be available to be spent in the town. The Electricity Department would lose traction current sales of some £5,000pa, potentially resulting in increased charges for other consumers. Finally the tramways undertaking paid other Council Departments such as the Treasurer's, Clerk's and Surveyor's Offices £1,800 pa for services rendered. In comparison the cost of continuing to work the tramways under the present conditions was around £5,000 per year. Replacing the trams with petrol buses would not relieve the situation as they would, at best, do no more than meet their own working expenses and loan charges, whilst the existing loan charges on the tramways would still have to be met.

*The ageing and unyielding trams caused growing problems as motor vehicles became more common from 1926 and the tramlines in the middle of the road caused difficulties and created hazards, e.g. in Mill Street and Taff Street. The wooden setts between the rails were slippery in wet weather whilst their warping made them both difficult to replace and caused deformation to the rails. The uneven track bed, broken rails and the age of the vehicles all combined to make the tramcars really clank and rattle.*
*Dr H.G.A. Hughes writing in November 2009*

Councillor Colenso Jones stated that, in view of the recent losses, the public were asking why the Council did not abandon the tramways. He thought that the report provided an answer. There would be no reduction of the Sinking Fund payments, even if the tramways were scrapped, until 1934. Abandonment would mean paying £9,000 a year for nothing for the next 5 or 6 years. The tramways were big ratepayers. The report required some digesting but the public should know that to scrap the tramways now was an impossible financial proposition. Councillor D.L. Davies said that they could not do without the trams. They ran a public utility service and were the only means of conveying workmen to their work. It was eventually decided that the officials should prepare a summary of the reports with a view to presenting the position to the public.

In the newspaper's editorial under the heading "Percy and the trams" reference was made to a previous comment in that column made on 17 March 1928:

*"Scrapping the trams might be more expensive than even running at a loss".*

The writer felt that Mr Teasdel's report bore out that statement:

*"The cost per annum for ten years if trams were abandoned would be £9,969 per year, as against an estimated loss, if the cars are carried on, of £5,000 per annum and there is a chance if things improve of this sum being reduced.*
*So to scrap the trams at the present moment would add to the already heavy burdens of the ratepayers.*
*The loan charges will have to be met in any case and if the trams are scrapped that will have to come out of the rates. There are several other matters in Mr Teasdel's report, such as loss of £950 a year to local rates, maintenance of roads £571 a year and last but not least the £20,000 a year paid to the 138 employees of the Tramways Dept., and which it may be assumed is largely spent in the town would be stopped and these men would have to find other work.*
*So for the present it would be a suicidal policy to scrap the trams".*

Based on the Parliamentary Agent's advice it was resolved on 9 October 1928 to apply for powers to replace the tramways with motor buses and operate a network of services within, but not beyond, the UDC boundaries. Alfred Baker, former General Manager of Birmingham Corporation Tramways, was engaged to report on the resolution's proposals and to support the Council's Bill before the Parliamentary Committee. However, both the selection of this gentleman and the speed with which his work was completed suggests that he had been approached earlier. Mr Baker had made the first tram to railless electric traction conversion in the UK on 26 November 1922 when trolley

# Pontypridd UDC Tramways System Track Map

Tram track shown at maximum extent c. 1927

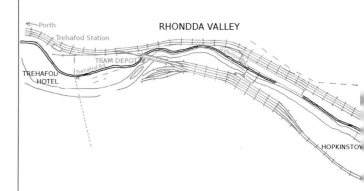

# Key to Map

| | |
|---|---|
| ———————————— | **Tram track** |
| –·–·–·–·–·–·–·– | **Authorised Tramway Extension** |
| – – – – – – – – | **Other Roads and Streets** |
| —+—+—+—+—+— | **Railway (precise track layout not shown)** |
| ···················· | **UDC Boundary** |

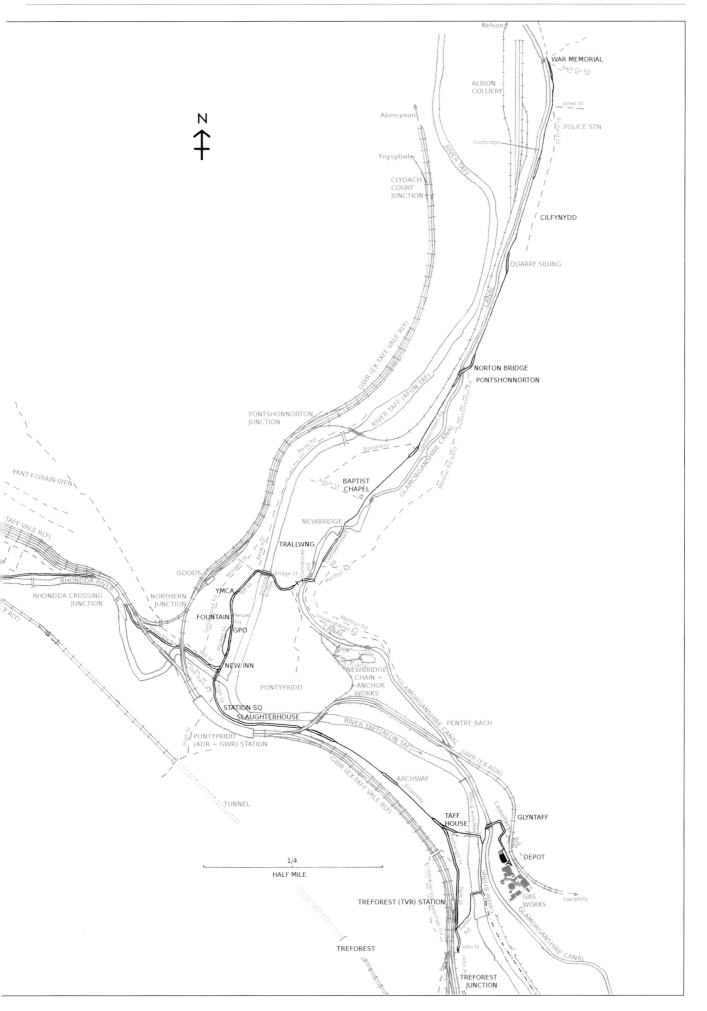

omnibuses began to run on Birmingham's Old Square – Nechells route. He was an early enthusiast of railless electric traction which he saw as the ideal substitute for life-expired single track and passing loop tramways, where the width of the road made reconstruction with double track impossible or where traffic volumes did not warrant such an investment. Municipal transport managers of the time often took on consultancy work for other operators and Alfred Baker, who had retired in February but was retained as an advisor until August 1928, was one of the most experienced in the country, having headed the Nottingham, London County Council and Birmingham undertakings in his career. During his tenure at Birmingham he had advised Darlington to convert its tramways to trolley vehicle operation. His report with a similar recommendation was delivered on 19 October 1928.

A special meeting of the full Council considered Mr Baker's report on 30 October 1928 in conjunction with their Parliamentary Agents advice as how to pursue his recommendations. They decided to:

a) Seek powers to run trolley vehicles along the Council's existing tramway routes and to run motor omnibuses throughout the District;

b) Insert a clause in the Bill giving authority to the Council to enter into agreement with neighbouring Authorities for the working and management etc. of any services which such Authorities are or may be empowered to provide;

c) Insert a clause in the Bill giving authorising the Council to charge fares in accordance with the provisions of the Council's Tramways (Temporary Increase of Charges) Order, 1927;

d) Instruct the Tramways Engineer to submit a detailed estimate of the cost involved by the above decisions (a), and also a list of routes along which it is proposed to run omnibuses;

e) Appoint a Subcommittee to inspect the trolley vehicle system in operation in Birmingham and to interview Mr Baker generally on the above proposals.

This Subcommittee suggested that, in addition to Birmingham, they should visit Chesterfield, Doncaster, Mexborough and Wolverhampton where trolley vehicles were already in operation. Despite the financial situation these municipal jaunts to admittedly not the most attractive towns in the British Isles were approved. Mr Teasdel's suggestion that the proposed trolley vehicle route should be extended from the existing Treforest tramways terminus to a point in Llantwit Road opposite Oakwood Street was, however, not adopted.

In November 1928 the Clerk was instructed to arrange for films showing the construction and operation of trolley vehicle systems at one or more local cinemas, an example being shown after the normal programme at the Palladium Cinema the following month.

In December 1928 the Electricity and Tramways Committee considered if there could be any financial benefit from introducing a through tram service Treforest – Trehafod, although the track layout would require a reversal at the junction with Mill Street. It was decided to operate the through service for a one month trial period, the Treforest – Cilfynydd service continuing to run with an increased speed.

At a special Council meeting on 11 December 1928 it was resolved that a Bill should be promoted in the next session of Parliament:

a) To empower the Council to provide and work trolley vehicles along certain routes in the district and to confer upon the Council all necessary and convenient powers with regard to the provision and working thereof, including power to apply to the MoT for authority to work such vehicles on other routes in the district and elsewhere;

b) To confer powers upon the Council with regard to the running of omnibuses in the district;

c) To make further provision as to the fares to be taken by the Council in connection with their tramway undertaking and to provide for the abandonment of such part of the undertaking as is rendered unnecessary by the proposed trolley vehicles and omnibuses;

d) To empower the Council to borrow money for the purposes of the Bill and to make further provision with regard to borrowing, reborrowing and repayment of money by the Council and other financial and miscellaneous matter.

A few hundred yards short of Cilfynydd Common terminus and the nearby Albion Colliery, the crew of tram 21 pose for the cameraman in front of Thomas & James garage in early 1930. No. 21 was built in 1908 by the United Electric Car Co. Ltd. and mounted on Mountain & Gibson bogie trucks. The short top cover was added at some date between 1910 and 1914. The rear platform steps are already folded up for the return journey and the destination display changed to Treforest. (National Tramway Museum [photographer Dr H.A. Whitcombe])

# THE CONVERSION PROGRAMME

*By late 1928 the newspaper letters column was full of comments about the proposed Parliamentary Bill. The correspondents were in agreement that the tramways were antiquated, whilst there was some concern that any new solution would be a burden on the rates, but the majority seemed indifferent.*

Official notification that a Bill would be promoted appeared in the press just before Christmas 1928 together with an invitation to a public meeting.

The statutory public meeting on 7 January 1929 saw the trolley vehicle proposals approved by a large majority although a few letters against continued to appear in the newspapers.

The Pontypridd Legal & Parliamentary Committee was kept busy in the first quarter of 1929 as reactions to the proposed Bill arrived. Glamorgan County Council was concerned about road reinstatement when the tramways were abandoned, whereas neighbouring authorities including Caerphilly, Cardiff and Gellygaer sought protection from the Bill and the right to enter into joint operating agreements. The GWR and RT were completely opposed. The situation was confused in respect of the various local motorbus operators, a joint petition against the Bill being received from Goughs Garage Co., Imperial Motor Co., Cridland Ltd., and Tresilian Motors Ltd. They were in full agreement on one point: the trolley vehicles should not be given the same protection as the tramways they replaced. It was decided to continue the negotiations with several petitioners in London prior to the start of the Parliamentary hearing on 4 March 1929 and to engage the services of Mr F.G. Thomas, KC, as leading Counsel, and Alfred Baker, amongst others. Despite a meeting with the neighbouring authorities by mid-March 1929 petitions against the Bill had been received from Caerphilly UDC and Llantrisant & Llantwit Fadre Rural DC.

The Clerk warned the Legal & Parliamentary Committee Meeting of 12 March 1929 that the Pontypridd Markets Fairs & Town Hall Co. would object to trolley vehicles (or motorbuses) running through Market Street on any Market or Fair Day. At the same meeting Mr W.B. Cownie, RT Managing Director, stated that through running was essential and that he was very much in favour of trolley vehicles. He would like to convert the Porth – Trehafod tram route to trolley vehicle operation as soon as

---

## URBAN DISTRICT OF PONTYPRIDD.
## Pontypridd Urban District Council Bill.

IN PURSUANCE of the Borough Funds Acts 1872 and 1903 NOTICE IS HEREBY GIVEN:—

1. That the Council of the Urban District of Pontypridd have resolved in accordance with the provisions of the Borough Funds Act 1872 to promote in the present Session of Parliament a Bill the title of which is "A Bill to empower the Pontypridd Urban District Council to provide and work trolley vehicles and omnibuses; and for other purposes."

2. That the objects of the said Bill are:—

(a) To empower the Council to provide and work trolley vehicles along certain routes in the district and to confer upon the Council all necessary and convenient powers with regard to the provision and working thereof, including power to apply to the Ministry of Transport for authority to work such vehicles on other routes in the district and elsewhere;

(b) To confer powers upon the Council with regard to the running of omnibuses in the district;

(c) To make further provision as to the fares to be taken by the Council in connection with their tramway undertaking and to provide for the abandonment of such part of that undertaking as is rendered unnecessary by the proposed trolley vehicles and omnibuses;

(d) To empower the Council to borrow money for the purposes of the Bill and to make further provision with regard to borrowing, reborrowing and repayment of money by the Council and other financial and miscellaneous matters.

3. That the said Bill has been duly deposited in Parliament and the date on which it was first deposited in either House of Parliament was the 17th day of December instant.

4. That copies of the said Bill may be inspected and extracts therefrom may be taken free of charge and copies of the Bill may be purchased at the price of Three shillings each at the Clerk's Offices in the Municipal Buildings, Pontypridd, between the hours of 10 in the forenoon and 5 in the afternoon on every week day for fourteen days after the date hereof.

5. That a Public Meeting of the local government electors of the Urban District of Pontypridd will be held at the Wesley Schoolroom, Gelliwastad Road, Pontypridd, in the district on Monday, the Seventh day of January, 1929, at Seven o'clock in the afternoon for the purpose of considering the question of the promotion of the Bill and a resolution or resolutions will be submitted to the Meeting in favour of the promotion of the Bill.

DATED this twenty-second day of December, 1928.
DAN EVANS,
Chairman of the Council.

possible but the company were lessees of the Rhondda UDC and were not free agents. He suggested that RT rent the line to Mill Street but withdrew his offer once he learned that the line in Trehafod needed relaying. He then suggested that the Company be allowed to run motorbuses between Porth and Pontypridd once the tram track was removed pending his company obtaining trolley vehicle powers, and that the Council run trolley vehicles from Mill Street to Trehafod, and that on the Rhondda side of the boundary he continue to run trams from Porth to Trehafod. Nonetheless the UDC agreed to consider the RT's suggestions regarding through running between Pontypridd and Porth, which led to the company withdrawing their initial opposition to the Bill.

The Bill reached the House of Lords in May 1929 and received the Royal Assent on 10 May 1929 as the Pontypridd Urban District Council Act 1929 granting the UDC authority to operate trolley vehicles over the existing tram routes, and to erect turning points at Cilfynydd, Treforest and Trehafod.

At the 14 May 1929 Electricity & Tramways Committee Meeting, a Tramways Subcommittee was re-elected to consider a site for a trolley vehicle and motor bus depot, and an offer from a Mr R.T. Richards to sell to the UDC 2,502 sq yds of land adjoining the generating station for this purpose. The General Manager, Mr Teasdel, was instructed to report on the condition of the permanent way to Cilfynydd and estimate how much longer it could be used without repairs, and on the construction of a trolley vehicle system and the introduction of motor bus services. He reported that the worst portions of track were from the Palladium Cinema in Taff Street (next to the YMCA) up Corn Stores Hill to Bonvilston Road Sidings, and between Quarry Sidings and Cilfynydd terminus. He estimated that the track would last 12-18 months.

Having made a number of enquiries in view of the mining subsidence and poor road surfaces of the area, he considered that 3-axle single-deck trolley vehicles would be the most suitable as they offered a smoother ride and a longer tyre life than 2-axle vehicles. The licence fee, at £67 4s, was also less than for double-deckers. He was already able to state his preference for a centre doorway design allowing as low loading as the type of chassis and MoT regulations would permit. He gave some detailed specifications which relate precisely to the design and fittings of the English Electric SD6WTB trolley vehicles as delivered. Some tramway traction poles would need to be reinforced and additional poles planted to support an estimated additional 5½ tons of trolley wire, although wall rosettes would be used wherever possible. At this time the Electricity & Tramways Department was maintaining 6 miles of traction feeders, 2.875 miles of negative return and 12 miles of trolley conductor wire.

The Tramways Subcommittee instructed Mr Teasdel to prepare an estimate of the cost of the proposed trolley vehicle system and motor buses, this being submitted on 29 June 1929 (see table alongside).

As a further incentive, the Electricity Department, following continual complaints about traction current charges, reduced the price per unit from 1.29d to 1.25d effective 1 July 1929.

The Tramways Subcommittee recommended that the UDC convert its tramways to trolley vehicle operation and introduce motor bus services in accordance with the powers conferred upon them by the 1929 Act. A total of ten trolley vehicles would be needed and it was proposed that loan sanction be sought for their cost. The Transport Manager pointed out that seven vehicles (six on Saturdays plus one spare) would suffice for the

Treforest – Cilfynydd route, and suggested that the option of three more should be taken up when needed, as it was already evident that conversion of the Trehafod route would not be completed at the same time. Tenders were thus invited for just seven trolley vehicles to the design suggested in his report of 7 June 1929. It was estimated that six months would be needed to construct the trolley vehicle system and acquire the vehicles.

They also suggested that motorbuses be introduced on a route to Rhydyfelin and a number of workmen's services, requiring four petrol buses. As first priority depot accommodation for 15 vehicles of each type with provision for subsequent extensions should be built near the existing Glyntaff Tram Depot, for which a £5,000 loan should be sought.

The Treasurer was instructed to negotiate the following loans:

| | Amount of loan to be negotiated £ | Amount authorised by the Council's Act £ | Purpose |
|---|---|---|---|
| (1) | 5,000 | 5,000 | Buildings |
| (2) | 6,000 | 15,000 | Four motor buses |
| (3) | 13,650 | 19,500 | Seven trolley vehicles |
| (4) | 5,972 | 5,972 | Electrical equipment for working trolley vehicles |
| | £30,622 | £45,472 | |

The loan for electrical equipment was estimated as being divided as follows: Treforest – Cilfynydd including access to Glyntaff Depot £4,415; Mill Street – Trehafod £1,557.

Pontypridd Council accepted all the Subcommittee's recommendations and tenders were invited for the overhead equipment and vehicles.

| Particulars of Work | Estimated cost £ | Loan period authorised by the Act Years |
|---|---|---|
| (a) Trolley Vehicles | 19,500 | 10 |
| (b) Electrical equipment and construction of works necessary for trolley vehicles | 5,972 | 20 |
| (c) Road reconstruction and tram track removal | 21,900 | 20 |
| (d) Construction or adaption of buildings for trolley vehicles and motor buses | 5,000 | 25 |
| (e) Motor buses | 15,000 | |
| Total estimated cost as provided by the Act | 67,372 | |

By 2 July 1929 agreement had been reached with Mr Richards for the Council to buy his site adjoining the generating station for £525 as the location of the new depot.

During September and October 1929 the tramway traction poles were tested as to their ability to support the additional weight of trolleybus equipment. The majority were satisfactory but some would need replacement or strengthening. It was estimated that some 64 additional new traction poles would have to be planted, over 10 miles of trolley wire run, and over 500 fittings attached. As almost 75% of this work would be necessary within the next 6 months, it was deemed impossible for the undertaking's own employees to carry out the conversion and keep the system going.

Full plans of the proposals were sent to the MoT on 3 October 1929 and they immediately requested further information relating to curves, gradients, etc. By January 1930 the MoT confirmed that they had no immediate objection to the proposed arrangements and turning points.

On 12 November 1929 the Electricity & Tramways Committee (ETC) resolved to invite tenders for conversion of the overhead equipment for trackless trolleys. They accepted Mr Teasdel's recommendation that trams should cease running through Market Street, as the trolley wire there had worn thin and conversion to trolley vehicle operation was not foreseen. The full Council was, however, not yet convinced and only in June 1930 was the trolley wire cut down, and the three traction poles and three rosettes removed for use elsewhere. Tenders for trolley vehicles were invited by 2 December 1929, the specifications being sent to manufacturers at a charge of £1 1s per copy, and eight responses including one from Richard Garrett & Sons Ltd., Leiston, for their OS type 3-axle single-deck design, were received. At the Council Meeting of 7 January 1930 the tender of English Electric Co. Ltd., Preston, as recommended by Mr Teasdel, for seven 32-seat vehicles at £1,667 10s each was accepted.

A location for the Cilfynydd trolley vehicle terminus proved difficult to find, the only suitable site being by the Albion Garage where a reversing triangle into Park Place (just south of Jones Street) was proposed. This was 100 yards short of the tram terminus and the Albion Colliery entrance, the key traffic objective. In February 1930 Glamorgan County Council released plans to widen the road near the tram terminus necessitating replanting eight traction poles 18ft further back to the new footpath. The road would then be 30ft wide at its narrowest part, which meant that under MoT regulations the bracket arms attached to these traction poles would have to be replaced by span wire construction requiring eight additional poles on the opposite side of the road. This road widening created an alternative site for a terminus between the junction of Pant-du Road with Cilfynydd Road and the junction with the lane leading up to Cilfynydd Common immediately in front of Cilfynydd War Memorial, opposite the Albion Colliery. By removing the base of the mound on which the War Memorial stood, sufficient space would be available for a turning circle, needing five more traction poles and about 400 yards of trolley wire.

On 3 March 1930 Mr Teasdel met the Glamorgan County Surveyor at Cilfynydd to discuss the location. As the site was on rising ground offering poor visibility approaching from the north on this, the main Merthyr Tydfil – Cardiff road, the Surveyor was not in favour. He suggested a turning circle rather than a reverser where the road widened at the junction of Jones Street and Richard Street with Cilfynydd Road, known as The Square, some 200 yards short of the tram terminus, and failing this the reverser into Park Place near the Albion Garage.

MoT permission to remove part of the mound in front of the Memorial to provide at least 60ft for a turning circle was received at the beginning of April 1930. The Electricity & Tramways Committee approved the plan on 8 April 1930 and on 11 April 1930 the Surveyor removed his objections.

Three experienced firms were asked to quote for the overhead equipment and by early March 1930 British Insulated Cable Co. (BICC) had tendered at £9,600 and Messrs Clough, Smith & Co. at £9,179 whilst R.W. Blackwell & Co. asked to be excused from quoting. These figures were considerably above the £5,972 estimated by the late Alfred Baker and shown in the Bill, not least as it had been calculated that only some 58 additional traction poles would be needed. Both companies considered that all curves needed to be strengthened and added that the MoT now required the use of span wire construction on streets more than 24ft wide. BICC felt that 120 new medium poles and 80 new heavy ones would be required. Clough, Smith specified 121 medium and 89 heavy poles, and added that 94 existing poles would have to be repositioned. Clough, Smith sent an engineer to Pontypridd for four days to survey both tram routes looking for possible economies. He found that many of the tramway traction poles were rusted inside and recommended replacement with new light poles. He also recommended the replacement of worn conductor wire.

The trolley springs on Pontypridd's trams were adjusted to give an upwards pressure of 4 lb whereas the trolley vehicles, in view of their higher speed, would have a pressure of 30-35 lb per boom, greatly increasing the strain on the overhead equipment. The extra weight in copper wire and fittings on the Treforest – Cilfynydd line was estimated at over 8 tons.

**Brush built car 30 stands in Park Street, Treforest, just north of the junction with Forest Road. It will be noted that trolleybus overhead equipment is already in place on the single bracket arm, and that the tram is collecting current from the trolleybus positive wire. (Photographer's name not recorded)**

| Allocation Original Tender | Cilfynydd – Treforest £6,002 | Trehafod £3,177 |
|---|---|---|
| Rebates in respect of new positive side feed cables, painting, permanent reinstating and bridge troughing: (letter to Mr Teasdel 20 January 1930) | £238 12s 6d £5,763 7s 6d | £27 2s 6d £2,949 17s 6d |
| Difference in value between 121 medium and 89 heavy poles (original tender) and 32 light, 111 medium and 77 heavy poles referred to in our covering letter: | ADD £105 1s £5,868 8s 6d | DEDUCT £112 19s £2,836 18s 6d |
| Rebates in respect of reduced number of poles to be removed and re-erected: | £58 5s 6d £5,810 3s | £81 3s 6d £2,755 15s |
| Rebates in respect of line abandoned in Cardiff Road, Canal Bridge, and Forest Road, and revised lay out of the reverser at Treforest terminus: | £193 5s 1d £5,616 17s 11d | £2,755 15s |
| Removing existing tramway trolley wires and replacing them with 3/0 SWG cadmium trolley wire: | £1,232 13s 3d | £638 14s 2d |

Mr Teasdel accordingly suggested some economies. Rather than retain the two access routes to Glyntaff Depot used by the trams he proposed that the southernmost, from Cardiff Road (on the east side of River Taff) to Forest Road, which ran southwest-northeast from Park Street to Castle Inn Bridge on the west side of the river and then across the bridge, should not be converted for trolley vehicles and that access should be solely across Machine Bridge which carried the A4058 just east of St. Dubritius RC Church. At a period when posters for Overseas Settlement were hung in the Central Library he went on to suggest that direct labour be used to change the side feeds, paint traction poles, reinstate the pavement, and to prepare bridge troughings.

Clough, Smith & Co. agreed to employ UDC workmen at Council rates and hire the tower wagon at 2s 3d per hour with driver. They specified solid drawn poles made by Mannesmann in Newport and were prepared to employ the permanent way gang for pole planting.

On this basis Clough, Smith submitted a revised calculation:

On this basis Mr Teasdel recommended that the work on the Treforest to Cilfynydd section be placed with Messrs

Clough, Smith & Co. Ltd. but that pending a commitment from Rhondda Tramways Co. (RT), work on the Trehafod section be postponed. Clough, Smith's tender at £6,849 11s 2d (less a credit of £500 for used trolley wire and fittings) for the overhead equipment on the one route was accepted on 4 March 1930. The still uncertain stance of the RT towards trolley vehicle operation led to a decision to defer any conversion of the Trehafod route. It was resolved that the Chairman, Clerk and Engineer should meet Rhondda UDC and urge them to take immediate steps to obtain powers enabling their lessees, the RT, to operate trolley vehicles, at least on the Trehafod – Porth section, to link up with Pontypridd's system between Trehafod and Mill Street.

All tramway wiring was replaced. Traction poles at curves and termini were replaced by new British Mannesman weldless stepped poles although many traction poles in acceptable condition elsewhere were retained. The section insulators, negative sections and insulated crossings were to Clough, Smith's own designs and fitted with non-hammering ends to ensure against crystallisation at the trolley wire ends. In Clough, Smith' s experience grooved trolley wire had a shorter life due to the reduced wearing surface on the side of the wire and according round gauge wire was used throughout. Where necessary guard wires were strung at least 3ft above the trolley wires (the MoT specified a minimum 2ft clearance). The contractor drew up detailed route plans of the overhead equipment needed with enlargements of the special work and discussed these with Mr Teasdel before construction commenced.

Easements of 1s pa per pole were agreed for four traction poles to be planted in John Place on the Crawshay Estate, off John Street, Treforest, to support the reversing triangle overhead wiring. In June 1930 it was pointed out that traction poles in Broadway could be planted in the front gardens on the boundary line of the portions of such gardens as they were owned by PUDC although inevitably one was erected in a private allotment garden!

The Engineers & Surveyors Department reported on the results of their call for tenders for a trolley vehicle and motor bus garage on 4 March 1930. The contract was for the supply and construction of two steel-framed buildings each 70 ft × 60 ft separated by a fireproof party wall. Corrugated asbestos cement sheeting roofs with glazed lights and ventilators were foreseen with the walls in no. 18 BWG corrugated iron. Large "Coburn" patent sliding doors and numerous windows with hoppers for ventilation would be provided. It was assumed that direct labour would be used for excavation, surface water drains, concrete stanchion foundations, reinforced concrete floors, construction of pits, building party wall and the provision of a rainwater tank, an estimated additional £1,065. As the majority of tenders received were less than the £1,872 estimate, it was decided to use "Robertson Protected Metal", a superior type of sheeting with a steel core covered with asphalt and asbestos felt as it was longer-lasting and required little maintenance. As no painting would be needed, £100 would be saved. It was decided to ask the three lowest tenderers to revise their estimates on this basis with the work to be carried out by direct labour and subsequently the lowest tender from Messrs Braithwaite & Co., Westminster, at £1,904 was accepted.

By the beginning of June 1930 the bracket arms and tie rods had been changed at Police Row, Cilfynydd Road and Cemetery Road, and at Clifynydd five bracket arms had been removed and

A line-up of six of the seven English Electric SD6WTB single deckers on the north side of the Glyntaff Depot premises prior to the opening ceremony on 18 September 1930. The building and chimneys in the background were all part of Pontypridd UDC's rubbish incinerator, which provided electricity for first the trams and subsequently the trolleybuses.

two re-fixed on new poles in preparation for the trolley vehicles. The height of all bracket arms on the Treforest and Cilfynydd route was adjusted in accordance with the Regulations. Work continued throughout the month and by the beginning of July 1930 all traction poles had been planted and Clough, Smith were hanging the overhead wiring. Priority was given to the Glyntaff Depot to Treforest terminus and Broadway sections so that they could be used for training purposes once vehicles arrived.

In late June 1930 members of the Tramways Department inspected the chassis, bodies and contactor gear at English Electric's Preston works. The traction motor tests proved most satisfactory, the 60bhp motor being sparkless at 100% overload, and after a full load test the temperatures were well below the specified standard. English Electric hoped to have a vehicle ready for test running by mid-July 1930 and to deliver the first two vehicles to Pontypridd by the beginning of August, enabling driver training to start. The remainder would follow by the end of the month. As this would permit services to start in early September it was decided to inaugurate the system on 4 September 1930. The company wondered if a special ceremony would be appropriate as Pontypridd UDC would be opening the first modern trolley vehicle system in Wales, and suggested that perhaps the Minister of Transport, Mr Herbert Morrison, could be invited. The Council took up this idea, but the Minister could not accept the invitation. By then Mr Teasdel had seen that the system was unlikely to be ready on 4 September and suggested that the ceremony be postponed to 18 September 1930.

The new single-deck English Electric trolleybuses were delivered by railway to the Barry Railway goods yard, which was situated between St. Mark's Church, Pwllgwaun and Lanelay Crescent, Maesycoed, in two batches. One or possibly two vehicles arrived in the second half of July 1930 with the rest following in early August. Driver training began in August 1930, the vehicle trailing a slipper in contact with the tram rail, as the trolleybus wiring was not completed. It is known that these training trips included excursions on the Trehafod route.

By the beginning of September 1930 Clough, Smith had almost completed the conversion although ongoing adjustments were made based on the experience with test runs. The side feeds from the section boxes and negative returns were still incomplete. Over the next few weeks new section feeder cables were run or the existing ones overhauled and replaced at each section, and negative feed cables from the overhead line to the negative feeders were connected at the bottom of Corn Stores Hill, Brewery Lane and the Generating Station. Painting of the new traction poles and some older ones was only completed in early October. Mr Teasdel again asked the Electricity & Tramways Committee to press RT to convert the Trehafod to Porth section of their system for trolley vehicles, so that work on Pontypridd UDC's portion could start and tramway operation cease. He added that it would prove expensive to operate three forms of traction although there were insufficient petrol or trolley vehicles to maintain a service to Porth.

On 9 September 1930 the ETC resolved that a Transport Committee, made up of Councillors from the Cilfynydd, Graig, Town, Trallwn, Rhondda and Treforest Wards, and the Chairman of the ETC, be appointed to consider and report direct to the Council on all public transport matters.

The MoT Inspection of the line and vehicles was made on Tuesday 16 September 1930 by Cols. Trench and Woodhouse. They drew attention to a number of old traction poles showing signs of stress and which required replacement, and suggested that the junction of Broadway and Fothergill Street would be improved by reducing the size of the central triangle. In respect of the vehicles, the Inspectors insisted that they be equipped with a brake warning light and an illuminated registration number at the rear. Subject to these points being rectified they sanctioned the start of trolley vehicle operations and the necessary certificate was issued on 30 September 1930:

*The Minister of Transport hereby certifies that the under-mentioned Route authorised to be equipped for the purpose of working trackless trolley vehicles by the Pontypridd Urban District Council Act, 1929, has been inspected by Colonel A.C. Trench, the Officer appointed for the purpose by the Minister and that the said Route is fit for public traffic (that is to say)*
*Route No. 1. 3 miles 2 furlongs 8 chains or thereabouts in length commencing in the Cardiff – Merthyr main road at the point opposite the entrance to the Albion Colliery at Cilfynydd passing in a southerly direction along that road to Norton Bridge, along Coedpenmaen Road (i.e. crossing Pont Shon-Norton Bridge over the Glamorganshire Canal), Corn Stores Hill (i.e. crossing over the Glamorganshire Canal at locks by Canal Place and Heol-y-Dwyrain), Bridge Street, Taff Street, High Street, Broadway, Fothergill Street and Park Street (i.e. immediately north of Treforest Junction), and terminating in that road at a point opposite John Street.*

As an immediate solution English Electric added the registration number to the illuminated rear destination blind of each trolleybus whilst the undertaking fitted a triangular Power Brake warning, which showed a red light when the driver applied the brake, to one vehicle at a cost £4 1s. Street lighting was soon installed at Cilfynydd turning circle and the Treforest reverser.

The route was ceremonially opened by former miner Mr Thomas Mardy Jones, Pontypridd's MP, on Thursday 18 September 1930 watched by representatives from practically all the municipalities in South Wales. He stated that "with the trolleybus we have got the best of both worlds", namely the economy of electric traction and the manoeuvrability of the motorbus. The *Pontypridd Observer* noted *"The company embarked on the buses and the new system was inaugurated by Mr Mardy Jones MP, who pressed a button and so started the cars. The visitors went over the whole system to Cilfynydd and then returned to the 'New Inn' where they were entertained to luncheon by the contractors"*. Pontypridd was to remain the sole trolleybus operator in Wales until Llanelly opened its system on 26 December 1932.

After the opening ceremony the trolleybuses went on the road at 1.30pm, but it proved impossible to maintain a 7½-minute service, and the Traffic Superintendent endeavoured to despatch vehicles at regular intervals. An attempt to run the same service the next day also failed as the 32-seat single-deck trolleybuses could not cope with the number of passengers wishing to travel (the double-deck trams they replaced had 52 seats).

**Glyntaff Depot, opening journey and dignitaries 18 September 1930. (David Beilby collection [English Electric])**

MINISTRY OF TRANSPORT
Whitehall Gardens,
London, SW1
The Secretary,
Ministry of Transport.


Sir,
I have the honour to report for the information of the Minister of Transport that, in accordance with the appointment of the 21st. August, 1930, I made an inspection on the 16th. September of trolley vehicle routes No.1 and 1C. and a portion of route No. 1.B, of the Pontypridd Urban District Council Transport Department.

Route No.1 commences with a turning circle near the Albion Colliery Cilfynydd and traverses Cilfynydd Road, Coedpenmaen Road, Taff Street, High Street, Broadway, Fothergill Street, and Park Street to a turning triangle in John Street, total length 3¼ miles.

Routes Nos. 1C and 1B join No. 1 at the junction of Fothergill Street and Broadway and proceed by Machine Bridge, Glyntaff Canal Bridge to the tramway depot, total length about three furlongs. These routes are to used only as a means of access for vehicles to the depot and passengers will not be carried thereon.

A tramway exists along practically the whole length of the routes inspected. The tram service will be discontinued when the trolley vehicles are put in service, but the tramlines on routes 1B and 1C and on the route 1 from the Fothergill St. junction in Taff Street cannot be taken up for the present owing to through running arrangements with the Rhondda trams on the proposed trolley vehicle route No. 2. Along the remainder of route No. 1 the tramlines will be removed in the near future in accordance with road reconstruction programmes.

Roadways are narrow in several portions of the route and there are several sharp turns and short steep gradients. Special care will be needed at the entrance to John Street, the bridges over the river and canal when entering the depot, and the canal and river bridges at the foot of Cornstores Hill. Traffic is heavy but I have no doubt that the trolley vehicles can with care be operated as safely as the trams and with much less inconvenience and delay both to other traffic and to themselves.

Road surfaces are generally of the tarmac type in good condition; the setts on the tramway track will be removed when the rails are taken up.

There is a narrow bridge under the railway near Pontypridd Station where there is only just room for two wide vehicles to meet, with a footpath on one side only. This bridge is to be reconstructed shortly when the roadway will be widened. The turning circle at the Cilfynydd terminus is across the main road. Diameter is 63ft and is adequate without much margin. A white line and other marks will be provided to assist drivers at this point. The turn must he made with the vehicle empty, and the conductor must alight to warn approaching traffic. Adequate lighting is to be provided at this point.

The turning triangle at the John Street terminus is in a short dead end road and traffic interferences will be negligible but special care will he needed on emerging from John Street into Park Street after the turn, and at this point also the conductor must give warning of the main road traffic. The short dead end into which the vehicles reverse requires resurfacing, which is to be done, and additional lighting is to be provided at this point also.
The overhead work is 3/0 swg circular cadmium copper on composition bolts with porcelain insulators. The span wires are specially galvanised by the Crapo process which is stated to give results of specially high protective capacity to the metal.

A considerable number of new poles have been installed, in addition to which some of the old tramway poles have been reinforced at the top section by an angle welded to the back. Construction is both span and bracket, the longest brackets being 18ft.

In Park Street one bracket pole appeared to be overloaded and span wire suspension will be arranged for this, as also on the Treforest side of the G.W. Newport Bridge. The bracket pole opposite No. 51 Police Row, Cilfynydd Road also show signs of weakness and will be replaced either by a new pole or by span wire construction.

The suspension arrangements of a certain number of bracket arm poles which carry street lamps, do not provide for triple insulation between the positive trolley wire and the pole as required by regulations. The suspension on these poles should be re-arranged to provide for this.

In one or two places minor defects in the overhead equipment require attention and the Engineer undertook to have these dealt with forthwith.

Extensive guarding arrangements have been necessary along some portions of the route and these as completed appear to be adequate. The representatives of the Post Office, who was present at my inspection, expressed himself as satisfied.

The Surveyor of the Council was present at my inspection and had no remarks to make either on behalf of the Council or the Glamorgan County Council.

The works are well constructed and in good order and subject to the minor points noted above I recommend the route be approved for passenger traffic.

I recommend that the following speeds be authorised:-

4 miles an hour.
When rounding the turning circle at Cilfynydd.
When passing under the G.W. Newport line bridge.
When entering and leaving John Street.

8 miles an hour.
When approaching and traversing Norton Canal Bridge.
Between the top of Cornstores Hill and the junction of Bridge Street with Taff Street.

18 miles an hour.
Between Coedpenmaen Post Office and top of Cornstores Hill.
In Taff Street and High Street.
In Broadway from High Street to G.W. Newport Line bridge In Fothergill Street .and Park Street.
At all other points speed not to exceed 16 miles an hour.

Also that compulsory stops be made:-
Before crossing Norton Bridge on the southbound journey.
At top of Cornstores Hill on the southbound journey.
At junction of Bridge Street and Taff Street.
At Bridge over River Rhondda in High Street on northbound journey.
In Station Square Pontypridd Station.
At junction of Fothergill Street and Broadway.

As routes 1C and 1B are not to be used for passenger traffic I do not specify speeds thereon, but special care and low speed will be necessary at the junction of Machine Bridge and the Cardiff Road, and between this point and the Depot, also while rounding the junction between Fothergill Street and Machine Bridge. I suggested that this junction might be improved by the reduction of one end of the central triangle. This would involve destruction of a tree but the Surveyor undertook to ask the Council to consider the matter.

I have the honour to be,
Sir,
Your obedient Servant,

(Sgd.) A. C. TRENCH.
Colonel.

When visiting the Treforest — Cilfynydd trolley vehicle route of the Pontypridd Urban District Council on 16th. September, I also inspected the trolley vehicles which the Council proposed to use.

These are single-deck 32-seater 6-wheel vehicles with central entrance, constructed throughout by the English Electric Company Limited, of which seven have been purchased.

The overall length is 27ft 7in. maximum width 7ft 5¾in. and height to the top of the trolley base, which is of the Estler type and carried by the body sides, independent of the roof, is 10ft 11½in. The rear overhang complies with requirements, as does the underclearance when laden, the least dimension of which is 10¾in. under the front axle. Three differentials are fitted, and the rear bogie is of the Thorneycroft type. The track is 6ft 5¼in. front and rear, tyres are 36in. x 8in. inflated to 100 lb pressure. The turning circle, laden, was measured to be 57ft. I was informed that the weight, fully laden, is 9tons. 14cwt . 2qrs, of which 3tons 17cwt 3qrs is carried by the front axle.

ELECTRICAL EQUIPMENT — The motor is single wound, of E.E.C. manufacture, rated at 60bhp carried amidships, and geared so that a motor speed of 1760rpm corresponds to a road speed of 20 miles an hour. Access to the brushes is easy.

A controller, worked by foot operates contactors fixed in the driver's cabin; there are six steps on the controller, the last of which weakens the field of the motor. Acceleration is automatic, up to the point at which the controller is held. The contactors are inoperative when the hand brake is applied, and the reversing switch is interlocked with the control pedal. The reversing switch handle serves also to operate the trolley wire and skate changeover switch, thus ensuring the controller is in the "Off" position when the skate is being placed on the rail. All power cables are well protected with rubber hose where run in proximity to metal work. The rheostats, which are below the body, appeared to be insufficiently protected against mud and water. If it is found in practice that the insulation resistance is lowered through this cause additional protection should be provided.

BRAKES — Westinghouse air brakes are fitted with independent brake cylinders for all six wheels. The compressor, located under the body, cuts in and out at 50lb and 75lb pressure respectively, and runs quietly. The air pipes are of steel, with stout rubber connections to the cylinders, and are well protected. The hand brakes acts on the four rear wheels and is not equalised, reliance being placed on correct adjustment. The brake drums are all 17in. diameter, with separate shoe paths for air and hand brakes in the four rear drums.
A rheostatic brake is also provided, its controller, which has two steps, being pneumatically operated during the first portion of the stroke of the brake pedal.
Brake tests, carried out at speeds varying between 15 and 18 miles an hour with a fully laden vehicle on wet tarmac and setts gave the following retardations, which may be regarded as satisfactory.

Foot brake only (rheostatic and air)  12.9 f.s.s.
Hand brake only                        5.0 f.s.s.
Rheostatic brake only              5.8 f.s.s.

The output of the compressor was found to be sufficient for frequent operations of the air brake.

BODYWORK, ETC. — The seating and interior arrangements are convenient and comply with regulations. With the vehicle laden, the entrance step is 11in. from the ground. Metal treads on the lowest step should he replaced by insulating material.
The sideguards are about 8in. clear of the ground with the vehicle laden; this clearance should he reduced to 5in.
The driver's equipment included a speedometer, electric horn, and electric windscreen wiper. Facilities for signalling to overtaking traffic are fair, but a driving mirror is required. The speedometer and brake pressure gauges should be illuminated; this can be arranged without difficulty by an alteration to the hood over the Neon pilot light. Safety glass is not fitted in the driver's cab; I suggest that the windscreen, at any rate, of future vehicles should be of this material. Fireproof protection is needed over the arc chute of one of the circuit breakers, the opening of which is close to a group of cables.
The driver's seat affords good vision, and a reasonably comfortable driving position, but the brake pedal is awkward to operate for the first portion of its stroke. Its shank should be set to bring it into a more convenient position.
The lighting of the vehicle is satisfactory, but, arrangements should be made to illuminate the rear number plate. A battery is fitted supplying current for emergency head, tail, and interior lighting, and also for the horn to screen wiper. Subject to rectification of the points denoted by letters A to H in the margin, I recommend that their use for public service be sanctioned.

(intd.) A. G. T.
19th., September, 1930

## Smallest British Trolleybus Operators

| Place | Route Miles | Vehicles | Dates of operation |
|---|---|---|---|
| Birmingham | 2.44* | 16* | 26 November 1922 – 30 June 1951 |
| Dundee | 1.25 | 2 | 5 September 1912 – 13 May 1914 |
| Grimsby | 1.5* | 5* | 3 October 1926 – 4 June 1960 |
| Halifax | 2.5 | 3 | 20 July 1921 – 24 October 1926 |
| Oldham | 1.5 | 2 | 26 August 1925 – 5 September 1926 |
| Pontypridd | 3.3 | 9 | 18 September 1930 – 31 January 1957 |
| Ramsbottom | 3.5 | 7 | 14 August 1913 – 31 March 1931 |
| West Hartlepool | 3.27 | 7 | 28 February 1924 – 2 April 1953 |
| York | 1.5 | 4 | 22 December 1920 – 31 December 1929 and 6 October 1931 – 5 January 1935 |

Route mileages and number of vehicles are shown for the operator's maximum size or that prevailing in 1930 (the latter denoted with an asterisk *).

Cost and traction current supply considerations had led to a decision not to operate the Pontypridd UDC (PUDC) tramcars used on the Trehafod route out of the RT's Porth depot, necessitating retention of the tram track between Glyntaff Depot and Mill Street. Track removal elsewhere did not start immediately. On Saturday 20 September 1930 it was decided to use four tramcars between Treforest and Cilfynydd to supplement the six trolleybuses. It proved impossible to run to timetable due to the continuing road works at Cilfynydd terminus and the different speeds of the trams and the trolleybuses. A round trip journey Treforest-Cilfynydd on weekdays was scheduled to take 45 minutes, compared to one hour by tram, but drivers could not keep to this time. Two tramcars were kept in service but although they provided additional capacity they also held up the trolleybuses on narrow streets. To avoid too many gaps in the service the tramcars were used on short workings as far as possible.

After two weeks trial services were being worked with six trolleybuses and one of the four ex-LGOC K-type double-decker motorbuses purchased in May 1930 rather than trams, but timings remained irregular. Trolleybuses had to be withdrawn due to teething troubles. As the drivers became more familiar

with their work and problems with the overhead equipment decreased, an effort was made to run a 10-minute service 5.00am – 7.30am with five trolleybuses, a 7-minute service 8.00am – 10am and 12.30 – 6.30pm, with six trolleybuses and a K-type motorbus. From 10.00am – 12.30pm and 6.30pm – finish an 8-minute service with six trolleybuses. This meant a round trip journey in 48 minutes (an average speed of 8.8mph compared with 6.6mph of the trams); however, it was felt that if this solution proved successful and subject to introducing specified stopping places rather than stopping anywhere the public wish to get on, an effort would be made to reduce the time to 45 minutes. It was noted that a reduced workmen's service was being run due to the Albion Colliery being idle.

*Some road bridges created problems for the trolleybuses, even though trams had none. One such was the railway bridge by Mill Street School. Trams ran from Pontypridd's Tumble up to Porth in the Rhondda. Only trial runs were made by trolleybuses. I myself rode trolleybuses from 'Castell Ifor Inn' in Pwllgwaun on two (unscheduled) occasions up to Gyfeillon near Capel Rhondda, Hopkinstown.*

*The advent of the trolleybuses was universally welcomed by the residents of Pontypridd. They were seen as a huge step forward in travelling comfort compared to the trams whilst the introduction of the new blue and primrose livery made them appear really modern. The trolleybuses were also seen as evidence that the economic situation must be improving.*

Dr. H.G.A. Hughes writing in November 2009

On 3 October 1930 the Pontypridd Transport Committee discussed proposals to convert the Trehafod tram route to trolley vehicle operation with Mr Richardson, General Manager, Rhondda Tramways Co., as road improvements had already started at Gyfeillon. Mr Richardson said that if it was going to be some time before the Rhondda route could be converted, petrol buses would be run in the interim. He felt that it would be better to obtain the vehicles to augment the present service rather than buy additional trackless vehicles now, and later have to obtain petrol buses. A motorbus service would need seven PUDC and 6 six RT vehicles.

On 9 October 1930 Mr Teasdel reported to the Transport Committee on the number of trolley vehicles that would be required if the tramways were abandoned:

English Electric single decker 3 in Taff Street at the bus stop outside Barclays Bank, heading south shortly after the commencement of trolleybus operation. The tram tracks remain intact including the junction for the single line into Market Street. Peter Smith collection (Photographer's name not recorded)

The daily run out had been:

|  | Early AM Workmen's | Ordinary Service | After 1.00 pm |
|---|---|---|---|
| Treforest – Cilfynydd | 5 | 6 | 8 |
| Pontypridd – Porth | 5 | 4 | 5 |
|  | 10 | 10 | 13 |

On Saturdays 16 trams had been in regular use, 10 on the Treforest – Cilfynydd route, and six on the Rhondda (Trehafod) route. The RT also used two cars in the early mornings, four during ordinary hours of traffic and six on Saturdays. Although the double-deck trams offered 20 more seats than the single-deck trolleybuses, Mr Teasdel pointed out that their higher operating speed meant that seven trolleybuses equated to 8 tramcars.

Questioned as to his preference for single-deckers, Mr Teasdel referred to the overbridges on the Rhondda route but assuming that these difficulties could be overcome there were economic considerations. He estimated that a double-deck trolleybus weighed around 9½ tons and ran on heavy-duty tyres. Each vehicle had seven tyres which would cost £21 15s each or £2 7s per tyre more than for single-deckers. The licence fee would be £96, the larger traction motors would take more power, and they would run for 90% of the time with a poor load factor. He felt that these large heavy vehicles were only suitable for places where there was a continuous good load factor, and that for Pontypridd single-decker trolleybuses were best and most economical.

When the time came for trams to be completely abandoned and the service operated entirely by trackless trolley vehicles, he estimated that some 16 vehicles would be required, 10 for normal service, a further five for peak periods and one reserve. The additional vehicles were estimated to cost around £1,600 each. The number of motorbuses for an interim service was of course dependent on the outcome of the RT's planning. Mr Teasdel suggested that if there was any prospect of the company converting their Porth tram route within the next 18 months or so, PUDC should strive to carry on with the trams, spending as little as possible on track maintenance. Elsewhere the tram rails should be removed as soon as possible.

This all led to a meeting between the Company's Managing Director, Mr Cownie, and the Chairman, Clerk and Transport Engineer in London on 17 February 1931. The next day the Transport Committee recommended to the full Council that the tramway between Mill Street and Trehafod should be abandoned and replaced temporarily with motorbuses prior to a conversion to trolley vehicles. Following the Council's formal decision in January 1931 the RT was informed of the pending abandonment and asked if they were prepared to agree to operate a joint bus service in lieu of the tramway. The Transport Committee recommended the introduction of a through motorbus service between Pontypridd and Porth, and that the Clerk be instructed to prepare a new agreement with the RT. It is difficult to ascertain with hindsight when it became clear to the UDC that the RT had decided to replace their trams with motorbuses rather than trolleybuses. Nonetheless the thought of a jointly operated urban trolleybus network in the area is fascinating.

On 29 October 1930 the Transport Committee considered the Transport Engineer's Report of Revised Stopping Places on the Treforest-Cilfynydd trolley vehicle route. There were now 28 intermediate stops (5 compulsory) whereas there had been 34 intermediate stops (17 compulsory), the stops at the Observer Office, Motor Station, Post Office, 'Maltsters Arms', Church Road and Burton's Cilfynydd Road having been done away with.

| | | | |
|---|---|---|---|
| F | Treforest terminus | F R | West Street |
| R | Treforest Station Entrance | F R | Common Road |
| C | *Bush Hotel* | | (on down only) |
| F C | Taff House | R | Newbridge |
| R | Rock House | F R | Baptist Chapel |
| F R | Taff Vale Park | R | Bonvilston Road |
| F R | Archway | F R | Bonvilston Road |
| R | Office Loop | R | Taff Vale |
| R | Slaughterhouse | F R | Norton Bridge |
| F C | Station Square | R | Police Row (top end) |
| C | Rhondda Bridge | F R | Quarry Siding |
| | (into town) | R | *Albion Hotel* |
| R | *New Inn Hotel* | R | Workmen's Hall |
| F C | Fountain | R | Richard Street |
| R | YMCA | F | Cilfynydd Terminus |
| F R | Berw Road | | |

| | |
|---|---|
| F | fare stage |
| R | request stop |
| C | compulsory stop |

In November 1930 Mr Teasdel suggested that four more trolleybuses be purchased for the Treforest – Cilfynydd route. A decision was deferred however – within a month Guy Motors Ltd. offered to supply such vehicles and to send a double-deck trolleybus on trial. The offer of a trial vehicle was accepted but the question of new vehicles remained deferred. News of a possible fleet expansion spread fast amongst manufacturers as in January 1931 Bristol Tramways and Carriage Co. Ltd. offered one of their new trolleybuses on trial. Having consulted the Committee Chairman Councillor Davies, the Transport Manager accepted this offer and the Bristol E demonstrator HY2391 arrived on 27 March 1931. An initial test run on 1 April 1931 with 2 tons of ballast to represent a passenger load showed that the Bristol consumed an average 3.18 units per mile.

The last trams on the Treforest and Cilfynydd route probably ran during February 1931 (the Transport Manager's report of 13 February 1931 refers to their continuing use on Saturday evenings) having providing possibly a unique example of a scheduled service operated jointly by trolley vehicles, trams and motorbuses. This date coincides with the entry into service of Guy BTX60 (fleet number 8) double-decker trolley vehicle and the arrival of three Bristol B motorbuses (fleet numbers 6-8). The Surveyor reported considerable damage to the road surface by the frequent passage of trolley vehicles on the Cilfynydd route and recommended that the disused tram track be removed as soon as possible to permit road reconstruction.

Verbal comments a wireless interference from the trolley vehicles started in October 1930, and Post Office Engineers asked what proposals there were to fit a device to combat the interference. Mr Teasdel had taken up the matter with a number of other operators. The general view at that time seemed to be as expressed by Darlington Corporation Transport:

*"That when the Engineer brought the matter before his Committee they decided to refer it to the Municipal Tramway Association, with a view to arranging a proper investigation, by the BBC or the GPO, for the whole of the electric traction industry, instead of each undertaking carrying out independent experiments".*

No. 2 crosses Victoria Bridge en route to Treforest shortly after the commencement of trolleybus operation. Behind the trolleybus beyond the bridge runs Ceridwen Terrace whilst on the right is 'The Maltsters' public house. (*Tramway & Railway World*)

In February 1931 Mr Teasdel was instructed to submit a report upon the advisability or otherwise of placing the Council's Transport Undertaking under management separate from the Electricity Undertaking. In March 1931 David Lewis Davies, Chairman of the Transport Committee, was elected as the Labour MP for Pontypridd.

The trolley vehicles were not proving entirely trouble-free. At 10.20pm on 6 February 1931 the Guy BTX60 demonstrator dewired at the dip, known as The Swamp, in Coedpenmaen Road. The driver braked hard to avoid the flailing trolley booms damaging the overhead equipment resulting in the vehicle skidding on the stone setts into a traction pole. Considerable damage was done to the rear platform and stairs. By mid-February 1931 garage working shifts were rearranged to permit urgent repairs to the English Electric vehicles at night. The following month ten serious dewirements occurred, four involving the Guy, and records show that three trolley vehicles had contactor troubles and a further three punctures. Despite this Guy Motors asked if the Council were prepared to buy the BTX60 demonstrator for £1,750. The Transport Committee recommended its purchase subject to Mr Teasdel negotiating a lower price, and there being no payment in respect of the mileage run. Guy reduced their price to £1,700 and extended the guarantee to two years, and this offer was accepted.

On 31 March 1931 a bracket arm was bent and other damage done to the overhead lines at the 'Albion Hotel'. The traction power had to be cut off 11.25 – 11.50pm during which time trolleybuses were turned at Quarry Sidings, presumably by shunting backwards and forwards several times, benefiting from the wide lateral deviation provided by the Estler trolley base.

Mr J.E. Teasdel, the Council's Electrical Engineer and Tramways Manager, died on 11 April 1931. As a token of respect it was decided that no deduction be made from the wages of transport employees who attending his funeral.

Pontypridd UDC trams continued to operate on the Mill Street – Trehafod – Porth joint service until the replacement motorbuses arrived, the remaining careworn tramcars being withdrawn without ceremony on 30 August 1931. In the final month of operation 114,899 passengers were carried providing £880 revenue and the cars ran 14,967 miles. Much of the overhead equipment was removed the following day in connection with the ongoing road widening, whilst all the tramway permanent way had been removed from the streets of Pontypridd by the end of 1932, a considerable quantity of rail being sold to Erith UDC Tramways in Kent.

A partially dismantled tram and English Electric single-deck trolleybus 4 at Glyntaff Depot. The registration TG385 is evident in the rear destination box above the rear windows. (David Bowler collection)

# Rhondda Tramways Co. Ltd.

The Pontypridd and Rhondda Valley Tramway Company between the Pontypridd and Rhondda UDC boundary at Trehafod and Porth Square was acquired by Rhondda UDC in 1904. The UDC then leased the tramway to the National Electric Construction Co. Ltd. (NEC) which from 1906 traded locally as the Rhondda Tramways Co. Ltd. (RT). The UDC built a network of single track and passing loop electric tramways of 3ft 6in. gauge, as used by both the horse tramway and Pontypridd's electric tramways, comprising almost 21 route miles. The network was operated in its entirety by the RT using, at maximum extent, 54 two axle cars. The tram depot and power station was at Porth although latterly the power station was given up and high frequency AC electricity was purchased from the South Wales Power Co. Ltd. The main converter station had three rotary converters (two of 500kW and one of 750kW) with substations at Treorchy (400kW) and Pontygwaith (400kW).

The electric tramways opened progressively as follows:

Trehafod – Partridge Road 11 July 1908
Porth – Pontygwaith 11 July 1908
Partridge Road – Pentre 2 September 1908
Pontygwaith – Ferndale 2 September 1908
Pentre – Treherbert 12 September 1908
Porth – Partridge Road via Dinas, Penygraig, Tonypandy
   5 November 1908
Ferndale – Maerdy 30 March 1912
Treherbert – Blaenrhondda 30 March 1912
Penygraig – Williamstown 30 March 1912

NEC, the parent company, had been founded in 1897 as the National Electric Free Wiring Co. Ltd., the "Free" referring to the installation of copper wiring into domestic households free of charge, only the materials used being chargeable. The NEC title was introduced in 1903. In addition to its power supply interests the company operated a wide range of passenger transport investments which, in addition to the Rhondda Tramways, included the diminutive Dewsbury, Ossett and Soothill Nether Tramways, the Musselburgh & District Electric Light & Traction Co. Ltd., and the Torquay Tramways Co. Ltd., as well as the subsequent tramway replacement motorbus and trolleybus operators such as City of Oxford Motor Services Ltd., Devon General Omnibus & Touring Co. Ltd. and the Mexborough & Swinton Traction Co. Ltd. In the late 1920s the NEC, following the lead of the British Electric Traction and Tilling Groups, encouraged local railway companies to take on one third of the ownership of each of its subsidiaries. This was seen as avoiding wasteful competition with the railway companies' own bus services, in essence the GWR in this part of South Wales.

In late 1931 practically all the NEC's share capital passed to the BET Group although the company and its subsidiaries remained a separate entity until BET was acquired by the Transport Holding Company, the predecessor to the state-owned National Bus Company, on 1 March 1968.

Trackless trolley vehicles were introduced between the tram terminus at Williamstown and Gilfach Goch, Nicholls Terrace (Rhondda UDC and Llantrisant & Llantwit Fadre RDC boundary) on 22 December 1914 via Tonyrefail, Hendreforgan, Garden City and Gilfach, to serve recently opened coal mines. Although not a foregone conclusion at this early date in the development of railless traction, the NEC installed a pair of parallel conductor wires, horizontal to each other, as was to become conventional practice. There was a depot at Tonyrefail for the 6 Daimler/Brush single-deck trolley vehicles, 55-60 in the tramway fleet numbering system. The 4.63 mile long route suffered from mining subsidence, the poor road surface associated with a rural area and steep hills. These challenges combined with a run-away accident led to the service being withdrawn in mid-March 1915. The temporary closure became permanent and the vehicles were sold to Clough, Smith & Co. for use by the Teesside Railless Traction Board (fleet numbers 11-16, registration AJ5866-71) in May 1920.

The RT started motorbus services in 1920, the second route to be introduced being that following the ill-fated trolleybus line in January 1921. Expansion continued with a service between Pontypridd and Cardiff opening in 1924, followed by Pontypridd and Porthcawl in 1925. By the time tramway conversion was being discussed there were over 70 motorbuses in the fleet. A through tram service between the Rhondda Valley and Pontypridd had commenced on 14 July 1919. The introduction of a joint motorbus service with Pontypridd UDC on 1 September 1931 constituted the first of many joint working agreements between RT and neighbouring authorities.

Rhondda UDC promoted a Parliamentary Bill in December 1932 for the abandonment of their tramways and the termination of the lease to the Rhondda Tramways Co. Ltd. The Bill also provided for the operation of motorbus services by the Company and to enable the Council to acquire the motorbus undertaking and operate their own services. The Rhondda tramways were abandoned on 2 February 1934 and replaced by 30 AEC Regent diesel buses.

Despite their Chairman's stated enthusiasm for trolley vehicles and the economic necessity of retaining a through service between the Rhondda and Pontypridd, it is assumed that the RT had sound economic reasons for not converting their tram services to trolleybus operation. First and foremost the tramway track and infrastructure was owned by Rhondda UDC and leased by the company. The area's economic recession meant that UDC was not in a position to finance the conversion of its tramways to trolleybus operation. Prior to the 1926 General Strike, the RT had served collieries employing 48,700 men but by 1933 this figure had fallen to 29,530 whilst some 12,000 people had left the two Rhondda Valleys to seek their fortunes elsewhere. Receipts per mile fell from 20.33d in 1923, to 12.06d in 1926 and again to 10.22d in 1931. The lack of commercial incentive for the company to contribute towards the conversion was further hampered by the UDC's option to purchase the company at specific dates making additional long term investment, whether in trolleybus equipment or tramways, of little interest. Furthermore it is noteworthy that the NEC and the BET Group were never greatly interested in converting their tramway investments to trolleybus operation, the Mexborough & Swinton Tramways Co. providing the sole exception.

Another challenge to trolleybus operation in the Rhondda Valleys were a number of low railway bridges over the main routes which although providing sufficient clearance for covered-top tramcars did not offer sufficient space for double-deck trolleybuses and their overhead equipment. The frequency of mining subsidence affecting buildings and roads would also have continued to trouble the traction poles and power supply. Finally the recollections of the Gilfach trackless trolley vehicles were far from positive!

# Pontypridd UDC

N

## Key to Map

———— **Trolleybus Overhead Wiring**

–·–·– **Proposed Trolleybus Extension**

·······+······ **Former Tram Route not Converted to Trolleybus Operation**

– – – **Other Roads and Streets**

–+–+–+– **Railway (precise track layout not shown)**

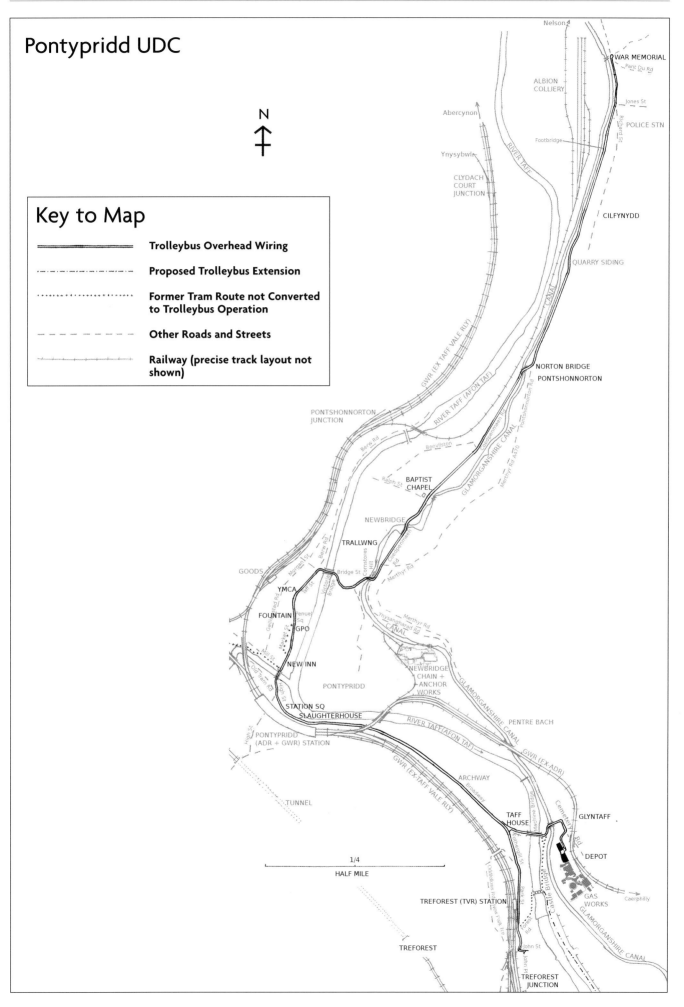

1/4
HALF MILE

# THE GREAT DEPRESSION

*It is essential to put the first decade of trolleybus operations in Pontypridd into their socio-economic context if the challenges facing the UDC Transport Department are to be fully understood. The American stock market crash in 1929 provoked a global economic depression. Although the UK had still not recovered from the effects of the First World War, the nation did not suffer as badly as many other countries The overall picture of the British economy in the 1930s was bleak, however, the effects of the depression were uneven: some parts of the country and some industries fared better than others. The South Wales Valleys, dependent on a single industry, coal, which was already in decline, fared badly, experiencing mass unemployment and poverty.*

In 1931 Britain left the Gold Standard which until then had assured the value of the currency and protected the country from inflation. Combined with a devaluation of the pound, interest rates fell making exports more competitive and leading to a modest economic recovery. Although this provoked a fall in unemployment from 1934 onwards it did nothing to help South Wales. Unemployment in the Principality as a whole never fell below 15% from 1927-38! It was above 20% from 1929-37 and even touched 38% in 1932. In 1934 unemployment amongst school leavers in Pontypridd reached 92% for boys and 97% for girls. By the late 1930s the population of Pontypridd was about 44,000 whilst almost 500,000 people left the Valleys during the inter-war years to try and find work elsewhere.

Unemployment benefit for insured workers was cut by 10% in 1931 forcing many families to seek poor law relief, which was subject to the dreaded means test, paid for by local ratepayers, who were hard-pressed themselves. In February 1932 a soup kitchen opened at Richard Street, Cilfynydd, whilst to celebrate King George V's Silver Jubilee in 1935 needy families received a free pair of boots from the UDC. In 1934 the cut in benefit was reinstated and two years later an Unemployment Assistance Board was set up to look after workers who had exhausted their insurance benefits. The stagnant high levels of unemployment in parts of the UK prompted the government to designate a number of Special Areas, including South Wales, in December 1934 where government investment was used in

**Guy BTX 60 no. 8 stands in Cilfynydd Road at Cilfynydd Square bus stop ready to head south towards Treforest. There is still a bus stop at this point today but the ornate telephone cabin has gone. Richard Street climbs away to the left. The building just in front of the trolleybus is the County Police Station built in 1901. (Peter Smith Collection)**

an effort to combat the depression. These efforts had little effect and it was only the stimulus of rearmament in the second half of the decade, e.g. the start of construction of the Treforest Industrial Estate in early 1937, followed by the outbreak of the Second World War which really reduced unemployment.

In this harsh environment Pontypridd's Councillors and the undertaking's professional management endeavoured to ensure that their new investments provided a public service at the lowest possible cost. One can but marvel at the manner they operated a trolleybus system on a shoestring whilst on occasion some of their methods, particularly in respect of the labour force, seem totally unacceptable by today's standards.

Upon the death of Mr Teasdel, the Traffic Superintendent, Adam Armstrong, was entrusted with the management of the Transport Department and its 121 employees with the title Acting Traffic Manager. Gwilym Evans, Deputy Electrical Engineer and Manager, was appointed Acting Engineer and Manager.

The trolleybuses were proving popular: on Saturday nights the undertaking was operating a 5-minute service Treforest – Cilfynydd using eight trolleybuses and two motorbuses. Average receipts per mile in March 1931 were 12.93d (compared to 12.51d in 1930) against costs of 10.086d excluding loan charges. This popularity, however, also brought headaches, the Car Shed Superintendent complaining:

*"On Friday night last (19 June 1931) the switches were operated a couple of times on the Corn Stores Hill which was due to the buses being overloaded to the extent of between 100 and 115 passengers. This bus was operating the circuit breakers on Saturday and Monday after the above mentioned trouble, which necessitated me keeping it in. On making enquiries I find that certain of the drivers are foolish to move their levers in the speed notches on the controller when going up Corn Stores Hill. This gave me the clue to the trouble. I have had the shunt field resistance taken off the controller and found one of the elements had got burnt out. I have now connected without this one element and the vehicle is working OK. The defective element I have sent off to the Guy People for repairs. On Saturday the Bristol trolleybus was overloaded again, and which gave trouble on the road. This overloading of the double-deck trolley buses will be a serious matter, and if the driver loses himself when the breakers are operating may cause serious trouble".*

Within a few months of the start of trolleybus operations there were numerous reports of slack running wires requiring retensioning. This took place in April 1931 at John Street to Fothergill Street, Taff House over Machine Bridge, and Taff House to Broadway Sections, whilst the curves near the 'Maltsters' and the 'Queen's Hotel', which were prone to cause dewirements, were eased. In May at Broadway Section to PCNR railway bridge, all four wires, Cilfynydd Terminus to Police Station all wires, Police Station to Burton's Section down lines & Burton's Section to Norton Bridge down lines. In June 1931 between Cilfynydd Police Station and Norton Bridge Section, and also between Bridge Street and the old RV Brewery Garage, Coedpenmaen Road. A bracket arm was changed for a longer one near the Coedpenmaen Schools to improve the running of the line. In July 1931 further sections

were tightened including Victoria Bridge, requiring 8½in. to be taken out of each line, and Berw Road to 'New Inn', 1ft 6in. out of each line. Additional pull-offs to improve the line at curves were installed at Norton Bridge, Berw Road, and near Canal Bridge, Coedpenmaen Road. Attention was given to side feeder cables and fittings at various points. During July and August 1931 the up and down lines from the PCNR bridge to the Abattoir were re-tensioned and the curves improved at Norton Bridge, two additional traction poles being planted for this purpose. A defective bracket arm behind Treforest railway signal box was replaced by a longer one, and a bracket arm removed and a span substituted at Norton Bridge.

After a long delay the MoT inspected the Bristol E double-deck trolleybus (HY2391) on 18 June 1931 and it entered passenger service on 20 June 1931. First reports indicate that it ran very smoothly, was easy to drive and no trouble at all to handle. Comparative tests in July/August 1931 showed the following power consumption statistics:

| | | |
|---|---|---|
| English Electric SD6WTB (1) | 32 seats | 1.46 units per mile (0.0456 p/passenger seat mile) |
| Guy BTX60 (8) | 59 seats | 1.434 units (0.0243) |
| Bristol E (9) | 60 seats | 2.271 units (0.0378) |

In September 1931 cheap fares for the unemployed travelling to/from the Labour Exchange were introduced as a six-month experiment (it was extended in February 1932 and then successively until the outbreak of the Second World War), valid as follows: Tuesday & Thursdays 9am – 1pm; Wednesdays 9am – 1pm / 2pm – 5pm; and Fridays 9am – 1pm / 2pm – 8pm.

A fault occurred on the Cilfynydd traction feeder cable on 13 August 1931 and on testing was found to be down both ways from Norton Bridge section pillar. The fault on the lower side was located on the Bridge and repaired. Several faults were found toward Cilfynydd, and in Police Row, some 10 yards of cable had almost entirely disappeared. The armour around the cable showed evidence of pick-axe damage, presumably in the recent road works. Current was off on Cilfynydd route from 09.50 – 10.05am on 13 August 1931 due to guard wires having been pulled down near the 'Albion Hotel'.

Guy offered the undertaking a second double-deck BTX60 ex-demonstrator trolleybus for £1,600 delivered. They stated that it was similar to number 8, in perfect condition and painted dark blue. It is possible that this was the vehicle tested by the London United Tramways on their initial Teddington-Kingston trolleybus line in March 1931, and subsequently loaned to Birmingham City Tramways for one week in April 1931 where it was registered OG9886 and potentially finished in the city's blue livery. Thereafter the vehicle returned to Guy Motors and does not appear to have been used again until sold to Llanelly & District in January 1935.

After some twelve month's experience the English Electric trolleybuses were still proving unsatisfactory with many breakdowns, defects and high maintenance costs. The manufacturer's representatives visited the depot on 10 September 1931 with the Chairman of the Council, Chairman of the Transport Committee, and Councillor J. Jones deputising for the Chairman of the Electricity Committee. As a result English Electric offered to carry out remedial work at their own expense

**1930 English Electric SD6WTB 2 approaches the Bedw Road stop as it climbs the rise in Cilfynydd Road heading south probably in 1932. A Commercial Motor Services (the trading name of Jones Brothers, Treharris) motorbus recedes into the distance on one of their services from Pontypridd. On 1 November 1945, Jones Brothers' stage carriage business was sold to the UDCs of Caerphilly, Gelligaer and Pontypridd, and the West Monmouthshire Omnibus Board, who jointly ran the ex-Jones Brothers' services. (Peter Smith Collection)**

and sent three men who by mid-October 1931 had worked some 550 hours and carried out the following:

*Trolleybuses 1, 4, 5, 6: Front bulkhead strengthened with angle irons wood cased. Front corner pillars of driver's cab strengthened with iron frames, eight gusset plates fixed to rails, underframe of cab strengthened, 26 steel gusset plates bolted and screwed to pillars, sills and floor of main saloon, rear ends and longitudinal seat brackets strengthened, drop windows eased.*

*6: rear springing softened by the removal of two leaves from each spring.*

*4: Resistances re-graded to improve the starting and braking.*

*1, 4, 6: Broken outrigger brackets replaced by new.*

New contact tips and copper braids were fitted to the contactors, and new type of electrical brake (as exhibited at the Commercial Motor Show in November 1931) were fitted, all the repairs being completed by February 1932.

Work continued on improving the overhead wiring layout, specifically at the sharp curve leading from Machine Bridge to Fothergill Street and near the 'Ivor Arms'. Some repairs to slight damage caused by trolleys were made at various points, including frogs by Taff House, a broken ear at Treforest terminus, a hanger near the Abattoir, insulated bolts at Norton Bridge, an ear in Cardiff Road, and ears and insulators near West Street and 'Ivor Arms'.

The undertaking's advertising contractors, Frank Mason, suggested in September 1931 that in view of the reduced advertising space on the single-deck trolleybuses compared to the double-deck trams, the minimum rent of £160pa in the existing contract should be waived until all the double-deck buses were in service. The Council accepted their offer of 66⅔% of the advertising receipts (some £200 at that time), effective 31 August 1931, whilst efforts were made to transfer the enamel plate advertisements from the recently withdrawn trams to double-deck Guy BTX60 trolleybus 8.

There were complaints that the trolleybuses were interfering with wireless reception. The Electricity Committee asked the Clerk to contact the BBC for information about recent experiments with suppressors, and to enquire if the BBC would contribute to the cost of fitting such equipment. Early in 1932 the BBC replied that they would assist as far as practicable in designing suppressors but that they were unable to make any financial contribution. The quotation for stopper coils on one trolleybus, exclusive of fitting and altering cables, was £14.

The end of tramway operation meant that 7-8 men were surplus to requirements. In an effort to reduce the Department's costs to a minimum by November 1931 three conductors were dismissed and two drivers downgraded to conductors. Part-time working was introduced in the maintenance and repair workshop. Two employees were laid-off whilst the three smiths were stood-off for one week in every three. A further three employees were required to take one day off per week in lieu of Sunday duty and four others had their working week reduced from 47 to 39½ hours, leading to a reduction of maintenance employee hours by 60 (£4 10s) per week. Trolleybus Electrician, B. Roberts was required to take one day off per week in lieu of Sunday duty, working 9am to 2pm instead of 8.30am to 2.30pm. The two trolleybus overhead linesmen were employed for a portion of their time on Electricity Department work at no charge to the Transport Department for these hours. Work on

Driver Alfred Workman poses with Bristol E 9 at Cilfynydd Common terminus. His grandson, Bernard Stogden, worked as a trolleybus conductor from his seventeeth birthday until called-up for National Service in the early 1950s, returning later to drive motorbuses for Pontypridd UDC. (Bernard Stogden [Grandson of Alfred Workman] Collection)

the trolleybus overhead wiring was often carried out on Sundays with the current off, and henceforth the linesmen had to compensate these hours during the week instead of receiving overtime payments.

Again with costs in mind Mr Armstrong asked for the Committee's guidance in handling the sole remaining conductress (the other having been on the sick-list for over four months). Some of the (male) drivers had complained that the conductresses were unable to assist in shunting and that they apparently did not notice when something was wrong. Accordingly, they worked solely on trolleybuses. Two tyres had recently been destroyed in this manner and a trolleybus reversed into a traction pole. In a pique of chauvinism he added: *"A conductor would probably have noticed this, whereas the conductress did not."* The remaining conductress had asked for her duties to coincide with the same driver as she was afraid to go home alone at midnight. She admitted it was out of place for a girl to attend to the various duties other than collecting fares and apparently added that she thought there would be little trouble in getting other work, something that seems unlikely considering the economic hardships of the time.

A Bristol Tramways (BTCC) representative called on Mr Evans on 15 December 1931 to ask if there was any interest in purchasing their trolleybus demonstrator (HY2391). The licence was about to expire and should there be no interest Bristol asked for its return by the end of the year. The Transport Committee reviewed the situation on 17 December 1931. The trolleybus had been delivered on 27 March 1931 for trial without any obligation, and was inspected and passed for service on 18 June 1931. It had been in use since 19 June 1931, had run about 13,500 miles and had proved very satisfactory in service. BTCC had paid the licence fee whilst the usual mileage rate for a vehicle of this capacity on loan was 4½d per mile or £253 2s 6d. No charge has been made for this but was usually considered in the price if purchased. The asking price was £2,200. The Acting Transport Manager & Engineer reported that, after some discussion, the representative at first agreed to £1,950 before agreeing to recommend its sale at £1,935. The Acting Traffic Manager added that if the trolleybus was returned it would be impossible to maintain services and that another vehicle would

be needed. The Council resolved that they were prepared to purchase the vehicle if suitable terms could be arranged, but not at the proposed figure. BTCC renewed the licence until 24 March 1932 and the trolleybus remained in daily service; however, an official reaction from the company was only received in March 1932 when they informed the undertaking that they were prepared to accept £1,750 for the vehicle. It was agreed to purchase at this amount but that efforts should continue to obtain yet a further reduction.

The average speed of the trolleybuses by now was 8.8mph in the morning, 8.25mph at mid-day and 7.92mph in the evening. The low evening figure was attributed to the need to fit the trolleybuses between the parallel motorbus service between Berw Road and Taff House, in order to provide a 5-minute service on the busiest portion of the route, without using more than 5 trolleybuses to provide a 10-minute service throughout.

No doubt endeavouring to benefit from the company's improved reputation following their repairs under guarantee to the single-deck trolleybuses, in January 1932 English Electric invited the Department to visit their test track at Preston where they could inspect the double-deck AEC/EE 663T trolleybus exhibited at the November 1931 Commercial Vehicle Exhibition. Alternately it could be loaned for testing in Pontypridd. This vehicle (prototype chassis AEC663T001) had been equipped with a new English Electric highbridge body to satisfy Revised Conditions of Fitness Regulations, featuring a half cab and dummy radiator, a front exit equipped with folding doors (in addition to the rear open platform) and twin staircases. Although the Acting Transport Manager expressed interest the Council was not in favour and there is no evidence whatsoever to support some commentators' views that an AEC663T demonstrator ran in Pontypridd. In May 1932 it went to Southend-on-Sea and was subsequently purchased by that undertaking receiving registration number JN2086.

Dewirement reports for January 1932 showed that there had been problems at the Depot, in John Street, at Taff House, the Slaughterhouse, 'The Maltsters', and Corn Stores Hill. In many cases these could be attributed to the poor road surface but also insufficient care in examining the trolley heads after a dewirement and before replacing the wheels on the wire. An additional traction pole was planted in Norton Dip and a span wire strung in place of a bracket arm in order to improve the line whilst a new bridle was fixed at the Broadway Section. A quantity of redundant overhead material was removed from the former Trehafod tram route, overhauled and made fit for further use.

By March 1932 the whole tram track had been removed from Cilfynydd terminus to Quarry Sidings and the full width of the road resurfaced with bituminous material. Work continued from Pontshonnorton to Quarry Sidings. Until now the negative return on some portions of the system had been by way of the tram track, however, as the rails were gradually removed it was necessary to seek alternative solutions. Near the Fair Field and in Fothergill Street the negative trolley wires were connected to the underground insulated returns.

At the beginning of February 1932 it was decided to designate the Acting Traffic Manager, Mr Armstrong, as the Transport Manager, but that the existing management arrangements should continue until April 1932, despite the administrative difficulties of the split-responsibilities with the Acting Electrical Engineer, Mr Evans, who was then given the title of Electrical and Transport Engineer.

The NJIC for the Tramway Industry decided to reduce wages from 4 April 1932 by ½d per hour for drivers, and by 1s per week for conductors under 21 years of age (no change for those over 21). The Transport Manager asked for instructions in respect of Sunday work. When Sunday tram services started on 7 February 1926 it was decided to pay time and a half for the first 4 hours and thereafter time and a quarter. The new agreement stated that all Sunday work should be paid at time and a quarter.

In March 1932 it was decided to remove the traction pole in the pavement in front of Hemmings Butcher, Taff Street, Pontypridd, and replace it with a wall rosette, whilst in April the pole opposite Halfords was removed being similarly replaced by a new span and wall rosette.

Although the undertaking never failed to show a gross working profit, in April 1932 Mr Armstrong drew attention to the heavy burden of loan and interest charges, e.g. trolleybuses £2,822 pa. A fare increase was necessary, but this required the Traffic Commissioners' approval in the case of the petrol buses. The Council was free to increase trolleybus fares, subject to them not exceeding the statutory maximum granted by the MoT. He prepared a new fares list for the Transport Committee's July meeting; however, as the slump deepened they were reluctant to add to the population's hardship and chose not to approve the increases. Receipts fell and crews were reminded not to miss a single fare-paying passenger. In May 1932 the Maritime Colliery closed down and other collieries lost 77 shifts. The population was decreasing too: in 1925 it was estimated that 49,490 lived in Pontypridd but by June 1931 this had fallen to 42,950.

|  | May 1931 | May 1932 |
|---|---|---|
| Passengers | £193,433 | £143,358 |
| Receipts | £1,397 | £1,111 |
| Daily average | £45 1s 7d | £35 16s 10d |
| Mileage | 27,687 | 22,482 |
| Receipts per mile | 12.11d | 11.86d |

Average expenditure per mile excluding loan charges:

| | |
|---|---|
| Traffic costs | 5.502d |
| Maintenance | 6.575d |
| Total | 12.079d |

As the undertaking's financial situation worsened, the Transport Manager had no alternative but to submit a further list of proposals in November 1932, containing even greater increases. In the meantime, in July 1932 he had been able to negotiate a ⅛d per unit price reduction for traction current arguing that the undertaking was paying 1.25d per unit whereas the average price of 67 undertakings was 0.786d per unit in year ending 31 March 1931. A further economy was achieved by moving the transport ticket office from the municipal building to Glyntaff Depot.

The two double-deck trolleybuses were decorated for the Pontypridd Civic and Hospital Week events of 8-10 September 1932.

Mr Armstrong's further fare proposals were discussed at the Transport Committee Meeting of 15 November 1932 but more details were requested, these being provided at the 16 December 1932 meeting.

The old and new fares were compared, the Transport Committee deciding on a number of adjustments to avoid hardship.

The Traffic Commissioners confirmed the fare changes in mid-March 1933 and they were brought into operation on both motorbuses and trolleybuses on Monday 3 April 1933. Local printer Mr P.S. Phillips printed 5,000 copies of a fares booklet free of charge with advertisements to defray his costs and the undertaking offered them for sale at 1d per copy. In the light of experience with the new fares, in May 1933 a 2d stage between Taff House and Berw Road instead of 2½d was introduced as there was a 1½d fare from Taff House to Fountain, a short distance away. As workmen travelling to town from points between Common Road and Bonvilston Road were being penalised, a 1½d single and 2d return Workmen's Stage between Station Square and Bonvilston Road was introduced.

The positive trolley wire in the up line by Burton's Section, Cilfynydd, broke at 3pm on 18 September 1932 although the repairs did not delay services. Four ears were damaged and street lighting lines broken at 9am on 5 October 1932 when a trolleybus skidded on Broadway. In late November 1932 Taff House junction was modified to ease trolleybus running into Fothergill Street. The double crossings were taken out and both the up and down lines were made straight through from Broadway into Fothergill Street. On 15 December 1932 the up positive wire at the Broadway section breaker parted, but no delays resulted as anchor ears had been fitted at a number of section breakers to prevent broken lines falling to the ground.

Upon completion of the tram track removal the Transport Committee considered that the trolleybus services could be speeded up to such an extent that at least one of the trolleybuses could be dispensed with. The Transport Manager was instructed to dispense with one vehicle forthwith and to maintain the present service with the remaining fleet. In an effort to identify which one the costs of single versus double-deck trolleybuses were compared:

|  | 60-seater pa | 32-seater pa | difference pa |
|---|---|---|---|
| Wages | No difference | | |
| Road Licence | £96 | £57 12s | £38 8s |
| Insurance | £38 | £29 12s | £8 8s |
| Energy (approx) | 2¼d per mile | 1.9d per mile | 0.35d per mile |

It was estimated that the single-deck trolleybuses were running 200,000 miles pa and the double-deckers 67,580 miles pa. If the two double-deck trolleybuses were withdrawn they would have to be replaced by four single-deckers, but no action was taken. Mr Armstrong reported on 17 February 1933 that since speeding up the service on 2 January 1933 and 23 January 1933 respectively, the trolleybuses were now running 49½ bus hours per week less on weekdays and 6¼ hours less on Sundays, saving some £330 4s in wages pa.

**PRESENT FARES**         **DETAILS OF SUGGESTED ALTERATIONS**

**Ordinary fares**
Treforest – Cilfynydd
**1d.**

| | |
|---|---|
| Treforest terminus – Archway | cancelled |
| Taff Vale Park – Station Square | no change |
| Station Square – West Street | cancelled |
| Fountain – Common Road | cancelled |
| Berw Road – Baptist Chapel | cancelled |
| West Street – Bonvilston Road | cancelled |
| Baptist Chapel – Norton Bridge | cancelled |
| Bonvilston Road – Quarry Sidings | cancelled |
| Norton Bridge – Cilfynydd terminus | cancelled |

**1½d.**

| | |
|---|---|
| Treforest terminus – *New Inn Hotel* | Shortened to Treforest – Station Square; a return trip was increased to 3d from 2½d. |
| Taff House – Fountain | Stage unchanged but a return trips was increased to 3d from 2½d. |
| Archway – Berw Road | New stage. Introduced to meet the need for a 1½d stage from Archway. |
| Station Square – Baptist Chapel | Stage unchanged but a return journey would now cost 3d instead of 2½d. |
| Fountain – Bonvilston Road | ditto |
| Common Road – Norton Bridge | ditto |
| Baptist Chapel – Quarry Sidings | ditto |
| Bonvilston Road – Cilfynydd | ditto |

**2d.**

| | |
|---|---|
| Treforest terminus – West Street | Shortened to Treforest – Fountain increasing a return journey by ½d. |
| Archway – Baptist Chapel | Stage unchanged but ½d increase on return journey. |
| Station Square – Norton Bridge | ditto |
| Fountain – Cilfynydd | Shortened to Berw Road, also ½d increase on a return journey between the new stage points. Present 3½d return fare less than that pre-war. |

**2½d.**

| | |
|---|---|
| Treforest – Baptist Chapel | New Fares (previously no 2½d ordinary single stage) |
| Taff House – Norton Bridge | ditto |
| Archway – Quarry Sidings | ditto |
| Station Square – Cilfynydd | At present 3d single, 4d return. New fare gives a 1d increase on return journey. The present 4d return is too low and equated to the pre-World War One fare, i.e. 2d each way. |

**3d.**

| | |
|---|---|
| Treforest – Bonvilston Road | New Stage. Treforest – Norton Bridge. Archway – Cilfynydd. Lengthened stages with no returns. |
| Station Square – Cilfynydd | New 2½d single earning an extra 1d (see 2½d fares). |

**Workmen's fares**

| | Single | Return | |
|---|---|---|---|
| Treforest – Mill Street | 1½d | 2d | No change |
| Station Square – Common Road | 1½d | 2d | Used to be Station Square |
| Mill Street – Baptist Chapel | 1½d | 2d | to Baptist Chapel |
| Fountain – Bonvilston Road | 1½d | 2d | No change |
| Common Road – Norton Bridge | 1½d | 2d | No change |
| Bonvilston Road – Cilfynydd | 1½d | 2d | No change |
| Brook Street – Mill Street | 1½d | 2d | New |
| Castle Inn Bridge – Station Square | ½d | 2d | New for workmen |
| Castle Inn Bridge – Mill Street | 1½d | 2d | New for workmen |
| Central Square – Station Square | ½d | 2d | New for workmen |
| Treforest – Baptist Chapel | 2d | 3d | Cut from Bonvilston Road |
| Station Square – Cilfynydd | 2d | 3d | No change |
| Treforest – Cilfynydd | 3d | 5d | Transport Committee left the return fare unchanged at 4d. |

On 16 December 1932 Mr C.J. Gwyther, Middle Street, Pontypridd, died as a result of injuries sustained as he attempted to board a trolleybus. The inquest returned a verdict of accidental death and no blame was attached to the crew.

On 26 January 1933 the up positive wire broke at Cilfynydd Police Station but again there was no delay. The guard wires were pulled down on to the trolley wires at Norton Bridge Corner on 4 February 1933 at 9.15am due to a dewirement. The circuit breaker on no. 3 traction feeder opened causing a 4 minute delay. As a result further anchor wires were fitted.

Between 24 and 27 February 1933 heavy snowstorms wreaked havoc with the timetable. On Friday 24 February the trolleybuses could not move through the snow due to side-skidding; the power was repeatedly off for periods of up to 30 minutes as the South Wales Power Co.'s wires were down, and also for periods of up to 3½ hours due to the supply failing from the Generating Station, Treforest. In early March a bracket arm at the curve in Albion Road damaged in the blizzard was changed and the curve at the same point eased.

Mr Armstrong replied on 10 March 1933 to calls to reduce costs. He admitted that overhead charges varied considerably between 0.138d and 0.662d per mile, the higher amount being due to repairs to the tower wagon. The cost of work on the underground feeders was allocated to the overhead and these required much attention; indeed the Post Office (GPO) engineer remained dissatisfied with their condition where they were laid close to underground telephone cables. It would be impossible to adhere to any arbitrary percentage reductions as revenue continued to fall, the pits losing 65 shifts in the month ending March 1933. The withdrawal of Sunday services was considered; however, a Subcommittee rejected this recommending that the Treforest – Cilfynydd service should run every 20 minutes, instead of every 15 minutes, requiring two trolleybuses instead of three. They also decided that the cost of maintenance and repair of the underground traction mains should be charged to the Electricity Department. Vehicle and overhead equipment maintenance, repair and cleaning were to be reduced by 25%.

There had been problems with contactor coils overheating and burning out. English Electric suggested some modifications, and when their specialist called on 16 March 1933 he offered to send a full set of modified coils on trial. At the driver's request windscreen wipers were fitted to the trolleybuses.

The Transport Manager suggested that a trolleybus be decorated for the Pontypridd Hospital in the week commencing 26 June 1933.

On 10 April 1933 tests were made by the GPO using a portable radio to establish the extent of radio interference, both on a trolleybus and at different points along the route. The interference was particularly bad along Coedpenmaen Road although there was an improvement when trolleybus No. 1 was fitted with stopper coils. The same vehicle was taken out on Sunday morning 21 May 1933 fitted with filters placed in circuit with the compressor motor, the interference from which had not been cut out by the stopper coils. Several listeners in Treforest and Coedpenmaen Road stated that this was a great improvement on previous tests, although this did not necessarily mean that when a full trolleybus service was running, and all vehicles equipped with filters, that listening would not be affected. BTH quoted £20 per set or £17 18s each for six for their Wireless Interference Eliminators.

The Electricity Committee deferred consideration of a further reduction in power charges on 29 May 1933 for 6 months.

In mid-September 1933 Mr Armstrong repeated that the price of 1⅛d per unit was still too high. According to MTTA returns, the average price of 21 undertakings taking less than one million units pa was 0.991d per unit. Newport was paying only 0.8d plus a coal clause and Cardiff, a much larger operator, only 0.64d per unit. Although the Electrical Department was able to respond with a list of 6 undertakings taking over 1 million units where the charge was 1d per unit or more; in October 1933 it was agreed to reduce the charge to 1d per unit. Based on the number of units taken in the year ending 31 March 1933 this would amount to a reduction of £305 16s 9d.

On Thursday 9 December 1933 a bracket arm near the signal box on the Broadway was damaged by the last trolleybus running into the depot. It was replaced that same night causing no delay to traffic. The Tabernacle traction pillar was replaced as the existing one was overheating at full load. Also in early December 1933 there was much work to locate and repair faults on the negative return cable in Ynysangharad Road. Several short lengths were put in to cut out the defective portions.

The District Joint Industrial Council for the Tramway and Transport Industry wrote in January 1934 that they were considering ending the temporary reduction of drivers' and young conductors' wages introduced on 4 April 1932. The PUDC representative was instructed to oppose reversion to the former rates. By now the complement of traffic employees had fallen somewhat to 70 drivers and conductors (73 in 1932), 4 inspectors and 2 part-time clerks. There were complaints about the temperature in the garage: over an eight-day period in December this had averaged 32°F but a heating system was only added the following July. In March 1934 the TGWU requested, on behalf of trolleybus drivers, that the street lighting in Cilfynydd Road at Norton Bridge and the 'Albion Hotel', be improved.

The Rhondda Tramways Company's last trams ran on 1 February 1934 and were replaced by motorbuses. There was no more mention of trolley vehicles.

By February 1934 an extra trolleybus left the depot at 9.45 pm on Sundays to give a 10-minute service from 9.55 to 10.35 pm for workmen on the Cilfynydd section.

In April 1934 trolley wires parted on four separate occasions of which three were at the Broadway, 'Crown Hotel' and 'Bonvilston Hotel' section breakers, and the fourth in the John Street crossing frog. That month line fittings were changed at the Depot, Broadway, Norton Bridge, Taff House and John Street and the down line 'Crown Hotel' section breaker. The down line wire parted in the fitting at Burton's section break on the evening of 16 May 1934. The high number of breakages was attributed to the fittings used by Clough Smith and it was decided to change all negative fittings and sections in the near future. The insulation resistance of the negative return cables between the Generating Station and the Corn Stores Hill were brought up to give a Me-Ohm test, and satisfied GPO requirements. Work was continuing on the return cables between the generating station and the sub-station, as these were also in bad condition. Work continued on the Broadway negative return cable, a new cable being suspended across the river at Brewery Lane.

A further test to establish if stopper coils and suppressor units on trolleybuses were of any benefit was made on Sunday 6 May 1934 with GPO engineers present. Three trolleybuses were taken out: one untreated, another fitted with stopper coils in the main cables on the roof, and the third fitted with suppressor units in the compressor and contactor circuits. A degree of noise

Bristol E 9 / Beadle at Glyntaff Depot decorated for George V's 1935 Silver Jubilee. Glyntaff Depot. The galvanised corrugated iron building to the left of the trolleybus is where the trolleybuses were housed. St Mary's Church Glyntaff is in the background to the right. Note the jumper cables coming from the northbound trolley wires attached to the bracket arm on the right hand side of the photograph, providing traction power to the physically-isolated single pair of wires leading into the building. (Peter Smith Collection [PUDCTD])

was selected as standard, i.e. the noise produced when the apparatus causing the noise is untreated and was designated as 100%.

i) Running from Broadway to Bridge Street
no noise at a distance of ¾ mile from the route.

ii) Running from the *Ivor Arms Hotel* to the *Bonvilston Hotel*
untreated trolleybus – 2 slight clicks
stopper coil trolleybus – no traction motor noise but 2 clicks at 50% signal strength
suppressor units trolleybus – a rushing noise at 70% signal strength as the vehicle passed and a few loud clicks afterwards.

iii) Trolleybuses driven separately to turning point at *Bonvilston Hotel*
untreated trolleybus – clicks at 30% to 50% signal strength reducing with distance
stopper coil trolleybus – no noise
suppressor units trolleybus – clicks at 30% to 40% and rushing noise at 40% to 50% signal strength (this was difficult to account for, because as far as can be ascertained, the trolleybuses were not then running).

iv) Trolleybus running down the Corn Stores Hill
untreated trolleybus – clicks at 100% – 150% signal strength and rushing noise at 120% – 100% signal strength after the vehicle went out of sight.
stopper coil trolleybus – clicks at 20% signal strength
suppressor units trolleybus – clicks at 70%-120%.

The GPO expert felt that stopper coils were the most effective means of minimising interference but these had been designed to prevent medium wave radio interference and were ineffective for long wave. Experiments were underway with stopper coils for both wavelengths and it was deemed better to wait before investing in a solution. Only in September 1935 were anti-interference devices to cut out long wave radio interference ordered from The Standard Telephones and Cables Co. Ltd.

As the electric tower wagon was now in a poor state and its battery life-expired, in June 1934 the Engineer obtained tenders, varying between £715 and £805, for an electric or petrol driven replacement. As a new battery for the existing wagon was available at £263-£353 he decided to retain the vehicle and purchase a new battery. However, on 21 October 1934 the armature shaft of the electric motor sheared off, and a horse-drawn wagon had to be used until it was repaired. It re-entered service on 14 December 1934. In April 1935 the tenders of BTCC for a 1-ton petrol lorry chassis at £194 15s, and Rawlinsons Ltd., Blackburn, for a lorry body with 3-section telescopic tower at £185 5s, were accepted.

On Sunday evening 30 September 1934 an underground cable fault developed on no. 1 traction feeder at 10.05 pm cutting off supplies on the Treforest Section beyond Broadway. Replacement motorbuses were put on as there was a Town Hall Concert that evening. The faulty section of the cable, the Machine Bridge, was isolated and power restored at 10.57pm. The cable was repaired the following day.

By November 1934 the 'New Inn' sections were changed and a more efficient type of section insulator installed. Towards the end of November 1934 Bristol E 9 was off the road with recurrent Hardy Spicer propeller shaft knocking and wear caused by the inability to retain the grease packing. This problem had first been noticed in mid-1932 and attributed to a

Station Square, Pontypridd, following installation of traffic island and rewiring in September 1935. Sardis Road with a Western Welsh single deck Leyland motorbus is in the left background whilst High Street descends on the right. In the apex of the junction is the 'Clarence Hotel' with the County Cinema behind. (Cy Yandell Collection)

lack of lubrication to the ball bearing in the third differential of the leading rear axle. The opportunity was taken to repair 9' s roof at the same time.

The no. 2 traction feeder failed on 3 December 1934 from 3.40pm to 4.07pm when two insulator bolts broke on the same span on the Rhondda Road lines feeding Pwllgwaun Colliery. No. 2 feeder was again out of commission on 21 December 1934 from 8.07pm to 8.20pm due to a trolley boom on no. 9 becoming live under the PCNR Bridge and causing a short circuit. Also in December 1934 the section breaker at the Old Bridge was replaced. On Saturday 15 December 1934 the booms of trolleybus 5 left the wires near the Burton's section breaker, pulled down two bays of guard wires, and struck the bracket arm. The top section of the traction pole was badly bent and the pole had to be replaced.

From January 1935, a 7½-minute trolleybus service was operated for concert goers between 9.50 and 10.30pm on Sunday evenings. Despite objections from the union, who felt that it was removing overtime from platform staff, the additional trolleybus was manned by shed hands, one being already on duty and the other being brought in one hour early, to avoid calling in a driver and conductor for just an hour's work.

In February 1935 the section insulators were replaced at Burton Sections and 'Bonvilston Hotel', and the wood troughing under the PCNR Bridge was repaired and creosoted. It was decided in April 1935 to progressively move telegraph poles and traction poles to the rear of the footpath in order to improve street lighting on Police Row, Norton Bridge.

On Thursday 28 March 1935 the negative trolley wire inside the crossing frog at John Street terminus broke, and as the positive wire had broken at the same location in February 1935 a new crossing was installed. With the installation of a new type of section insulator at Norton Bridge sections on Sunday 17 March 1935, the entire route had been re-equipped, greatly reducing the number of trolley wire breakages. New trolley wire was also run over the Rhondda Bridge, Taff Street.

There was an accident at Norton Bridge Road, Pontshonnorton on Saturday evening 23 March 1935 resulting in the death of Mrs Rose Bevan. A double-deck trolleybus heading towards Pontypridd at about 8.43pm passed a motorbus travelling in the opposite direction. The trolleybus driver Isaac Evans sounded his horn as he passed but then noticed Mrs Bevan in the centre of the road some 15ft ahead, crossing from the canal side of the road. He braked and swerved to the offside. If she had continued across the road she would have escaped; but

Another view of Bristol E 9 at Glyntaff Depot decorated for the 1935 Silver Jubilee with Jack John, Rolling Stock Superintendent, standing in front on the nearside. Note the pair of trolley wires coming in from the left of the photograph from the former tram depot and tied-off to the traction pole on the right. Trolleybuses had to depole and rewire to gain access to or from either depot building at this time. (Cy Yandell Collection [PUDCTD])

The 1931 Guy BTX60 No. 8 is seen here in Coedpenmaen Road at the junction with Foundry Place. Mrs Morley, wife of the cobbler whose shop was behind the house ("ley" of the cobbler's name can be read above the arched brickwork) is scrubbing her doorstep. Prices sweetshop advertising Lyons Tea and Gold Flake tobacco is on the left by the trolleybus, and the girder bridge over the Glamorganshire canal can be seen in the background. Something has attracted the attention of a number of youngsters, all wearing boots with their socks slipped down to their ankles, whilst a number of PUDCTD staff are in attendance. (Peter Smith Collection)

turned back, and despite another swerve by the trolleybus she was caught by the offside corner, knocked down and sustained severe injuries from which she died ninety minutes later. The driver was exonerated from all blame. The Coroner pointed out that the gas street lighting was insufficient and that trolleybuses should be fitted with speedometers. These had originally been fitted but had proved unsatisfactory. The MoT responded that speedometers had been compulsory in all new trolley vehicles since 1932. Subsequently four traction poles were moved from the curb line to the back of the path along Police Row.

The prevailing trolleybus schedules were based on an average speed of 9mph off-peak and 8.8mph during peak hours, but congestion in the town centre meant that schedules could not be maintained within the stipulated speed limits. Arguing that since the limits had been laid down, the tram track had been removed and other road improvements made, application was made to the MoT in March 1935 for an increase in the maximum speed from 16mph to 20mph. This was granted on 12 July 1935.

On 21 May 1935 the Transport Committee under its new Chairman, Councillor D.T. Jones, considered complaints from other road users and the police that the compulsory trolleybus stop at the Rhondda Bridge, High Street, inwards, held up vehicles behind. This induced drivers of these vehicles to overtake without being able to see any traffic coming out of Mill Street. It was decided to contact the MoT.

The traction pole outside the premises of Maison Samuel, 21 Taff Street, Pontypridd was removed in May 1935 by mutual agreement and replaced with a wall rosette on the premises of Messrs Thomas & Evans Ltd. nearby subject to a wayleave of 2s pa.

The northbound lines at Station Square were diverted around an experimental traffic island in September 1935 requiring two additional traction poles and a Bundy Clock installed for the trolleybus and Rhydyfelin routes. During the month of October

1935 trolleybuses suffered a broken chassis spring, a damaged wing, and six trolley heads pulled off and damaged. There were no trolley wire breakages or interruptions in service. Line fittings were changed at Cilfynydd Road, Abattoir, Station Square, John Street and Taff House. "Flash" tests were made on all sections of lines, and all lines inspected. However, on 2 November 1935 power was cut off for 45 minutes owing to a wire breakage in Park Street Treforest caused by a dewirement. Cables feeding the overhead lines at the Burton's and Broadway section breaks parted on 27 and 31 December 1935 respectively, but there were no delays and repairs were carried out immediately.

Mr Armstrong, Transport Manager, suggested that all smoking restrictions should be abolished as there were insufficient seats for smokers! Pontypridd was one of the few operators with such restrictions at that time, namely no smoking in the upper saloon on double-deckers or in the front compartment of centre entrance vehicles. The matter was complicated by the number of inter-running agreements on motorbus services. In January 1936 all smoking restrictions on PUDC vehicles were cancelled.

In March 1936 Mr Armstrong drew the Transport Committee's attention to the price of traction current, the average fuel/energy costs per mile being:

|  | January 1936 | February 1936 |
|---|---|---|
| Oil fuel | 1.043d | 1.018d |
| Petrol | 2.235d | 2.276d |
| Trolleybus | 2.369d | 2.306d |

In December 1934 the undertaking took 51,628 units, falling to 50,394 in December 1935. If all petrol buses were operated under similar conditions as those between Treforest and Cilfynydd, the average fuel cost per mile would be much reduced, as on routes such as Penycoedcae, Maesycoed and Common fuel consumption was high. On the Porth route (which was comparable to the trolleybus route) 32-seater petrol buses ran 6.5 miles per gallon, which at 1s 0¾d per gallon gave a fuel cost of 1.9d per bus mile. Double-deck diesel buses were returning 11 miles per gallon, which at 1s 0¼d per gallon gave a fuel cost of 1.1d per bus mile. Comparison with the trolleybuses' energy cost of 2.3d per mile indicated that the charge of one penny per unit was too high. The Transport Committee asked the Electricity Committee to reduce the charge for traction current. Having made a profit of over £10,000 in the preceding year, the Electricity Committee decided on 12 May 1936 that they would consider reducing the price from 1d to 0.8d per unit provided that at least 500,000 units were taken annually; however, the matter was left pending a review of all electricity charges. Applicable from 1 July 1936 the traction current price fell 25% to 0.75d per unit.

It was found that the body framing of Guy BTX60 trolleybus 8, particularly behind the lower panels, had almost rotted away. By January 1936 the panelling had been partly removed and it became evident that the repairs would require a time-consuming thorough job, confirming the need of an additional building behind the bus depot for maintenance purposes. In June 1936 the Transport Manager was instructed to submit an estimate of the cost of repair and maintenance to eight, and to make a comparison with the maintenance costs of other small transport undertakings. By 17 July 1936 it was known that the repairs had cost £116 14s 10d, involving extensive repairs to the roof, reconstruction of the nearside, and a considerable amount of work to the body offside, the chassis, floors and seats. The entrance stanchions and handrails were relined with Doverite; the trolley booms and electrical equipment were thoroughly overhauled, and the vehicle painted and varnished inside and outside.

English Electric approached the Council once again with an offer to loan them one of their latest double-deck trolleybuses. As in 1932 the offer was declined.

A comparison of the relative costs of repairs and maintenance of trolley vehicles in various undertakings prepared by the Transport (Engineering) Department showed:

| Name | Total Capital | Miles Run | Cost per mile |
|---|---|---|---|
| 1. Ashton under Lyne | 33,914 | 194,374 | 2.789d |
| 2. Derby | | 1,922,693 | 2.513d |
| 3. Maidstone | 47,894 | 419,863 | 2.417d |
| 4. Wolverhampton | 600,778 | 3,900,424 | 2.044d |
| 5. Pontypridd | 35,395 | 266,657 | 2.02d |
| 6. Nottingham | 381,278 | 3,035,132 | 1.981d |
| 7. Walsall | 93,109 | 632,720 | 1.878d |
| 8. Grimsby | 16,297 | 263,980 | 1.791d |
| 9. Ipswich | 188,570 | 1,645,056 | 1.717d |
| 10. West Hartlepool | 78,927 | 579,481 | 1.65d |
| 11. Chesterfield | 50,545 | 606,806 | 1.52d |
| 12. Portsmouth | 74,060 | 243,122 | 1.503d |
| 13. Birmingham | 170,585 | 1,530,487 | 1.454d |
| 14. St. Helens | 63,068 | 825,835 | 1.325d |
| 15. Darlington | 125,273 | 1,296,666 | 1.27d |

An attempt to use the battery tower wagon whilst the new tower wagon was under repair had confirmed that it was life-expired and it was suggested that a 2-ton lorry be purchased upon which the tower could be mounted when the newer chassis was out of service. The lowest of three tenders came from BTCC who offered a second-hand overhauled chassis at £100, to which would have to be added a new radiator mask at £3 10s and about £30 to £35 for a locally-built cab and body. The Bristol offer was made in conjunction with their tender for a double-deck motorbus. Mr G.J. Evans, Electrical and Transport Engineer, recommended the purchase of both motorbus and tower wagon chassis. The Bristol chassis was delivered by mid-

English Electric single-decker trolleybus 7 re-entered service at the end of 1936 after a complete overhaul of the body, repairs to the electrical equipment and Estler trolley base, and a repaint using Lewis Berger's "Kemitone" synthetic paints, which were deemed to give the best of the synthetic finishes yet tried, at a total cost of £77. This photograph was taken in Glyntaff Depot yard with the GWR (ex-ADR) railway line in the background for use in Messrs Berger's advertising. (Roy Marshall Collection [Berger Paints])

Harry Nichols and his colleague with Bristol E 9, decorated for the Coronation of King George VI in May 1937, pose at John Street terminus Treforest. Long Row Terrace, Meadow Street is in the background to the right. The unused service number box above the driver's cab once again provides the basis for the photographs of the new King and his Queen. The large sidelights or spotlights above the driver's windscreen at the top of the nearside and offside front pillars are still in place, providing evidence that the body had not yet been rebuilt. (Cy Yandell Collection)

July 1937 but the firm which had successfully tendered to build a cab and body was now too busy to carry out the work. Rather than wait, the work was entrusted to Messrs W. Lewis & Sons Ltd., Cardiff, although more expensive at £62 10s.

On Saturday 29 February 1936 the booms of trolleybus 9 caught under the PCNR bridge pulling off the positive head and leading to two journeys being lost. The overhead line proved to be in perfect condition. An overhead wiring bracket arm outside the garage was damaged by trolleybus 4 on 23 March 1936.

Together with a member of the GPO Engineering Department further trials were made on Sunday morning 10 May 1936 aimed at reducing the wireless interference caused by trolleybuses. In addition to the mains suppressor coils already fitted to trolleybus 1, a filter arrangement was connected up. This vehicle and an untreated trolleybus were run up and down Park Street in turn, while observations were made on a wireless set in the GPO van and on a Marconi mains radio in a private house in Castle Street. On both sets there was a noticeable reduction in the noise caused by the trolleybus fitted with a suppressor compared with the untreated one.

At 8.16am on Saturday 2 May 1936 a fault developed in the negative return cables at the YMCA causing a delay of 17 minutes.

A trolleybus was struck by lightning on 20 June 1936 blowing a switch and causing a minor fire, whilst a fire at the 'Park Hotel' disorganised services from 5.40 – 9pm on 23 June 1936. Trolleybuses on the Cilfynydd portion of the route were

withdrawn and replaced with a skeleton motorbus service; Treforest trolleybuses were turned at Station Square. Services through the town were resumed between 7.30 and 8pm. The power was off for 48 minutes on Tuesday 14 July 1936 during which two motorbuses endeavoured to maintain services. That same day, at midday, trolleybus 5 brought down three bays of street lighting between the 'Bonvilston Hotel' and the Baptist Chapel but no defect could be found in the overhead wires. On Friday 7 August 1936 the positive "up" trolley wire at the Police Station Sections at Cilfynydd was broken by trolleybus 8. The trolley head was jammed in the overhead wire and the bus lost one trip.

The uncrowned King, Edward VIII, later known as the Duke of Windsor, who identified himself very much with the hardships of South Wales, visited Pontypridd on 18 November 1936 and traffic was disrupted during his departure from 12 noon until 12.40pm. Ominously just two weeks later at the full Council meeting delegates were selected to attend the Glamorganshire County Council Air Raid Precautions Scheme in Cardiff.

Following many complaints from drivers about poor visibility in the dark along Pontshonorton Road and the fatal accident in March 1935, a report on trolleybus headlights was requested in December 1936. After contacting a number of other operators the Electrical Engineer responded that earlier trolley vehicles, including those in Pontypridd, were generally equipped with interior and exterior lighting fed by traction current. Such headlamps were considered inadequate except where there was good street lighting. Some undertakings had achieved improvements by using: GEC long series system with 60W lamps in place of 40W (a trial on trolleybus 6 had provided a limited improvement); GEC long series system with 60W lamps combined with special headlamp fittings supplied by Messrs Sanders of Birmingham; separate low tension lighting, with dynamo and battery for the head, side and tail lamps, horn and wiper, but with the continued use of the traction supply for the interior lighting (considered effective although conversion was expensive); and/or separate spot or fog lamps for use in fog or on badly lit roads.

He commented that headlamps working from DC traction current could not be focussed to produce a directional beam, South Lancashire Transport for example using a 48W cadmium yellow fog lamp at each bottom corner of the dash. Although more recent trolleybuses were fitted with low tension dynamo and battery equipment, as used on motor vehicles, it would be difficult and expensive to convert the existing trolleybus fleet. The other eight trolleybuses were fitted with Phillip's 100-volt 60W traction lamps and new reflectors which together provided some improvement. The work was completed by October 1937; however, on 2 October 1937 new Road Vehicles Lighting Regulations came into effect and Mr Evans then set about fitting dipping arrangements to the headlamps.

On Wednesday 30 December 1936 at 9.37pm the positive trolley wire at Burton's section feeder, Cilfynydd broke. The loose end of this wire fell over the negative line causing a dead short. This resulted in the supply being off with a consequent delay to traffic on this section from 9.37pm until 10.12pm.

The Coronation Day of George VI was planned for 12 May 1937, the date previously foreseen for Edward VII's Coronation. The undertaking carried some 1,300 children from Cilfynydd, Norton Bridge and Hawthorn, to and from the cinema free of charge as a contribution to the Coronation festivities. The town was decorated with bunting, union flags and strings of coloured fairy lights whilst a golden crown containing some 200 small light bulbs had been placed on top of the ornamental arches supporting the trolleybus equipment over Victoria Bridge. Bristol trolleybus 9 was specially decorated and illuminated for the occasion.

Work to replace the section insulators at Burton's Cilfynydd and move the pillar closer to the supporting traction pole was completed on 25 March 1937. Trolleybus 5 re-entered service following a thorough overhaul of the electrical equipment, reconditioning of the saloon windows, seats, floors, panels and doors, and a repaint and varnish, again using Berger paints, on the same date.

Mr Armstrong, the Transport Manager, was due to retire on 30 June 1938 whilst the Electrical and Transport Engineer, Mr G.J. Evans, would also retire about two years later. The Transport Committee debated the continuing need to manage the transport undertaking's commercial and engineering sections separately in May 1937. Following a Subcommittee review it was felt that upon Mr Evan's retirement the administration and control of the traffic side of the undertaking could be entrusted to Mr John Powell, then Transport Clerk, and Chief Inspector Freeman. It was decided that effective 1 July 1938 and until Mr Evan's retirement, Mr Powell would be appointed to the position of Transport Manager at a salary of £312 pa rising at the end of one year to £330 pa, and that Chief Inspector Freeman be appointed Traffic Superintendent at a salary of £286 pa, rising at the end of one year to £300 pa.

In early August 1937 there were a series of complaints about low voltage at Cilfynydd. Drivers noted that the air brake compressor motors were running very slowly and had difficulty in building up pressure whilst there were problems operating contactors. It was necessary to withdraw Bristol 9 from service twice owing to the line voltage being too low to attract the plungers to make contact with the interlocking arrangement.

Following a report of damage to telephone cables in Broadway due to electrolytic action possibly caused by leakage of trolleybus traction current, a fault developed on no. 2 Traction feeder at a joint box in one of the cable pits in Broadway on 25 August 1937. The cable was repaired by inserting four yards of new cable but on testing another fault was discovered and subsequently traced to a point near the Broadway section pillar. On cutting this out the cable remained defective as it was found that water had percolated along the cable for more than 50 yards. As the cable was in the roadway it was deemed costly to replace it in that position and conduits for new cables were laid beneath the pavement. Instructions were issued that if at any period when supply difficulties were experienced the load was to be taken via the Gas Yard rotary converter in the town centre.

There were several cases of overhead damage during August 1937. The records indicate that these generally only involved new drivers or those who also drove motorbuses. Many occurred on the last journey into the depot! It was noted that older, steadier drivers were practically dewirement free. At 9.20pm on Sunday 22 August 1937, trolleybus 8 suffered a dewirement which pulled off its trolleyhead causing considerable delay until a replacement trolleybus could be sent out.

Probably in an effort to clear their remaining trolleybus stock, BTCC offered a range of spares, including a Bull 80hp motor with eddy current brakes, reversing controller, braking master controller, a set of resistance boxes, accelerating panel, line contactor panel, two circuit breakers, a polarity indicator, and various smaller items for the Bristol E trolleybus at £87, just 25% of their normal price. The offer was accepted, it being noted that a motor armature rewind alone would cost more than the total amount asked.

Trolleybus 2 re-entered service on 9 October 1937 following a complete overhaul of the bodywork, electrics and mechanical equipment and a repaint with Berger paints.

Trolleybus 1 collided with a traction pole near Workmen's Hall, Cilfynydd, on 11 October 1937 requiring a replacement pole

English Electric single-decker 4 heads towards Cilfynydd at the junction of Taff Street and Market Street in the late 1930s. Hepworth the tailors, once the UK's largest clothing manufacturer and now trading as Next plc, advertise "holiday wear". (Peter Smith Collection)

with bracket arm, etc, and repairs to the trolleybus together totalling £39. As the overhaul of one trolleybus had just been completed and no. 4, the next in line for similar treatment had not been withdrawn, it was decided to dock 1 instead.

On 17 September 1937 the Transport Manager reported that the NJIC for the Road Passenger Transport Industry had applied for an increase of 4s per week of 48 hours which he estimated would increase costs for drivers and conductors alone by £860 pa. The application was coupled to an increase in the number of days of leave, from 8 to 12, adding a further £190 pa to wage costs. He feared serious effects on the undertaking. The last NJIC award had been made subject to the right of appeal by undertakings who considered they were not in a financial position to pay the increase and Pontypridd had successfully appealed. The wage award finally granted and adopted by MTTA was 2s per week from the beginning of December 1937 subject to no further revisions of wages or conditions being considered for a further 2 years. This increase was estimated to increase costs by £480 to £500 pa.

In the financial year ending 31 March 1937 there had been a net loss on the transport system of £700, excluding the call upon rates to meet the annual repayment of debt still outstanding on the scrapped tramways. Mr Armstrong recommended that the Council should decide if an appeal against the award should be made, which none of the smaller municipal transport undertakings in South Wales and Monmouthshire had accepted (although Cardiff and Newport Corporations had). However, following consideration by a Subcommittee it was decided to grant the award.

By November 1937 there were delays in the body shop and arrears of maintenance, trolleybus 1 awaiting substantial reconstruction following its collision with a traction pole and no. 6 also needing attention following collision damage. After a visit by the Transport Subcommittee to the former tram shed on 13 January 1938 estimates were requested for alterations to provide a paint shop and repair shop at the lower portion of the building; an extension of the trolleybus garage at the western end; and a roof above the open space between the tram shed and the trolleybus garage. These showed that alterations to the former tram shed for painting and repairing vehicles would cost £313. It was decided on 21 June 1938 to proceed with sliding doors and partitions for the paint shop and workshop; however, nothing was ever done about extending the trolleybus garage space.

By May 1938 the *Pontypridd Observer* was expressing concerns at the deplorable state of trolleybuses 3, 4 and 6 which, they wrote, compared unfavourably with Rhondda Transport's motorbuses. The newspaper urged the Department to offer some of the unemployed a job in an accelerated rejuvenation of the fleet. Trolleybus 4 re-entered service on 28 July 1938 after a partial bodywork overhaul followed by a complete paint and varnish at a cost of £59. The newspaper hoped that trolleybuses 3 and 6 would soon benefit from the same treatment.

Road works in the vicinity of the PCNR bridge on Broadway necessitated changes to the overhead wiring in February 1938; four new traction poles were planted and the position of another was altered in readiness for the change. In connection with road improvements at Norton Bridge Junction the overhead line was altered in April 1938 and a traction pole replanted. On Sundays 10 and 17 April 1938 the negative and positive wires were renewed between Burton's Section and Cilfynydd Police Station. The old wire had been in use for seven years and worn very thin. Owing to road improvements at

Llanbradach Hill, Treforest, one traction pole was repositioned and another removed. At 11am on Saturday 30 April 1938 the positive wire on the Broadway Sections broke on the outside of the anchor wire causing it to fall to the ground. Repairs were carried out and traffic was not delayed. In the summer new side-feeds were run and connected up on the Broadway Section.

Quotations were obtained from English Electric Ltd. and Messrs Waveney Co. Ltd., in September 1938 for a double-deck body to suit the original English Electric single-deck chassis. English Electric stated that their chassis would be able to carry a double-deck body but that the speed would be reduced and consequently it would be advisable to replace the electrical equipment by a more modern, higher power type.

**English Electric**

| One 62-seat double-deck rear entrance | |
|---|---|
| composite body | £1,083 10s 0d |
| Trolleys and trolley heads | £66 14s 0d |
| 80 HP motor | £485 |
| Low pressure lighting | £93 |
| TOTAL | £1,728 4s 0d |
| Extra for all metal body | £85 17s |

**Waveney**

| Body only | £915 |
|---|---|

Such a conversion did not appear to be an economic proposition and in the Transport Manager's view, it would be better to buy a new double-decker vehicle. On 20 September 1938 the Transport Committee resolved not to convert a single-deck trolleybus into a double-deck trolleybus. At the beginning of October 1938 English Electric Co. Ltd. wrote to offer a new 56-seater double-deck trolleybus on hire until the end of the year at a charge of 5d per mile, subject to a minimum 6,000 miles being operated and the Council taking out full comprehensive insurance and covering all other costs. The offer was not followed up.

On Monday 24 October 1938 at 5pm the negative trolley wire in Bridge Street, near the junction with West Street, burnt through as trolleybus 9 passed beneath heading towards town. All repairs had been completed by 5.25pm.

The Transport Manager complained that the ticketing system did not always enable an Inspector to detect a misused ticket. Conductors did not always accurately punch tickets as the stage numbers were printed very narrowly, and the same style of ticket was issued for single and return passengers, the single being punched once and the return twice. An ordinary single ticket could be sold again as a return after a second hole had been punched in it. As all returns were cancelled with the same type of round punch-hole on the return journey, an Inspector had no means of ensuring that a return ticket had been cancelled on that particular bus. In collusion with a conductor, a passenger could travel as often as he wished with an expired return ticket. Finally even a conductor had to rely on his memory of the passenger as to whether an ordinary cancellation punch-hole in a return ticket was one which he had made himself.

Having inspected the TIM ticket issuing machines then in use in Cardiff it was decided that printed value tickets and bell punch were still the most suitable method for Pontypridd. Effective 1 February 1939 special return tickets were ordered where necessary, with wider stage numbers so that accurate

Trallwn Canal Bridge with the 'Queen's Hotel' public house on the right and further down the road on the same side, the Llanover Hotel at the top of Cornstores Hill. In the distance is the spire of St. Catherine's Church which housed the Town Clock wound weekly by PUDC staff. (Photographer not known)

Trallwn, junction with West Street and Bridge Street. The road to the right led to the Brown & Lennox steelworks which produced, amongst other things, much of the anchor chaining used by the Royal Navy and British merchant shipping. (Photographer not known)

punching could be insisted upon and the existing ticket stocks were used up as singles. Stage numbers were included in subsequent issues of the timetable booklets, whilst it was proposed to display on each bus a route diagram showing fare stages and numbers, so that passengers would be able to see that their ticket had been correctly punched. Returns were no longer cancelled by punching, but by hand nippers. A stock of nippers was ordered so that each conductor on duty would have a pair giving a distinctive design of cancellation cut, the nippers being changed daily. Conductors going on duty were required to nip a certain section of the waybill with his nippers and all return tickets cancelled by him would bear the corresponding cut.

The supply from no. 2 traction feeder failed on Saturday 19 November 1938 from 9.50pm until 10.10pm due to a negative trolley wire breakage outside the YMCA. Both trolley wires in the southbound line from the 'New Inn' for 72 yards down Taff Street towards Liptons were found to be badly worn and were renewed. On 23 November 1938 at 08.15am a broken trolley wire near Church Road, Coedpenmaen, and a burnt off positive side feed at Norton Bridge caused the positive wire, down line, to be dead from Norton Bridge to Church Road. Trolleybuses used the other pair of wires. On 30 November 1938 a positive wire broke near Quarry Siding, Cilfynydd but there were no delays. On Saturday 3 December 1938 at the 'Crown Hotel' section breaker the negative trolley wire on the up line broke inside the splicing ear although the wire did not fall to the ground as it was held up by the anchor wire.

On Sunday 18 December 1938 Broadway was closed for bridge alterations. The trolleybuses were replaced for the day by motorbuses running via Wood Road. As the Post Office telephone lines above the trolleybus overhead wiring had been removed, the guard wires in Bridge Street were removed in February 1939.

The major overhaul of bodywork, framework and panels inside and outside, including roofs, floors, chassis cab and platform, seats and interior decoration, on trolleybus 1 was completed in February 1939. All windows were re-fixed with new mouldings and the electrical equipment overhauled, and the trolleybus painted and varnished. The total cost was £176. Although he did not recommend buying new trolleybuses, Mr Powell pointed out that there were difficulties coping with traffic on the trolleybus route if one of the double-deck vehicles was out of service. There were only four double-deck

motorbuses in the fleet at that time and they were all needed on the Porth route on Saturday evenings. He suggested another double-deck motorbus.

A joint meeting of the Electricity and Transport Departments on 4 May 1939 discussed the increasing threat of hostilities. As a first step it was decided to purchase spare plant and arrange alternative supplies. Provision was to be made for: first aid, fire fighting, protection of employees, protection of plant and buildings, gas detection and decontamination, and communications. It was decided to cover over and sandbag a length of the pits in the depot and cut deep trenches behind. All staff were to receive first aid training and some fire fighting instruction. All roof lights and windows were to be obscured with an opaque colour wash and where it was essential to have daylight illumination moveable blinds were to be provided.

On Sunday 2 April 1939, 650 yards of positive trolley wire were hung between Norton Bridge and Burton's section feeder to replace worn wire, the negative wire being renewed on 23 April 1939. A further 200 yards of both positive and negative wire between Cilfynydd Police Station and Albion Garage were renewed on 30 April 1939. The two section insulators near the Abbatoir, Broadway were changed, the old ones being retained for repair and further use. On Sunday 7 May 1939 the up positive trolley wire from 'Crown Hotel' to the Old Swan Lodging House Treforest (80 yards) was renewed. On 14 May 1939 the 'Crown Hotel' positive section breaker was replaced, the old one being taken down for repairs, and about 20 yards of positive trolley wire on the down line was also renewed at the Cilfynydd terminus. On Sunday 4 June 1939 wires were slewed into their permanent position under the new PCNR railway bridge on the Broadway.

In April 1939 a review of the benefits of introducing weekly tickets was carried out although 68 of the 93 undertakings in the MTTA did not issue such tickets. The request had come from regular riders to town from Cilfynydd although the fare was 2d or 2½d single – below the minimum fare at which it was usual to issue weekly tickets. The Transport Manager suggested a trial of a sixpenny four-journey ticket but only on the trolleybus route. Such tickets would permit two return journeys on one day between any two points on the route of issue. The tickets would be issued on any bus up to 9am with only one journey on the ticket being available after 3pm. The recommendation was adopted for a trial period of 6 weeks, effective Monday 4 September 1939.

# CHAPTER FIVE

# WARTIME

*In early September 1939 five squads were formed to handle emergency repairs to plant and overhead equipment caused by enemy action. All street lighting ceased from 5pm on 1 September 1939 whilst bus lighting was reduced and masked. Effective Sunday 17 September 1939 the motorbus timetables were reduced and passengers were encouraged to use the parallel trolleybus services wherever possible. It was announced that every effort would be made to operate the normal trolleybus service between Treforest and Cilfynydd throughout the week but that there would be no motorbus duplicates during busy periods.*

At the Traffic Commissioners' request motorbus mileage was reduced by 25% (more than that would have involved essential workmen's services) effective Sunday 17 September 1939 and passengers were encouraged to use the parallel trolleybus services wherever possible.

Most employees were already working until 10 or 11pm to cover the essential work caused by the prelude to war. Anticipating a call-up of staff to serve with the forces (22 conductors were 25 years old or less) a list was compiled of women suitable to work as conductresses, the Transport Manager adding: "We do not want girls of the "flapper" type for this kind of work, and our recommendation is that we restrict applicants to widows or unmarried women of the ages 20-25 inclusive".

On 21 November 1939 Councillor Powderhill urged the Transport Committee to consider extending the trolleybus system as he envisaged that oil supplies would soon be disrupted. This was underlined by a further rise in petrol prices to 1s 5¼d per gallon. Messrs Evans and Powell were instructed to investigate.

In an initial response Mr Powell reported on 12 December 1939 that trolleybuses were not a feasible proposition on services such as Maesycoed, Wood Road and Graigwen due to the steep narrow roads whilst they could not be run to Trehafod and Porth due to the through running agreement with Rhondda Transport Co. (although later in the war the MoWT had no concerns about enforcing changes to such agreements). The low railway bridge on Llantwit Road just south of John Street, ruled out an extension beyond the Treforest terminus. In his opinion solely the Rhydyfelin service was worth considering; however, he was convinced that no approval would be granted to erect overhead equipment along the main Cardiff road. It is unclear why he held this conviction as the UDC already ran trolleybuses on other portions of the A470 Cardiff-Merthyr trunk road; elsewhere trolleybus routes were extended along main roads into the 1960s and in any case special wartime circumstances prevailed.

The disused course of the Doctor's canal, which from a wharf and winding hole immediately to the south of the Hide & Skin Market, ran roughly parallel with Cardiff Road and the Glamorganshire Canal to a junction with the main canal at Dynea, offered an alternative route. The climb up to the Old Canal Road by the Market would need regrading and reconstruction whilst to join up to the existing depot access line on the east side of Machine Bridge and run behind Cardiff Road Houses (near Castle Inn Bridge) the lane leading out to the Old Canal would also require improvements. The canal had been progressively filled in as the course for a proposed tramway extension, however, this meant that the road surface would have to be made capable of carrying loaded trolleybuses weighing up to 12 tons.

On 4 January 1940 the Transport Manager presented his estimate for an extension from the Machine Bridge, Treforest along the Doctor's Canal to the Dynea end of Poplar Road, Rhydyfelin. Construction would require an MoT Provisional Order which he feared would be difficult to get at that time. His lack of enthusiasm was evident as several other operators were able to get approval for trolleybus route extensions during the war.

A service every 10 minutes on weekdays between Cilfynydd and Rhydyfelin would be combined with a 10-minute service between Church Road (near Bonvilston Road) and the existing John Street, Treforest terminus to provide a 5-minute frequency on the busy section between Bonvilston Road and Taff House. As an alternative to running to Church Road where the road layout would have required a reversing triangle rather than a turning circle, the Berw Road motorbus service could be replaced by trolleybuses. In order to meet traffic requirements on Saturdays the service between terminal points and the town would be increased to every 7½ minutes frequency (less than was already being provided, even in wartime, from Cilfynydd).

The trolleybus fleet would have to be increased from nine to 14 vehicles (eight for Cilfynydd-Rhydyfelin and six for Berw Road – Treforest) which, with two spares, indicated an order for seven new double-deck trolleybuses. Quotations showed a cost of £2,600 each although it is unknown which manufacturer would have been able to deliver new vehicles by this time in the war and no details of the quotations have been found.

The Surveyor found that the lane from Machine Bridge behind Cardiff Road Houses (Emily's Row) was unsuitable for larger vehicles. The alternatives were to operate along the main Cardiff road for just over half a mile to the Ebenezer Chapel, involving road works valued at £2,000, which he again emphasised would probably be vigorously opposed by the

No. 4 stands at the John Street terminus in Treforest. On the left the bridge over Llantwit Road carried the GWR (ex-Taff Vale Railway) main line from Merthyr Tydfil to Cardiff. (The late W.J. Haynes, courtesy BTS Library)

County Road Authorities, or constructing a suitable road junction from Cardiff Road to the Old Doctor's canal near the Hide & Skin Market, Treforest, at an estimated £4,000. Together with electrical equipment and vehicles, the extension was estimated to cost a total of £25,200.

Although the aim had been to reduce dependency on imported fuel the Transport Manager could not stop himself adding that he already had sufficient spare motorbus rolling stock. Revenue would never cover the added capital burden and heavy calls on the rates would be inevitable; indeed revenue might fall as the route along the Old Doctor's Canal avoided the busy stop at the junction of Dyffryn Road and Cardiff Road. He added that apart from the wartime difficulties, the time was ripe to consider Pontypridd's future transport policy.

One is left with the impression that any extension proposals were shown in an as unfavourable light as possible, and on 9 January 1940 the Transport Committee decided to take no further action, at least for the time being, and placed their faith in the possible use of producer gas for motorbuses.

Messrs Frank Mason & Co. Ltd., the undertaking's advertising contractor since its inception, enquired if the Council wished to renew its contract which was due to expire at the end of 1939 and extend this to include a position on the rear platform panel. Net advertising revenue had reached about £141 pa of which £56 was earned by the outside panels. The Manager felt that this could be increased to a figure representing the purchase price of a new vehicle every five or six years. He considered Masons to be a reliable firm that covered around 90% of all transport advertising in the UK, whilst he had no concerns about introducing a rear advertising space which could increase revenue by 3s per bus per week. As a result of this recommendation the contract was renewed for a further three years from 1 January 1940.

The six-week trial of a 6d four-journey daily ticket on the trolleybus route started on 4 September 1939. Weekly sales soon rose to about 150 and as there was no appreciable effect on revenue the experiment was allowed to run its course. When the trial ended on 14 October 1939 it was decided to retain them for trolleybus journeys but not to extend their use to other services in view of the war.

As an aid to "black-out" driving white lines were painted on some unclassified roads including the trolleybus route along Coedpenmaen Road from Corn Stores Hill to Merthyr Road.

The outbreak of war had started to influence the cost of living and the NJIC for the Transport Industry granted a war wage of 4s per week to adult employees with smaller increases for youths from the week commencing 10 December 1939. As an indication of the Council's appreciation of the staff's efforts in handling heavy loads and the "black-out", services were suspended on Christmas Day 1939 and crews granted the day off with eight hours pay. Trolleybus ticket sales rose in October 1939 to 200,798 with 25,472 miles run and £1,441 revenue versus 156,133 sold with 20,296 miles run and £1,113 revenue in October 1938.

On Sundays 5 November and 12 November 1939 the height of the trolley wires at Cilfynydd turning circle was increased, the circle reformed and several insulating bolts changed. On Sunday 19 November 1939 the positive trolley wire at John Street reverser which had worn very thin was replaced. During the month the side feeds to the Slaughter House section feeder were repaired, an old traction pole on Llanbradach Hill was removed and the overhead equipment transferred to the new pole.

The undertaking's ticket supplier, H. Hunt & Co. Ltd. Nottingham, increased their prices by 1d per thousand tickets (ca. 16%) and stated all further increases in the price of paper would lead to commensurate increases at the rate of 1/8 d per thousand for each £1 per ton increase in the price of paper. There was no purpose in disputing the war-related increase as the price of paper was controlled by the Paper Control Commissioners.

The first call-up of 1940 involved men up to 28 years of age, affecting 22 employees. Advertisements were placed in January 1940 inviting applications from persons exempt from military service and from men between 42 and 50 years of age, to fill conducting vacancies as they occurred due to regular staff leaving for war service. It was stipulated that these were temporary appointments, on a week to week basis for the duration of the war and not within the scope of the pension scheme.

Single-deck trolleybus 7 ran into the rear of an unlit stationary lorry at Police Row, Cilfynydd at 6 am on 22 January 1940. The driver's cab and equipment was seriously damaged, the front dash and cab floor being torn off, although the driver was uninjured. The conductor was thrown off his feet and off work for several days but the two passengers on board escaped injury but for minor cuts. Replacement parts and labour totalled almost £135. Trolleybus 3 re-entered service on 1 February 1940 after a thorough overhaul including the bodywork, panels, roof, floor, windows doors seats etc. with new pillars and renewal of other defective items.

Snow storms and frozen roads disorganised services in late January and early February 1940; indeed on Monday 29 January 1940 ice on the overhead prevented trolleybuses running until the afternoon. Motorbuses were substituted, the RTC granting a supplementary ration of fuel. Thereafter a trolleybus was run though the night in icy weather to keep the wires clear.

Increasing traffic meant that employees had built up a substantial backlog of unused holiday entitlement whilst a shortage of labour was rapidly developing. This was aggravated by the Transport Committee's decision on 13 February 1940 that any employee called up for military service should be permitted to take the holiday to which they were entitled before reporting to the forces. It was noted that from Saturday 17 February 1940 there would be insufficient conductors to cover normal requirements. Some 65 applications had been received for the positions of temporary conductors of whom 24 were deemed suitable and their names were placed on the waiting list, the positions being allocated amongst the seven Wards of the District. The Labour Exchange pointed out that any unemployed person undergoing job training would be disqualified from unemployment benefit and it was agreed that in this case the undertaking would reimburse the amount lost for up to three weeks.

Until now no lighting restrictions had been introduced on the trolleybuses, but experiments were made on a motorbus with a set of shaded interior fittings, acquired from Bristol Tramways. Tests showed that the light intensity fulfilled the Emergency Powers (Defence) Regulations conditions, and after an inspection by the Police Superintendent on 6 March 1940 the whole fleet was so equipped by 31 March 1940.

The undertaking's policies with the Municipal Mutual Insurance Ltd. were due to expire on 31 March 1940. Having considered seven tenders the most favourable offer was that from the existing insurer at £10 for each trolley vehicle plus 4s per seat (a reduction of 1s per seat on the prevailing rate or £17 3s for the entire trolleybus fleet). The matter was decided when the company offered a 5% discount for a 3-year contract and the policies were renewed.

In connection with the forthcoming retirement of Mr G.J. Evans, Electrical and Transport Engineer on 2 August 1940, the Staff Committee suggested that the duties should be divided. It was pointed out that the relationship between the two departments began inside the depot where Electricity Department employees were working, using transport equipment and for which the Transport Department apparently received no credit. Along the trolleybus route traction poles were used to support brackets carrying electricity service lines, street lighting lines, and street lighting fittings used for public lighting. In suggesting an appropriate new organisation it was noted that Pontypridd's transport department was not large enough for two modes of traction and that diesel oil remained the cheapest fuel even in wartime although it was noted that trolleybuses had several major advantages. In April 1940 they suggested that the Transport Department should be headed by a Transport Manager with a Traffic Superintendent, responsible for inspectors, drivers and conductors, and an Engineer, responsible for the depot, fleet maintenance, etc, as direct reports.

New trolley wires fitted near the crossing frog at Taff House. A fault in the positive side feeder at the 'New Inn' section break on Friday 26 April 1940 was immediately repaired and arrangements made for renewal.

The MoT issued an Order (No. 594) restricting the number of lower-deck standing passengers to eight from Monday 20 May 1940 which it was feared would create difficulties at peak periods particularly between the town centre and Cilfynydd. It was noted that every serviceable trolleybus was in use.

The Government cancelled the Whitsun 1940 holiday and it was decided to pay time-and-a-quarter in respect of Whit Monday. Only a week later on Sunday 19 May 1940 two special trains carrying over 500 children and their teachers from Kent and the Medway Towns, part of a major evacuation to Wales that day, arrived to a warm welcome from thousands of residents and the Salvation Army band. Pontypridd soon became used to the arrival of youngsters, each with a card identity tag, laden with gas masks, school satchels, bags and parcels. Soon after the last British troops had been taken off the Dunkirk beaches another 1,000 children arrived from Acton and London's East End.

Mr Powell sought the Transport Committee's views on the hours of application of workmen's fares which were only issued up to 8.00 am, 12.30 – 3pm, and 8.30 – 11.30pm. War conditions were changing working hours, e.g. some collieries were starting at 9.00am, the Chain Works had introduced a shift starting at 8pm, and there were similar problems on Sundays where workmen's fares were not available until 8.30pm. Conductors were instructed to use their discretion. In September 1940 it was decided that workmen's fares would be available on Sundays from the first journey until 3pm in addition to the period after 8.30pm, whilst for the duration of the war apprentices' tickets, would also be available to passengers not earning more than 15s a week.

It was decided to introduce a special fare for school children during their summer holiday as they now had fewer opportunities to go to the seaside. A 1d return fare was offered from all stops in the PUDC area to Ynysangharad Park entrance (West Street for the Cilfynydd end, and 'New Inn' for the Treforest end) during the August school holidays on Monday, Tuesday, Thursday and Fridays, issuable 9.30am – 12.30pm and 3.00 – 4.30pm, and available for return at any time on the day of issue. This facility with slight changes as to the times of applicability was repeated each summer until at least 1950.

The Transport Manager had hoped that reduced services would make an improved maintenance programme possible, but the shortage of vehicles meant that there was no opportunity to take vehicles out of service. Certain workmen's fares takings had increased by 10-12% compared to 1939, whilst with the arrival of evacuees the school load was much increased. He suggested that two double-deck motorbuses be bought.

On Saturday 8 June 1940 a fault occurred on the No. 2 traction feeder and traced to opposite the entrance of the trolleybus depot building near the generating station. At the beginning of June 1940 the trolley wires at Cilfynydd turning circle were replaced whilst during the month two lengths of trolley wire about 40 yards long opposite the Abattoir and around the curve at Norton Bridge were renewed.

After just a few days' prior warning from the MPTA that an application for increased wages had been received from the Employees' side, it was learned that the NJIC for the Road Passenger Transport Industry had awarded a further 3s per week for drivers, conductors and certain adult depot employees, with smaller increases for youths, effective 4 July 1940. An inexorable series of increases followed to keep pace with wartime inflation. In April 1941 and February 1942 increases of 4s per week were granted (women receiving only 90% thereof); 4s 6d per week in July 1943 following strikes in Derby, Nottingham, Reading, the Thames Valley and Yorkshire, and in May 1944 an increase of 5s per week. This last increase also introduced improved

**English Electric SD6WTB 4 stands at John Street terminus, Treforest, during the Second World War. Note the headlamp masks. (The late W.J. Haynes, courtesy BTS Library)**

Bristol E No. 9 stands in wartime livery and equipped with headlamp masks at Glyntaff Depot with the open-fronted galvanised corrugated iron trolleybus depot building in the background. Bristol GO6G motorbuses 21 and 22 are just visible to the left and Bristol K5G 29 is on the right. (Courtesy: Bristol Vintage Bus Group (Allan Macfarlane))

conditions nationwide, including 12 days holiday with pay to all employees after 12 months' service; and a guaranteed 48-hour working week. Time on stand-by was included for either overtime or spread-overs, whilst for rest day work a guarantee of not less than four hours, or six if work be performed, at time and a quarter, was introduced.

A false air raid alert was caused on 8 July 1940 by flashing from trolleybuses running into the depot. Henceforth, before removing the trolley wheels from the overhead wires, the main lighting circuit had to be switched off, and not be switched on again until the trolleys' wheels had been rewired. The effect of this was to have only the emergency switch on, which, with the interior emergency lights out of commission, gave head and tail lights only.

On 2 August 1940 the positive trolley wire beneath the PCNR bridge in Broadway broke interrupting the nos 1 and 2 Traction Feeders and delaying traffic 10.10 – 10.40pm. The positive trolley wire down line broke at the Broadway section breaker at about 3.30 pm on 16 August 1940 due to a faulty positive section insulator. This was changed the following Sunday morning and about 40 yards of badly worn trolley wire replaced.

On 14 August 1940 Cilfynydd British Legion invited evacuees billeted locally and children of members of HM Forces, the merchant service or ex-servicemen, to a free performance at the Palladium Cinema. Special trolleybuses carried the children to town and back free of charge.

Compared with many other industrial areas of Britain the population was fortunate not to suffer hardship and damage as a result of bombing raids, but the threat of imminent destruction was always prevalent. During the summer of 1940 there were some 300 air raid warnings in the Pontypridd area, 138 in September alone, and many more warnings later on. A high explosive bomb fell on Cilfynydd Common at 1.30am on 12 July 1940 close to the Albion Colliery where 1,300 men were underground. The German *Luftwaffe* had identified Treforest Trading Estate as a target and aimed at Upper Boat Power Station although Mynydd Mayo was hit instead. Bombs also fell in Hopkinstown and in Cilfynydd during other raids whilst people were killed in Porth and further up the Rhondda Valley later in the war.

When war broke out the Government instructed that during an air raid alert all traffic must stop, amending this later to permit motorists to continue *"if there was a good reason for doing so"*. The Transport Department interpreted that the clearance of people from a town without adequate air raid shelters, and the conveyance of workmen to/from their work, constituted two good reasons for continuing to operate although other authorities had taken a different stance. Mr Powell was of the view that he couldn't instruct crews to keep running, citing:

a.  Siren sounded when there was a Saturday night queue of several hundred at Mill Street with no adequate shelters in the vicinity. Common sense was to clear the traffic.

b.  Workmen delayed on the way to work when no risk of aerial activity. The crews continued to operate.

c.  Siren sounded just before finishing time involving vehicles remaining out until 3 – 4 am at a cost which would become prohibitive if regularly repeated. It had been arranged with the Military and Police Authorities that under such circumstances the vehicles required to clear those stranded in town would remain in service but the remainder run into the depot.

In September 1940 it was agreed with the Police that vehicles would proceed normally during air raid alarms until circumstances compelled them to stop. It was acknowledged that during alarms during hours of darkness, drivers could not be expected to maintain schedules and that they would be entitled to reduce speed to approx 6 mph with appropriate extensions to running times and service frequency. The "black-out" reliefs provided on certain duties during the winter of 1939-40 were repeated in the coming winter. Work at the depot continued as normal but with an observer to give warning to take cover as necessary.

Mr Powell added that conductors, despite having battery lamps, could not be expected to issue the full range of tickets

English Electric SD6WTB 4 stands at John Street terminus, Treforest, during the Second World War. This view shows the wartime white edging applied to the mudguards and the lifeguards, as well as the headlamp masks. (The late W.J. Haynes, courtesy BTS Library)

Kingston upon Hull Corporation Transport 3, a 1937 Leyland TB4 with Weymann composite bodywork, poses on Victoria Bridge facing north towards Cilfynydd in that undertaking's azure blue and matt blue wartime livery. Four such vehicles were loaned to Pontypridd from August 1941 until August 1942. On the other side of the bridge the overhead wiring turns left into Taff Street whilst Morgan Street is straight ahead. 'The Bridge' public house stands on the corner of Berw Road where the Police Station is now located. Llanwood School is in the background. (Photographer's name not recorded)

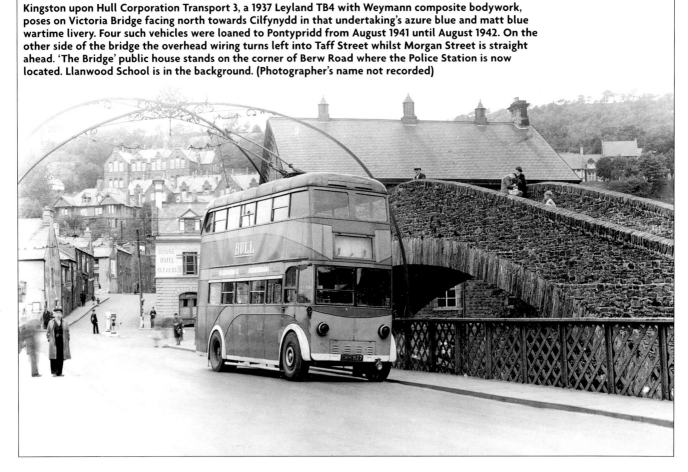

and give change when all interior lights were switched off. He suggested that passengers should tender the exact fare whilst in the "black-out" a 2d flat fare should apply with the exception of 1d stages, and the acceptance of return fares and workmen's fares. This was not implemented; not least as such a change on motorbuses would not have received RTC approval. Needless to say, revenue began to suffer from evening traffic reductions due to the frequent air raid warnings.

In view of the increasing number of alarms, on 10 September 1940 the Transport Manager asked the Transport Committee for decisions on fitting splinter-proof netting or an alternative to vehicle windows, and supplying traffic staff with steel helmets. Despite the urgency a decision was referred to the Subcommittee who subsequently recommended that windows be treated with an anti-shatter paint that offered some protection for 3 months at an estimated cost of £15. On 12 November 1940 the Transport Committee decided to take no action as the MoT advised that they were looking into a national solution. The General Manager was instructed to obtain a cheaper specimen toughened fibre helmet (9s against 12s each for steel helmet) and to discuss its suitability with the employees' representatives. Only in January 1941 was it decided to buy sufficient fabric netting for the entire fleet but a decision as to the right moment to fit it to the windows was left to the Manager.

On 15 September 1940 the press reported that the Ministry of Home Security had stated that flashes from trolleybuses and electric trains offered no guidance to enemy aircraft. An enquiry confirmed that there had been a test by the Air Ministry who were satisfied that any flashes were valueless for aircraft navigation and location purposes. Nonetheless in May 1941 a sample guard was ordered for fitting above special work in the overhead wiring where flashes frequently occurred and mounted above the crossover at Taff House junction in June.

In October 1940 it was decided to station an Inspector at Mill Street for the majority of the "black-out" hours, following complaints from crews that there had been a lack of direction during air raid alarms and no standard response.

The Transport Manager recommended that drivers, conductors and the 17 depot staff not employed under the conditions of the Electricity Supply Industry (which foresaw such a payment) receive eight hours' pay on Christmas Day 1940. He was proud of the way the staff had maintained services in the town, in contrast with certain other places, and thus saved the Department much revenue.

There was a fault on nos 2 and 3 traction feeders in Gas Yard Substation on Tuesday evening 5 November 1940 but this caused no delays. However, the following evening a dewirement at 6.15pm outside the Workmen's Hall Cilfynydd brought down the guard wires for some distance, and these entangled in the trolley wires delaying traffic from 6.47 – 7.24 pm. The dewirement was due to an insulated bolt stripping its thread allowing the trolley wire to sag excessively.

A trolleybus was found to be "live" on 5 February 1941 probably due to the snow and run into the depot. The next day tests showed that the lowest reading was 2 million ohms, 25,000 ohms above the BoT limit.

The undertaking's uniform suppliers warned that there would be several months' delay to the delivery of the 1941 order due to a shortage of buttons! Rather than ask crews to cut the buttons off their existing uniforms, the TGWU asked them to send in any spare buttons.

In May 1941 Kingston upon Hull's General Manager Mr G.H. Pulfrey informed his Transport Committee that the city had a surplus of trolleybuses due to the combined effects of evacuation, conscription and the reduced operating mileage enforced by government restrictions. He obtained their authority to exchange the surplus trolleybuses for motorbuses on a permanent or temporary basis. Mr Pulfrey approached a number of undertakings - however, although several would have been interested in purchasing them, none were interested in an exchange. The following month, in June 1941, Mr Pulfrey sought approval to convert the Anlaby Road tram route to trolleybus operation, as the track was in a poor state and sufficient trolleybuses were in stock, subject to the return of any loaned trolleybuses.

On 10 June 1941 Mr Powell drew the Pontypridd Transport Committee's attention to the fact that Hull had a number of 54-seater trolleybuses for hire. He felt that this could be profitable and would enable the undertaking to systematically overhaul its own trolleybus fleet. He was instructed to investigate and he visited Hull, accompanied by the Rolling Stock Superintendant, shortly afterwards to inspect a sample vehicle. By 8 July 1941 the Clerk was authorised to complete an agreement for the hire of four double-deck trolleybuses at £25 per bus per calendar month for a minimum period of six months. These materialised as two-axle Leyland TB4 vehicles equipped with Weymann H28/26R composite bodies, Hull fleet numbers 1-4, originally delivered in June and July 1937. They were the first two-axle trolleybuses in Pontypridd. The loan conditions were based on an LPTB Heads of Agreement with a clause that the vehicles were to be returned to Hull immediately if they were required by reason of enemy action or any other emergency.

Hull trolleybus 1 and 2 left on tow for Pontypridd travelling through the Brecon Beacons, the highest point reached by a trolleybus in Wales, on 19 August 1941 followed by 3 and 4 on 26 August 1941. It is believed that the tow was carried out by suitably equipped Pontypridd Bristol B motorbuses. The Hull trolleybuses entered service in Pontypridd almost immediately.

In May 1941 it was decided to employ conductresses should men not be available. Three women were appointed for training, one of which, Mrs Devereux, a widow, had previously conducted for six years with a very good record. Based on an Industrial Court Decision, they were paid 90% of the adult male conductors' rate for the first six months of service, thereafter the full pay and increments applicable to adult males. By now the PUDC commencing rate was 1s 3$\frac{1}{8}$d per hour increasing to 1s 4$\frac{1}{4}$d after 3 months and to 1s 5$\frac{3}{8}$d after 6 months.

There was a growing shortage of drivers; current staff already working at the limit of capacity. The Ministry of Labour indicated that the chance of engaging new drivers was remote whilst all conductors interested in driver training had been recruited. Some operators were able to get their drivers released from the forces and Mr Powell enquired if this was possible, the undertaking subsequently benefiting from three such temporary releases. The shortage of labour led the Transport Manager to ask for instructions on 4 December 1941 as to the employment of married women as conductresses. One male conductor who had already been trained as a trolleybus driver had agreed to motorbus training, one conductor was prepared to train on both and one conductor was prepared to undertake trolleybus training only. This was insufficient to meet the foreseen challenges. In January 1942

| STOPPING PLACE | REMARK |
| --- | --- |
| Treforest Terminus<br>*Commercial Hotel*<br>(Goods Station Gates) | Discontinue. |
| Treforest Passenger Stn<br>*Bush Hotel* | Both are important loading points<br>which cannot be changed. |
| Taff House | MoT Compulsory Stop, fare stage and important loading point. Cannot be altered. |
| Rock House | Used extensively by Park Infants School children, who would have to walk either to Taff Vale Park or Taff House if discontinued. |
| Taff Vale Park | Fare Stage. |
| Archway | Used extensively by people coming down the steps from Wood Road and by adjacent houses along Broadway. |
| Observer Office | 100 yards on the Pontypridd side of the Observer Office. Retain as residents of the Pontypridd end of Broadway might have to walk some 300 yds back to the Archway or walk into town instead of riding. |
| Abattoir | Discontinue. |
| Station Square | Cannot be altered. |
| *New Inn* | Cannot be altered. |
| Fountain | Cannot be altered. |
| YMCA | Discontinue. |
| Berw Road | Compulsory MoT Stop, Fare Stage and important loading point. |
| West Street | Extensively used by ordinary passengers and by Chain Works employees; therefore cannot be altered. |
| Common Road | Compulsory MoT Stop, Fare Stage and used extensively by ordinary traffic. |
| New Bridge<br>Baptist Chapel | Suggest 1 stop by Coedpenmaen Post Office, if Police and Surveyor will agree<br>(road junction may be an objection that this is contrary to MoT procedure). |
| *Bonvilston Hotel* | Sufficiently used as to warrant retention. |
| Church Road | Discontinue. |
| Bonvilston Road | Fare Stage and important loading point. Cannot alter. |
| "Swamp" | Fairly frequently used. To discontinue would mean people from adjacent houses would have to walk 300 yds or more to the nearest stop on either side. |
| Norton Bridge | Compulsory MoT Stop, Fare Stage and heavy loading point. |
| Police Row | Discontinue. |
| "Managers"<br>Quarry Siding<br>*Albion Hotel*<br>Workmen's Hall<br>Richard St.<br>Cilfynydd terminus | Cannot be discontinued, well used. |

the Transport Committee agreed to the employment of married women as conductresses.

In principle all men 18-41 years of age were liable to conscription unless they were employed on civilian work of importance to the war effort (Protected Work) in which case they could not be called up once they had reached a certain age. Until late 1941 most work in passenger transport was considered a Reserved Occupation, and the majority of grades were protected from 25 and the remainder from 35 years of age. Employers could ask for the deferment of call-up for men in reserved occupations but outside the reserved age.

In late 1941 the Schedule of Reserved Occupations and Protected Work was revised whereby undertakings had to apply for protection through the RTC to the Ministry of Labour and National Service by 30 April 1941 and Pontypridd's application had been granted. Under the Essential Work (General Provisions) Order 1941, an undertaking could be scheduled as being engaged upon essential work, the effect of which was to deprive employees of their right to leave for other employment except by permission of the National Service Officer. Mr Powell was concerned that there were certain key personnel whose resignations could jeopardize the maintenance of services; however, if the Department was to register it would lose the right to dismiss an employee except for serious misconduct.

The Government asked that business and statistical information should not be published as this could provide the enemy with guidance as to the success or otherwise of their air attacks. The MPTA recommended that publication of passenger traffic and operational statistics should cease until the end of the war. The Council decided that this information was to be withheld from the press and Minutes of Transport Committee.

On Saturday 16 August 1941 at 10.20pm the driver of a trolleybus moving slowly along Taff Street towards Treforest felt a bump and heard a crushing sound. He immediately stopped and with the aid of a torch found a dead man beneath the vehicle.

The Home Guard was given a stock of 7,200 two penny vouchers in September 1941, paid for by the UDC's three trading undertakings, for distribution at their discretion, but they were advised to approach business and industry for sponsorship of further supplies. In October a similar request from the Air Training Corps (ATC) was received and passed to the Council for decision. The Transport Department preferred a system other than vouchers as they already had Home Guard, ARP and Fire Watching, Military, Employment Exchange vouchers to deal with. Vouchers slowed down the work of the conductor and subsequently required checking, sorting and accounting. A Transport Subcommittee recommended that a stock of prepaid single 2d tickets be sold to the ATC. The fare voucher scheme continued until the stand down of the Home Guard on 3 December 1944.

During the evening of 2 March 1942 trolleybus 3 (Driver Riddick) rode up on to the pavement in Broadway, Treforest,

English Electric SD6WTB No. 4 stands in the Glyntaff Depot area in wartime livery. The registration number can be seen both at the base of the rear panels and, as required by the MoT, in the former rear destination box where it could be illuminated. The overhead wiring layout warrants closer inspection with both the reversing triangle in front of the trolleybus depot entrance; the previously physically-isolated line from the erstwhile tramcar shed coming in from the left is evident. (Peter Smith Collection)

damaging the front of Mr Jones butcher's shop. The trolleybus suffered a dented front panel, and a broken front offside headlamp and mask.

On 27 January 1942 the Transport Committee considered the number of trolleybus stops and uncollected fares. Mr Powell felt that the 29 stops between the two termini were too many although it would be unrealistic to aim for the theoretical ideal of a stop every 400 yards. He added that if four of the 20 stops between Cilfynydd and the town centre were discontinued, the Conductor would have 2 minutes less time to collect the fares. He suggested a reduction to 22 stops (an average of one every 266 yards) with most being "if required" only.

Although the number of uncollected fares had become a national problem due to wartime conditions making it difficult to train and supervise conducting staff with the abnormally heavy traffic, Pontypridd had the further challenge of very short stages and inexperienced staff.

The undertaking used "jumpers" to the maximum extent but the number of spare conductors was limited by national agreement and a 48-hour week had to be guaranteed. The use of a fixed roadside conductor at major stops, sometimes handling 1,000 passengers an hour, to issue tickets and handle cash was problematic in the "black-out", particularly if buses arrived full and the passengers could not get on or demanded their money back. They had considered rostering more conductors than vehicles on the road, one collecting fares from the queue at the terminus before joining the bus with "his" passengers, and the arriving conductor going to the head of the queue to await the next bus. The busiest trolleybus stops were Old Bridge (inward from Cilfynydd) and Coedpenmaen (outward from town).

He further suggested Acting Inspector (appointed year by year) Bernard Egan be made a Temporary Inspector for the duration of the war at Inspector's wages, Conductor/Driver George Ludlow be used for temporary ticket checking duties, and also for Acting Traffic Inspector for the annual holiday period of 1942, and that Senior Conductress Mrs Devereux be appointed Temporary Ticket Checker.

At about 7.50pm on Sunday evening, 15 February 1942, a conductress put £5 of silver into her ticket box under the stairs of one of the Hull trolleybuses en route to Treforest. At the "Swamp" on her 9.36pm trip from Treforest to Cilfynydd, she put in another 5s silver and took out some tickets from her box. Some boys were sitting inside, one of whom remarked "There's a lot of money". When she came to the top of the stairs at Norton Bridge she saw two of the boys on the platform but when she got downstairs they had gone back inside. She did not return to her box again until 11.20pm when she found the silver missing. One of the boys could be identified and the matter handed over to the police, although the conductress was informed that she would be held responsible for the missing cash as she had not used one of the locks and keys issued free for greater ticket box security. Municipal Mutual Insurance Ltd. agreed to accept the claim as "cash in transit" but indicated that a condition of any future payment would be a proper locked box or cupboard. Under these circumstances the conductress was not required to refund the stolen cash.

Under the Regulation of Traffic (Formation of Queues) Order 1942 passengers waiting for a bus were required to queue whilst the MoWT recommended that stops should be staggered to ensure that queues for different places were kept separate. The Surveyor was authorised to erect "Queue here for ..." signs;

The City of Portsmouth Passenger Transport Department loaned all four of their 3-axle trolleybuses to Pontypridd UDC for various periods between August 1942 and April 1946 to assist the undertaking with the wartime surge in traffic. No. 215 in the Portsmouth fleet was a 1934 AEC663T with MCCW all-metal body and is seen in Park Street, Treforest, in wartime livery. The number displayed in the service number box has no relevance.
(The late W.J. Haynes, courtesy BTS Library)

however, as up to 6 services were using the same stop in Taff Street it was decided that these should be staggered:

a. **Buses running from Old Bridge to Station Square direction**

| | |
|---|---|
| Old Bridge | Trolleybus stop |
| Fountain | Trolleybuses to Treforest |
| Opposite *New Inn Hotel* | Trolleybuses to Treforest by Liptons and Gamlins shops |
| Station Square | Trolleybuses to Treforest by John's Café |

b. **Buses running from Station Square into High Street/Taff Street**

| | |
|---|---|
| Station Square | Trolleybuses to Cilfynydd nearest island |
| Fountain | Trolleybuses to Cilfynydd |
| Berw Road corner | Queue for Cilfynydd parallel with PUDC club |

On 20 March 1942 two senior schoolgirls "larking about" broke an upper-deck window on trolleybus 8. The replacement cost 12s and the parents of each girl were each sent a bill for 6s. One didn't reply whilst the other, who had seven children and the only son working off sick, offered to pay in due course. As nothing further was heard, prosecution was threatened. The Transport Committee resolved on 12 May 1942 that unless the schoolgirls attended an interview and paid for the repairs within the stipulated period, their school bus passes would be cancelled and immediate Police Court Proceedings instituted.

Although Workmen's Weekly Tickets were foreseen as including just six return journeys it had become practice to accept them for a seventh return journey in the case of Sunday workers, whilst in addition night workers travelling to the collieries on Friday for their pay were allowed a free journey. As checks were difficult, it was decided that Weekly Tickets would only be issued on Mondays and expire on the following Saturday irrespective of whether the tickets had been fully used or not. Sunday travel on a Weekly Ticket was only permitted if another travel day of the week was sacrificed. The free "pay ride" for colliery night workers continued, as these Weeklies had a special "night worker" punch mark.

By 1942 the worst of the air raids had passed and throughout the country many evacuees returned home. In Pontypridd they were soon replaced by American troops, some being stationed in Cilfynydd, where they soon established themselves in the community as generous visitors!

Although Hull asked in March 1942 that the hire of their trolleybuses should cease on 30 April 1942 it proved possible to informally arrange an extension, as the conversion of the 2.09-mile long Anlaby Road tram route, carried out by the undertaking's own staff, was proving protracted. A prerequisite of trolleybus operation was the return of Leyland TB4s 1-4. Nonetheless by June 1942 it was evident that they would soon have to be returned and it was decided that if it was impossible to hire replacement trolleybuses the RTC should be asked for additional petrol to operate motorbuses until trolleybuses could be obtained. Concurrently a letter from the MPTA was received asking if any new trolleybuses would be needed between June 1943 and June 1944 as a production plan was in preparation. It also asked if any purchase would be made from revenue or if a loan would be necessary. PUDC services were

now running fully loaded for 19-20 hours per day: having considered the conditions four double-deckers were requested, which, if the heavy loadings continued, could be purchased from revenue. Mr Powell suggested, however, that licences to acquire these vehicles should also grant the right to borrow should there be insufficient reserves at the time of delivery. He felt that the vehicle position in 1943-44 would be acute irrespective of whether the war continued or not, and even if subsequently the vehicles were not required in Pontypridd, rolling stock at that time would be at such a premium that he had no doubt whatsoever that reserving four trolleybuses was a safe investment.

However, by mid-July 1942 it was learned that it might be possible to hire a number of Portsmouth trolleybuses. Ben Hall, the Portsmouth General Manager suggested that a deputation from Pontypridd UDC should meet the Portsmouth Transport Committee. In case the hoped-for Portsmouth loan should not go ahead, the RTC was approached about London Transport (LPTB) motorbuses which were available for hire. The RTC allocated two London AEC Regent ST class motorbuses, ST310 and ST369, and an additional fuel ration for use on the Treforest-Cilfynydd timetable although efforts continued to arrange a loan of Portsmouth trolleybuses.

The two LPTB motorbuses went into service between Treforest and Cilfynydd route at the beginning of August enabling work to start on preparing the first two Hull trolleybuses for their return. They departed on 10 August 1942, followed by the remaining two on 17 August 1942. In Hull, trolleybuses took over the Anlaby Road route on 6 September 1942 with numbers 1-4 together with 5-12 allocated to the service.

It proved possible to reach agreement with Portsmouth despite the fact that, according to Mr Powell, the city had no real wish to hire any trolley vehicles. He believed that it was only due to Portsmouth's public-spiritedness and the offer to return their trolleybuses within 72 hours should they have any difficulties that eventually prompted them to loan vehicles to Pontypridd. Interestingly, the four loaned vehicles were all non-standard prototypes in the Portsmouth fleet and had been in open storage, out of service, since early 1940. As a result of heavy bombing and the evacuation of much of the civilian population the Portsmouth undertaking had a considerable surplus of motorbuses and trolleybuses at that time!

The Portsmouth hire terms were the same as those of Hull at £25 per vehicle per month; however, they offered a better commercial proposition having 60 seats compared to 54 on the Hull trolleybuses. The first two Portsmouth trolleybuses, 212 and 215 in that city's fleet numbering system, arrived on 8 August 1942 and once they were ready for service the LPTB motorbuses were taken off the trolleybus route. The other two trolleybuses, 213 and 214, arrived on 14 August 1942. The hired vehicles were towed to Pontypridd via Newbury, Oxford, Gloucester (then the lowest bridging point on the River Severn), Abergavenny, Brecon and Merthyr Tydfil, presumably to avoid low bridges.

On 21 August 1942 it was learned that the MoWT had allocated Pontypridd two, not four, new trolleybuses for delivery in 1943. They would have Karrier chassis but the bodybuilder was not yet known. Mr Powell pointed out to the Transport Committee that with English Electric, Guy and Bristol trolley vehicles already in the fleet, various different types of trolley vehicles on loan from Portsmouth, and a variety of different motorbuses the undertaking had to forego the advantage of standardisation and that this was causing complex maintenance issues.

A wartime view of Bristol E 9 in the Glyntaff Depot area. The body shows the results of the thorough overhaul given in the late 1930s. (Peter Smith Collection)

Mr Powell visited Hull on 6 October 1942 as there were questions of liability for certain work and renewals necessary on the vehicles at the time of their return, including resistances, brake equipment, etc. which could only be solved on the spot. Pontypridd had purchased a number of spares for use on the Hull trolleybuses which were now no longer required. Agreement was reached to share the cost of a resistance section and that Hull would reimburse Pontypridd at the prevailing price (some £60-70).

The trolleybus traction supply came from a 500kW rotary converter in the generating station and two of the same capacity in the gas yard substation. By 1941 the one at the generating station was rarely used for traction purposes and normally those in gas yard used, although they occasionally fed Pwllgwaun Colliery and supplied the Council's normal DC demand over and above the rated output of the steam plant. The rotary converters were used as "stand-by" plant for the steam turbine and reciprocating engines. This meant that if the steam plant failed the rotaries were immediate run up and the load that was on the steam plant transferred to them. This might happen only once in 12 months with the result that a very high maximum demand was recorded, perhaps only for a few hours, and yet an exceptionally high fixed charge was incurred for 12 months. This was also useful when the steam plant was being overhauled or if anything happened to the canal and circulating water was lost.

The advertising contract with Messrs Frank Mason & Co. Ltd., due to expire at the end of 1942, was renewed for a further three years. The UDC received $66^2/_3\%$ of the advertising revenue (about £250 pa) but advertising was proving difficult to get.

There was a continuing problem with the issuance of workmen's fares outside the stipulated hours which had been aligned with those of Rhondda Transport. The undertaking had shown flexibility applying the principle "was the *work* a direct result of the war emergency?"; they had issued few exceptions but it was getting increasingly complicated applications from colliery officials were refused as their working hours had not varied because of the war. Mr Powell sought guidance from his Transport Committee. "Are we to grant workmen's fares to war workers travelling to and from work outside regulation hours for the issue of workmen's fares? If so, is such concession to be allowed to full-time workers and part-time workers which are now being handled in increasing quantities?" If yes, the Transport Committee was asked to draft a scheme disturbing existing regulations as little as possible.

A meeting with the RTC took place in November 1942. The RTC could not criticise the withdrawal of all workmen's fares after 8am, except for people who had special permits as this would be meeting the MoWT requirements. Mr Powell explained that this was impractical for local conditions. The MoWT felt that workmen's fares should be available to appropriate persons employed on a late turn of duty "who, but for this fact, would commence work at a time which would entitle them to obtain a workman's ticket during the normal hours of issue". Fearing that the MoWT would compel the undertaking to comply with its direction, Mr Powell suggested that workmen's fares be granted outside regulation hours to workers (male, female, full and part-time) travelling directly as a result of wartime conditions and otherwise complying with the conditions of workmen's services at special fares. A special permit was required, application forms being provided by the employer or trade union.

Motorbus services after 9pm were withdrawn in December 1942 although there were some later workmen's journeys. The *Pontypridd Observer* found this inconsistent, suggesting that the trolleybuses should also run in at 9pm! The trolleybuses timetable remained unchanged for a few weeks until it was clear how the revised Porth timetable would connect with the Treforest – Cilfynydd service. Thereafter some reductions to the trolleybus evening service were made due to tyre shortages: from Treforest after 10pm to 10.45 every 15 minutes then 11.15; from Cilfynydd every 15 minutes 10.30 – 11.15 with a last journey at 11.40pm.

Another of the Portsmouth trolleybuses loaned to Pontypridd during the Second World War was 1934 AEC663T 212 with English Electric composite body, seen here at the Treforest terminus in John Street. In April 1938, Portsmouth renumbered its trolleybus fleet by adding 200 to the original fleet number. An additional figure was transferred in advance of the existing fleet number on the front and rear panels, causing the number to be offset, and this can be clearly seen on the photograph. These vehicles were considered surplus to requirements in the naval city due to their lack of traction batteries. (The late W.J. Haynes, courtesy BTS Library)

In February 1943 it was learned that increased interior lighting would become permissible under an Amendment to the Lighting Orders but that this would not apply to areas within 12 miles of the coast, including the Bristol Channel and Severn Estuary. As Pontypridd was on the border line an application to implement the increases was made to the police.

Following the MoWT's relaxation of the limit of standing passengers from five to 12 Municipal Mutual Insurance Ltd. agreed to renew the undertaking's policies on the present basis for a further three years but with cover for the new higher number at no additional charge.

The MoWT informed the undertaking that the chassis for the two new trolleybuses would now only be ready in March 1944. This meant that the thorough overhaul of Pontypridd's own trolleybuses, underway since hired vehicles had been available, would need to be expedited. It was essential that the Portsmouth trolleybuses be retained until the local fleet renewals were further advanced, particularly as it had been learned that it might be necessary to increase the trolleybus run-out to feed the railways with traffic that at that time was being conveyed 20-30 miles by road. Two trolleybuses were sufficiently complete for electrical and mechanical work to start; however, in order to speed this up it was decided to appoint an additional Trolleybus Garage Hand who could handle routine maintenance whilst a more experienced Hand pressed on with the overhaul and renewal work.

In May 1943 application was made for two more new double-decker trolleybuses for the MoWT 1944-45 production programme, to be purchased from revenue (as preferred by the Ministry). By now trolleybuses were running more miles than the entire motorbus network with a maximum of 11 vehicles out on the road Monday-Friday and 12 on Saturdays!

In May 1943 three 550 yard lengths of trolley wire on the Corn Stores to 'Bonvilston Hotel' section were renewed, whilst in August/September 2,000 yards of new trolley wire were run between the Old Bridge Sections and the 'New Inn' Sections.

During the evening of 13 October 1943 a Cilfynydd-bound trolleybus skidded on the wet road surface in Taff Street, mounted the pavement and crashed into W. Vetta's shop. The shop front was seriously damaged but there were no injuries to the passengers or crew.

The MoWT granted Pontypridd two trolleybuses in the 1944-45 programme, bringing the number on order up to four, whilst the undertaking provisionally requested two more in the 1945-46 programme. Consent for the latter was given in May 1944 and the order was again placed with Karrier with the bodybuilder to be advised later. It was estimated that the four trolleybuses, at £3,000 each, together with four new motorbuses would take £21,400 out of the surplus cash which stood at ca. £44,000 at the end of September 1943. The Deputy Treasurer suggested it would be prudent to cover these amounts with a loan sanction in view of an expected demand for Excess Profits Tax.

The Pontypridd undertaking was at last profitable and it was important to consider future financial policy, Glasgow being cited as the model municipal undertaking offering efficient service at cheap fares and substantial rate relief. The question was not the controversial subject of rate relief; however, it was felt that one of the secrets of Glasgow's success was being free from debt. Pontypridd's net debt at 31 March 1943 had fallen to £19,159 and Mr Powell considered that his first, achievable aim was to reduce this to zero.

Portsmouth AEC663T 212 with English Electric composite body, waits at the Treforest terminus in John Street prior to departure on another journey to Cilfynydd. The offset fleet number, the result of the April 1938 Portsmouth trolleybus fleet renumbering, can be seen on the front panel. The trolleybus is equipped with headlamp masks, but there is no evidence on this or other photographs of white paint on the vehicle's extremities, e.g. mudguards and side life guard rails, to fulfil wartime "black-out" restrictions. (The late W.J. Haynes, courtesy BTS Library)

London Transport ex-Tilling 2ST7 AEC Regent ST949 as used on the trolleybus route seen whilst on hire to PUDCTD (temporary fleet number P3). (Peter Smith collection)

### Cumulative Balances on Revenue Account over the preceding 6 financial years:

|      | Cumulative Rate Aid |            |         | Cumulative loss in carrying on Undertaking |
|------|---------------------|------------|---------|--------------------------------------------|
| 1938 | £128,630            | Deficiency | £4,694  | -£133,324                                  |
| 1939 | £133,830            | Deficiency | £5,353  | -£138,583                                  |
| 1940 | £138,630            | Surplus    | £1,209  | -£137,421                                  |
| 1941 | £141,100            | Surplus    | £8,918  | -£132,182                                  |
| 1942 | £143,540            | Surplus    | £27,242 | -£116,298                                  |
| 1943 | £143,540            | Surplus    | £35,551 | -£107,989                                  |

To the end of year 1942-43 capital expenditure to the extent of £13,268 had been met from revenue, so that the true revenue loss to that date was £94,721.

Outstanding debt at 31 March 1943 after deducting sinking funds in hand was £19,159. Repayment of the Loans Pool amount of the above (£13,533) could be accelerated.

In 1943-44 the undertaking paid £2,000 for rate relief.

As 1944 opened the MoWT, Ministry of Labour and operators considered the direction of labour to transport undertakings. This required that a proper wage be paid during the training of conductors and conductresses, effective from 17 December 1943. Adults were to be engaged at not less than pre-war commencing rates £2 9s 6d per week, juniors as above £2 7s and junior females 90% of adult male £2 4s 6d. It was becoming evident that the shortage of drivers would make it difficult to give traffic staff their annual holidays in 1944. An understanding

was reached with the local TGWU that the work done over 22 duties was to be shared over 20 duties and under this arrangement the traffic staff would be paid for all time worked over 48 hours.

In March 1944 it was learned that the two trolleybus chassis allotted in 1942 which should have gone to the bodybuilders in that month would now only be ready in June, this later being put back to the first week of July 1944. The strain on the undertaking increased in April 1944 when up to four motorbuses were loaned to Caerphilly UDC, who had lost 9 buses in a fire at their garage. They remained on loan until the end of September 1944.

April 1944 witnessed two trolleybus mishaps. On 11 April 1944 a trolleybus heading towards Cilfynydd was seen to be emitting flames as it crossed Victoria Bridge. Passengers were transferred to a following trolleybus. Potentially more serious, at 9.20pm on 25 April 1944 Portsmouth AEC663T trolleybus 212 ran away down Corn Stores Hill; fortunately the driver reacted correctly and the vehicle was eventually brought to a stop half way across Victoria Bridge. A similar incident involving a tramcar had occurred at the same location in May 1919 but had ended with the vehicle crashing into a grocers on the other side of the bridge. The Transport Committee congratulated the driver and issued a reminder, which had to be signed by all drivers, that the compulsory stop at the corner of Corn Stores Hill had to be observed.

Following an investigation it was found that 212 had suffered an air brake failure when approaching the top of Corn Stores Hill owing to a small rubber washer sticking in the release valve supplying air to the rear brakes. The Driver stated that the brakes operated normally when he left the Baptist Chapel, and it was not until he prepared to halt at the Corn Stores Stop that

An unidentified Portsmouth vehicle with MCCW bodywork descends Fothergill Street, Treforest, at Druid's Row, namely the row of terraced houses on the left hand side of the road. Druid's Row is believed to have been built on an ancient druidical site. The larger building on the right opposite the traction pole with a side bracket arm is the former Cecil Cinema, and the 'Crown Hotel' is the public house with the roofed doorway. Note how the traction pole bases have been painted white to aid drivers in the "black-out". (Photographer's name not recorded)

he found himself in difficulties. It could not be explained why the remaining brake power which pulled up the trolleybus in half the length of the bridge, despite the runaway speed down the hill, did not hold the vehicle at the top of the hill with the slight up gradient there to assist it. However, it was evident that the way in which the driver stuck to his post and steered his bus avoided what might have been a serious accident. Investigations subsequently showed that the vehicle had been taken out of service twice earlier in the day owing to faulty brakes.

The Conductor jumped off, reportedly at the 'Maltsters', stating that he feared the trolleybus was going into the public house. Fortunately no one was injured. The cost of repairs to the vehicle were estimated at £2 15s to cover bent trolley booms and damage to the roof caused by flailing booms.

In May 1944 there were a series of faults on one of the traction mains between Mill Street and the Abattoir, repairs being made in early June. By July, however, the Electricity Department was having difficulties generating sufficient power due to the low water level in the canal and set about a scheme for pumping water from the River Taff. In June the trolley wire between the 'New Inn' and Abattoir sections was completely renewed, over 1,600 yards of new wire being run. Work on no. 2 traction feeder continued with two short sections renewed and further faults located. The rotary substation in Gas Yard was overhauled, the Factory Inspector recommending a number of alterations to the switchboard, and in accordance the last copper busbars connecting the battery to the switchboard were removed. This meant that supplies could no longer be sourced from the storage battery; in fact its general deterioration had by now removed its usefulness as an auxiliary or emergency source of supply.

Restoration of street lighting to pre-war standards began in January 1944 and by September the Electricity Department, anticipating permission for the reintroduction of centrally controlled street lighting, started work to make the main road lighting controllable from the Generating Station and the Gas Yard Substation. Along the trolleybus route from Parsons Bakery, Coedpenmaen Road, to Cilfynydd gas lighting prevailed. In fact half lighting was reintroduced from 17 September 1944 and the "black-out" ended completely on 24 April 1945.

A burst water main in Cilfynydd Road near the Albion Colliery disrupted trolleybus operation for over a week in mid-July 1944. It is un threderstood that motorbuses ran over the northern part of the route but no details are known as to where or how the trolleybuses were turned.

On 29 July 1944 the MoWT warned that conditions had so depleted LPTB's rolling stock that all vehicles on hire must be recalled. Pontypridd had received new motorbuses in April 1944 but six LPTB vehicles remained. It was agreed with LPTB to return two more buses on 3 September 1944 whilst the MoWT granted licences to increase the number of motorbuses on order from two to four. It was hoped that London could be persuaded to leave at least two of their motorbuses at Pontypridd. Since 1939 Pontypridd had received 19 new motorbuses in addition to hired vehicles. Although the undertaking was successful in both retaining the last four LPTB motorbuses on loan, and in increasing its order for four new double-decker motorbuses, there was so much traffic to Treforest Trading Estate that there were still insufficient double-deckers. By November 1944 withdrawal of the South Coast travel ban was imminent, and Mr Powell feared that Portsmouth could ask for their trolleybuses back in the spring. He suggested that the undertaking endeavour to acquire four more motorbuses to handle all eventualities at the Trading Estate (which by now was handling 10,000 passengers a day) and to provide relief on the Treforest-Cilfynydd route during "off-peak" hours until sufficient new trolleybuses arrived. At that time he anticipated the arrival of two trolleybuses shortly but feared that delivery of the remainder was "remote".

At about 7.25am on 19 December 1944 a trolleybus running towards Treforest dewired in dense fog by Park Schools. Passenger Frederick Millard of Treforest got out to assist the girl conductress at the driver's request. Whilst the conductress directed the traffic, Mr Millard, with the bamboo retrieval pole in his hand, was hit by a PUDC motorbus heading from Trehafod to the Trading Estate. The motorbus driver had just seen the trolleybus' emergency light and was preparing to stop when he hit the man. Mr Millard was taken to the Cottage Hospital in the Transport Department car where he was found to have a fractured leg. Mr Powell felt morally bound to assist the man and made good his loss of wages amounting to £10. The Insurance Company required proof of negligence on the part of the Department's staff but informally commented that if an *ex-gratia* payment was made they would reimburse.

In November 1944 authority was sought to acquire Gwernygerwn House, until then home of the Gas Works Manager, as office accommodation. Six rooms were suitable for offices and it was proposed to use four of them for the Manager, Rolling Stock Superintendent, Traffic Superintendent and a Clerk. One room was foreseen as a Meeting Room suitable for accommodating a Subcommittee or the frequent meetings with Union Representatives. New repair shops, mess room, garage for small vehicles and stores were needed due to the continuing fleet expansion. Mr Powell suggested building alongside the former tram depot on land recently acquired from Mr Richard Roberts using a portion of this new building for repair shops. A roof could be constructed between this new building and the old tram depot on the one side, and the trolleybus garage on the other, with the trolleybus garage extended backwards (there being ample land behind). A mess room was needed urgently, perhaps in the garden to Gwernygerwn House.

The year 1945 opened with severe winter weather conditions – indeed on 25 January 1945 no morning trolleybus service ran, as the two trolleybuses which had been running though the night had become snowbound by 4.30am. A snowplough-equipped motorbus provided a limited service. After a week of exceptionally cold weather during the evening of 1 February 1945 there were further heavy falls of snow and the Department again ran two trolleybuses throughout the night to help keep the roads open and prevent ice forming on the overhead wires. Pontypridd had the unique distinction of being the only Welsh municipality to continue to operate a regular interval service throughout the freezing weather. In recognition of the exceptional effort made by employees to cope with the snow storms the Transport Committee later paid £75 into a scheme agreed with the employees and the Union for communal use, e.g. sick fund, establish a library, etc.

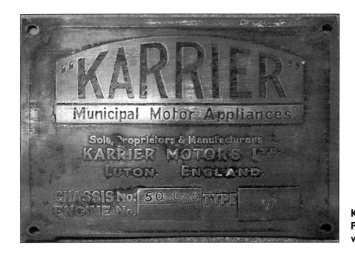

**Karrier maker's plate from chassis number 50085 used beneath Pontypridd's fleet number 10, the first Karrier W to enter service with the UDC. (Mike Crabtree)**

# A NEW FLEET ARRIVES

*In February and March 1945 respectively the first two Karrier W trolleybuses, to be numbered 10 and 11, arrived in Pontypridd painted in a matt undercoat as specified by the Ministry of Supply. They entered service as soon as they had been painted into the undertaking's livery. This meant that considering the existing fleet of English Electric SD6WTB (1-7), the Guy BTX60 (8) and Bristol E (9) trolleybuses and the four Portsmouth vehicles (212-215) on loan, the undertaking now had 15 trolleybuses at its disposal.*

Subject to supply difficulties it was decided to erect passenger waiting shelters, which would be supplied free of charge by an advertising agency, at the following stops on the trolleybus route: Taff House, Treforest; Station Square, for outward traffic to Cilfynydd; 'New Inn', Town Centre; Baptist Chapel, for inward traffic to town; Norton Bridge; Quarry Siding, Cilfynydd inward; Richard Street, Cilfynydd inward; and Workmen's Hall, Cilfynydd inward.

At the end of April 1945 there was a further breakdown on the no. 2 traction feeder in the Broadway section; having isolated a section of cable between Park Schools and Taff House, the fault was localised and the feeder brought back into service by 9 June 1945. Owing to the dangerous state of a traction pole in Mill Street, the overhead line equipment was altered to span suspension between St. Catherine's Chambers and the County Buildings. Worn trolley wire between Taff House and Treforest terminus was renewed in June 1945 and by the beginning of

September 1945 the trolley wires on Broadway section had been renewed.

There was a fatal accident involving a trolleybus at Coedpenmaen on 10 March 1945. Mr Seth Tucker ruined a pair of trousers pulling the deceased from under the trolleybus and was reimbursed £1 5s for their replacement.

By May 1945 there was a shortage of drivers and it was expected that the Ministry of Labour and National Service would direct drivers from North Wales to Pontypridd. Some 50 employees were still with the Forces and with their return imminent Mr Powell asked for instructions as to how current staff should be dismissed as the serving employees returned. His suggestion that those employees directed to the undertaking by the Essential Works Order, and then retired employees who had returned to work be released first, was agreed on 13 November 1945. Thereafter, in sequence, part-timers, females and temporary would be laid-off.

The 1945 Weymann body on Karrier W 11 looks particularly austere from this angle. The trolleybus is standing in Station Square in front of Pontypridd GPO and Sorting Office. (Peter Smith Collection)

The Karrier W trolleybus especially decorated and illuminated for VJ Day stands in John Street, Treforest. (Cy Yandell collection)

Circumstances would soon show that the excess of employees was but temporary!

The Electricity Department supplied trolleybus traction power at ¾d per unit, but the meters were on the out-going side of the generators with the result that any losses incurred in supplying the electricity were borne by that Department. It was mutually agreed to add 10% to the cost of each unit, backdated to 1 January 1945, whilst the Electricity Department endeavoured to improve their metering arrangements.

Hostilities in mainland Europe came to an end at the beginning of May 1945. Three days of public holiday were granted starting on Tuesday 8 May 1945 with "VE" (Victory in Europe) Day. As darkness fell the town centre was illuminated by festoons of coloured lights hung from the traction poles, the centre piece being the King's crown made in the Transport Department's blacksmith's shop lit up in red, white, blue and green attached to the ornamental arches supporting the trolleybus equipment over Victoria Bridge. In order to cope with the expected high number of passengers and the fact that 6-8 traffic employees were on holiday each week throughout the summer, employees were offered a day off with pay at the end of their annual holiday or eight hours pay in lieu for VE Day plus an additional two days holiday.

On 10 July 1945 the Transport Manager was instructed to look into the reinstatement of bus stops abandoned during the war, however the RTC recommended in November 1945 that this be left in abeyance pending a national agreement.

New conditions of service agreement for employees covered by the NJIC came into force in July 1945, the main change being that if a duty exceeded nine hours for a day, overtime had to be paid on the excess. This reduced scheduling flexibility which until then permitted duties slightly less than eight hours to compensate for a longer working day (usually a Saturday) to make up the 48 hour guaranteed working week. The rate for rest day working increased to time and a half. Together with other changes the result was a considerable increase in the undertaking's labour costs.

Owing to the larger fleet, the undertaking's advertising contractor Frank Mason & Co. Ltd. offered improved rates when their contract came up for renewal at the end of 1945. Mr Powell spoke highly of the relationship with Masons, who adhered to the Council's wish not to advertise alcoholic beverages or betting. At that time the undertaking was receiving two-thirds of the revenue collected, resulting in receipts of £285 in 1943-44 and £341 in 1944-45, with Masons bearing the costs of painting the advertisements, renovation, etc. Advertising on tickets raised an additional £3 10s per million tickets. Masons offered £750 for the existing fleet for a five-year period plus £20 pa for each double-decker or £5 for each single-decker acquired after the renewal date, representing virtually three-quarters of the revenue collected. Unfortunately this soon resulted in less income, the figure falling from £1,469 in 1945-46 to £714 in 1946-47 as the combined motorbus and trolleybus fleet reduced in size towards the end of the war and immediately thereafter as vehicles on loan to Pontypridd were returned to their owners.

At midnight on Tuesday 14 August 1945 it was announced that Japan had surrendered and public holidays were declared for "VJ" (Victory in Japan) Day on 15 August 1945 and the following day. Special schedules which had been prepared in advance were immediately put into effect whilst an earlier NJIC decision provided for eight hours pay on VJ Day, whether worked or not, plus time worked at plain rate; and eight hours pay on the second day whether worked or not, plus time worked at double rate. However, at 6.15am the crews announced that whilst they were prepared to operate the special schedules until 8.00am as workpeople were involved they were not prepared to work afterwards at the NJIC conditions. They insisted on three days off later for working the two VJ days. Although a departure from a National Agreement this was agreed to, enabling services to resume from 9.15am.

Gangs of council workmen restored the fairy lights between the GWR Station and Victoria Bridge, the latter again ornamented with a Victory Arch of coloured lamps and Crown.

An illuminated trolleybus approached beneath the King's Crown lit up on the ornamental arches supporting the trolleybus equipment over Victoria Bridge. A tower wagon lorry is on standby in front of the 1861 Tabernacle chapel, now Pontypridd's Museum and Tourist Information Centre. (Cy Yandell collection)

A trolleybus, believed to be Karrier 11, was decorated and illuminated for the holiday.

Two more Karrier W trolleybuses, numbers 12 and 13, arrived in August 1945 bringing the fleet up to four, and Sunbeam MS3 trolleybuses 213 and 214 were returned to Portsmouth.

At the outbreak of war an experiment with 6d four-journey tickets on the trolleybus route had started with the intention of extending the trial to motorbus routes. Although retained on the trolleybuses the MoWT refused an extension during wartime. On 22 May 1946 permission was granted to introduce 6d four-journey ticket on all services.

In November 1945 a length of trolley wire near 'Albion Hotel', Cilfynydd, was renewed and the section insulators changed.

There was a further fault on no. 2. Traction Feeder, located to the branch cable in Mill Street feeding the Pwllgwaun Colliery and 67 yards were renewed.

In March 1946 some 112 yards of trolley wire near Quarry Road, Cilfynydd were replaced.

Following the arrival of two more Karrier W trolleybuses, fleet numbers 14 and 15, in late February and early March 1946 it was decided to return the remaining two Portsmouth trolleybuses (AEC 663T 212 and 215) by the end of April. The Deferred Maintenance Charge for the Portsmouth vehicles was £122 10s 2d, which Mr Powell considered very reasonable, and was settled in September 1946. On 14 May 1946 the Transport Committee decided that with six new Karrier trolleybuses in

Roe-bodied Karrier W 14 of 1946 loads in Taff Street outside Lipton's store, a national chain of grocers and tea merchants. The driver, in his summer dust jacket, has his right hand on the handbrake ready for the "off". A poster in Lipton's window encourages passers-by to "Register with Lipton", a clear indication that food rationing was still in operation. Nonetheless at least one of the ladies standing outside the shop wears a pleated raincoat and headscarf – the latest fashion of the time. (BTS Library (the late W.J. Haynes))

63

**Having reversed into John Place, No. 12 prepares to pull forward to the loading point at the John Street, Treforest terminus. The nearside upper-deck panels feature a large hand-painted advertisement. (Omnibus Society)**

stock and two more due in July 1946 they should advertise the Bristol E (9) and three single-deck trolleybuses for sale. The proceeds were used towards reducing the outstanding debt on motorbuses.

The shortage of traffic staff was becoming an increasing concern. The undertaking ceased to be scheduled under the Essential Work (General Provisions) Orders, 1942 and 1944, from 15 May 1946, whilst that same month Section 19 of the Road Traffic Act 1930 governing hours of duty, which had been suspended during the war, was reintroduced. Nonetheless the post-war recovery hardly offered an economic boom for the "man in the street" – some 2,235 persons in Pontypridd were unemployed on 13 May 1946 whilst 36 cases of South African peaches arrived as a gift to the town. Soon afterwards costs increased when, following TGWU pressure, Pontypridd was regarded as a Group 1 municipal undertaking leading to higher commencing pay rates of £4 17s and £4 13s per week respectively for Drivers and Conductors.

Victory celebrations, including sports events, a ball and fireworks display, were held 8-15 June 1946. Although fuel economies prohibited illuminated advertisements or shop windows, as on VE and VJ Days coloured lights were hung along Taff Street, High Street, Bridge Street and on Victoria Bridge whilst illuminated trolleybus 11 reappeared.

The Transport Manager was instructed in June 1946 to report on the possibility of restoring pre-war services. He complained about a number of misleading newspaper reports. When war broke out the MoT had directed a 50% reduction in mileage but Pontypridd had been able to maintain 75%-80% of mileage, indeed thanks to the trolleybuses it had been possible to actually increase the frequency and capacity on the Treforest – Cilfynydd route whilst larger capacity motorbuses had been

used on other routes. This saved Pontypridd from the acute transport difficulties experienced in most towns despite the load trebling in volume, a 20 hours service day, and the age of the fleet in 1939. As far as the trolleybus route was concerned, the increased frequency, compared with pre-war, had been maintained and the single-deckers were being gradually replaced with double-deckers at a cost of £24,000. There had been a request for a new service to Oaklands, Cilfynydd although the area was only 500 yards from the trolleybus route and thus uneconomic to operate.

Although the Transport Committee wished to introduce Transfer Tickets enabling passengers to continue on any other PUDCT service, on 4 June 1946 the full Council introduced more interchange restrictions permitting solely "passengers on the Llantwit Road service who purchase sixpenny four-journey tickets be allowed to use such tickets for return journeys from Pontypridd to Treforest on trolley vehicles".

Conductresses continued to be systematically replaced by men and the complement had fallen from a wartime peak of 50 to 20 by September 1946 of which three were married and thus due for early release. In order to dismiss the other 17 it would be necessary to employ men other than those who had been with the undertaking before being called up for the Forces there was a long waiting list. All employees, about 60 in number, engaged during the war were regarded as temporary, and Mr Powell felt that the situation had to be clarified. He prepared a Duty Schedule eliminating overtime as far as possible, basing duties on a 48-hour week, with six working days and one rest day. This resulted in a total of 62 duties needing to be manned (trolleybus 12, motorbus 30, factory and reliefs 20).

Amongst the staff at that time there were 61 drivers qualified for trolleybuses and motorbuses; five conductors returned from the forces trained to drive trolleybuses and eight persons medically examined and undergoing trolleybus driver training (total 74). There were 20 conductresses (three being married women), 16 permanent male conductors (including those trained for driving) and 38 other male conductors (total 74). He asked the Council to decide whether to place all temporary male drivers and conductors on the permanent register, or give instructions on recruiting men to replace the conductresses, i.e. according waiting list, ex-servicemen, etc.

On 10 September 1946 it was decided to speed up the dismissal of conductresses to enable male labour to be taken on from the waiting list. All male drivers and conductors serving in a temporary capacity were transferred to the permanent register. In view of their imminent dismissal, three or four conductresses had recently been absent, apparently due to illness. Mr Powell asked the Transport Committee to consider the case of Mrs Devereux who, he stated, had done a good job as the Female Inspector and Welfare Liaison Officer between the Manager and the female staff. She now felt uncomfortable to be working in the offices as the number of conductresses fell (to just 11 by 16 November 1946) and he wondered if she should revert to her position as Head Conductress or look for a better solution. On 12 November 1946 he was instructed to terminate her employment when this was deemed expedient, but thereafter she was to be employed for a further six months in the Transport Office at the same rate of pay with occasional conductor duties.

On 16 September 1946 the traction power supply was interrupted due to a breakdown of the Pwllgwaun Colliery plant which was also fed from the no. 2 Traction Feeder. Also in September 1940, having repainted the traction poles at Cilfynydd and started work at Broadway, painting ceased when the pole painter was recalled to Forces! Guard wires were renewed in Cilfynydd as requested by the GPO.

It had been agreed with the Electricity Committee on 7 July 1945 that the Transport Department should pay an additional 10% for traction current to cover the conversion losses incurred by the use of a rotary converter. In September 1946 Mr Powell asked for a review, commenting that other transport undertakings were not asked to bear these losses. The UDC Electrical Engineer and Manager thought the charge reasonable; however, if such a reduction would improve the efficiency of the trolleybus service or enable the undertaking to present a case to the Traffic Commissioners for a trolleybus route extension, the request could be justified. On 8 October 1946 the Electricity Committee rejected the request.

The delivery of the last two Karrier W's (subsequently given fleet numbers 8 and 9 as the Bristol and Guy ex-demonstrators had by then been withdrawn) was imminent, meaning that the undertaking would have a fleet of eight new double-decker trolleybuses available. Hoping to profit from the post-war shortage of new vehicles, all nine pre-war trolleybuses were offered for sale at the end of 1946. Mr Felix Cunuder, the Works Superintendent Trams and Trolleybuses (he was only promoted to Engineer from May 1947) of Cardiff Corporation Transport, visited Pontypridd in November 1946, for an initial inspection of the vehicles. Cardiff's tram to trolleybus conversion scheme had been interrupted by the war and trams had continued to run along Bute Street to Pier Head until the tracks were declared unsafe. On 28 April 1946 motorbuses were substituted between Mill Lane and Pier Head. It had always been the intention to convert this route to trolleybus operation although a low railway bridge, carrying the London mainline and the lines out of Cardiff General Station to Cardiff Queen Street Station, at the

north end of Bute Street would require the use of single-deck vehicles. Five three axle single-deck AEC/East Lancashire trolleybuses had been ordered in 1945 but their delivery seemed unlikely before 1948-9. Cardiff had rejected an allocation of Sunbeam two axle chassis so the availability of Pontypridd vehicles was timely.

Following a trial run on English Electric 4, Mr Cunuder recommended that none of the vehicles should be bought due to their poor condition and outdated electrical equipment. The state of the vehicles is confirmed by Cy Yandell's recollections of a single-deck trolleybus running past the 'Bonvilston Hotel' in Coedpenmaen Road with sparks flying out underneath. As far as the single-deckers were concerned, he considered that if they were bought the superimposed Estler trolley bases would have to be replaced to enable them to pass beneath a railway bridge at East Canal Wharf, which was on the route of one of the two city centre terminal loops proposed for the Pier Head route (which was subsequently not approved by the MoT). The lighting arrangements were unsuitable, the interior lighting and headlights being supplied with traction power from the overhead but the side and tail lighting was supplied by a 6-volt battery. There was no dynamo to recharge the battery and they had to be renewed about every two days. The Bristol E double-decker was rejected as too high for service in Cardiff, whilst the Guy BTX 60 was considered underpowered and lacked air brakes.

Despite their poor condition, the Cardiff Transport Committee authorised the purchase of the entire fleet of single-deckers together with a quantity of spares, as they were desperate for any trolleybuses they could get in order to release motorbuses that were being used to supplement the tram services. In early 1947 the Pontypridd UDC Transport Committee Chairman and the Transport Manager visited Cardiff to discuss the sale with the right to accept any reasonable offer. By the end of March 1947 all seven single-deck trolleybuses were stored out of use at the depot and the sale was agreed in April 1947

The Cardiff Minutes record that Pontypridd 1 and 6, then in the process of a major chassis and body overhaul, were bought for £1,000 each, and the other five for £200 each to include any spares that they (2-5 and 7) immediately needed. Those vehicles in a roadworthy condition were towed as far as Cardiff's Llandaff Fields trolleybus terminus and then run under power to Clare Road Depot. By the first week of June 1947, five had been transferred to Cardiff with the remaining two following within the next couple of weeks.

The Cardiff Transport Committee allocated £2,500 for the purchase of the seven vehicles and a maximum of £4,000 to cover their purchase and reinstatement. However, the final total expenditure for acquisition, making them roadworthy and repainting was £4,504 12s 6d plus a further £22 5s 6d for additional spares. They ran in Cardiff until the arrival of new single-deck vehicles in 1949 being known, amongst other euphemisms, as "religious buses" as, reportedly according to the Lord Mayor, *"Pontypridd had knocked the hell out of them"*.

The Clerk was instructed on 12 November 1946 to apply to borrow £6,000 for two new double-deck trolley vehicles. Owing to increased labour and material costs, Park Royal's figure for the trolleybus bodies on the Karrier W's 8 and 9 had increased from £1,328 12s 6d to £1,595 each. The Finance Committee pointed out that all the Council's Trading Committees had recorded deficits over their lifetimes, but the Transport Committee had the highest. The Pontypridd UDC Act 1929 foresaw that all surpluses should be used for rate relief. In case of the undertaking's nationalisation, what was to be done about the still outstanding deficits that were met out of the rates? The Finance Committee suggested that henceforth all surpluses should be transferred for rate relief and not used to purchase new vehicles.

The NJIC for the Road Passenger Transport Industry applied in November 1946 for improved conditions including 40 hour working week to be paid at the rate of the present 48-hour week, overtime "added rates", more "spread-over" payments, special rates for Sundays and work on Good Fridays, night work, also increased annual holidays. The estimated additional costs were £8,000 – £10,000 pa. Effective from 1 April 1947, the working week was reduced to 44 hours in six days but with no reduction in the weekly rate of pay and with a minimum daily duty tour of seven hours and a maximum of 8½ hours. In addition the Sunday rate was increased to time and a half (instead of time and a quarter). Mr Powell commented that the award would mean that labour costs would increase from ca. 60% to 78% above pre-war levels although the undertaking was still running at pre-war fares. Material costs had gone up by between 50% and 400% according to the item. The concentration on an industrial load (8,060 persons working at Treforest Trading Estate alone) for one hour every morning and evening had made the load factor more uneconomic.

The AEU requested a shorter, 44-hour working week for their members in June 1947, as they were governed by the Electricity NJIC and not by the Transport NJIC. Mr Powell commented that there were five different trade unions in the depot at that time involving varying conditions that were as confusing as they were difficult to operate. Uniformity would offer substantial advantages. He suggested offering a 44-hour week at the same

conditions as those granted under the NJIC for Transport. However, there were difficulties in reducing the working week for depot craftsmen from 48 to 44 hours as they needed to be on duty for morning and afternoon peaks Monday – Friday. Thursday afternoons were easier as it was a half-day closing in the shops. Due to heavy amount of maintenance work and every vehicle being required at some time of the day, painting and bodywork repairs were in arrears, with chassis problems on the horizon. Mr Powell thought of dividing maintenance into three sections, engines, chassis and bodywork, with a Charge Hand heading each section, the additional cost according to DJIC Schedule being 2d an hour. He suggested offering a flat amount of 7s 6d per week.

In January 1947 quotations were invited for replacing the austerity wooden seating in some of the motorbuses; however, the Karrier W trolleybuses retained their wooden slatted seats on both decks until withdrawal. Warning notices appeared on the trolleybuses warning passengers, especially miners and other workers wearing hob-nailed boots, of the lack of grip on the staircase step steel-stripping until these could be replaced with non-slip material.

The winter weather conditions reduced revenue by about £500 per week and made it difficult to maintain services, although all workmen's services were operated except for those between 6 – 6.45am on Thursday 6 February 1947. Some traffic employees had to work all night and were paid overtime rates plus 5s refreshments allowance. Priority boarding for workers was discontinued.

At a Joint Meeting of the Electricity and Transport Subcommittees on 14 February 1947 government plans to

Heavy snow falls in the winter of 1947 meant that motorbuses had to replace trolleybuses on a number of occasions. Here Bristol K5G is seen at the junction of Market Street with Taff Street. The running wires, like everything else, are laden with snow! (Cy Yandell collection)

nationalise electricity and transport undertakings were discussed. In a remarkably advanced ecological view it was agreed that every effort would be made to retain the refuse-burning Treforest Destructor. The MPTA were endeavouring to retain the transport services as at present operated by Local Authorities, and here again it was felt that every effort on the part of this Association and other comparable responsible bodies should be encouraged and assisted.

There were more pressing problems for the power supply industry than nationalisation. The Government decided that from midnight on 12 February 1947 no electricity could be used by domestic and non-industrial consumers in the South Wales area between 9am and 12 noon and 2pm and 4pm. Power would be cut-off to such consumers between the hours specified unless they were supplied off the same feeder as industrial users. Additionally the actual voltage of supply to all consumers would be reduced by 5% throughout the day until further notice. This scheduled load shedding continued until 31 March 1947.

The Transport Act 1947 (effective 1 January 1948) established the British Transport Commission (BTC) with authority to carry goods and passengers by rail, road and inland waterway. Its objectives were defined as "to provide, or secure, or promote the provision of an efficient, adequate, economical and properly integrated system of public inland transport and port facilities within Great Britain ...". In the case of local authority undertakings taken over by the BTC, the Commission would assume responsibility for outstanding liabilities including the loan debt. Additional compensation aggregating not more than £2.5 million was also foreseen. Municipal undertakings would be able to request continued local authority transport operation, not as the individual undertakings then existing, but based upon "mergers" or Joint Boards; on a wider or traffic region basis, however, it would be necessary to prove efficient operation. A Pontypridd delegation joined a conference of East Glamorgan local authorities to work out details for the proposed operational organisation of road passenger transport in the area.

A new Bedford tower wagon and workshop arrived at the beginning of November 1947 and the Dennis-Stevens petrol electric tower wagon BO3639 (formerly 1920 motorbus 49) on loan from Cardiff Corporation Transport was returned. Cardiff withdrew it in December 1947.

There was a power breakdown on Wednesday 12 November 1947 from 8.40am 10.30am. Replacement motorbuses started running by 9am. It was stated that this was only the second time in the history of the trolleybuses that they had been off the road for such a long time.

Normal services operated on Christmas Eve, Boxing Day and Saturday 27 December 1947 but none on Christmas Day. However, on Christmas Eve, David John of Rhydyfelin was knocked down in Fothergill Street, Treforest and killed by a trolleybus heading towards Treforest. The Coroner exonerated the driver and recorded a verdict of Accidental Death.

The local branch of the Electrical Trades Union submitted a letter to the 9 February 1948 meeting of the Pontypridd Trades Council and Labour Party, suggesting that transport problems on the Treforest Trading Estate could be "effectively and permanently solved" by a trolleybus extension to include the Estate. It added that arguments that trolleybuses had to reduce speed to negotiate bends did not apply to the straight run between Machine Bridge and the Estate, whilst with the pending conversion of the town's power supply from DC to AC increased use of trolleybuses would ensure a new lease of life for the Council generating station. Furthermore the delivery time for

trolleybuses was much less than that prevailing for motorbuses. On the national scale anything that reduced the country's dependency on imported oil, payable from very limited currency reserves, would be beneficial.

The idea was submitted to the Labour Party group on the Council and at the 2 March 1948 meeting, upon the motion of Councillor John Howell JP and seconded unanimously, it was resolved that the Clerk, Transport Manager, Surveyor and Electrical Engineer should investigate improving services between Pontypridd and the Estate by introducing trolleybuses. In an effort to avoid the "bottleneck" at Upper Boat, a route through Poplar Road, Rhydyfelin was suggested, with the option of continuing further south to the Nantgarw Colliery, which was soon to reopen.

By the beginning of December 1947 the undertaking was once again confronted by a series of wage claims from both maintenance and platform staff. This pointed towards the necessity of increasing revenue despite the undertaking having paid £46,335 between 1943 and 1947 in excess profits tax! Inflation had caused costs to soar:

| Specimen Items | Percentage above pre-war |
| --- | --- |
| Trolleybus costs per bus mile | 91% |
| Motorbus | 87% |
| Crew wages | 63% |
| Craftsmen's rates | 58%-60% |
| Tyres | 336% |

Mr Powell felt that trolleybus operating costs per mile compared with other operators (1946-47) showed the disadvantages of having a small system with short routes traversing sharp bends:

| | |
| --- | --- |
| Pontypridd | 21.00d |
| Manchester | 20.772d |
| Bournemouth | 20.41d |
| Hull | 19.65d |
| Wolverhampton | 19.487d |
| Reading | 19.037d |
| Portsmouth | 17.384d |

He added that the average speed of trolleybuses was 9.06mph and crew costs 5.91d per trolleybus mile, the cost per mile decreasing as speed increased.

On 9 April 1948 the Transport Committee approved his proposals that the 1½d minimum should be discontinued, and a penny fare be introduced for a short journey of about half a mile with fares of 2d, 3d and 4d thereafter. There were similar increases to workmen's, schools and four-journey tickets. Apparently since the outbreak of the Second World War 33 municipal undertakings had increased their fares, in some cases more than once, whilst another six including Pontypridd were now considering increases. As far as the trolleybuses were concerned, the 1929 Act of Parliament allowed for a charge of 1½d per mile with a 2d minimum for ordinary fares, and 1d per mile with 1½ d minimum for workmen. A fare increase on the trolleybuses could thus be introduced sooner, if desired, than on the motorbuses which required RTC approval. Such an anomaly proved unnecessary and the new fares came into effect on Sunday 12 December 1948.

Following a review of the concession fares offered to old age pensioners in the area, an application was made to the Licensing Authority to offer half fares to OAPs resident within the urban

## SUMMARY OF OPERATING RESULTS 1938-1949

| Year ending | Total Mileage | Total Revenue | Revenue per Mile | | Ttl Working Costs Revenue A/C | Operating cost p/mile | | Gross Profit Revenue A/C | Net Profit (Note 1) | Excess Profits Tax | Cap. Expend. from Revenue |
|---|---|---|---|---|---|---|---|---|---|---|---|
| | | | Trolleybus | Motorbus | | Trolleybus | Motorbus | | | | |
| 31.03.1939 | 929,269 | £44,270 | 12.77d. | 11.30d. | £39,516 | 10.98d. | 10.26d. | £4,754 | -£1,212 | | £4 |
| 31.03.1940 | TB 274,208 | £48,940 | 14.58 | | £38,919 | 11.36 | | £10,021 | £3,838 | | £140 |
| 31.03.1941 | | £55,562 | | | £42,316 | | | £13,246 | £7,665 | | £1,635 |
| 31.03.1942 | 874,198 | £73,065 | 20.57d. | 20.01d. | £51,255 | 15.02d. | 13.74d. | £21,810 | £18,336 | £1,930 | £156 |
| 31.03.1943 | 894,679 | £85,735 | 24.02d. | 22.77d. | £60,278 | 17.90d. | 15.71d. | £25,007 | £21,496 | £16,098 | £7,328 |
| 31.03.1944 | 975,177 | £99,118 | 25.56d. | 23.99d. | £73,553 | 20.00d. | 17.38d. | £25,564 | £22,265 | £16,573 | £22,910 |
| 31.03.1945 | 1,068,980 | £108,230 | 29.00d. | 22.82d. | £79,978 | 20.26d. | 17.23d. | £28,252 | £25,968 | £14,300 | £18,739 |
| 31.03.1946 | 1,163,521 | £110,609 | 27.66d. | 21.39d. | £88,835 | 20.85d. | 17.58d. | £21,775 | £19,732 | £8,519 | £22,251 |
| 31.03.1947 | 1,246,969 | £113,303 | 28.80d. | 19.86d. | £101,178 | 21.00d. | 19.05d. | £12,125 | £10,367 | £7,214 | £2,143 |
| 31.03.1948 | 1,427,704 | £129,595 | 27.10d. | 19.19d. | £117,166 | 21.30d. | 18.13d. | £12,429 | £8,338 | | £2,862 |
| 31.03.1949 | 1,477,651 | £131,886 | 27.61d. | 21.31d. | £131,078 | 22.21d. | 21.06d. | £7,808 | £3,525 | | £1,715 |
| | | | | | | | | | £141,530 | £64,634 | £79,879 |
| 1940–49 | | | | | | | | | | £11,880 | |
| Post-war refund | | | | | | | | | | £52,754 | |
| Net Excess Profits Tax | | | | | | | | | | | |

Note 1: Net Profit after interest and debt repayments
Note 2: A Deferred Repair Fund was started in 1942-43 but not continued.
Note 3: Excess Profits Tax was repealed in 1946

area on the Council's internal services. The application was granted at the beginning of March 1949, despite objections from Western Welsh Omnibus Co. Ltd. and Rhondda Transport, on the basis that other undertakings had already been granted such permission. The concession was not available between 8.00am and 9.00am, 12.45 and 2.15pm, or 4.30 and 6pm on Mondays to Fridays, nor on Saturdays. It was not available to OAPs receiving any form of company pension (effectively ruling out retired PUDCT employees) and required production of an authorisation card.

On 1 April 1948 the UDC electricity undertaking was nationalised. Frustratingly the new tower wagon passed to the South Wales Electricity Board (SWALEB). Ominously, in a review of 45 years' local authority ownership, it was mentioned that almost the whole of the original DC mains system laid down in 1903-1907 was still in use.

A spare BTH Type 207 A3 traction motor, as used on Karrier Ws 8, 9, 12-15 was ordered in May 1948 for delivery in ca. 12 months time at a cost of £301 5s.

In summer 1948 insurance was arranged with Municipal Mutual Insurance Ltd. to cover the UDC against damage caused by electrolytic action on the underground traction feeder cables at a cost of £1 per mile. Soon afterwards the company paid £259 2s 2d to the GPO in respect of damage some time previously.

Although there had been some relaxation in lighting restrictions, the aim of a 25% reduction in power consumption for lighting, compared to pre-war, continued. The MoT considered that lighting should be provided at road junctions where there were many pedestrians after dark, for bollards, obstructions, traffic signals and above important traffic signs; where road repair was in progress, on the main traffic routes and at named points recommended by the police. Over the next 18 months "Cats' Eyes" were added along the A470 through the urban area, whilst permanent white plastic lines impregnated with reflecting powdered glass were laid from Cilfynydd trolleybus terminus to the Royal Oak, Pontshonnorton, and later as far as the Machine Bridge, Treforest.

The Engineers & Surveyors Department received a letter from Divisional Road Engineer MoT Cardiff, in early September 1948 referring to proposals to extend the existing trolleybus route to Nantgarw making use of the disused Cardiff Railway (CR). "The question of the extended use by trolleybuses of the proposed new trunk road raises an important principle and requires very careful consideration in consultation with the Department's Railway Division. You mention in your letter dated 8 June 1948 to the Planning Officer, East Glamorgan Joint Planning Committee that one of the proposals you have in mind is to use the line of the old Cardiff Railway for the future trolleybus route. This route is, in fact, being explored for the line of the new (A470 Cardiff – Merthyr Tydfil) trunk road and there is every likelihood that it will be ultimately accepted. It is suggested, therefore, in the circumstances that you defer considerations for extending the trolleybus route until the route of the new road is determined, which I hope will not be very long delayed". It will be recalled that the CR had been frustrated in its ambitions to tap the valuable coal traffic from the Taff Vale Railway through a junction at Treforest and its northern extension, had only been used by a local service between Cardiff (Rhymney) and Rhydyfelin from 1911 until 1931. The railway remained derelict until construction of the NCB coke ovens at Nantgarw began in summer 1948 but the line beyond towards Treforest was never reinstated.

Karrier W no. 14 with Roe composite body loads passengers in Taff Street heading north on 15 July 1949. On the skyline in the background can be seen the roof of the popular Palladium Cinema and cafe. The cinema closed in 1961 and was demolished to make way for a supermarket. The three spheres indicating a pawnbroker hang ominously above a first floor window behind the trolleybus. (Roy Marshall)

## Proposals to extend trolleybuses to Rhydyfelin, Treforest Trading Estate and Nantgarw

By 1937 when construction of the Treforest Industrial Estate began, the trunk Cardiff Road traversed a built-up area from Glyntaff to Upper Boat, and although narrow in places was served by a 10-minute motorbus service for most of the day (7½ minutes on Saturdays). The Second World War led to a huge expansion of workmen's traffic to and from the Estate, whilst from summer 1948 work started to redevelop Nantgarw Colliery less than a third of a mile beyond the Industrial Estate. Throughout much of the trolleybus era these three possible sources of traffic provided the catalyst for two serious attempts to build an additional trolleybus route.

The 1940 proposals referred to an extension from the Machine Bridge, Treforest, to the Dynea end of Poplar Road, Rhydyfelin, replacing the Berw Road – Rhydyfelin motorbus route as then operated. As initially foreseen the trolleybuses would have run along Cardiff Road as far as Dyffryn Road, turned northeast and climbed Dyffryn Road over the Old Doctor's Canal and past the Round Houses, possibly as far as Oak Street. The Treforest Industrial Estate had not yet become a traffic objective. Owing to concerns about trolleybuses using Cardiff Road the estimates as presented for the Transport Committee's approval assumed that the line would turn off Cardiff Road at either the Hide & Skin Market, Treforest, on the east side of the River Taff about a quarter of a mile south of Machine Bridge, or at the Ebenezer Chapel a further third of a mile south to join the course of the former Doctor's Canal. It will be recalled that the UDC had been granted powers to build a light railway from the Machine Bridge, Treforest, following the course of the canal to Pont-y-Glyn and then southwards to Maesaraul and Dynea, to Upper Boat close to the Melin-

Gorrwg Foundry in 1920 and that these had been partially renewed in 1927.

The 1948 extension would have continued beyond Dyffryn Road south southeast to the west of Rhydyfelin following the Cardiff trunk road, through Hawthorne, to Upper Boat. It would have passed through the entire length of the Treforest Trading Estate (formerly known as an Industrial Estate) and then swung northeast at its southern end along Oxford Street and beneath the GWR ex-Cardiff Railway (CR) bridge towards the village of Nantgarw. The terminus is likely to have been at the entrance to the new Nantgarw Colliery in Quarry Street where there is also a school. No additional concerns were raised about trolleybuses using Cardiff Road; however, as an alternative to following the narrow main road through Upper Boat, a route through Poplar Road, Rhydyfelin was suggested. At some stage the option of building a road, possibly solely for trolleybuses, along the route of the disused CR was proposed although it is not known whether this related solely to 1) an Upper Boat "by-pass" or 2) from the 'Dyffryn Arms' public house, Rhydyfelin, to Upper Boat, or 3) Poplar Road to Upper Boat.

In 1948 the sole Pontypridd UDC motorbus route passing through Nantgarw was the Pontypridd – Caerphilly service operated jointly with Caerphilly UDC. However, the Treforest Trading Estate traffic still demanded a large fleet of motorbuses especially to cater for peak hour workmen's traffic. There would no doubt have been objections from both Rhondda Transport and Western Welsh, who operated a Cardiff – Pontypridd service, to trolleybuses running beyond the Trading Estate to and from Nantgarw.

In late 1948 trials began with four Bell Punch "Ultimate" ticket machines on the in-town services. The undertaking was now carrying 20 million passengers annually, which would have needed some 65 separate ticket values if machines were not used, whilst the trolleybus route alone had 12 different values and 44 different point-to-point fares. Use of traditional Bell Punch tickets and administration of their sale was labour intensive: mechanisation would remove the necessity of a night shift in the Ticket Office. Following a demonstration to the Transport Committee on 11 January 1949, it was decided to standardise on the "Ultimate" for short distance routes. In June 1949 Bell Punch's quotation of £20 pa for the hire of each "Ultimate" ticket machine was accepted.

Early in 1949 the AEU requested improved lighting to replace the hand-lamps still used in Glyntaff depot, where few improvements had taken place since the tramways had opened. Much of the overhaul work was carried out in the former tram depot, a three-bay building, with half of one bay walled-off lengthwise as the Fitting Shop. The rest of the building was open at the end and understandably the men also complained about the damp and cold working conditions. Mr Powell felt that the situation could be improved if the existing wall was moved to screen the whole instead of half the bay, and roller shutters fitted to the building entrance. It would not be necessary to move the wall for the whole length of the building as one third of it had been done in 1938 to accommodate the Paint Shop. New stores and mess room were completed in May 1949 at a cost of £8,116 for the buildings and £556 for the equipment.

SWALEB reported in June 1949 that the traction pole at 70 Taff Street was in a bad condition and asked if it could be removed and replaced by a rosette on the premises of Haines Stores. As Haines were in agreement, and a replacement traction pole would cost approx £20, an easement of 1s pa was given.

Maidstone Corporation advertised a number of trolley vehicles for sale in November or December 1949, and enquiries were made into the possibility of obtaining loan sanction to cover the cost of buying one - but a purchase did not materialise. It is assumed that these were part of a cancelled order placed in January 1948 for five Sunbeam W chassis to be equipped with Northern Coachbuilders bodies and intended for a new trolleybus route to the Shepway housing estate. A downturn in the undertaking's finances forced Maidstone Council to change its policy in 1949, and it is likely that they endeavoured to place the vehicles with other operators. They were unsuccessful. The order with the coachbuilder was cancelled in mid-1950 and that with the chassis manufacturer, after prolonged negotiations and possibly a £500 cancellation fee, in 1951-52.

Pontypridd UDC's first tower wagon had been purchased by the tramways, but with the development of the electricity undertaking it was felt appropriate to charge proportionately to the use, made by each Department. The Council's Electricity Department had bought the current tower wagon and this had thus been passed to SWALEB upon nationalisation. SWALEB were now charging the Transport Department 8s 3d per hour for the wagon and driver, some £50-60 per month, and an effort was made to reduce the charge. By September 1950 SWALEB admitted that PUDCT had erroneously been paying the entire cost of the tower wagon and its crew standing by in case of a traction breakdown. It was agreed that the vehicle and crew would now be used for SWALEB work as far as possible, but with priority for traction work as required.

# Pontypridd UDC

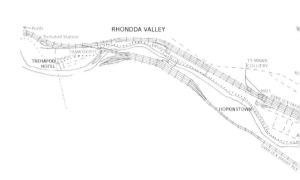

## Key to Map

| | |
|---|---|
| ━━━━━━━ | **Trolleybus Overhead Wiring** |
| ·························· | **Approved Trolleybus Route not Constructed** |
| ─ ·─ ·─ ·─ | **Proposed Trolleybus Extension** |
| ─ ─ ─ ─ | **Other Roads and Streets** |
| ─┼─┼─┼─┼─ | **Railway (precise track layout not shown)** |
| ·─·─·─·─·─· | **UDC Boundary** |

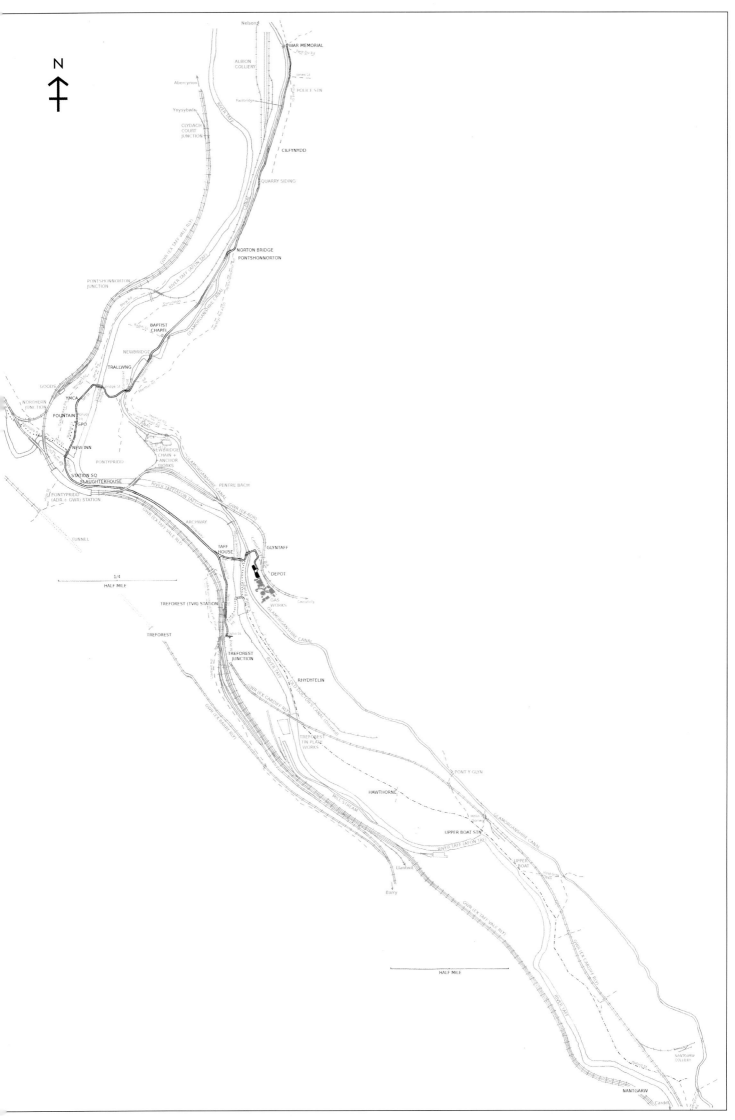

N

Nelsons

WAR MEMORIAL
Pant Du Rd
ALBION
COLLIERY
Jones St
Aberrynon
POLICE STN
Ynysybwl
Rackbridge
CLYDACH
COURT
JUNCTION
CILFYNYDD

RIVER TAFF

QUARRY SIDING

NORTON BRIDGE
PONTSHONNORTON

PONTSHONNORTON
JUNCTION

RIVER TAFF (AFON TAF)

GLAMORGANSHIRE CANAL

GWR (EX TAFF VALE RLY)

BAPTIST
CHAPEL

NEWBRIDGE

TRALLWNG

GOODS
YMCA
NORTHERN
JUNCTION
FOUNTAIN
GPO

NEW INN
PONTYPRIDD

NEWBRIDGE
CHAIN +
ANCHOR
WORKS

GLAMORGANSHIRE CANAL

STATION SQ
SLAUGHTERHOUSE
PENTRE BACH
PONTYPRIDD
(ADR + GWR) STATION
RIVER TAFF (AFON TAF)

GWR (EX ADR)
ARCHWAY
TUNNEL
GWR (EX TAFF VALE RLY)

1/4

HALF MILE

TAFF
HOUSE
GLYNTAFF

DEPOT
Caerphilly
GAS
WORKS

GLAMORGANSHIRE CANAL

TREFOREST (TVR) STATION

TREFOREST

TREFOREST
JUNCTION

RHYDYFELIN

RIVER TAFF (AFON TAF)

GWR (EX CARDIFF RLY)

GLAMORGANSHIRE CANAL (Disused)

GWR (EX BARRY RLY)

TREFOREST
TIN PLATE
WORKS

PONT Y GLYN

HAWTHORNE

MILE STREAM

UPPER BOAT STN

GLAMORGANSHIRE CANAL

RIVER TAFF (AFON TAF)

UPPER
BOAT

Llantwit

Barry

GWR (EX TAFF VALE RLY)

HALF MILE

GWR (EX CARDIFF RLY)

RIVER TAFF

NANTGARW
COLLIERY

NANTGARW

Cardiff

The well-known motorbus and trolleybus photographer, and transport professional, Roy Marshall, captured Karrier W/Weymann UH30/26R No. 10 climbing Victoria Bridge beneath the ornate gantry on 15 March 1949. He well recalls selling a negative to the Sunbeam Trolleybus Co., successors to Karrier, presumably for advertising purposes. (Roy Marshall)

Mr Powell then complained about the cost of repainting traction poles: although the undertaking had provided the paint it had been charged over £600 for 330 poles! SWALEB were prepared to reduce their charges as follows: traction poles carrying trolleybus equipment, street lighting and SWALEB equipment, the Board would absorb one third of the painting cost; poles carrying trolleybus equipment and SWALEB equipment, the Board would absorb half the painting cost. This was estimated to reduce the cost by 40%.

This arrangement was entered into strictly without prejudice to the question of whether the Board had any statutory right to increase the electricity tariff for traction purposes. The Clerk was looking into this and in the meantime payment for the repainting was withheld. SWALEB asked if the Department was prepared to pay something and was told that if the Council agreed, they would be prepared to certify 50% of accounts rendered pending agreement with the Treasurer on final figures. It was also suggested that more than one hundred disused traction poles on former tram routes belonging to the Transport Department between Mill Street and Trehafod, along Cardiff Road from Machine Bridge to Castle Inn Bridge, Treforest and up Forest Road, should be sold to SWALEB.

On 10 January 1950 SWALEB gave notice that they were reviewing the price of traction current supplied to their customers based on either a 5-year agreement on a two part tariff at industrial rates or a new national tariff. SWALEB were immediately informed that the Transport Department would require financial consideration in respect of their use of some

260 traction poles for carrying cables, service lines, etc., as well as over 100 street lamps. These poles were between Treforest and Cilfynydd, from the Depot via Machine Bridge to Taff House, and between Pontypridd and Trehafod and via Cardiff Road and Castle Inn Bridge to Forest Road along former tramways. In September 1950 it was decided to sell those traction poles no longer required by the Transport or Surveyor's Department for street lighting purposes to SWALEB.

The first evidence of falling traffic revenues had started to be felt in South Wales whilst as at 31 December 1949 in Pontypridd motorbus services continued to lose money (£5,591 loss) although the trolleybuses remained profitable (+£2,218). Mr Powell felt that a high quality service at a higher price would be better than cutting services; thus there could be a number of stages unaffected by the December 1948 increase, which could now accommodate a fare increase. In his report of 10 May 1950 he drew attention to the fact that figures indicated that operations were yielding a gross profit of about £4,000 pa but a net loss after meeting interest and loan repayments of ca. £4,500.

Operating costs had doubled since 1939 but fares had only gone up by about $33\frac{1}{3}$%. The main increases were traffic expenses, primarily labour, although repairs and maintenance had also increased considerably, again reflecting higher labour costs. He added that heavy peak traffic requiring additional traffic staff was also particularly costly. Body rebuilding was also a challenge due to the poor quality timber used in the wartime and immediate post-war vehicle bodies (and

The Weymann-bodied Karrier Ws, fleet Nos 10 and 11, were the only vehicles in the post-war fleet to have English Electric control equipment. No. 11 is seen outside 'The Greyhound Inn' on the Tumble, Station Square, on 15 July 1949. (Roy Marshall)

Karrier W No. 12 with Park Royal body passes the 'New Inn' in Taff Street heading towards Cilfynydd on 15 September 1949. The junction of Taff Street (which continues into High Street) and Mill Street can be seen two buildings to the rear of the trolleybus. (Roy Marshall)

In immaculate condition Karrier W 12 with Park Royal body pauses at the Park Gates (Ynysangharad Park) stop. The building in the background had considerable local significance: it was the home of the Pontypridd Rugby Club. In the distance, above the front dome of No. 12, can be seen the obelisk erected on Pontypridd Common to the memory of the fallen in the First World War. (John Carter [Photographer C. Carter])

acknowledged as such by MoT Vehicle Examiners). The opportunities for economies were few, whilst pending increases for traction power and uncertainties whether the MoT would be releasing fuel for private hire purposes, made financial planning difficult.

Despite progressive fleet replacement there were still nine motorbuses over 20 years old in service whilst there were only eight trolleybuses and no reserves! The undertaking had 276 employees: 172 platform, 74 maintenance, 8 inspectors and 22 administrative staff.

**LOAD FACTOR**

| | Trolleybus | Motorbus |
|---|---|---|
| 1. Total bus hours in service | 26,373 | 98,477 |
| 2. Fleet strength | 8 | 58 |
| 3. Standard max hours per bus pa | 6,000 | 6,000 |
| 4. Max hours for fleet | 48,000 | 348,000 |
| 5. Load factor | 55% | 28% |

In respect of an assault on a conductor for non-payment of fares, the Clerk reported that the only trolleybus fares under which a summons could be taken out were those in the Council's Bye-Laws dating from 1905 and applicable to the tramways. He was accordingly instructed to prepare a new version. These draft Trolleybus Bye-Laws were adopted by the Transport Committee on 12 December 1950 and confirmation was sought from the MoT.

In the six months ending 20 September 1950 motorbus services made a loss of £9,423 but trolleybuses registered a profit of £1,225. As an economy in October 1950 motorbus schedules were reduced - however, the Sunday trolleybus service was cut from 10 to 12-minute frequency after 4pm whilst on Wednesdays the 7 minute frequency was reduced to 8 from 3.30 – 6.00pm.

An industry application in September 1950 for an additional 3d per hour was referred to the Independent Tribunal which resulted in an award of 7s 6d per week for Drivers, Conductors, and skilled maintenance workers with 6s 6d for the remainder, for a 44-hour week. The various wage increases did little to slow the unprecedented number of resignations that typified the transport industry as a whole, as men left for more remunerative jobs in industry, where craftsmen could expect a basic 3s 6d per hour. This avoided any redundancies at the end of the annual holiday period, but did lead to some uneconomic journeys being withdrawn.

Icy road conditions and poor visibility typified the first few days of 1951 making time keeping impossible in the early mornings. Following a request from the TGWU it was decided to fit nearside rear view mirrors to all vehicles in the fleet.

Messrs Frank Mason & Co. Ltd. were currently paying £1,080 pa for the undertaking's advertising rights, and as the contract approached its expiry date the Council let it be known that they expected a substantially higher offer. Masons asked if the UDC would reconsider its refusal to carry brewer's advertisements (27 whole spaces being vacant) and offered £1,200 pa for five years or £1,500 pa including brewer's adverts. The latter offer was accepted in March 1951, indeed in September 1952 the Transport Committee went so far as to allow advertising spaces to be let to football pools promoters.

Mr Powell was concerned by the spiralling costs and wages. Average operating costs per mile in October 1950 had reached 22.82d for motorbuses and 24.06d for trolleybuses whereas revenue (which he chose to quote for the undertaking as a whole) was 24.02 per bus mile. He complained of having to run services through hilly, congested side streets, but warned that to operate these economically would mean charging fares that many passengers could not or would not pay. As economy measures he suggested the introduction of a 1½d minimum

New panelling in front of the rear axle has removed the "P" of the undertaking's title in this view of Roe-bodied Karrier W 15 (FTG698) in Bridge Street outside Cohen's the opticians and Marenghi's Café. (Roy Marshall)

'The Greyhound Inn' has been recently revamped as 'The Skinny Dog' but 'The White Hart' public house and commercial hotel currently stands empty. Karrier W 9 with Park Royal composite body stands in The Tumble on its way to Treforest on a warm (note the driver's jacket hanging behind the nearside windscreen) 15 July 1949. The banner advertisement on the upper-deck side panels features Corona carbonated drinks, the brand name of two Porth grocers William Thomas and William Evans, who built up a market for soft drinks towards the end of the 19th century, prompted by the growing influence of the temperance movement in South Wales. Their nationwide success was, no doubt, due to their policy of providing a delivery service to the door, just like a baker or milkman. (Roy Marshall)

single fare for adults (1d children), and higher fares from 1pm on Saturdays until the last bus on Sunday (the period when higher wages were paid). Workmen's cheap day returns should be abolished and all concession fares, e.g. for the blind and OAPs, withdrawn, although in the latter case he did not expect any appreciable increase in revenue.

He acknowledged that losses on the Treforest Trading Estate services (by 1952 these were losing £9,000– £10,000 pa) were the root of the financial situation, and commented on the economies that could be achieved by working the system with one form of transport i.e. disposing of the trolleybuses. There was a costly duplication of rolling stock and operational charges between Taff House, Treforest and Pontypridd. Along Berw Road there was much non-remunerative mileage which, if transferred along Coedpenmaen Road, would enable the Rhydyfelin and Cilfynydd services to be linked with less vehicles than the total number of motor buses and trolleybuses used on these two separate routes.

Increased fares, which basically brought fares up to the statutory maximum rate per mile, viz. 1½d per mile and 2d minimum for ordinary passengers, and 1d per mile with 1½d minimum for workpeople, were discussed in June 1951. The Council immediately approved the proposals for introduction from September 1951, but MoT approval was only forthcoming at the end of the year:

**Treforest**

| 1d | Taff House | | | | | |
|----|----|----|----|----|----|----|
| 1½d | 1d | Archway | | | | |
| 2½d | 2d | 1½d | Station Square | | | |
| 3d | 2½d | 2d | 1d | Old Bridge | | |
| 3d | 3d | 3d | 2d | 1½d | Baptist Chapel | |
| 4d | 4d | 3d | 3d | 2d | 1½d | Norton Bridge |
| 5d | 5d | 4½d | 4d | 3d | 2½d | 1½d | Cilfynydd |

Special fare: Cilfynydd terminus – Quarry Siding 1d
Four-journey Tickets: 10d

Children under 15 years of age, half fare with minimum charge of one penny single, odd half pence counted to the penny above.

**Workpeople's Returns**

| | |
|---|---|
| Treforest Terminus – Berw Road (Old Bridge) | 3d return |
| Archway – Baptist Chapel | 3d return |
| Station Square – Norton Bridge | 3d return |
| Baptist Chapel – Cilfynydd | 3d return |
| Treforest Terminus – Baptist Chapel | 4d return |
| Station Square – Cilfynydd Terminus | 5d return |
| Treforest Terminus – Cilfynydd Terminus | 7d return |

**Transfer Returns**

| | |
|---|---|
| Bonvilston Road – Great Western Colliery | 5d return |
| Treforest terminus – Great Western Colliery | 5d return |
| Cilfynydd – Great Western Colliery | 7d return |
| Treforest terminus – Trehafod | 7d return |
| Cilfynydd Terminus – Trehafod | 8d return |
| Treforest Terminus – Coedcae Colliery | 8d return |
| Bonvilston Road – Coedcae Colliery | 7d return |
| Cilfynydd Terminus – Coedcae Colliery | 9d return |
| Rhydyfelin – Cilfynydd (via Town) | 8d return |

As the annual holiday period (20 April – 13 October 1951), during which a maximum of 13 men would be on leave at any one time, a shortage of platform crews was anticipated. The lack of suitable labour resulted in a review of the female labour policy. In May 1951 recruitment of conductresses recommenced but at male rates of pay. They were provided with a dust coat instead of a complete uniform. Over the last few years Mrs Devereux had been working as Supervisor of the Staff Canteen with two ex-conductresses as assistants, these assistants were now put back on the road with their seniority position established.

At 1.55pm on Sunday 15 April 1951 a driver having difficulty in starting his motorbus went for the duty shift hand for assistance. On going into the trolleybus garage to look for him he found the board supporting the garage electricity fuses and switches was in flames. He immediately grabbed an adjacent fire extinguisher and put out the fire. The duty inspector sent for Jack John, the Rolling Stock Superintendent who on arrival at the Depot discovered that a changeover switch, which connected the garage to a 460-volt supply when the 500-volt traction supply was switched off at night, had not been changed back to the 500-volt circuit for the start of the trolleybus service at 1.25pm. As a result the first trolleybus to move out from the garage on the 460-volt supply had caused a flash-back which was maintained across the fuses and set the board alight.

The Secretary of the Pontypridd Shopping Week, Festival of Britain Celebrations Committee asked whether the Council would be prepared to decorate a trolleybus for the week 31 August – 7 September 1951. This was agreed with the Finance Committee, all expenses being charged to the Festival Account. National pride was damaged when during its week in service a union flag was stolen from the decorated vehicle.

Always on the outlook for economies, in September 1951 Mr Powell referred to five stops in just 350 yards along Broadway, Treforest, namely Taff House, Rock House (trolleybuses only), Taff Vale Park (trolleybuses only), Archway and the Observer Office (trolleybuses only). He suggested that these should be amended to Taff House, Taff Vale Park (trolleybuses only) and Alexandra Road; however, this provoked a petition from Broadway residents objecting to the withdrawal of the Observer Office stop. As a result in April 1952 an alternative solution was implemented; northbound stops: Taff House, 'Danygraig Arms' (trolleybuses only), and Alexander Road (Treforest side); southbound stops: Alexander Road (Pontypridd side) (trolleybuses only), Alexander Road (Treforest side), 'Danygraig Arms' (trolleybuses only), and Taff House.

Each locality in the SWALEB area was allotted a primary or secondary "day of hazard" upon which the electricity supply could be cut if load shedding became necessary. Short notice (1-2 minutes in advance) warnings of a pending area power cut were usually broadcast on national radio, each part of the country being identified by a numerical code.

At the public inquiry into the undertaking's financial position held on 22 October 1951, Mr Powell again stated that he felt that Pontypridd was not big enough to warrant two forms of road transport. He added that this required the undertaking to keep duplicate maintenance staffs, whilst the corkscrew nature of the route through the town resulted in proportionately higher trolleybus overhead equipment costs. In view of the prevailing fuel shortages and electricity load shedding he added that trolleybuses were also at risk from power cuts. He believed that substantial savings could be achieved if the entire network was re-planned and the trolleybus system eliminated.

The Albion colliery slagheaps dominate the background as Roe-bodied Karrier W 14 waits at Cilfynydd Common terminus on 6 August 1951. (Roy Marshall)

Roe-bodied Karrier W 14 uses the reversing triangle at John Place, the Treforest terminus. Over sixty years later the scene has not changed but for the disappearance of the trolleybus and related equipment. (Peter Smith collection)

Karrier W 9 pauses outside the YMCA with the Palladium Cinema immediately beyond to allow three Pontypridd UDC motorbuses, led by 1949 Bristol K6G No. 55 (HTX610) with Beadle H30/26R bodywork, to pass. The County, Palladium, Park, Town Hall and White Palace cinemas in Pontypridd competed with each other offering two shows a night changing twice a week. Note the negative feed to the overhead line above motorbus 55. The single-deck motorbus disappearing out of the picture is Bristol L5G No. 16. (Cy Yandell collection)

In October 1951 Mr Powell reported that an increasing number of faults and heavy repair bills could be expected in respect of the trolleybus feeder cables which were now over 40 years old. SWALEB had stated that many sections required renewal. The Board were informed that when economic conditions improved the UDC might well consider rerouting certain services and abandoning trolleybuses. SWALEB were asked to estimate the cost of repairs to keep the trolleybuses operating through the winter and responded with a figure of £2,000 – £3,000. The Transport Manager was instructed to investigate how this figure had been reached and to engage Mr G.J. Evans, the Council's former Electrical Engineer as a consultant. On 19 November 1951 Messrs Evans and Powell met SWALEB representatives. The Transport Department took the view that the condition of the feeders and SWALEB's estimate indicated maintenance arrears which should not have been allowed to accumulate. Before spending £3,000 the Department should prepare a scheme for reorganising services and trolleybus abandonment. The Board made it clear that they did not want to lose the traction load.

Mr Powell added in his report that the world oil supply situation, not least due to the Korean War, suggested caution before any decision on abandoning trolleybus operations. In April 1952, 7½d more tax was put on petrol and diesel oil. There were also signs of expansion in the Trading Estate, and as trolleybus replacement might involve the use of three or four more motorbuses in all day service, it was suggested to wait a little before making a definite break with electric traction. In an effort to minimise costs it was proposed that where the replacement of long lengths of cable was contemplated (in one area a length of 490 yards was involved) there should be further tests to ascertain whether any parts of the existing cable could be retained and only actual faulty sections replaced. It was also agreed the Board would further investigate the faulty negative cables.

In SWALEB's estimates they had included work which would maintain supplies independently from Treforest Generating Station and Gas Yard Substation, so that if one failed the other would be available. As the most likely interruption, other than a fault in the Transport Department's own cables, would be a general shut down or power cut, it was felt that the risk of relying solely upon the Gas Yard Substation for trolleybuses could be taken. On this amended basis the SWALEB Engineer felt that £2,000 should easily cover the costs. It was agreed that work should be tacked in stages according to urgency, and that in any case the amount of work for the financial year 1951-52 should not exceed £1,000. However, the detailed financial reports for these years, which have survived, provide no evidence that the work was ever carried out.

No. 14 stops outside 'The Greyhound Inn' on the Tumble in Station Square opposite the railway station. A tile representation of a greyhound can be seen on the wall of the public house just in front of the trolleybus's upper-saloon front windows. John Carter (Photographer C. Carter)

The conductor poses for the photographer during the layover at Cilfynydd Common War Memorial terminus. (BTS Library [Photographer R.F. Mack])

# RUNDOWN AND CLOSURE

*Although there is no indication of how good or bad the feelings between personalities who had all once worked for Pontypridd UDC might have been, on the official level the relationship between the Council and the SWALEB was becoming strained as negotiations were increasingly influenced by the inflexibility of a national organisation.*

No. 8 joins The Tumble from High Street. The second floor window of the Criterion Restaurant, now known as the Morgan Tavern, is visible behind the trolleybus and beyond that the cast iron tracery of a Regency building now demolished. The 'White Hart Hotel' public house served Webbs Welsh Ales brewed in Aberbeeg. (John Carter [Photographer C. Carter])

In June 1952 the UDC suggested to SWALEB that retrospectively from 1 April 1950, SWALEB should pay the UDC £200 pa for the use of their traction poles (the Council to maintain the poles and SWALEB to have an option to purchase such poles should trolleybus operation be discontinued), £30 pa for use of the transport canteen and 5s per week for garaging the tower wagon. The UDC was prepared in principle to accept traction current charges being based on the maximum demand plus a unit charge, but subject to SWALEB agreeing to the following formula. The maximum demand for 1950-51 was to be considered as 172kW, that for 1951-52 to be 176kW (although the highest recorded was 212kW), whilst for 1952-53 SWALEB was to consider Saturdays as "off-peak load" and charge at one-third of excess over the weekday maximum demand. Although it was difficult to give an accurate figure of the benefits of the above proposals, the Treasurer estimated that the UDC would gain £700-750 for the two years ended 31 March 1952 compared to the original proposals, whilst for 1952-53 and subsequent years a gain of about £450 could be expected.

The Road Safety Committee asked for a specially decorated trolleybus bearing appropriate slogans for Road Safety Week 27 January – 2 February 1952.

Owing to repeated vandalism the Transport Department toilet at Cilfynydd trolleybus terminus was removed, and arrangements were made with a private householder for the use of toilet facilities at 12s 6d pa.

On 15 July 1952 it was learned that the SWALEB had accepted the Council's proposals that they should pay £200 pa for the use of the traction poles, but this amount was to cover any existing and future attachments. The UDC was to maintain and paint the poles. In the event of the Council discontinuing trolleybuses and SWALEB taking up the option to purchase any poles that they might require, SWALEB would relieve the Council of any liability for reinstatement of the public highways in connection with such poles. The Council would not be obliged to renew any poles not required for transport purposes. The Transport Manager's prior approval was required before any attachment was made, all attachments were made at the

Board's risk, and the Board was to take all reasonable steps to keep their attachments and fittings on the Council's poles free from corrosive action. The conditions for continuing to use the canteen and garage the tower wagon were accepted.

In respect of traction current charges the SWALEB tariff detailed in their letter of 23 March 1950 was accepted and would be paid by the Council from 1 April 1952, provided that during "off-peak" hours, kilowatts of maximum demand incurred in excess of the maximum demand during "on-peak" hours, would be charged at the rate of £1 16s 8d pa per kilowatt of such excess maximum demand; the unit and fuel charges to be the same for units consumed during both "off-peak" and "on-peak" periods. ("On-peak" periods were defined as 7am – 7pm Monday – Friday inclusive, "off-peak" all others). Concessional fares were withdrawn immediately although SWALEB was able to use up any tickets already issued.

In October 1952 a proposal to abolish all workmen's fares was accepted and the Transport Manager instructed to submit the alternatives, to apply on all routes (not just those within the UDC area), for approval by the licensing authorities. Questioned as to the possible inter-availability of pensioner's fares on jointly operated routes, it was learned that neighbouring authorities only granted concessions on locally operated routes at a charge of 5s. It was accordingly decided that PUDC would also apply a charge of 5s for an annual pass or authorisation card for half-fare travel on their routes.

In November 1952, without consultation, SWALEB increased charges for overhead linesmen by between 6d and 10d per hour resulting in the Transport Manager ceasing to authorise their accounts for payment. Seeking an explanation he was told that the increase was due to an instruction from SWALEB's head office in respect of all contracting work. PUDCT responded that trolleybus overhead work was not conventional contracting work and that the new rate was well above that paid for

overhead traction linesmen nationally. They added that if overhead maintenance was to be so increased in cost, then there would have to be a suitable increase in the amount paid by the Board for the use of PUDCT traction poles, etc. In response to pressure for payment, SWALEB was informed that the Department was prepared to settle outstanding accounts at the rate per hour for linesmen applicable prior to November 1952 and to negotiate the difference at the appropriate level.

Severe weather, frost and snow, dislocated services 26 November – 3 December 1952.

Increased wages, commodities and fuel costs led Mr Powell to submit new fares for the Transport Committee's approval in January 1953 as follows:

| | |
|---|---|
| Up to 0.5 mile | 1d |
| 0.6 miles to 5 miles | 1.8d per mile |
| 5.1 miles to 7.5 miles | 1.7d per mile |
| Returns from 5d single fare upwards are rated at 66.66% of single fares. | |

The previous fare increases which had been approved by the Council for introduction from September 1951 could only be introduced at the end of 1951 due to MoT concerns generally about local authority fare increases. The result was just three months' additional revenue in the 1951/52 financial year instead of 7 months as foreseen. In consequence there was a net loss of £11,500 for the 1951/52 financial year plus the costs of further wage increases (in total additional costs of £16,000 pa) incurred in the meantime. By now operating costs per mile for trolleybuses were 164% above pre-war (motorbuses 141%) but fares were only 75% above the pre-war levels. The intended fare increases would bring them up to around 100%. The position was not peculiar to Pontypridd, indeed out of 96 municipal undertakings 81 were loss-making in the preceding financial year.

Park Royal bodied Karrier W 13 (FTG235) enters Station Square from High Street with the 'White Hart Hotel' and 'The Greyhound Inn' on the Tumble to the right. In the background a Western Welsh AEC motorbus with ECW double-deck body waits in Sardis Road. Whiterock housing estate is on the hillside in the background. (Cy Yandell collection)

A little girl in her school uniform dress of the period has just alighted from No. 9 at Park Gates (Ynysangharad Park) in Bridge Street. The 33-acre public park lies between Ynysangharad House and the erstwhile Brown Lennox Chain and Anchor works. It was laid out in the Edwardian style as a War Memorial and opened on 6 August 1923. The 'Queen's Hotel' and Cornstores Hill are in the background. (John Carter [Photographer C. Carter])

Anticipating that the new fares would be approved, in June 1953 the Celtic Press, the only printer having the special small type necessary for this kind of work, was given an order for 250 faretable booklets. However, in July 1953 the MoT queried the applicability of the fares to trolleybuses. The legal situation was clarified in cooperation with the Town Clerk and the MoT decided to grant the Order under Defence Regulation 56 which authorised the increased rate per mile to both trolleybuses and motorbuses.

In preparation for the Coronation of Queen Elizabeth II the Council set aside £200 for the customary decorations and lighting, and asked the Transport Department to decorate a trolleybus. Karrier 11 reappeared decorated with bunting, flags and lights. It is believed that a portrait of the new Queen and Prince Phillip with laurel leaf embellishments was fitted to the upper-deck front panels obscuring the destination screen. Local children were fascinated by the illuminated trolleybus and rushed to the roadside to see it. One keen youngster running into the road for a better view was knocked down by the

trolleybus but fortunately not seriously hurt. Despite an appeal from the Unions to suspend services on Coronation Day 2 June 1953, a skeleton service was operated as several functions took place throughout the town. Employees off-duty on Coronation Day were granted a holiday with pay for that day; those who had to work were paid at the rate of time a half with a day off in-lieu. A Conductor in the latter days of the system recalled:

*"If the booms came off the running wires and were too high to reach from road level, the driver would open the rear emergency window and use the extra height gained from there to hook the poles and bring them down to a lower level and pass the bamboo back to the conductor".*

On Monday 10 August 1953 a driver bringing a trolleybus into the depot de-wired at 11.35pm at Machine Bridge. This blew the circuit breakers in the Power Station and due to the rearrangement of shifts there was nobody to replace the

Another view taken at the Park Gates (Ynysangharad Park) stop in Bridge Street. The light-coloured building with a bay window overlooking Bridge Street was the home of the Pontypridd Rugby Club. (John Carter [Photographer C. Carter])

Karrier 9 overtakes Rhondda no. 269 (LNY 350) a 1952 AEC Regent III / Weymann H30/26R motorbus waiting at the Porth stop at the junction of Taff Street with Mill Street. The Bundy recorder clock was located at the top of a lane just to the front nearside of the motorbus. (Peter Smith collection [Photographer W.A. Camwell])

breaker, with the result that the Power Station Superintendent had to be called out thereby delaying bringing the rest of the trolleybuses back into the depot. As no report was received by the Traffic Superintendent on the Tuesday he sent word to the driver to say that this was wanted. As there was still no reply the driver was interviewed by the Transport Manager on Saturday 15 August 1953. Asked why he had not submitted a report he answered that he had asked an Inspector to get a report form

but the Inspector had not done so. Mr Powell believed that the dewirement had occurred because the driver had been rushing to get into the depot and go home. The driver was suspended. Arrangements were made with the Electricity Authority to ensure that the circuit breaker would not operate without someone on duty to replace it.

A meeting took place in November 1953 between representatives of the Council, MoT and Police, regarding the Station Square trolleybus stop for Treforest. It was decided that this was to be moved to a point opposite the Post Office (below the Rhydyfelin bus stop) on the understanding that the MoT's representatives would, if necessary, add road markings prohibiting vehicles other than PUDC buses stopping at the spot.

The Industrial Court awarded increases to drivers, conductors and depot employees of 4s per week of 44 hours for adults (with proportional increases for juveniles) in December 1953. In addition employees were granted five Bank Holidays pa, instead of four, payable at time-and-a half rate, the additional one being Good Friday. It was felt that the Department could meet these increased costs from existing revenue. However, the Federation of Municipal Passenger Transport Employees immediately requested a further pay increase, the NJIC awarding an additional 3s from 5 March 1954. The effects of the two wage increases led to a £5,000 increase in costs to the undertaking as a whole.

There were problems with ice and snow in January 1954: the first trolleybus out of the depot at 5.00am being replaced with a motorbus as the frogs were frozen.

On 18 May 1954 Weymann bodied No. 10 starts to climb High Street outside Montague Burton the tailors. The shop is extant. Standing at the bus stop for Porth, opposite the junction with Mill Street, is Pontypridd UDC Bristol K6A motorbus 41 equipped with a Park Royal body. The Pontypridd – Porth motorbus service was operated jointly by Pontypridd UDC and Rhondda Transport, as in tramway days. In the early 1930s there were advanced plans to convert the Porth tram route to trolleybus operation. (Peter Smith Collection [Photographer John Meredith])

Pit head baths at the Great Western Colliery opened on 8 February 1954 after which only one of the nine collieries served by the undertaking was without this facility. Henceforth colliers tended to travel ten minutes earlier to their shift to change clothing and vice versa for the return, except for those who preferred not to use the baths. The need to equip vehicles with wooden slatted seats to carry passengers with dirty work clothing had almost disappeared.

Owing to historical reasons as former UDC trading departments, Gas and Electricity Board employees had been carried on duty for any distance on one route at a 2d flat fare using pre-paid tickets. The flat fare concession was withdrawn but at the Boards' request they were sold 1d, 1½d and 2d pre-paid tickets and their entitled employees tendered pre-paid tickets equivalent to the ordinary fare. Similar arrangements were introduced for GPO employees in March 1954.

At the 9 March 1954 Council meeting Mr Powell drew attention to the increased overhead equipment maintenance charges made by SWALEB. He suggested that the percentage increase of SWALEB charges should be calculated and then applied to the annual figure that they paid for use of the undertaking's traction poles.

Councillor Emrys Peck stated: "We have felt that this maintenance might become exorbitant. We have felt that we should scrap these trolleybuses on the Treforest-Cilfynydd route. The time is opportune when we should scrap the trolleybuses. I hope we have the necessary diesel driven buses to take their place. We have been talking about buses left in the transport yard – put them into operation from Rhydyfelin to Cilfynydd and thus eliminate this heavy electricity cost". Mr F.J.C. Warner commented, "The time has come to examine the question of scrapping our trolleybus system, and I think we should ask the Transport Manager to report on the matter. I do think that trolleybuses are out of date in Pontypridd and I think the town would be served better without them". Mr J. Stallard referring to the cost of petrol and the possible increase in the price of it remarked: "Before we start talking about scrapping, I think we should know what we are going to scrap. We should have a full report on the matter". It was agreed that the Transport Manager should present a report on the trolleybus undertaking and that a deputation meet the Electricity Board as suggested by the Transport Manager.

Mr Powell reported on 9 April 1954 that a letter had been sent to SWALEB seeking an identical increase as that which had been applied to the overhead maintenance charges applicable to the annual amount that they paid for the use of the Department's traction poles. He added that where the Board was replacing its DC equipment on the traction poles with AC equipment, this led to the poles supporting five cables instead of the previous two. Despite a reminder being sent in July 1954 there was no response from SWALEB, and on 12 October 1954 the Transport Committee decided that if no retrospective concession was forthcoming the Council would increase its charge for the use of their traction poles, and that the extra charge would be fixed and imposed as soon as possible.

He went on to consider the question: "Should the trolleybuses be scrapped?" Since 1950 he had indicated from time to time that Pontypridd was not large enough to support both a motorbus and trolleybus network, particularly at the prevailing high operating costs. The Traffic Superintendent had already prepared timetables for a link-up of Rhydyfelin and Cilfynydd routes on a through service which would require less vehicles than required for the separate operation of these two routes but other circumstances had intervened. Over the same period there had been successive increases on fuel tax totalling 1s 9d per gallon, bringing the total tax payable up to 2s 6d per gallon, which in 1953 cost the Department roughly £15,000 pa on motorbus operation. The tariff discussions with SWALEB resulted in a rate per unit which was not unfavourable in itself, despite being based on the maximum demand system of charge which the Transport Manager regarded as unsatisfactory for electric traction supplies.

There remained a £3,000 loan debt outstanding on the trolleybuses of which £1,500 was due for repayment in the 1954-55 financial year and £1,000 during 1955-56. If the trolleybuses were to be withdrawn immediately, there would be insufficient motorbuses to meet the peak load. It would be necessary to buy four new motorbuses at a cost of £16,000, resulting in additional annual loan charges of £2,500. The peak load related particularly to the Treforest Trading Estate but this load was reducing and if it fell substantially there would be a surplus of motorbuses which would solve any question of a shortage of vehicles that the immediate scrapping of the trolleybuses would involve. The surplus on trolleybus operation of £6,000 represented a trolleybus operating cost per mile of 30.85d excluding loan charges compared to 27.69d for motorbuses - thus if the trolleybus route had been operated by motorbuses there would have been an even greater profit.

On this basis Mr Powell considered that there should be no rush to scrap the trolleybuses as the difference was too low to justify the further capital cost involved (c. 2d per mile). He recommended that no decision be made until the trolleybus loan debt had been repaid by which time it would be clearer how the Trading Estate traffic would develop. There were a number of provisos which could force an earlier decision, such as a tax cut on fuel oils, whilst any failure of the 50 year old feeder cables could lead to an immediate abandonment. Nonetheless the training of trolleybus drivers ceased, indeed by final abandonment there was only one trolleybus driver left who was unable to also drive motorbuses, and it became increasingly frequent for a driver to be at the steering wheel of both a trolleybus and a motorbus in a single shift. Dewirements became more frequent as drivers handled trolleybuses as if they were motorbuses, particularly in the case of a temporary substitution of a defective trolleybus by a motorbus and then a reinstatement all in one duty.

The Transport Committee accepted his recommendations and resolved that the matter be deferred until the loan charges outstanding on the trolleybuses had been repaid. Although he had never previously visited the Commercial Motor Show, Mr Powell sought authority to visit the 24 September – 2 October 1954 event particularly in view of the age of the motorbus fleet. He referred to recent developments such as the withdrawal of Bristol from the open market, the choice of all-metal or composite bodies and seating capacities.

The Federation of Municipal Passenger Transport Employers briefed its members about the serious shortage of platform staff throughout the industry (some 10,000 staff had resigned in 1953) which they attributed to unattractive working hours and pay. Pontypridd lost six members of the traffic staff in September 1954 alone whilst one year later there were 20 conductresses on the staff. The Federation posed the general question: where is the money going to come from to make employment more attractive? Accounts for the first half year of 1954 showed a sharp fall in receipts and a rise in expenditure, although the trolleybuses had made a net profit of £3,026 and motorbuses a

**1938 Red & White Albion Valkyrie SpPW141 (CAX378) with Duple B37C body, fleet number S1938, heads for the centre of Pontypridd as Karrier W 9 with Park Royal body climbs up over Victoria Bridge heading towards Cilfynydd hotly pursued by a Morris Commercial van. Coed-y-Lan Secondary Modern School can be seen in the background. (Dave Hall collection [Photographer C. Carter])**

loss of £4,518. There was a noticeable reduction in revenue in August 1954, totalling £1,465 of which £269 was suffered on the trolleybus route. All South Wales operators suffered similar reductions (up to 10%) which Mr Powell put down to the increased use of private cars, television, etc.

Effective from Sunday 28 November 1954 the NJIC granted wage increases of 8s per week to drivers and conductors with somewhat lower increases to maintenance workers. The figure was admittedly less than requested, but combined with payment at time-and-a-quarter after 1 pm Saturday, a higher night work allowance, and similar increases to craftsmen, the cost to the undertaking rose by an additional £7,700 pa. The increases of December 1953 and March 1954 had increased the wages bill by £4,000 and this was expected to lead to a deficit of £10,000. Mr Powell proposed new fares to increase revenues by £15,000 pa:

| 0.5 mile | 1½d |
|----------|-----|
| 0.9 mile | 2d |
| 1-3 miles | 2.2d per mile |
| 3-5 miles | 2d per mile |
| 5-7.5 miles | 1.9d per mile |

These proposals were approved by the Transport Committee on 11 January 1955, the application for increased fares was granted on 28 February 1955 and they were brought into operation on 20 March 1955. This was the first application made under the Transport Charges, etc. (Miscellaneous Provisions) Act 1954 which gave the Licensing Authority power of approval for both motorbus and trolley vehicle fares, without the necessity of a separate application to the MoT under the Local Acts. The result was a greatly expedited procedure which previously had often taken two months. Encouragingly traffic receipts for April 1955 showed an increase of £837 over April 1954 (£214 attributable to trolleybuses) compared with the £1,000 falls that had characterised the reports in the preceding financial year.

About 9.30pm on Thursday 10 February 1955 the Traffic Superintendent, out of uniform, boarded a trolleybus in Mill Street and went upstairs whilst the conductor was in the lower saloon collecting fares. Although there were four persons on the top deck until the time that the trolleybus reached Quarry

Siding, the conductor did not come upstairs to collect fares. As the trolleybus pulled into Quarry Siding stop, one of the four passengers upstairs, went downstairs to alight. The Traffic Superintendent followed him to the top of the stairs and looking down he saw the conductor smoking on the platform. The youth tendered his fare but received no ticket. The conductor was interviewed by the Traffic Superintendent and subsequently dismissed by the Transport Manager.

In May 1955 it was decided to place passenger waiting shelters outside the GPO at Station Square, 'New Inn Hotel', at the bottom of Richards Street, and near the Workmen's Hall, Cilfynydd, and at Treforest trolleybus terminus. There were already shelters along the trolleybus route at Cilfynydd Terminus, Quarry Siding (inward), Norton Bridge (inward) and Taff House, Treforest (inward).

At the beginning of June 1955 Mr Powell reminded the Transport Committee that in April 1954 they had decided to postpone any decision on the future of the trolleybuses until their loan charges had been repaid. As these charges would virtually disappear after the next financial year, he suggested that they should now decide its policy on this matter.

Although other trolleybus operators retained Karrier Ws with utility bodies in service for almost ten more years, e.g. Derby and South Shields, Mr Powell placed great store on the fact that they were now 9-10 years old and retained their original bodies. If trolleybuses were to be kept their bodywork required a thorough reconstruction or replacement, and their chassis and electrical equipment also needed a full overhaul at an estimated cost of £2,000 per vehicle. There were severe delays in the delivery of new vehicles, whether motorbus or trolleybus, in some cases between 12-24 months. He also drew attention to the state of the 50 year old underground traction feeder cables, the replacement of which would be very costly.

There are indications that by now motorbuses were operating at times on the trolleybus route; this seems to have been due to the trolleybuses being out of service due to a lack of trolley wheel collectors. Pontypridd was the last UK trolleybus operator to employ trolley wheels rather than skids with carbon inserts, presumably to avoid expense when the long-term aim was abandonment. Although a number of British tramway operators were still using trolley wheel collectors at this time,

The Omnibus Society toured the trolleybus system on Karrier W 11. The enthusiasts and their vehicle are seen at Glyntaff Depot prior to departure. Close observation of the hanger in the depot area exit wiring behind No. 11 reveals a rather primitive junction frog leading from the reverser in the entrance to the open-fronted trolleybus depot and the siding beyond. The chimney of the refuse destructor can be seen in the background. A stone placed under the offside front wheel serves as a chock! (Roy Marshall)

delivery of the wheels was reported as unreliable and protracted whilst there had been several price increases despite a fall in quality.

In March 1955 offers were received for new vehicles, the best being from Guy Motors at £2,113 each for double-deck chassis. There were already 16 Guy motorbuses in the fleet and these had performed well whilst there would be advantages in operating vehicles of one make. Mr Powell had been impressed with the Charles Roe bodies exhibited at the Commercial Motor Show and Roe had submitted the lowest tender. During 1956 three 17-year old double-deck motorbuses would need replacement whilst, should the trolleybus route close, further motorbuses would be needed. On weekdays the normal trolleybus run-out was six, with a fleet of eight vehicles; however, on Sundays there were sufficient motorbuses to cover the Cilfynydd – Treforest service. Accordingly on 7 July 1955 he recommended that provisional orders be placed for six double-deck Guy Arab motorbuses (the three motorbus replacements plus three for trolleybus replacement) with Charles Roe bodies for delivery in late 1956, to be followed by three more for trolleybus replacement in early 1957.

In July 1955 the SWALEB informed the Department that there were faults on No. 1 and 2 traction cables and that repair would require excavation work outside their ordinary maintenance contract. Mr Powell feared that the repairs might prove expensive, but without them the supply could fail and the service be interrupted with consequential loss of revenue. He was told to discuss the matter with SWALEB and report to the Transport Committee.

The relationship with SWALEB remained strained. From July 1955 SWALEB increased their charges for the use of their vehicles; the Council responded that in this case they would increase their hire charge to the Board for use of the UDC's tower wagon for trolleybus overhead maintenance. On 10 August 1955 SWALEB informed Mr Powell that they would cease to use the Gas Yard Substation for electricity supply purposes at the end of that month, upon the completion of their changeover from DC to AC. This substation of course remained indispensible for the trolleybuses as it was here that the AC was converted to DC traction current, and the Transport

Department's switchgear and circuit breakers were housed. SWALEB stated that keeping the substation operational and manned would cost about £40 per week. Mr Powell responded that the Council was entitled to a continuation of the supply it had always received, and it was for the Board to maintain it and to operate the equipment associated with the supply. He added that the Council was considering whether to continue trolleybus operation or not and that this would have an influence on whether SWALEB could continue to use the Transport Department's supporting poles. Under these circumstances it was felt that there should be no change to the charging system until the UDC had made a decision on the future of the trolleybuses, and this was promised by early October 1955.

No doubt this provoked a letter dated 6 October 1955 from SWALEB in respect of the Depot power supply. "As you know the present method of charging is not in compliance with the Board's Standard Tariffs, and it is our duty to apply the standard tariff as soon as possible. The maximum demand recorded is over 50kW; therefore, the Commercial Maximum Demand Tariff "B" automatically applies." SWALEB gave notice to terminate the then basis of charging on 31 December 1955 and to introduce Tariff "B" from that date.

It was decided to erect further passenger waiting shelters along the trolleybus route at the bottom of Richard Street, Cilfynydd (inwards); Workmen's Hall, Cilfynydd (inwards) and Baptist Chapel (inwards).

The undertaking was now 50 years old and a Jubilee Exhibition was staged in the YMCA. Mr Powell was quoted as saying "possibly the Transport Department has seen more "downs" than "ups" but one can[not] [sic] gainsay the fact that it has made valuable a contribution to the health, happiness and prosperity of the town". Prompted by the visit of some of their members to the Exhibition, the Omnibus Society visited Pontypridd on Sunday 17 June 1956. They were offered tea and light refreshments in the transport canteen.

In September 1955 the General Manager of Walsall Corporation Transport, Mr R. Edgley Cox, sought his Transport Committee's approval to inspect utility style trolley vehicles which were likely to be available for sale in Pontypridd and Wolverhampton as potential replacements for older vehicles.

Another view of the only known enthusiast's tour of the small Pontypridd system. Karrier W 11 is seen at Cilfynydd Common terminus on Sunday 17 June 1956. (Roy Marshall)

The trolley booms of the weary-looking service vehicle, No. 8, have been lowered to enable the Omnibus Society tour vehicle to pass at Cilfynydd turning circle. (Roy Marshall)

Heading south towards Pontypridd town centre, Roe-bodied Karrier W No. 14 is seen in Cilfynydd Road with Burton's feeder two traction poles to the rear. The Glamorgan canal is on the left running parallel with the road: today this is the A470 trunk road. In the distance are the spoil tips of the Albion colliery. It is this photograph, published in the 1968 Ian Allan book *Trolleybus Trails* by J. Joyce, that sparked the author's interest to find out more about the diminutive Pontypridd trolleybus system. (Colin W. Routh)

He added that these were of the wartime utility type. Following the inspection of two vehicles in Pontypridd, presumed to be 14 and 15, as they had Roe bodies almost identical to Walsall's own 330-3 but which he recorded as 1947 Sunbeams, he informed his Committee in October 1955 that they were in good condition but that he had learned that South Shields were also interested in purchasing them. He suggested that he and the Chairman negotiate with Pontypridd and South Shields and that the Committee give them authority to bid up to £550 for the pair. The Wolverhampton vehicles were discounted as being only suitable for spares. The Walsall records show that Pontypridd declined an offer of £300 each for the two Karriers; however, it was felt that an immediate offer of £500 for the two vehicles with an option to purchase the remaining six trolleybuses at £350 each upon the abandonment of the system, indicated as about 12 months hence, would be accepted.

On 8 November 1955 the Pontypridd Transport Committee considered the report of their Subcommittee into the effects of any future Council decision to cease operating trolleybuses and replace them with motorbuses. The Committee resolved that:

a. The offer of the Walsall Corporation for two trolley-buses (14 and 15) for the total sum of £1,000 be accepted;
b. Application be made for loan sanction in the sum of £56,500 for the purchase of nine new double-deck motorbuses and three new single-deck motorbuses
c. The Transport Manager endeavour to arrange for the abandonment of trolley vehicle operations to take effect by 31 October 1956;

d. Consequent upon b) and c) being achieved the follow-ing decisions be implemented, viz:
i) The Transport Manager inform SWALEB that the Council propose to discontinue using electric trolley-buses during the last quarter of 1956, and before arranging for the disposal of the traction poles and overhead equipment to request their observations thereon:
ii) The Surveyor, Treasurer and Transport Manager report jointly on the use of the trolleybus traction poles following abandonment.
iii) Walsall Corporation be given a first option to buy the remaining six trolleybuses at £350 each in November 1956.

Following withdrawal from service in December 1955, Karriers 14 and 15 were towed to Walsall, it is understood by the Sunbeam Trolleybus Company, by the end of the month. Following the fitting of upholstered seats to replace the wooden slatted seats with which they were still equipped, and repainting in Walsall's livery, the vehicles entered service in the Midlands town on 1 April and 27 March 1956 respectively, numbered 301 and 302. In Pontypridd, two Guy Arab IV double-deck motorbuses (69, 70) ordered a year earlier to replace two pre-war motorbuses, entered service on 1 January 1956 and provided partial trolleybus replacement.

On 9 December 1955 Mr Powell proposed increased fares based on a mileage system to meet increased labour costs; however, as this would be the second increase within 9 months he was unable to make any reliable estimates as to the effect

**Karrier W / Park Royal UH30/26R 13 crosses Victoria Bridge over the River Taff heading towards Treforest. (John Meredith)**

Treforest
| | | | | | | | |
|---|---|---|---|---|---|---|---|
| 2d | Taff House (0.4 miles) | | | | | | |
| 2d | 2d | Archway (+0.2 miles) | | | | | |
| 3d | 2½d | 2d | Station Square (+0.6 miles) | | | | |
| 5d (9d return) | 3d | 3d | 2d | Old Bridge (+0.4 miles) | | | |
| 6d (10d) | 5d (9d) | 4d (7d) | 2½d | 2d | Baptist Chapel (+0.4 miles) | | |
| 7d (1s) | 6d (10d) | 6d (10d) | 4d (7d) | 3d | 2d | Norton Bridge (+0.6 miles) | |
| 8d (1s 2d) | 8d (1s 2d) | 7d (1s) | 6d (10d) | 6d (10d) | 4d (7d) | 2½ d | Cilfynydd (+0.9 miles) |

**Special fare**

Bonvilston Road – Quarry Siding 2½d
Quarry Siding – Station Square 9d return
Quarry Siding – Cilfynydd terminus – 2d (0.5 miles)
Treforest Terminus – Fountain 8d return

**Four Journey tickets:**   1s 4d
Allows two return journeys per day e.g. to go home for lunch.

**Weekly tickets (one return journey per day)**

| **Single Fare** | **Weekly ticket** |
|---|---|
| 6d | 4s |
| 7d | 4s 8d |
| 8d | 5s 4d |

Weekly Tickets to be issued on Monday and Tuesdays only.
Available for one return journey daily Mondays – Saturdays inclusive. Not available on Sundays.

**Transfer weeklies**

| | |
|---|---|
| Bonvilston Road – Great Western colliery | 4s |
| Treforest Terminus – Great Western colliery | 4s 8d |
| Cilfynydd – Great Western colliery | 6s |
| Treforest terminus – Trehafod | 5s 4d |
| Cilfynydd Terminus – Trehafod | 6s 6d |
| Treforest Terminus – Coedcae colliery | 6s |
| Bonvilston Road – Coedcae colliery | 5s 4d |
| Cilfynydd Terminus – Coedcae colliery | 7s 9d |
| Sycamore St., Rhydyfelin – Cilfynydd (via town centre) | 6s 6d |
| Dynea, Rhydyfelin – Cilfynydd (via town centre) | 7s 9d |

Having backed into John Place beneath the Treforest reverser, the driver of Karrier W 8 turns to talk with his conductor in the lower-saloon nearside seat, before pulling forward to the boarding point in John Street (29 May 1956). (Roy Marshall)

this would have on revenue. The aim was to increase revenue by £8,000 – £9,000 as the two recent wage awards would cost £6,000 pa for drivers, conductors, semi and unskilled maintenance workers. There were outstanding applications for craftsmen and clerical staff likely to cost another £2,000. The Transport Committee approved the new fares, which required modifications to the Ultimate ticket machines, on 13 December 1955 and they were introduced on 4 March 1956.

## CILFYNYDD-TREFOREST TROLLEYBUS ROUTE:
## USE OF MOTORBUSES 1 APRIL 1955 - 31 MARCH 1956

| Month/ | Trolleybuses | | | | Motorbus |
|---|---|---|---|---|---|
| year | Hours in service | Miles run | Electric units | Cost | Mileage run |
| 04.55 | 2,719 | 21,758 | 43,490 | £215 | 1,861 |
| 05.55 | 2,791 | 22,329 | 42,490 | £211 | 1,339 |
| 06.55 | 2,733 | 21,855 | 45,770 | £223 | 1,656 |
| 07.55 | 2,746 | 21,794 | 40,110 | £216 | 1,993 |
| 08.55 | 2,808 | 22,463 | 42,280 | £225 | 1,716 |
| 09.55 | 2,722 | 21,779 | 43,400 | £229 | 1,853 |
| 10.55 | 2,682 | 21,456 | 40,540 | £218 | 2,426 |
| 11.55 | 2,635 | 21,083 | 45,480 | £242 | 1,595 |
| 12.55 | 2,652 | 21,216 | 43,380 | £230 | 2,914 |
| 01.56 | 1,881 | 15,049 | 35,230 | £198 | 8,606 |
| 02.56 | 1,631 | 13,048 | 25,620 | £159 | 9,625 |
| 03.56 | 2,477 | 19,814 | 39,060 | £213 | 4,724 |

Average consumption 1.997 units per mile
01-03.56 ETU Overtime Ban

At the beginning of 1956 the MoT enquired if the trolleybus speed limits and compulsory stopping places laid down in the Byelaws and their Regulations some years ago remained appropriate. The MoT was notified of the impending abandonment of trolleybus operation and that it would now be inappropriate to consider any changes.

An overtime ban in support of a wage claim in the electricity supply industry started on 21 January 1956, and effectively meant that the SWALEB linesmen who maintained the trolleybus overhead equipment withdrew their emergency coverage outside normal working hours. Trolleybus operation was limited to between approximately 7.30am and 4.30pm Monday – Friday to avoid any risk of a breakdown or emergency, e.g. a broken trolley wire falling live without tripping the substation circuit breaker, requiring the immediate assistance of linesmen. Motorbuses were used on trolleybus schedules. The exact date of the end of the overtime ban and a return to normal trolleybus operations has not been found, however, mileage returns suggest that this must have been in late February or early March 1956.

Mr Powell took this opportunity to reiterate his objections to a maximum demand tariff and asked SWALEB for an adjustment of the kW maximum demand charge. The undertaking was paying for the units of electricity actually used and the annual maximum demand tariff. The SWALEB system meant that the maximum demand tariff continued to be paid although some 3,000 trolleybus miles per week now had to be operated by motorbus, costing an additional £50-£60. SWALEB was inflexible and stated that the Department had benefited from an advantageous average price of 1.28d per unit during the last 3 months of 1955 and 1.35d thereafter, but did not address the fact that the undertaking now had to take its entire load off during the afternoon peak period.

As no local solution was forthcoming, on 13 March 1956 the Clerk was instructed to write to the SWALEB Chairman seeking a reduction in maximum demand charge for traction power during the period of the overtime ban to offset the additional costs of operating diesel buses.

SWALEB gave 3 months' notice in respect of the charges for supplying traction power at Gas Yard on 1 May 1956. "As from the date of the termination of this Notice we would normally require you to take supplies under our published tariffs which do not include "off peak" charges. As your present charges incorporate an Off Peak feature we are prepared to discuss with you the possibility of continuing to include a provision of this kind in the revised charges which will apply after 1 August 1956. Since we understand that you are likely to discontinue the use of trolleybuses later this year we think that any arrangement of this kind which we can agree upon could remain of an informal character and one of our representatives will be happy to call upon your Transport Manager to discuss the matter upon hearing from him".

The letter did not indicate what the proposed charges were likely to be but it was felt that there seemed to be a possibility of continuing to benefit from the prevailing negotiated "off peak" demand charge, under which the undertaking paid £1 16s 8d per kWh for "off peak" supplies instead of the standard rate of £5 10s per kWh. In his response Mr Powell suggested that the annual figure paid by SWALEB for use of the UDC's traction poles (£230 since 1 October 1953) should be increased to £275 pa

retrospective to the date of SWALEB's last increase, namely January 1956. He went on to ask how many traction poles would be needed by the Board in the event of trolleybus abandonment.

The SWALEB proposals of 9 May 1956 were:

| Component charge | Present | Proposed |
|---|---|---|
| Max. demand rate | £5 10s p/kWH on-peak £1 16s 8d p/kWH off-peak | £7 p/kWH on-peak £2 6s 8d off-peak |
| Unit charge | 0.66d per unit | Taper scale from 0.86d to 0.76d |
| Fuel clause | 0.0008d p/unit for each 1d rise or fall in coal from £1 18s per ton | 0.0007d p/unit for each 1d £3 per ton. |

SWALEB agreed to continue to informally use an off-peak maximum demand charge although not a feature of their future standard tariffs. Whilst regretting the necessity to replace trolleybuses with diesel buses during the ETU overtime embargo, SWALEB stated that they did not feel in any way responsible for the additional costs incurred.

As a result it was estimated that trolleybus power charges would increase by about £200 for the maximum demand charges and £300 on unit charges. The maximum demand could be based on a month (14s per kW) rather than a year, something Mr Powell felt important as trolleybuses might not operate for the entire 12 months (the newspapers quoted him as anticipating abandonment in October or November 1956), although he considered that a figure of 11s 8d to 12s would be fairer. In the

No. 8 waits immediately in front of the pedestrian crossing at 'The Greyhound Inn' on The Tumble, Station Square. (John Carter [Photographer C. Carter])

1946 Karrier W 9 with Park Royal body pulls away from 'The Greyhound Inn' stop on The Tumble, Station Square. No. 9 was sold to South Shields Corporation Transport for further service in April 1957. Note the colourful advertisement for Corona "fizzy" drinks produced by Thomas & Evans of Porth. (John Carter [Photographer C. Carter])

Seen in High Street on its way towards Cilfynydd, Karrier W 14 with Roe body overtakes a British Railways Scammell Mechanical Horse delivering parcels to Montague Burton the tailors. A Western Welsh AEC Regent with Brush body can be seen in the background, whilst a Pontypridd UDC Bristol B with Eastward & Kenning single-deck body turns into Mill Street. (John Carter [Photographer C. Carter])

**Karrier W/Weymann no. 11 is seen in The Tumble outside the 'Greyhound Inn'. (John Carter [Photographer C. Carter])**

light of all this he suggested on 7 June 1956 that the Transport Committee accept the new tariff from 1 August 1956, but change over to a monthly maximum demand, pleading that in view of the special circumstances leading to the trolleybus abandonment some reduction of this monthly rate should be made. This approach was authorised on 12 June 1956.

Provisional MoT consent for loan sanction to purchase trolleybus replacement motorbuses was received in June 1956; however, to keep loan charges as low as possible he suggested that the provisional order placed in July 1955 for six double-deckers and three single-deckers for delivery in late 1956, and 3 double-deckers for 1957, should be converted to firm orders for four double-deckers and three single-deckers for delivery in 1956 with the remainder still as provisional for 1957. Despite having placed this provisional order a year previously, Guy Motors advised that the chassis would only be completed in December 1956 – January 1957 with the bodies some 8 weeks later. By negotiation with the manufacturers, it proved possible to bring forward delivery of the 4 Guy Arab IV double-deckers to mid-November 1956.

The remaining trolleybuses were now in dire need of an overhaul, and in order to keep them running until the replacement motorbuses had been delivered it proved necessary to reduce their use as much as possible. This practice started on 1 August 1956 coinciding with the change to maximum demand traction power charging. It was warned that in the case of a breakdown, e.g. feeder failure, the Department would have to improvise as best they could.

Walsall Corporation was offered another two trolleybuses at the option price but as work on their housing development (for which extra vehicles were needed) had been held up they declined. Whilst at the MPTA Conference held at Southport in September 1956 the Chairman of the Transport Committee and Mr Powell spoke with R. Edgley Cox, the Walsall Manager, who

had promoted a policy of trolleybus extension after his appointment there on 1 June 1952. He could only confirm that they would not take up the option to buy more trolleybuses. Mr Powell was instructed to invite offers for the remaining trolleybuses in the technical press, such offers to be compared with tenders already received based on scrap and component value prices.

In the middle of Pontypridd trolleybuses' death throes, in July 1956 the Egyptian Government nationalised the Suez Canal, prompting Anglo-French military intervention as the Canal Company's concession did not expire until 1968. The resulting oil supply difficulties and fuel rationing led the Transport Committee to question the practicalities of continuing trolleybus operation. It was felt that the six remaining vehicles all needed a thorough reconstruction at a cost of £8,000 – £10,000, assuming sanction could be obtained. It was unclear how operations could continue whilst the trolleybuses were out of service for reconstruction. The 50 year old tramway feeder cables were still in use. There might not be a fault for many months but if a fault was to develop, its discovery and repair could cost several hundred pounds. They needed replacement, at an estimated cost of £6,000 per mile or £20,000 for the entire route (November 1955 figures), whilst the delivery time for new cables was 3-6 months. SWALEB retained attendants at Gas Yard Substation solely for the traction supply, and this would be reflected in the traction current tariff if trolleybus operation was to continue indefinitely. Last but not least, the undertaking had already committed itself financially to replacement motorbuses.

There was an Industrial Tribunal Award to drivers, conductors, and maintenance workers of 5s per week effective from 1 November 1956, and estimated to cost the Department an additional £3,000 pa, with a craftsmen's application still outstanding. This combined with impending diesel fuel rationing

The new kerb layout at Cilfynydd with the southbound overhead line above the pavement. (Peter Smith collection [PUDCTD])

led Mr Powell on 4 December 1956 to suggest cutting services by some 2,000 miles per week and again increasing fares on the following basis:

| | |
|---|---|
| 0.6 miles | 2d single |
| 0.7 – 0.9 miles | 3d single |
| 1-3.5 miles | 2.7d per mile |
| 3.6-5 miles | 2.4d per mile |

Return fares were available for single fares from 4d plus 66.66%. The Transport Committee approved both the service reductions and fare increase.

Mr Powell added that, perversely, it was impossible to make further economies whilst the trolleybuses were still operating, adding that the vehicles were in a poor state and that remedial work would be essential if trolleybus operations continued for any length of time. As they were not dependent on imported fuel, the undertaking was operating as much trolleybus mileage

The undertaking sent out a professional photographer on the final day of trolleybus operation, 31 January 1957, to record the passing of an era for posterity. The General Manager, John Powell, features in most of the shots. Here Karrier W 12 descends Fothergill Street past the 'Crown Hotel'. John Powell in raincoat and trilby hat stands on the left pointing towards the trolleybus. (PUDCTD)

Karrier W 9 passes the 'Crown Hotel' in Fothergill Street on 31 January 1957, the final day of trolleybus operation in Pontypridd. The gentleman with the battered hat, raincoat and rounded shoulders standing behind the traction pole on the right (beneath the "J" of R. J. Bown) is John Powell, the General Manager. The Traffic Superintendent, George Ludlow stands in uniform just behind the trolleybus. (PUDCTD)

Karrier W 8 in latter-day (post-June 1956) dark blue livery with aluminium painted roof descends Taff Street on 31 January 1957, the final day of trolleybus operation in Pontypridd. John Powell can again be seen on the corner of Market Street beneath the Ely sign attached to the 'New Inn'. The Traffic Superintendent, Herbert Ludlow, in uniform, steps out into the road. (PUDCTD)

as possible, and the trades union had been most accommodating in respect of drivers changing vehicle types in their duties, as trolleybus driver training had ceased. A supplementary fuel ration had already been requested should the trolleybus power supply fail. He recommended replacing the 7½-8-minute Monday-Friday frequency with a 10-minute one and the 6-minute frequency on Saturdays with an 8-minute frequency.

On 11 December 1956 Mr Powell reported on the difficulties in indefinitely extending trolleybus operation considering also the economics of the current fuel crisis. It was resolved to implement the Council's policy of replacing trolleybuses with diesel buses and to submit to the Traffic Commissioners applications for Road Service Licences for a Cilfynydd – Rhydyfelin motorbus service and to cover the portion of trolleybus route from Taff House to John Street, Treforest, with a Treforest – Craig-yr-Hesg service. Once the highest tender for the purchase of the remaining trolleybuses was known the Transport Manager was authorised to negotiate their sale, together with the remaining spares, in a manner that would give the Council the longest possible use of the trolley vehicles.

By the New Year two offers had been received for the remaining six Karrier Ws. South Shields Corporation offered £2,100 made up of £400 each for the four remaining vehicles with BTH electrical equipment (8, 9, 12, 13) and £250 for the two with EE equipment (10-11), and a negotiated price for the remaining spares. Doncaster Corporation offered £225 each for either two or four vehicles on slave tyres. South Shields subsequently agreed to take just the BTH-equipped trolleybuses and allow Pontypridd to retain them until the replacement motorbuses were in stock. The other two went to Doncaster, resulting in a total of £2,110 for the six plus £1,000 for the two sold to Walsall in 1955. The Department was very satisfied with the figures achieved. The Traffic

Commissioner was asked for additional fuel to permit trolleybus abandonment sometime in February 1957. The four new Guy Arab IV 6LW double-deckers with 55 seat Roe bodies costing £4,476 1s 6d in total each, fleet numbers 71-74 (UTX492-495) were delivered during January 1957 and entered service on 1 February 1957.

In view of the fuel rationing, trolleybus operations continued through January 1957 on a day-to-day basis, but a new difficulty arose with road works between Cilfynydd terminus and the Police Station. The widened footpath meant that the overhead wiring was above the new pavement, leading to safety concerns, whilst the narrowed carriageway meant that the lateral distance from the trolley base to the conductor wires was too great for satisfactory trolleybus operation. There were a number of dewirements and it proved impossible to swing out towards the crown of the road to overtake parked vehicles.

On Thursday 24 January 1957 the Surveyors Department advised that they were waiting to plant new street lighting columns at the new kerb line which would effectively prevent the passage of trolley booms. This would require slewing the running wires to a new position above the roadway on this section of the route, and, sooner or later, at Norton Bridge where road works were planned. To avoid such an expense at this late stage in the trolleybus system's life, a successful approach was made to the Traffic Commissioners for additional fuel supplies and in consultation with the Chairman of the Transport Committee it was decided to cease trolleybus operations on Thursday 31 January 1957 thereby avoiding any maximum demand charge complications.

No prior announcement of the abandonment was made to avoid any risk of souvenir hunters or vandals damaging the vehicles that had already been sold for service elsewhere. The only special activity on 31 January 1957 was an excursion by Mr

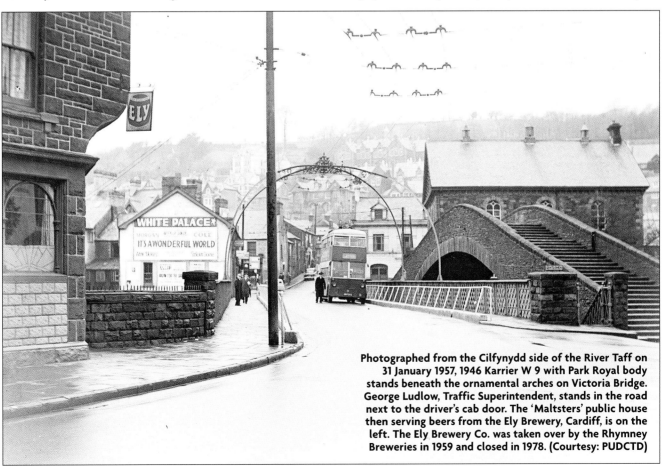

Photographed from the Cilfynydd side of the River Taff on 31 January 1957, 1946 Karrier W 9 with Park Royal body stands beneath the ornamental arches on Victoria Bridge. George Ludlow, Traffic Superintendent, stands in the road next to the driver's cab door. The 'Maltsters' public house then serving beers from the Ely Brewery, Cardiff, is on the left. The Ely Brewery Co. was taken over by the Rhymney Breweries in 1959 and closed in 1978. (Courtesy: PUDCTD)

Powell and an assistant to photograph the trolleybuses in service at various points on the route, often with a Departmental official visible in the same picture. As far as can be established, the trolleybuses ran the normal timetabled service until the end of the operating day. There is no record of which vehicle operated the final journey before returning to Glyntaff Depot although photographic evidence shows that at least nos. 8, 9 and 12 were in use on the final day. It is possible that 10 and 11 were taken out of service prematurely to enable an early departure to Doncaster (11 is known to have been operating on 9 January 1957).

In its Saturday 2 February 1957 the *Pontypridd Observer* reported:

### END OF THE ELECTRIC TROLLEY ERA

*How many people who rode on a Pontypridd trolley bus on Thursday realised they were doing so for the last time? Unless, of course, at some future date they pay a visit to Doncaster, South Shields or Walsall, where the displaced vehicles will be given a new lease of life after they have been overhauled and fitted with new bodies.*

*The end of the trolley-bus system in Pontypridd came even more quickly than was anticipated. It is true that the Pontypridd Council had decided upon the principle of withdrawing the trolley-buses, but it was thought that they would continue in operation for some time yet. Instead, it was decided to take the trolley-buses off the street this week, because road alterations and the erection of new street lighting at Cilfynydd made it impossible to run the trolleys without extensive and costly modification to the overhead line equipment at Cilfynydd and Norton Bridge.*

### CERTAINLY NOT!

*Despite information which has appeared in our columns recently explaining why the trolleys have to be replaced by motor buses, particularly at the present time, we ventured to ask the transport manager, Mr John Powell, if it were true he is anti-trolley bus.*

*His reply was: 'Certainly not. In fact, I am a staunch advocate of trolley buses, but they do not get a fair field of operation in Pontypridd. If we had a longer, wider and straighter route, with modern automatic rectifier sub-stations, and the up-to-date skid method of current collection from the overhead line, then trolley bus operation would be an entirely different proposition. As it is Pontypridd transport has to adapt itself to Pontypridd conditions as they exist today'.*

### MEMORIES

*The Treforest to Cilfynydd route, which now goes over to motor bus operation, was first served by electric tramcars. They started on March 6, 1905, and the first day's takings amounted to £42. When the first double-deck tramcars appeared they were nick-named "twicers". Electric trolley buses replaced the tramcars in September 1930. These quickly earned the familiar title "dodgems". Double-deck trolley buses were more extensively operated during the war years when our population temporarily increased as a result of evacuation. When the batch of new trolley vehicles now being replaced was acquired in 1944-45, all the chassis were equipped for double-deck bodies.*

### TWO SERVICES

*It is understood that following application for new licences, the Council proposes to operate a through bus service from Cilfynydd to Rhydyfelin (Dynea) via the town centre, and a separate route from the former Treforest trolley bus terminus to Craig-yr-Hesg, certain buses on which will run through to Ynysybwl.*

*Thus, once again the old order changeth yielding place to new!*

The remaining stores, excluding a second-hand traction motor, were offered at one-third of their list price subject to purchasers taking the lot appertaining to the respective vehicles. This was expected to realise about £120 plus £75 for the motor.

The Transport Department owned some 340 traction poles, however, only 82 were used exclusively for supporting trolleybus overhead equipment. Around half were used by the Transport Department, for street lighting and the Electricity Board or by the Transport Department and for street lighting. As far as the rest were concerned, some were used by the Electricity Board and the Transport Department, others only by the Electricity Board. SWALEB wanted to acquire some 92 poles of which 32 had street lighting fittings on them and on 12 of which Rediffusion Services Ltd. also had attachments.

It was decided that for both financial and safety reasons the trolleybus overhead line equipment should be dismantled and sold as soon as possible.

1  Only poles used exclusively by the Transport Department to be included in the proposed immediate disposal plan
2  Poles which will be used solely by SWALEB were to be sold at £5 per pole
3  Poles used for street lighting and by SWALEB were to be taken over by the Surveyor's Department who would agree a scheme with the Board for their continued use for public electricity supply purposes
4  The poles for immediate disposal (1) were to be marked in consultation with representative of the Surveyor's Department, Electricity Board and Transport Department
5  The Transport Manager was to supply details to the Electricity Board and Surveyor of the conditions governing Rediffusion Services Ltd. attachments
6  Easements arranged by the Transport Department for attachments which would still be required for street lighting purposes were to be taken over by the Surveyor's Department.

The overhead wiring equipment was offered for sale in situ in two lots comprising i) 16-17 miles of copper conductor wire with spans and miscellaneous accessories such as hangers, ears, insulated bolts, section insulators, frogs, street pavement section pillars and side feeds; and ii) the remaining traction poles not required by the Surveyor's Department or SWALEB.

The tender conditions foresaw payment in advance and that the purchaser was to provide all tools, equipment and vehicles for the dismantling, removal and, where necessary, reinstatement. The purchaser's supervisor was to oversee the work to ensure that it was carried out in an efficient and expeditious manner. Work in the main street of the town was to be done at a time to be agreed with the police. Any reinstatement work necessary was to be completed to the satisfaction of the Surveyor or private landowner as the case may be. Where roads had to be opened, the openings were to be watched, fenced and properly lit during hours of darkness. The purchaser was required to comply with all requests of the Police or Highway Authority and take out insurance to ensure that both the purchaser and the UDC were indemnified against all risks and claims that might occur because of the work.

The following specialists were invited to tender: John Cashmore Ltd., Newport; George Cohen & Co. Ltd.; Thomas Ward, Briton Ferry; Irwin & Jones (Cardiff) Ltd.; Metal Trading (Swansea) Ltd.; Messrs Zammit, Llanelly; Thompson & Company (Cardiff) Ltd.; and J.G. Jenkins Ltd., Morriston. Five tenders were received and it was agreed on 9 April 1957 that the highest tender from J & P. Zammit Ltd., Llanelly, in the sum of £3,061 10s be accepted.

There were 23 wall rosettes supporting the overhead wiring for which the Transport Department was paying annual easements. Except for those which would still be needed for street lighting purposes, the property owners were offered the alternative between just cutting the trolleybus equipment free of the rosette or its complete removal together with restoration of the wall to a satisfactory condition.

As much of the valuable traction power feeder cable was laid in bitumen compound it was irrecoverable; however, those portions originally laid or renewed in conduit were worth retrieving. This would prove a challenge as in some places the electricity supply cables lay in the same conduit as the traction cables. Arrangements were made with SWALEB to recover them when they had labour available subject to payment of their costs.

In early March 1957 SWALEB advised that they were not interested in recovering any underground cables, although they might attempt to recover some of their own DC cable, in which case they would handle the Transport Department's cables simultaneously, apportioning the cost.

Commencing on 1 February 1957 the Treforest – Cilfynydd service, operating between the same termini and to the same timetable, was operated entirely by motorbuses. Once new licences had been granted this was replaced by two superimposed services Rhydyfelin – Machine Bridge – Cilfynydd every 10 minutes during the day, and Treforest, John Street – Craig-yr-Hesg (Berw Road) every 15 minutes (10 minutes Wednesdays and Saturdays) with some journeys continuing to Ynysybwl. As a result of trolleybus abandonment the rating assessment of the undertaking and its property was immediately reduced from £2,415 to £1,997 with a further fall to £1,598 from 1 March 1957. On 18 March 1957 the cost of fuel went up by a further 1¼d per gallon increasing the Department's operating costs by £700 pa. The annual report, published in June 1957, showed that in the 1956-57 financial year for the period until 31 January 1957, the trolleybuses had made a profit of £3,414.

The last trolleybus to leave Pontypridd was on Friday 8 March 1957 for South Shields.

Roe-bodied Karrier W 15 is seen resting inside the trolleybus shed at Glyntaff Depot. (Peter Smith collection [photographer's name not recorded])

Heading towards Cilfynydd Karrier W No. 8 overtakes a horse and cart as it makes its way down Taff Street. Next to Hopkin Morgan bakers and confectioners is Leslie Stores which burnt down in about 1950. (D.A. Jones)

Karrer W 13 with Park Royal body, John Place, Treforest terminus. (D.A. Jones)

No. 14 takes on passengers in Taff Street southbound opposite the junction with Mill Street. (D.A. Jones)

On an overcast day Karrier W 15 with Roe body waits for departure time from Cilfynydd Common War Memorial terminus. The Memorial can be seen to the right hand side of number 15. The driver of a British Road Services Bedford pantechnicon sorts his load in the background. (D.A. Jones)

The driver of Karrier W 9 heading towards Treforest makes a clear hand signal as he pulls out in Taff Street at its junction with Gas Lane where the rotary converter substation was situated. Thomas & Evans grocers shop is visible behind the trolleybus. (D.A. Jones)

Karrier W / Weymann 11 stands inside the trolleybus shed at Glyntaff next to the firewall separating trolleybuses from motorbuses. (D.A. Jones)

# TROLLEYBUS FLEET DETAILS

Despite its small size Pontypridd UDC's trolleybus fleet, which never exceeded nine vehicles, was not lacking in interest. John Teasdel, the undertaking's General Manager at the time of the conversion of the tramways to trolleybus operation was convinced that 3-axle single-deck vehicles would be the most suitable and economical for the town's needs. The design and equipment of this initial fleet can be considered as amongst the first genuine trolleybuses rather than trackless trolley vehicles supplied to British operators. Passenger loads at peak times soon proved that double-deck vehicles were indispensable and two interesting bargains in the form of former demonstrators were soon acquired.

The importance of coal mining and steel to the war effort combined with the state of the ageing original fleet made it necessary to hire supplementary vehicles from other operators to cope with the growth in traffic.

Additional trolleybuses were requested as soon as the Ministry of War Transport (MoWT) began to issue permits for the limited number of vehicles to be produced; however, delivery only began a few months before the war in Europe was over. Pontypridd's entire trolleybus fleet was replaced by the end of 1946 with double-deck vehicles ordered during the hostilities. Pontypridd, unlike many other operators, never rebuilt or re-bodied these vehicles. This task was completed by their new owners enabling many ex-Pontypridd UDC trolleybuses to remain in service until the early 1960s.

## 1–7 English Electric SD6WTB

| Fleet No. | Reg. No. | Chassis type | No. | Elec. Eq. | Body | Into service | Withdrawn |
|---|---|---|---|---|---|---|---|
| 1 | TG379 | E. Electric SD6WTB | 127 | E. Electric | E. Electric | 18.09.1930 | 13.10.1946 |
| 2 | TG381 | E. Electric SD6WTB | 128 | E. Electric | E. Electric | 18.09.1930 | 13.10.1946 |
| 3 | TG383 | E. Electric SD6WTB | 129 | E. Electric | E. Electric | 18.09.1930 | 30.04.1947 |
| 4 | TG385 | E. Electric SD6WTB | 130 | E. Electric | E. Electric | 18.09.1930 | 30.04.1947 |
| 5 | TG387 | E. Electric SD6WTB | 131 | E. Electric | E. Electric | 18.09.1930 | 30.04.1947 |
| 6 | TG389 | E. Electric SD6WTB | 132 | E. Electric | E. Electric | 18.09.1930 | 30.04.1947 |
| 7 | TG391 | E. Electric SD6WTB | 133 | E. Electric | E. Electric | 18.09.1930 | 30.04.1947 |

Chassis: Three axle type English Electric SD6WTB manufactured by the English Electric Co. Ltd. at the Dick, Kerr works in Preston, Lancashire.
Motor: English Electric, Type DK 121 (60hp at 500 volts) series wound self-ventilated interpole.
Electrical equipment: English Electric manufactured by English Electric Co. Ltd. at their Phoenix Works, Bradford, Yorkshire.
Foot-operated controller: 5 notches and a weak-field notch.
Dewirement indicator: Neon pilot light.
Brakes: Westinghouse Brake & Saxby Signal Co. Ltd. compressed air, 2-stage rheostatic and hand brakes.
Body: English Electric B32C.
Length: 27ft 6 in. Width: 7ft 6in.

Height: 11ft to top of trolley base.
Wheelbase: 17ft giving a turning circle on either lock of 57ft.
Wheel track: front 6 ft 5¼in., rear 6 ft 5¼in.
Unladen weight: 7 tons 12cwt
Tyres: High pressure pneumatic 36 × 8 on all wheels.

The English Electric Co. Ltd. was formed in 1918, one of its constituent companies being Dick, Kerr which had previously manufactured trolley vehicle electrical equipment under its own name. English Electric continued to manufacture and market this equipment from its inception, many items continuing to be listed as "DK", reflecting the original Dick, Kerr design. Although Dick, Kerr and its related companies had built

English Electric SD6WTB no.7 stands at the Dick, Kerr works in Preston prior to despatch to Pontypridd by rail. The Estler Bros trolley base featuring both trolley poles superimposed on a single pivot is prominent on the roof. Note the destination display "Porth": a terminus that unfortunately never materialised. (David Beilby Collection [Alstom/English Electric Archive])

tramcar bodies since 1898 neither they nor English Electric ventured into the construction of trolley vehicle bodies until 1927 when a complete vehicle, incorporating English Electric electrical equipment and a Leyland chassis, was supplied to Bradford Corporation (that undertaking's 560). In 1929 they began to market complete vehicles. In 1930 English Electric decided to stop supplying complete vehicles and entered into a co-operative agreement with AEC to produce a new range of two-axle (661T, 662T) and three-axle (663T) trolleybuses although English Electric vehicles were built up to 1932. The Pontypridd SD6WTBs were the only English Electric 3-axle single-deck trolley vehicles built for the UK market.

**Chassis:** The rear bogie had a swivelling suspension intended to overcome any tendency to tilting during braking and to prevent torsional stresses in the springs. A double swivelling point is provided for the rear bogie in order to correct any tendency to tilt when braking thereby equalising wheel adhesion, making braking more efficient and relieving the springs of undue stress.

Pressed steel side frames braced with transoms, provided with outrigger brackets for supporting the body.

The steering gear was of the cam-operated type, the cam actuating a hardened pressed steel roller mounted between two ball bearings.

**Electrics:** Single traction motor located under the front saloon. The motor drive was transmitted to the rear axles through a cardan shaft and three differentials, giving a differential drive between the two wheels of each axle and between the two axles themselves.

The traction motor was geared so that a motor speed of 1,760rpm produced a road speed of 20mph (Cardiff gave their top speed as about 18mph).

Pedal operated contactor-type controller, placed by the side of the driver's seat. The master switch was of the drum type, it controlled the operation of the contactors and ensured that they opened and closed in the correct sequence. The contactors were built up of interchangeable parts and with adjustable contact fingers provided with removable tips, rendering maintenance relatively simple. Auxiliary contacts were also fitted, but as the current carried by the contactors was quite small, the arc when breaking the circuit was negligible. A current limit relay regulated the acceleration and protected the motor from overloads. The bank of contactors was mounted in a compact steel case lined with asbestos and fitted with a removable cover, each unit having a blowout device provided with a removable arc chute made out of heat-resisting material.

A battery or batteries provided power for emergency lighting in case the mains voltage was lost, and to operate the driver's horn and windscreen wiper.

The vehicle was equipped with a trailing current collection skate on the offside rear and appropriate changeover (overhead power collection to overhead/tram rail collection) switch which was operated by the reversing handle thus ensuring that the controller was always in the "Off" position when the skate was being placed in a rail.

**Brakes:** Two notch foot-operated pneumatically activated rheostatic brakes, a Westinghouse Brake & Saxby Signal Co. Ltd. air brake working independently on each of the six wheels and a hand brake on the rear bogie wheels.

The foot pedal served two functions. Initial depression of the foot pedal applied the electric rheostatic brake through two brake positions; further depression of the foot pedal whilst retaining rheostatic braking, applied air brakes on all six wheels, the air brake applying different shoes to the rear wheels to those applied by the hand brake. The brake drums were all of 17in. diameter.

The air brake compressor cut in and out at 50lb and 75lb pressure respectively. There were independent brake cylinders for all six wheels with one brake cylinder each side of the chassis forward of the front axle and two brake cylinders fitted to each rear axle.

The handbrake applied the brakes to the four rear wheels and was not equalised, reliance being placed on correct adjustment. The handbrake lever was to the offside of the driver's steering column.

**Bodywork:** Composite seven-bay single-deck construction including a wider central fourth bay and centre entrance and exit built by English Electric Co. Ltd. at Preston.

Brackets or extensions were bolted to the roof rail immediately above the body pillars between bays 1 and 2, bays 2 and 3, bays 3 and 4, and approximately half the way across the centre entrance and exit to support the four transverse girders of the exposed trolley gantry which was not in direct contact with the arched roof. A gutter ran around the base of the roof with drains running down the body pillar between bays 1 and 2, and immediately to the rear of the rearmost side windows, on both sides.

The Estler Bros trolley base was mounted on a gantry with four transverse supports secured to longitudinal rails fixed to the cant rails on each side above bay 3 and supported both trolley poles superimposed on a single pivot. To demonstrate the flexibility of the Estler trolley mountings, at the opening ceremony a vehicle was reversed on a straight portion of the route near the Cilfynydd terminus without removing the trolleys from the wires until the manoeuvre had been completed.

Platform handrails and stanchions were covered with black Doverite.

The rear and side of the body beneath the waistrail was divided horizontally, tramcar style, into waist and concave rocker panels, however, this division was not applied to the cab front. Glass louvres were fitted above the drop light windows in bays 2 and 6 on both sides of the vehicle. The rearmost side windows featured a radiused top corner and abutted wide rear corner pillars. There were two windows at the rear with broadly radiused external top corners surmounted by a destination box. The wide central combined entrance and exit was vestibuled and equipped with a two-leaf folding door at the top of the steps which slid forwards and which when open lay behind the front transverse panel. The rear leaf incorporated a downwards curving handrail.

There were two steps, i.e. three from street level, up to the position of the entrance doors. There were no further steps from the central platform into the front or rear saloon, i.e. a single floor line.

The transverse bulkheads to the front and rear of the entrance and exit area were glazed throughout but not equipped with internal separating doors. The front offside bulkhead glazing separating the rear compartment from the central entrance vestibule could be opened to display official notices, fares, etc.

**The rear passenger compartment, and central entrance and exit of one of the English Electric SD6WTB vehicles prior to delivery. (David Beilby Collection [Alstom/English Electric Archive])**

Four ventilators were mounted on the roof: on the nearside towards the front of bay 3 immediately behind the second support of the trolley gantry and towards the rear of bay 7 at the side of the inspection catwalk, and on the offside towards the front of bay 1 and towards the rear of bay 6 at the side of the inspection catwalk.

The imperceptibly curved front panel of the driver's cab was extremely shallow and did not even extend down to the height of the front axle. The main transverse chassis girders were visible beneath the front panel to the driver's cab.

The front registration number was painted centrally about two-thirds of the way down the front panel beneath the fleet number and English Electric winged symbol. The top half of the offside driver's windscreen opened outwards, with a wiper being affixed to the upper portion of the offside windscreen. There was a front hinged driver's cab door with recessed handle immediately above the front axle on each side, the upper three-quarters of the offside window therein having a vertically divided sliding "signalling" window. Fixed quarter lights preceded the cab door on each side. There were two glazed panels in the bulkhead behind the driver, that on the offside being vertically divided into two sliding panes to facilitate communication between the driver and conductor.

There were two lifeguard rails on each side. The lower rail on both sides extended between the front and second axles as did the upper rail on the offside. On the nearside the upper rail extended between the front axle and the central combined entrance and exit steps. There was no protection beneath the high-mounted, flat front panel to the driver's cab. The front and rear of the front mudguards, and the front and rear of the second and third wheel mudguards extended below the side body panels. Both front axle wheel hubs were equipped with a driver's step ring.

There was a single mudguard above the second and third axles. A mud flap hung between the second and third axle to reduce risk of stones and other street detritus thrown up by the wheels on the second axle damaging the bodywork or causing punctures to the tyres of the third axle.

A bamboo trolley retrieval pole was carried at the side of the roof on the nearside with three supporting hooks above the roof gutter fixed centrally above bays 1, 4 (the centre entrance and exit) and 6. Extended trolley boom retaining hooks with cross-bracing in an "X" form were placed at the end of the roof-mounted inspection catwalk.

**Lighting:** External lighting was two headlights mounted a little more than halfway up on the extreme nearside and offside of the front panel, the base being aligned with the horizontal division of the side panels, beneath the driver's windscreen and at the rear a single red "bulls-eye" light at the top of the primrose-painted rear corner cantrail or vent panel. The headlights were fed from the traction power supply (DC) but the rear lighting was supplied by a 6-volt battery. There was no means of recharging the battery on the vehicle and it was necessary to change the battery every 2–3 days for this purpose.

The rear registration number was painted or transferred centrally towards the base of the rear panel beneath the fleet number. The MoT Inspectors pointed out that the rear registration number had to be illuminated in hours of darkness. The registration details were added to the rear destination blind and henceforth displayed permanently in the illuminated rear destination box.

Internal lighting comprised a single circular globe light in the ceiling towards the front of bay 2 in the front saloon and two larger units towards the rear of bay 5 above the longitudinal seats in the rear saloon. The interior lighting was fed from the traction power supply (DC).

In an emergency, current was supplied to the headlights, rear light, interior lighting, the driver's horn and windscreen wiper from a 6-volt battery.

**Seating:** The front saloon seated 12 on transverse seats with rather square upper corners to the backs abutting on the central gangway and having no top rail, grab handles or stanchions; three passengers were accommodated on a wooden longitudinal seat in the entrance vestibule and the rear compartment provided seats for the remaining 17 passengers along the sides and back.

Horseshoe shaped grabs hung from Doverite covered longitudinal handrails running the length of the ceiling to the left and right of the gangway in the front and rear salons, and on the offside in the central platform area.

*Tramway & Railway World* recorded that 'the seats are upholstered and "provided with easily detachable covers, which are slipped over the normal covers when workmen are carried"'. Early reports referred to special loose upholstery covers to protect the seats when colliery services were being operated.

**Destination equipment:** A destination box capable of displaying a single line of information was mounted centrally in the primrose-painted panelling immediately above the driver's windscreen and at the rear centrally above the rear windows. Early views show that the rear destination box inevitably displayed the warning "six wheel brakes".

**Internal Livery:** The unlined ceiling constructed of tongue and groove planks was painted white. The floor of both compartments and the central entrance vestibule was covered with English oak hardwood slats. Saloon floors brown, platform floor grey.

The vehicles were equipped with Numa air bells. One bell push being mounted above the doorway in the central platform area, and one each in the centre of the ceiling in the front and rear saloons.

Black Doverite covered rods or rails protected the window panes in bays 1–7 both sides but these appear to have been removed at an early date.

**External Livery:** Blue and primrose yellow (see Appendix C).

**Subsequent alterations:** In August 1931 the undertaking met English Electric representatives to work out solutions to complaints and the company's fitters came to Pontypridd.

Pontypridd UDC Transport Department's woodworking shop at Glyntaff. Various body side members can be seen under construction. (Cy Yandell collection)

Some bodies were stayed and strengthened, broken outriggers replaced, springs modified, resistances retapped to improve and smooth starting, new contact tips fitted and "a new type of electric brake fitted". A power brake triangular warning sign lamp which illuminated when the driver applied the brakes was reportedly fitted to at least one vehicle but there is no photographic evidence of this. By October 1931 some 550 man-hours had been worked and the modifications were not completed until February 1932. Despite the manufacturer's efforts, by the late 1930s the undertaking commenced an ongoing programme of body reconstruction and chassis maintenance involved substantial work, the bodies for example being stripped to the ribbing. The drop light windows were replaced by half drop windows and the nearside driver's cab door was removed when the bodies were reconstructed. The contactor equipment was moved at the time from separate boxes into one box on the front bulkhead. At least trolleybus 3 returned to service with its front panel divided vertically down the centre into two panels. The rather square outer corners of the transverse seat backs were cut away to permit easier passage along the central gangway whilst some of the glazing in the transverse bulkheads was removed and the opening pane for official notices repositioned. It is evident that this work was carried out as men and equipment were available.

Dates of reconstruction:

| | |
|---|---|
| 1 | January 1938 – January 1939; December 1944 until sale |
| 2 | Unknown – October 1937 |
| 3 | January 1939 – January 1940 |
| 4 | December 1941 – October 1943 |
| 5 | Unknown – March 1937; December 1941 – April 1944 |
| 6 | December 1943 until sale |
| 7 | December 1936 – unknown |

Radio interference suppression coils were fitted to No. 1 as an experiment and subsequently to all the vehicles.

A small circular driver's rear view mirror was mounted externally two thirds of the way up the offside pillar of the cab.

Headlight dipping arrangements, improved headlight reflectors and 60W lamps were fitted from 1937. Possibly at the same time a small front side light also fed by battery was mounted in the front panel close to the offside headlight.

In December 1936 the Transport Department commenced a programme of body reconstruction and chassis maintenance encompassing the entire single-deck trolleybus fleet and involving substantial work spread out over almost ten years as only one vehicle could be taken out of service at one time. Internal body modifications included replacement of the drop lights with half drop windows, cutting away the rather square outer corners of the transverse seat backs to permit easier passage along the central gangway, removal of some of the glazing in the transverse bulkheads, and the repositioning of the opening pane for official notices. The interior of one of the English Electric SD6WTB vehicles is seen here after reconstruction. (Cy Yandell collection)

As a wartime lighting measure some if not all vehicles appear to have been equipped with hooks mounted centrally at the base of the rear panel for emergency acetylene or oil lamps independent of the power supply.

External advertising began to be displayed on the rear panels beneath the windows from 1940.

**Disposal:** In May 1946 it was decided to dispose of 3 EE WTB trolleybuses and the Bristol E double-decker as 6 Karrier W's were by now in stock with single-deckers 1 and 6 out of service for body reconstruction and major overhaul. It is likely that the vehicles were withdrawn from service progressively as the Karrier W fleet enlarged, it being recorded that by 1 April 1947 all the single-deckers were out of use at the depot.

Last taxation dates at Pontypridd (all for 12 months, by 1946 this was £57 12s pa):

1    31 December 1944 (re-taxed at Cardiff on 31 July 1947).
2    Early January 1946 (re-taxed at Cardiff on 13 August 1947).
3    9 January 1946 (re-taxed at Cardiff on 31 July 1947).
4    10 January 1947 (re-taxed at Cardiff from 1 July 1947).
5    8 January 1946 (re-taxed at Cardiff on 16 May 1947).
6    12 January 1943 (re-taxed at Cardiff on 3 July 1947).
7    9 January 1946 (re-taxed at Cardiff at end July 1947).

Reference to the dates of withdrawal from service in Pontypridd and entry into service in Cardiff indicate that tax refunds must have been received for several individual vehicles, e.g. 4, 5, 7.

Cardiff Corporation Transport's tram to trolleybus conversion scheme had been interrupted by the war and trams had continued to run along Bute Street to Pier Head until the tracks were declared unsafe. On 28 April 1946 motorbuses were substituted between Mill Lane and Pier Head. It had always been the intention to convert this route to trolleybus operation although a low railway bridge, carrying the London mainline and the lines out of Cardiff General Station to Cardiff Queen Street Station, at the north end of Bute Street would require the use of single-deck vehicles. Five three-axle single-deck AEC/East Lancashire trolleybuses had been ordered in 1945 but their delivery seemed unlikely before 1948–9. Cardiff had rejected an allocation of Sunbeam two-axle chassis so the availability of Pontypridd vehicles was timely.

Cardiff expressed an interest in the entire pre-war fleet and the vehicles were inspected by their engineer, Felix Cunuder, at Pontypridd in November 1946. Despite their age and generally poor condition, all seven single-deckers together with a quantity of spares were purchased in April 1947; however, the Bristol E was rejected as too high for service in Cardiff and the Guy BTX60 was considered underpowered and lacked air brakes.

Cardiff 235, formerly Pontypridd UDC 5, is seen turning out of Hayes Bridge Road into Mill Lane over the Glamorganshire Canal in grey wartime livery. Trolleybuses on service 16 terminated in Cardiff city centre by traversing Hayes Bridge Road, Mill Lane and Custom House Quay in an anti-clockwise direction before rejoining Bute Street. Please notice the battery-powered front side light mounted in the front panel between the offside headlight and the English Electric winged symbol. (John Carter [photographer C. Carter])

Cardiff "Doodlebug" 235 (Pontypridd 5) turns over the Glamorganshire Canal. Noteworthy is the renewed use of the rear destination box for its original purpose, the "TROLLEYBUS" warning in the rear offside window and information to passengers about the PAYE system in the nearside windows on each side of the central entrance and exit. (John Carter [photographer C. Carter])

Cardiff 236 having reversed into Bute Crescent, Pier Head. (M.P.M. Nimmo collection [photographer's name not recorded])

The Cardiff Transport Committee Minutes record that they were purchased as follows: numbers 1 and 6, then in the process of a major chassis and body overhaul, £1,000 each, and the remaining five vehicles at £200 each. It was a condition of the sale that Pontypridd would provide any spares available in their stores which might be required for any immediate attention to the five vehicles free of charge. By the beginning of June 1947 five vehicles had left for Cardiff with the remaining two, presumed to be 1 and 6, following by the end of the month.

The vehicles were overhauled in Cardiff and equipped with carbon insert slider trolley heads prior to entering service between April and August 1947. The temporary Bute Street motorbuses were replaced by trolleybuses on 17 August 1947 when the ex-Pontypridd EE WTBs began to run on service

16 Monument (St.Mary Street) – Bute Street – Pier Head, although they did occasionally run as specials on other services. Pontypridd 1 and 6 (Cardiff 231, 236) were finished in Cardiff's crimson lake and cream livery but the rest appeared in wartime grey, giving rise to the nickname of "Grey Ghosts" in addition to "Doodlebugs" (due to their low maximum speed of about 18mph and the similarity of the noise from their traction motors and gearing to that emitted by the pulse jet engine of the German Second World War V-1 flying bomb).

Originally the Cardiff Transport Committee allocated £2,500 for the purchase of the seven vehicles; however, this was subsequently increased to a maximum of £4,000. Total final expenditure for acquiring the vehicles, making them roadworthy and repainting was £4,504 12s 6d, plus a further £22 5s 6d for additional spares. In May 1949 232 (Pontypridd 2) was withdrawn to provide spares for the remaining vehicles. The rest were disposed of to Blair, Manchester in June and September 1950 for breaking up, the final three fetching £10 each.

These were the only second hand trolleybuses in the UK to be used in conjunction with a Pay As You Enter (PAYE) scheme although they did carry a conductor to ensure that the passengers dropped their flat fare into the collecting boxes. They were well suited for the PAYE system as the two collection units could be placed in the centre vestibule serving the front and rear compartments.

Although they lasted only a short time in Cardiff (all were gone by August 1950) they performed a useful task in relieving the post-war vehicle shortage by releasing motorbuses for services on other routes. They were replaced by five new BUT9641T/East Lancashire single-deckers (Cardiff 238–242) that arrived in July-August 1949.

In September 1952, Cardiff disposed of the remaining spare parts, valued at £272 14s 2d, as scrap.

Cardiff 236 (Pontypridd 6) in fleet livery, Glamorgan Canal Bridge terminus St. Mary Street. (M.P.M. Nimmo collection [photographer's name not recorded])

# 8 Guy BTX 60

| Fleet No. | Reg. No. | Chassis type | No. | Elec. Eq. | Body | Into service | Withdrawn |
|-----------|----------|--------------|-----|-----------|------|--------------|-----------|
| 8 | UK8948 | Guy BTX60 | 23447 | Rees Stevens | Guy | 22.01.1931 | 1946 |

Chassis: Three axle type Guy BTX 60 manufactured by Guy Motors Ltd., Fallings Park, Wolverhampton.
Guy drawing CB2347 dated 17 April 1930.
Motor: Front-mounted Rees-Stevens (60hp at 500 volts) compound wound, regenerative, built by Rees Roturbo Co. Ltd., Wednesfield Road, Wolverhampton.
Electrical equipment: Rees-Stevens patent employing controllers built by British Thomson-Houston Co. Ltd., Rugby, Warwickshire.
Dewirement indicator: Assumed to have been equipped with line-lights.
Brakes: Westinghouse pneumatic, Rees-Stevens regenerative, hand and rheostatic brakes.
Body: Guy H31/28R (30/29 according PUDCTD) drawing CB 2256 dated 7 January 1930.
Length: Nottingham records quote 26ft other sources show 25ft 9in. Width: 7ft 6in.
Wheelbase: Nottingham records quote 16ft 7in. other sources show 16ft 4½in. giving a turning circle on either lock of 60 ft.
Unladen weight: 7 tons 16cwt 1 qtr

Guy Motors produced Britain's first three-axle double-deck trolley vehicle, the BTX which was equipped with pneumatic tyres and regenerative braking, in 1926. The BTX60 (the suffixed digits indicating the nominal seating capacity of an appropriate body although other examples had 57 or 58 seats), was completed in January 1930 and demonstrated in Nottingham from June 1930 until at least October 1930. The vehicle was returned to Guy Motors in October or November 1930, being supplied to Pontypridd UDC as a demonstrator in January 1931, prior to which the trolley plank had been strengthened and the paraffin side lamps replaced by battery powered electric side lights. It was on hire to PUDCTD from 21

January 1931 at a rate of 4d per mile running 2,483.3 miles at an average 1.72 units per mile by 28 February 1931. After six weeks use Guy offered to sell the vehicle to the Council for £1,750. However, after negotiations it was bought for £1,700 with a 2-year guarantee, the hire charges being cancelled, in March 1931 and given fleet number 8.

**Chassis:** Based on the low frame Guy BX three-axle motorbus chassis with an offset transmission having the differential and worm cases on the nearside to permit a lower floor to the lower saloon. There was no third differential between the two rear driving axles but, as evidenced by drawings, both axles had differentials with universally-jointed driving shaft. Fully floating axles with a detachable rear bogie having double cantilever springs. Half elliptical front springs. On the front axle the swivel pins were mounted on taper roller bearings and thus easily adjustable for wear. Marles cam and roller steering. Chassis number 23447, weight approx 3 tons 18cwt.

**Electrics:** Guy Motors were granted the exclusive use of the Rees-Stevens patent system of trolley vehicle control by the Rees-Roturbo Manufacturing Co. Ltd. The Rees-Roturbo compound interpole traction motor was rated for 60hp at 500 volts, at 900–2,500rpm with capacity for heavy overload in accordance with British Standard specification No. 173/1928. Magnets of high permeability steel are fitted with laminated steel main poles. Aluminium end covers and ball and roller bearings reduced the weight of the motor to a minimum.

The traction motor was mounted between the chassis frame, over the front axle, in order that the commutator brushes could be inspected without using a pit, resulting in a high front lower saloon floor line which sloped towards the rear of the bus and a high-mounted driver's cab. It also resulted in a particularly long propeller shaft to the leading rear axle.

1930 Guy BTX 60, formerly a demonstrator but from March 1931 No. 8 in the Pontypridd UDC fleet, stands at Glyntaff Depot outside the corrugated iron trolleybus depot. Note separate wiring connections into both the trolleybus depot and the former tramcar shed (behind the photographer). (Peter Smith collection [photographer's name not recorded])

**Rear bogie detail of Guy BTX 60 No. 8. (BTS Library [PUDCTD records])**

The motor shunt circuit was never broken whilst the windings were designed to give a smooth and effective retarding effect when the vehicle was slowing down from high speeds on the level or when going down hills at normal speeds. *Tramway & Railway World* reported in May 1930 that the combination of shunt and series winding with regulating resistance gave an easy start and smooth acceleration.

As the motor field was excited by shunt as well as series windings, the series resistances, operated by way of the contactors by the foot pedal, had a greater effect on the speed control than in earlier vehicles. A resistance was automatically brought into circuit with the shunt winding during regenerative braking to prevent the voltage of the generator rising above line voltage when the vehicle was coasting with the power pedal in the "off" position and with the outside current supply cut off. A further resistance in the lighting circuits prevented the lamps being burned out when regenerative braking took place.

Regenerative braking was advantageous on flat routes at speeds of between 14–25mph. In this system when the vehicle was coasting at more than a certain speed the motor becomes a generator, setting up a counter electromotive force and returning current to the line. Immediately the motor became a generator and returned current to the line, a resistance was brought in with the line circuits to avoid damage to the lighting circuits.

The control gear consisted of a Stevens patent combined drum type controller and shunt regulator mounted on an aluminium case. The controller actuated a standard contactor panel. The power pedal control was mechanically interlocked with the reversing switch: the reversing switch hand lever could not be moved until current was cut off from the motor whilst the power pedal could not be depressed until the reversing switch was in the correct position. Radio interference choke coils were mounted in the master controller case.

**Brakes:** Foot brake applied on front and middle axle. Handbrake worked on rear axle only. Westinghouse Brake and Saxby Signal Co. Ltd. air brakes.

Power pedal to left, brake pedal to right.

No further details have been found.

**Bodywork:** Composite six-bay highbridge double-deck construction, enclosed forwards-ascending half-turn (90°) staircase with conventional semi-vestibuled open platform entrance and exit at the rear, built by Guy Motors, Fallings Park, Wolverhampton.

The domed roof somewhat overhung the front of the upper-saloon which had two windows with radiused outer corners and particularly wide front corner panels. The trolley base and poles were fitted in a conventional manner on a concealed roof-mounted gantry above bay 2. A gutter at the base of the nearside upper-deck panels above the open rear platform led to a drain descending down the rear pillar of bay 6.

The staircase and rear platform were integrated into the bodywork. The main transverse chassis girders were partially visible beneath the front panel to the driver's cab.

Half-drop openers were fitted to the lower saloon side windows in bays 1, 2, 3 and upper-deck bays 2, 4 and 6. Shallow

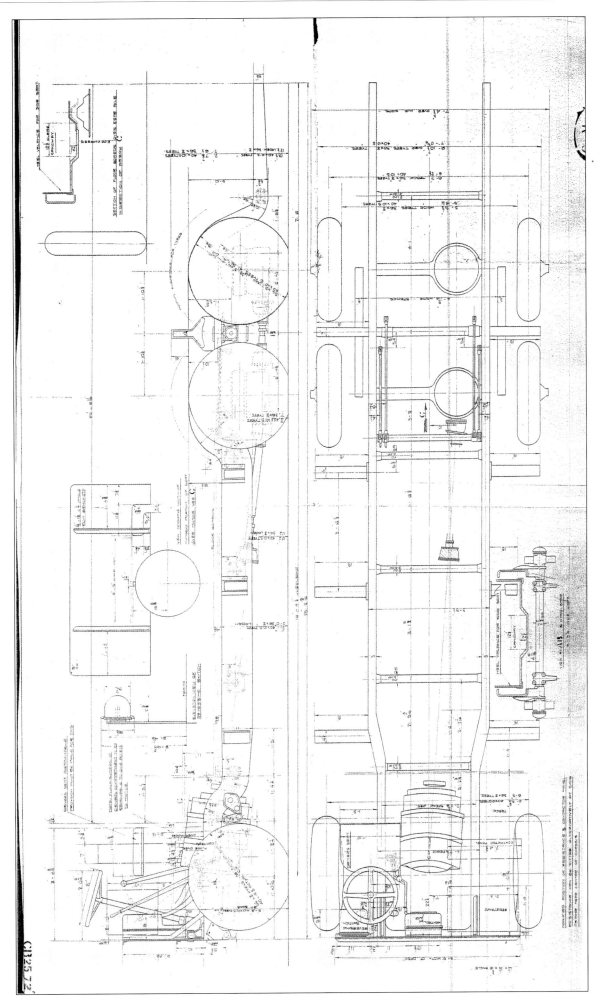

glass louvres were fitted above the opening side windows on both decks. The rearmost side windows to the upper saloon (offside and nearside) and lower-deck offside diffused glass window behind the staircase had large-radius corners to match those at the front and rear of the upper saloon and in the rear platform window. The upright rear elevation incorporated two large windows (the pane on the nearside presumably sliding transversely behind the fixed offside pane) to the upper saloon, which provided access to the trolley gantry and the upper-deck emergency exit, and two matching windows to the lower-deck open rear platform, all with radiused outer corners.

There was a single step from the rear platform into the lower saloon.

The "piano front" of the upper-deck curved forwards above the driver's cab, the vertical front elevation being equipped with a single-line destination box built into the panelling. This also resulted in an overhang above the driver's cab windscreen. The driver's cab, which protruded well forward of the upper-deck, was equipped with shallow opening windscreens on the off and nearside and a front hinged door on the offside. The equally shallow window (about 6in. shorter than the lower saloon side windows) in the offside cab door and its counterpart on the nearside was provided with a sliding "signalling" window. There were fixed quarter lights between the offside cab door and its matching nearside counterpart, and the cab front pillars. A small rectangular driver's rear view mirror was mounted externally half way up the offside front pillar of the cab. There were three glazed panels in the bulkhead behind the driver.

The high-mounted, flat front panel beneath the driver's cab windscreen was upright with rounded edges, its base being almost 1ft above the base of the lower saloon side panels. The front registration number plate was affixed to a protective shield that hung beneath the front panel between the dumb irons, level with the spotlight, and featuring a Guy maker's plate on the nearside, whilst that at the rear was applied with transfers at the top of the offside rear platform window.

The low body panels required solely a single lifeguard rail on each side, extending between the front and second axles. There was a one piece "fairing" over the rear wheels which left the bogie trunnion exposed to view whilst a mud flap hung between the second and third axle. There is no evidence that the vehicle ran in Pontypridd equipped with the chrome-plated hubcap covers with which it was equipped when demonstrated in Nottingham.

**Lighting:** External lighting was two headlights mounted half way up the flat front panel beneath the driver's windscreen on the extreme nearside and offside, two top-mounted circular front side lights hung from the overhang above the driver's cab windscreen whilst at the rear there was a single light at the top of the offside lower-deck corner panel and a red triangular reflector at the nearside base of the rear panel.

The side lamps, which had replaced the old fashioned paraffin "carriage lamps" at the top of the front panel evident when demonstrated in Nottingham, were powered by a 6-volt NiFe battery with 45 ampere per hour capacity. It is possible that the electric driver's horn was powered from the same source.

The manufacturer's literature states: "Should the poles leave the wires the lighting system of the bus (interior and exterior) does not fail", indicating that the vehicle was equipped with some form of emergency or standby battery lighting.

It is believed that the interior lamps were fitted with circular chromed surrounds and opaque glass diffusers mounted along the ceiling on each side.

**Seating:** No details of the seating layout have come to light; however, based on what is known about similar Guy BTX demonstrators of the period used in Birmingham and Llanelly, and limited photographic evidence, it is possible that in the lower saloon there was a longitudinal bench seat for 6 passengers on the rear nearside and one for five passengers on the offside. Guy favoured a rearwards facing bench seat for five passengers behind the driver's cab bulkhead and thus there would have been three rows of forwards facing double transverse seats. In the upper saloon there were eight double transverse seats on the nearside, six on the offside and a transverse seat for three passengers at the rear above the open rear platform.

Moquette covered seats with curved backs.

**Destination equipment:** A destination box capable of displaying a single-line of information was mounted centrally in the upright panelling at the front of the driver's cab roof and at the rear in the primrose-painted panel immediately above the rear platform window.

**Internal Livery:** The ceilings were white probably with stained and varnished window surrounds.

Floors grey.

**External Livery:** The demonstrator was supplied in a basic Pontypridd livery of blue and primrose yellow (see Appendix C).

A gold fleet number, shaded blue, 8 was affixed centrally on the front panel aligned with the base of the headlamps and beneath the oval Guy "Indian Chief" maker's plate, and on the rear panel beneath the rear platform window.

**Subsequent alterations:** As the result of a dewirement in Coedpenmaen Road on 6 February 1931 No. 8 skidded and collided with a traction pole causing considerable damage to the rear platform and stairs.

In 1936 the nearside body was rebuilt and extensive repairs were made to the roof.

The differentials on this vehicle proved troublesome perhaps due to inadequate lubrication; indeed by the late 1930s the crown wheel was averaging only a two-year lifetime.

During negotiations to hire four Hull trolleybuses in 1941, the undertaking was offered and purchased a complete rear assembly for £10 (Hull operated Guy BX motorbuses having similar components).

There were problems with the Hardy Spicer inter-axle propeller shaft in 1943 resulting in eight being taken out of service in June 1943. The replacement arrived with a tapered flange instead of a splined flange and the vehicle was still off the road in mid-September 1943.

**Disposal:** Pontypridd withdrew the vehicle in 1946. It was sold to Miss Jenkins, Bryntail Farm, Pontypridd for £40 in March 1947 for use as a static caravan at Porthcawl.

## 9 Bristol E

| Fleet No. | Reg. No. | Chassis type | No. | Elec. Eq. | Body | No. | Into service | Withdrawn |
|---|---|---|---|---|---|---|---|---|
| 9 | HY2391 | Bristol E | 102 | BTH | Beadle | 114 | 20.06.1931 | 1946 |

Chassis: Three axle type Bristol E manufactured by the Bristol Tramways & Carriage Co. Ltd., Motor Constructional Works, Bath Road, Brislington, Bristol 4.

Motor: Bull Motors Ltd., Milton Road, Stowmarket, Suffolk, a subsidiary of E.R. and F. Turner Ltd., Ipswich, RV 700B (80hp at 500 volts) and built in their Ipswich factory.

Electrical equipment: British Thomson-Houston Co. Ltd., Rugby, Warwickshire. Foot-operated contactor controller with 5 resistance and 2 field shunt notches.

Dewirement indicator: Assumed to have been equipped with line-lights.

Brakes: Westinghouse compressed air, Bull eddy current, 2-stage rheostatic and hand brakes.

Body: John C. Beadle Co. Ltd., Spital Street, Dartford, Kent H32/28R. Beadle drawing number DO 5142. Body number 114.

Length: 28ft 0in. Width: 7ft 6in.

Height: 15ft 2½in.

Wheelbase: 17ft 0in.

Unladen weight: 8 tons 0cwt

The Bristol Tramways & Carriage Co. Ltd. (BTCC), the bus and tramway operator in that city and a large surrounding area, began to produce its own motor bus chassis in 1908. New manufacturing premises (The Motor Constructional Works) were established in 1912 in Bath Road, Brislington, a short distance south of the tram depot.

Prompted by the interest in large-capacity double-deck motor buses on three-axle chassis the works built two prototype type C three axle motor bus chassis, C101 and C102,

powered by a Bristol HW six-cylinder petrol engine and fitted with B type radiator, in 1929. No purchasers were found but an enquiry was received from Doncaster Corporation Transport, an established Bristol motor bus customer, as to the possibility of the company manufacturing a trolleybus.

Although BTCC felt that the motor bus would ultimately replace electric street traction, a general lack of business due to the industrial recession encouraged them to reconstruct motor bus chassis C102 as a prototype three axle trolleybus chassis, numbered E101. This trolleybus chassis was displayed, unbodied, at the 1929 Commercial Motor Show. In 1930 chassis E101 received a Beadle H33/27R body built on Roe frames and finished in Doncaster livery but with BTCC ownership details, registered DT 2620. In late August 1930, E101 was hired to Doncaster Corporation Transport licensed as a demonstrator. In April 1932 the demonstrator was purchased by Doncaster and given fleet number 31.

Motor bus chassis C101 was reconstructed as trolleybus chassis E102 during 1930 and despatched to Dartford where it received a Beadle H33/27R body, returning to Bristol during January 1931. It was tested extensively in Brislington tram depot yard, an additional pair of wires being strung above the tram track fan in front of the building. At some stage in this period E102 was registered for use of the public highway, receiving the Bristol registration mark HY 2391, and was tested after tram services had finished for the night in Bath Road reportedly reaching Victoria Street, just short of Bristol city centre, using the tramway overhead wire and a skate device for the current return connection.

Bristol E chassis E102 was sent to John C. Beadle, Dartford, Kent, in late 1930 where it received a composite H33/27R body. The absence of trolley gear suggests that this is an official Beadle's photograph taken in Dartford. (Bristol Vintage Bus Group, Phil Sposito [BTCC Archives])

Pontypridd UDC was not only a good Bristol motorbus customer but had recently introduced trolleybuses on one of its two tram routes with the second conversion pending. E102 was offered for hire to Pontypridd UDC in January 1931 and delivered on 27 March 1931. There then followed a considerable delay until the MoT sent an official to carry out an inspection and tilt test which provoked complaints from the Transport Department. The MoT inspection was made on 18 June 1931 and the vehicle entered passenger service on 20 June 1931. It proved most satisfactory and by 17 December 1931 it had run 13,500 miles. In December 1931 Bristol offered it for sale to Pontypridd at £2,200 which prompted a period of negotiations during which time Bristol paid for it to be relicenced until 24 March 1932. It was purchased in March 1932 for £1,735 and given fleet number 9.

**Chassis:** Deep channel pressing frame in 3% nickel steel based on the spectacle frame Bristol C three axle motorbus chassis. The maximum section was 11in. deep, 3in. wide and ¼in. thick.

The chassis was 3ft 10in. wide for much of its length but widened to 4ft 1in. to the rear of the rear pair of wheels

beneath the platform, and narrowed progressively to just 2ft 2¼in. beneath the driver's cab area.

The front axle was a heavy nickel chrome stamping. The stub axles were mounted on taper roller bearings to reduce the steering effort. The steering connections were alloy steel tubes fitted with spring-loaded ball joints. Maximum angle of steering lock was 45°.

The rear axle bogie was carried on a nickel chrome tube secured to the frame by cast steel brackets, each axle end having independent movement. A spherical attachment was used between the spring and axle brackets to avoid undue strain to the spring ends. The spherical bearings were large enclosed and well-lubricated gun-metal pads.

The traction motor was coupled to the leading rear axle by a two-part propeller shaft, a centre bearing being carried by the transverse cross-member between the chassis frame. The front section of the shaft sloped at an angle from the rear of the motor to the centre bearing. There were three differentials; the third differential was mounted on the front of the leading rear axle, the drive passing through to the third axle by a short telescopic shaft and universal joint.

Bristol E chassis E102 in Brislington tram depot yard. Arno's Court Triumphal Arch, built about 1760 from Bath stone, is visible in the background above the rear bogie. Both the tram depot (a listed building) and the arch still survive. (Bristol Vintage Bus Group, Phil Sposito [BTCC Archives])

Bristol E chassis E102 in Brislington tram depot yard. Houses in Bloomfield Road are visible over the wall. (Bristol Vintage Bus Group, Phil Sposito [BTCC Archives])

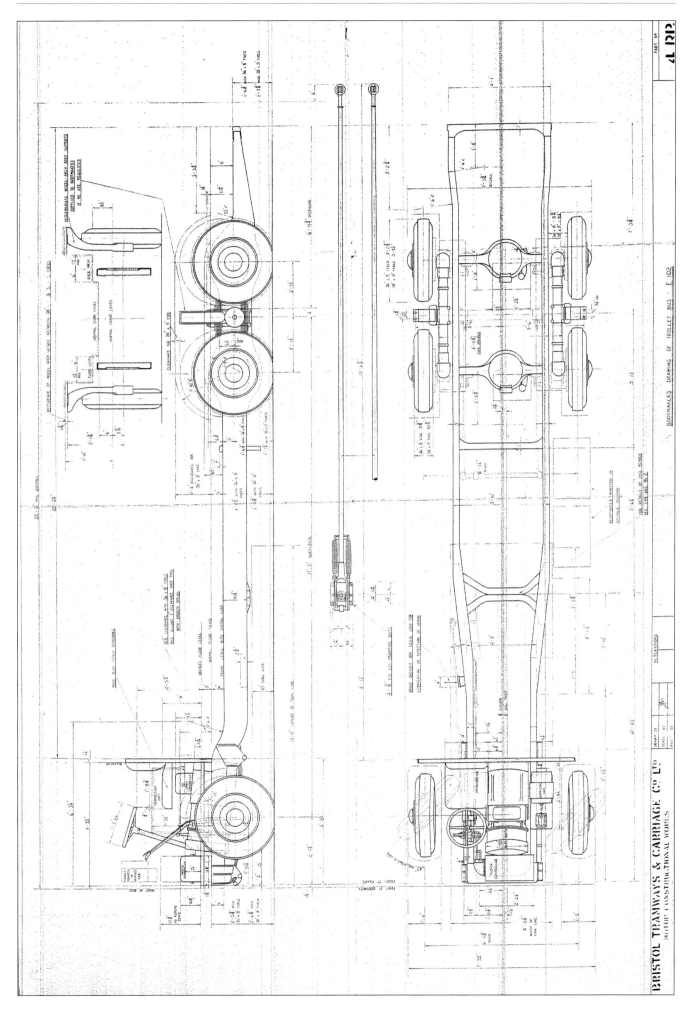

**Electrics:** The light-weight Bull motor was rated at 80hp, 1,250rpm British Engineering Standards Association Traction rating and was sparkless up to at least 100% overload. The magnet frame was an octagonal box type steel casting to which a light steel plate extension was welded at the commutator end to carry a light alloy bracket to which was attached the eddy current brake. Bull cooperated with Richard Garrett & Sons Ltd., Leiston, Suffolk, in the manufacture of trolleybus traction motors.

The motor windings embodied a high percentage of asbestos and mica insulation, the field coils consisting of asbestos and cotton covered square strip. The armature was mounted on a light weight cast steel spider with removable shaft and the armature windings were insulated in the slot portions with a bakelised wrap containing alternate layers of mica and bakelised paper, the end windings were insulated with mica and cotton tape treated with heat resisting enamel. The end windings were carried on cast steel spiders which were arranged to prevent dirt or moisture finding their way into the windings from the ventilating ducts through the armature core. The commutator was built on a cast steel hub; the risers being integral with the commutator segments. The complete armature was shrouded with a canvas wrap treated with heat resisting enamel and 16 gauge steel wire bands were fitted.

A ventilating fan was fitted on the rear end of the motor consisting of a light-weight alloy casting bolted to a facing on the rear end winding carrier. The rear end bracket was a carefully designed and ribbed light alloy casting of ample strength.

Roller bearings were provided at both ends with an additional double thrust bearing at the commutator end. These bearings were mounted in separate cast steel housings and it was possible to remove the armature completely from the motor without dismantling the bearing assemblies.

The Bull patent totally enclosed brush gear took up a small proportion of the commutator periphery, the mechanism being completely enclosed against dirt or accidental arcing by the patent die-cast brush construction. The complete box could be quickly removed from the brush arm by means of a suitable key. The brush springs could be tensioned by means of a key without removing the box. A radial adjustment was provided for the brush arm to compensate for commutator wear. The brush arm was insulated with paxolin and an arc resisting composition disc between the box and the face of the rocker. The brush rocker was a lightweight channel section aluminium alloy casting. The rocker was split and clamped upon a seating, provided in the end bracket, by means of two bolts at opposite diameters.

The traction motor was mounted, tilted upwards towards the front of the vehicle, between the chassis frame over the front axle and protruding 7½in. at its highest point above the driver's cab floor line which itself was some 5in. above the lower saloon floor line. It also resulted in a particularly long propeller shaft to the leading rear axle.

The master controller was mounted transversely in the driver's cab immediately in front of the traction motor with the potentiometer under the driver's seat.

The resistances were attached to the nearside chassis frame immediately in front of the leading rear axle.

**Brakes:** Eddy current brakes (controller no. 6635), a Westinghouse Brake & Saxby Signal Co. Ltd. compensating air brake working independently on each of the rear bogie wheels and a hand brake on the rear bogie wheels. No brakes on front wheels.

Metropolitan-Vickers compressor motor series wound DC ½hp 500–550-volt at 700rpm serial No. 53637/2/3 maintained a working pressure of 100 lb per square inch. The control switch was operated by the pressure in the reservoir, the motor starting when the pressure fell to 75 lb per square inch and cutting out when 100 lb was reached. The Westinghouse compressor and substantial Metropolitan-Vickers motor were mounted on a platform on the nearside of the driver's cab between the traction motor and the side panel.

Operation of the driver's brake pedal supplied pressure as required to cylinders on each axle bracket. A piston 5in. in diameter was coupled by a short connecting rod to each brake cam lever. The pistons had a 2¾in. stroke. An adjustor was fitted to each brake shoe to compensate wear of the brake drums and linings.

The Bull eddy current brake consisted of a cast steel rotor mounted upon a tapered extension at the commutator end of the motor shaft. The rim was designed to expand freely when hot without excessive conduction of heat to the shaft and bearings, and without distorting or cracking the rotor spokes. This was accomplished by allowing the ribbed rotor to float on four steel pegs fitted to the periphery of thin steel discs upon which the rotor was centred. The rotor revolved in a multi-polar magnetic field without frictional contact; braking torque was obtained by exciting the brake field through a potentiometer brake controller which caused short circuit currents to flow in the rotor thereby developing a heavy braking torque. The energy absorbed was dissipated in heating the rotor; the heat being carried away by the air current induced by a light alloy cast fan mounted on the forward end of the motor shaft. The light weight potentiometer controller consisted of a resistance placed across the supply mains on depressing the eddy current brake pedal. A brush arm then traversed a stationary commutator in the controller to which the potentiometer resistance was connected. This gradually increased the potential applied to the brake magnets until the desired braking had been obtained. Braking torque was maintained down to a low road speed.

The handbrake lever was on the nearside of the driver's steering column.

**Bodywork:** Composite six-bay highbridge double-deck construction, enclosed forwards-ascending half-turn (90°) staircase with conventional semi-vestibuled open platform entrance and exit at the rear, built by John C. Beadle Co. Ltd., Spital Street, Dartford, Kent.

The domed roof overhung the slightly v-shaped front of the upper-saloon which had two wide rectangular fixed front windows. The trolley base and 19ft 6¾in. long poles were fitted in a conventional manner on a concealed roof-mounted gantry above bay 2. A gutter ran around the base of the roof with drains descending down the front pillar of bay 1 and the rear pillar of bay 6 on both sides.

The staircase and rear platform were integrated into the bodywork. There was one step up onto the rear platform and a further step up into the lower saloon. The staircase had seven steps from the platform to the upper-deck including a 90° turn (no landing) each riser being equipped with a rectangular metal protection at its base.

The main transverse chassis girders were partially visible beneath the front panel to the driver's cab.

Another official view of the Bristol E demonstrator following the addition of its Beadle H33/27R body. The body was finished in the basic Bristol Tramways & Carriage Co. Ltd. livery of dark ultramarine blue and ivory white. The prominent service number box on the driver's cab roof was retained, unused following the vehicle's purchase by Pontypridd UDC whilst photographs show that it served as a basis for the decorations carried to celebrate King George V's Silver Jubilee in 1935. It had definitely gone following the body reconstruction carried out in the late 1930s. (Peter Smith collection [BTCC Archives])

Lower saloon interior view of Bristol E 9. The lamp fitting masks show this to be a wartime view. (photographers name not recorded)

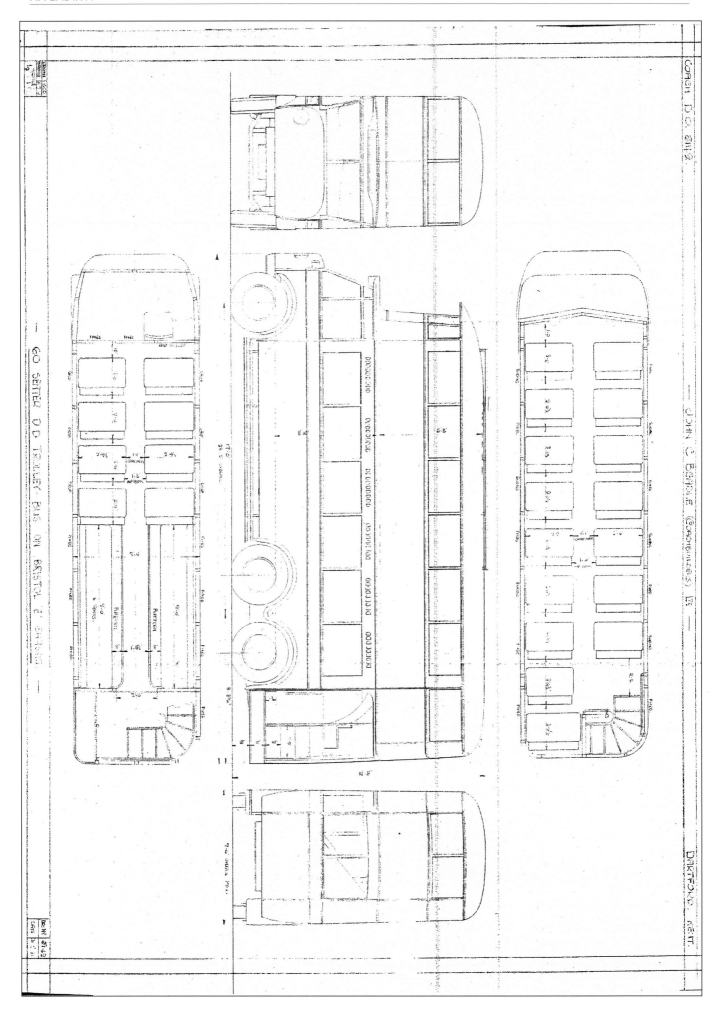

The front pillar of bay 1 and the rear pillar of bay 6 on the nearside and offside of both decks were considerably wider than the other window pillars whilst the upper-deck rear corner pillars were particularly wide. Half-drop openers were fitted to the lower saloon side windows in bays 1, 2, 3 on both sides. The windows in bays 1, 3, 5 of the nearside and bays 2, 4, 6 of the offside of the upper saloon were each equipped with two panes divided vertically, the pane towards the front of the vehicles sliding backwards in front of the fixed rear pane. All the upper saloon windows were 1ft 9½in. deep. There was also a single offside lower-deck window with fixed pane behind the staircase. The upright rear elevation incorporated two large windows to the upper saloon, and two matching windows to the lower-deck open rear platform. The nearside windows in each case were somewhat wider (2ft 3in.) than those on the offside (1ft 9½in.). There was a single step up to the rear platform and a further step into the lower saloon. The base of the rear platform panels was cut away on the offside by a depth of several inches to provide easier access to the spare wheel carried beneath the platform.

The slightly v-shaped "piano front" panelling of the upper-deck flared gently forwards at its base to abut the flat roof of the driver's cab which overhung the windscreen and supported a centrally-mounted single-line destination indicator box built into a curved fairing. The driver's cab, which protruded well forward of the upper-deck, was equipped with opening windscreens on the off and nearside and a front hinged door on the offside. The opening upper panes of the windscreen were slightly v-shaped, being deeper at the centre of each pane. The large window in the offside cab door and its counterpart on the nearside was divided vertically into two panes, that towards the front of the vehicle sliding backwards in front of the fixed rear pane, for driver signalling and cab ventilation purposes. There were fixed quarter lights between the offside cab door and its matching nearside counterpart, and the cab front pillars. A small rectangular driver's rear view mirror was mounted externally two thirds of the way up the offside front pillar of the cab. There were three deep glazed panels in the bulkhead behind the driver, that on the offside divided vertically into two sliding panes, and each equipped with roll down blinds.

The high-mounted, flat front panel beneath the driver's cab windscreen was upright with rounded edges, its base being almost 1ft above the base of the lower saloon side panels. The front registration number plate was affixed to a protective shield that hung beneath the front panel between the dumb irons, level with the front axle wheel hubs, whilst that at the rear was applied with transfers at the top of the nearside rear platform window.

The lower-deck waistband, i.e. below the windows, was noticeably deep.

There were separate wheel arches in the side panels over the second and third axles with a mud flap hanging between. There were two lifeguard rails on each side extending between the front and second axles, although there was no protection beneath the high-mounted, bulbous front panel to the driver's cab.

**Lighting:** External lighting was two headlights mounted on the extremities of the curved panel each side of the outline "radiator" with large sidelights or spotlights on the cream-painted panels above the driver's windscreen, at the top of the nearside and offside front pillars.

The position of the rear light is not known and nothing is evident on the limited number of photographs showing the rear of the vehicle.

In the lower saloon rectangular lamp fittings were located centrally on the bulkhead behind the driver's cab above the glazed panels, and centrally above the side windows in bays 2, 3, 4 and 5 on each side. In the upper saloon circular globe lamp fittings were located towards the rear of bays 1–6 on both sides of the ceiling.

The saloon lighting was supplied by batteries and not directly from the traction supply.

**Seating:** The lower saloon had a 6-person inwards-facing bench seat on each side over the rear axles and 4 rows of forwards-facing double seats. The upper saloon had 7 rows of double seats on the offside and 9 rows on the nearside, the ninth seat at the rear of the upper saloon above the open platform also accommodating two passengers. There was a metal kicking panel at the base of driver's cab bulkhead.

The seats had leather covered cushions and backs with painted toprail.

Vertical handrails rose up behind the second and fourth seat on the nearside and the first and third seat as well as in front of the longitudinal seat on the offside of the lower saloon and the fifth and sixth seat on the nearside and second, third and fourth seat on the offside of the upper saloon. The driver's seat was covered in leather.

A continual longitudinal handrail hung from the lower saloon ceiling on the nearside of the central gangway with a counterpart on the offside above the first three rows of seats and above the longitudinal seat.

In the lower saloon there were conductor's bell pushes on the wooden window surrounds centrally above the windows in bay 2 nearside and bays 1 and 3 offside. Their location in the upper saloon is not known.

**Destination equipment:** A destination box capable of displaying a single-line of information was mounted centrally above the driver's cab windscreen and towards the nearside at the top of the blue-painted upper-deck rear panels beneath the upper saloon rear windows.

**Internal Livery:** The ceilings were white. Floors grey. The lower saloon gangway floor was covered with hardwood slats.

The windows were surrounded by stained and varnished wood frames.

Black Doverite covered rods or rails protected the window panes in bays 1–6 and the rearmost windows on both sides of the upper saloon, as well as the front upper saloon windows.

**External Livery:** The demonstrator was delivered in the basic Bristol Tramways & Carriage Co. Ltd. livery of dark ultramarine blue and ivory white but subsequently repainted into Pontypridd UDC livery. See Appendix C.

**Subsequent alterations:** There is evidence that Bristol 9 suffered from propeller shaft and coupling problems from summer 1932, possibly due to a malfunction of the splined portion of the propeller shaft provided to accommodate lengthening or shortening of the shaft as a result of spring deflection. The original propeller shaft was sent to Bristol for repair in late August 1932 and subsequently replaced by one of Hardy Spicer manufacture. By 1934 Mr Evans was again in contact with Bristol Tramways about propeller shaft problems which earned the rebuke that E101 was still operating with its original shaft and no reported problems.

9 received a thorough body overhaul in the late 1930s, probably in late 1937 following the purchase of a quantity of Bristol spares. The separate wheel arches over the rear bogie and panel between the two wheels were replaced by a continuous wheel arch over both wheels with a "V"-shaped panel hanging between the wheels. Ventilation louvres were added at the base of the nearside lower-deck panels in bays 2 and 3 to improve ventilation to the resistances attached to the nearside chassis frame. The sliding panes in bays 1, 3, 5 of the nearside upper saloon were replaced by a fixed pane in bay 1 and half-drop openers in bays 3 and 5. Those in bays 2, 4, 6 of the offside of the upper saloon were replaced by half-drop openers in bays 2 and 4, and a fixed pane in bay 6. The lower-deck offside window behind the staircase was replaced with panelling.

Probably at the same time a rear registration number plate was added at the base of the rear panels on the offside in addition to the registration details already applied to the rear platform window.

The two large sidelights or spotlights on the white-painted panels above the driver's windscreen were removed in the late 1930s and replaced by conventional, smaller sidelights on stalks at waistband height.

**Disposal:** Pontypridd withdrew the vehicle in 1946. It was inspected by Cardiff Corporation Transport's engineer, Felix Cunuder, in November 1946 as to its suitability for further operation on their Bute Street route but being a double-deck vehicle was too high. On the occasion of his visit 9 was out of service with the main resistance burnt out, in addition the worm wheel on the leading rear axle was worn although the replacement part had reportedly already been purchased. It is likely that the vehicle never re-entered service.

9 was sold to Mr J.D. Brown on 8 July 1947 for £33 10s with the stipulation that it was not to be used for human habitation in the Pontypridd area and subject to a payment to India Tyre and Rubber Co. Ltd. of the valuation of the tyres on the vehicle. It is believed to have been sold for use as a static caravan or farm outhouse on Anglesey and reportedly survived until at least 1967.

The obligatory tilt test of Bristol E No. 9 outside Glyntaff tram car shed. The open front of a tram is visible on the right of the photograph. (PUDCTD)

## 8–15 Karrier W

| Fleet No. | Reg. No. | Chassis type | No. | Elec. Eq. | Body | No. | Into service | Withdrawn |
|---|---|---|---|---|---|---|---|---|
| 8 | GNY301 | Karrier W | 50352 | BTH | Park Royal | 32534 | 07.12.1946 | 31.01.1957 |
| 9 | GNY302 | Karrier W | 50353 | BTH | Park Royal | 32535 | 07.12.1946 | 31.01.1957 |
| 10 | FNY983 | Karrier W | 50085 | E. Electric | Weymann | C8021 | 27.02.1945 | 31.01.1957 |
| 11 | FNY984 | Karrier W | 50086 | E. Electric | Weymann | C8022 | 28.03.1945 | 31.01.1957 |
| 12 | FTG234 | Karrier W | 50192 | BTH | Park Royal | 29218 | 31.08.1945 | 31.01.1957 |
| 13 | FTG235 | Karrier W | 50191 | BTH | Park Royal | 29219 | 31.08.1945 | 31.01.1957 |
| 14 | FTG697 | Karrier W | 50312 | BTH | Roe | GO2089 | 01.03.1946 | 12.1955 |
| 15 | FTG698 | Karrier W | 50313 | BTH | Roe | GO2090 | 08.03.1946 | 12.1955 |

Chassis: Two axle wartime utility type Karrier W marketed by Commer-Karrier, Biscot Road, Luton, Bedfordshire and manufactured by Karrier Motors Ltd. at the Sunbeam trolleybus factory, Moorfield Road, Wolverhampton.

Motor: 8–9 British Thomson-Houston Co. Ltd., Rugby, Type 207 A3 (85hp at 550 volts) compound-wound, non-regenerative, stabilised rheostatic control.

10–11 English Electric Co. Ltd., Bradford, Type EE406/8M (80hp at 550 volts) compound-wound, non-regenerative, stabilised rheostatic control.

12–13 British Thomson-Houston Co. Ltd., Rugby, Type 207 A3 (85hp at 550 volts) compound-wound, non-regenerative, stabilised rheostatic control.

14–15 British Thomson-Houston Co. Ltd., Rugby, Type 207 A3 (85hp at 550 volts) compound-wound, non-regenerative.

Electrical equipment: 8–9, 12–15 British Thomson-Houston Co. Ltd., Rugby, Warwickshire. Contactor control

10–11 English Electric Co. Ltd., Preston, Lancashire.

Dewirement indicator: Assumed to have been fitted with line-lights.

Brakes: Compressed air and rheostatic brakes on brake pedal. Hand.

Body: 8–9 Park Royal Coachworks Ltd., Abbey Road, Park Royal, Willesden, London NW10.

10–11 Weymann Motor Bodies Ltd., Addlestone, Surrey.
12–13 Park Royal Coachworks Ltd., Abbey Road, Park Royal, Willesden, London NW10.
14–15 Charles H. Roe Ltd., Crossgates, Leeds, Yorkshire. all UH30/26R.

Length: 26ft Width: 7ft 6in. Wheelbase: 16ft 3in.
Wheel track: front 6ft 6in., rear 5ft 9¼in.
Unladen weight: 8–9, 12–13 7 tons 7cwt 3qtrs
10–11 7 tons ?cwts ?qtrs
14–15 7 tons ?cwts ?qtrs

Tyres: front wheels 36 × 8in.; rear wheels 9 × 20in.

The Ministry of War Transport (MoWT) issued permits to operators allowing them to purchase vehicles and their component parts. These permits were converted into orders and sent from the MoWT to the Ministry of Supply (MoS) who held lists of approved suppliers, to whom they sent the orders according to their rationing system. The operator could then decide to 'take it or leave it', there were no further options. From 1 January 1946, operators were free to order bodywork without permits although chassis allocations remained in force.

Final cost:
8–9 £3,341
10–11 £2,976
12–13 £2,968
14–15 £3,032

Karrier W / Park Royal 9 stands in John Place beneath the reverser at Treforest terminus, the southernmost point on the Pontypridd system. (Cy Yandell collection [photographer's name not recorded])

The 1945 Weymann body on Karrier W 11 looks particularly austere from this angle. The trolleybus is standing in Station Square in front of Pontypridd GPO and Sorting Office. (Peter Smith collection [photographer's name not recorded])

Karrier W 14 of 1946 loads in Taff Street outside Lipton's store on a cold wet day. The two Roe-bodied trolleybuses, 14 and 15, were taken out of service in November 1955 for sale to Walsall Corporation Transport. Similar to vehicles in Walsall's own fleet, 14 and 15 were considered to be in the best condition of all the Karriers at Pontypridd which warranted a sale price of £500 each with the option to buy the remaining trolleybus fleet in due course. (Peter Smith collection [photographer's name not recorded])

**Chassis:** Standard basic wartime chassis for use beneath double-deck or (with a longer wheelbase) single-deck bodies incorporating salient features of the pre-war Sunbeam MF2 and Karrier E4 chassis. There is no evidence to suggest that these chassis were designated W4, i.e. Wartime 4-wheel, to differentiate from a three-axle standard wartime chassis once under consideration. The surviving Karrier chassis plates from the driver's cab clearly show that Pontypridd's examples were designated as Karrier W. The chassis frame employed deep channel section side-members braced with large diameter tubular cross members. Full depth channel section members across the centre of the frame ensured torsional rigidity. The whole of the frame structure was bolted together with high tensile steel bolts fitted in reamed holes.

Conventional front axle with forged steel hubs mounted on taper roller bearings, similar bearings being used to take the thrust of the king pins. Double roller cam and roller steering unit of robust dimensions for heavy-duty use.

Chassis length: 25ft 7in. Chassis frame width: front 3ft 3⅞in., rear 3ft 8in.

Overall width (over tyres): 7ft 5⅝in.

The underslung worm type rear axle had fully floating shafts, the main axle casing being a nickel steel drop-forging. The differential was housed in a drop-forged steel casing on which the phosphor-bronze worm wheel which meshed with a hardened steel worm was also mounted. The differential casing was offset towards the nearside of the chassis to permit a low and unobstructed centre gangway. The steel hubs were mounted on roller bearings. The driving shafts were machined from heat treated nickel chrome molybdenum steel, the hub driving flanges being forged solid with the shafts removing the necessity for splining the hub end of each shaft.

The axle gear ratio was 9.7 to 1.

The short transmission shaft was equipped with a needle roller universal joint at each end. The slide, due to axle movement, was taken through a large diameter splined sleeve at the forward end of the shaft, and end thrust through a ball thrust bearing mounted in the end case of the motor thus relieving the armature of any load. The driving torque reaction is taken through the rear road springs.

The laminated road springs were 3½in. wide, the front springs were 44in. in length and the rear springs 59¾in., these dimensions being between the spring eyes. The eyes of the main plates were forged solid, and on the rear springs the main plates were of the divided type, having inner eyes to provide a positive location for the axle. The spring shackle pins were protected on the wearing surfaces with a deposit of hard chrome to reduce wear.

The motor-driven compressor unit for the air brakes was mounted on an insulated base on the off side main frame side member. The compressor had a displacement of 5 cubic ft per minute. The compressor motor was totally enclosed and operated direct from the line voltage. An electric governor, also mounted on an insulated base, controlled the operation of the motor and automatically cut out when the pressure in the air reservoir reached 80 lb per sq.in., and cut in again when the pressure fell to 65 lb per sq.in.

**Electrics:** Compound-wound traction motor with rheostatic braking operating in conjunction with the mechanical braking system. The traction motor was mounted between the chassis frames towards the rear and just ahead of the rear axle, enabling it to be carried lower in the frame than was then

Karrier W chassis photographed at Sunbeam's Wolverhampton works to show the typical layout of the electrical equipment, in this case of BTH manufacture. (*Modern Transport* 27 June 1941)

normal practice so that low-height double-deck bodies could be fitted, and offset to the nearside. The contactor switchgear was mounted on a single panel in a cabinet on the nearside of the front bulkhead in the driver's cab, with the master controller under the driver's seat. Those vehicles with BTH equipment (12–13) had a removable panel in the nearside of the front bulkhead to give access to the rear of the contactor cabinet.

There was a 12-volt dynamo on the commutator end of the traction motor. A speedometer of the electrical "tachometer" type was fitted, the generator portion being mounted on and driven from the forward end of the traction motor.

All equipped with Rheostatic Brake Co. resistances and Brecknell Willis lightweight trolleybases. In accordance with the undertaking's policy the booms were equipped with trolley wheel heads.

There was one main bank of resistances between the chassis frames ahead of the motor. The shunt resistance was mounted on the external face of the chassis nearside (approximately beneath bay 3 of the body). There is no evidence that these trolleybuses were equipped with traction battery manoeuvring equipment.

**Brakes:** Compressed air, hand and rheostatic brakes.

The compressor and air reservoir, complete with a safety valve and drain cock, were bolted directly to the offside external face of the mainframe member. There was one air-brake cylinder on top of each king pin and one cylinder attached to each side of the chassis cross-member ahead of the rear axle. An anti-freezing unit was fitted on the suction side of the compressor. Seamless steel tubing incorporating drainage was used for the pipeline. There were insulators in the pipeline between the motor-driven compressor and reservoir. The dash panel of the driver's cab was equipped with two gauges to indicate reservoir and brake cylinder pressure. There was an air brake governor in the cab.

The brake drums on both front and rear wheels were 17in. in diameter, the front shoes being 3in. and the rear shoes 6in. wide. The hand brake was of the "pull on" type and operated on the same set of shoes in the rear axle as the foot brakes and through the same cam gear.

Electrical rheostatic braking was operated from the same pedal as the air brake and was effective at all speeds down to 3 or 4mph. Approximately the first 1½in. of pedal travel was used to obtain rheostatic braking whilst further pedal travel brought in the air-operated mechanical brakes.

The handbrake lever was to the offside of the driver's steering column.

**Bodywork:** Composite five-bay highbridge double-deck utility construction, enclosed forwards-ascending half-turn (90°) staircase with conventional semi-vestibuled open platform entrance and exit at the rear, designed to specifications approved by the MoS. The National Federation of Vehicle Trades and Operators Joint technical and Advisory Committee was set up to agree the specifications for utilitarian bodies that could be built using the minimum of material and labour. In order to optimise the use of available materials and reduce the amount of labour required, hardwoods were only used for the main body framing, the longitudinal rails being of pitch pine. Exterior panelling, including the roof, was of 20-gauge swg steel whilst panels were shaped rather than beaten resulting in noticeably angular roof domes.

Metal louvres were fitted above the upper and lower-deck saloon side windows, and above the upper-saloon front windows. Half-drop openers with central gripper fixed to the top rail of the upper pane were fitted to the side windows as follows (there being variations between batches and body builders):

8–9 in bays 1, 3 and 5 of the upper saloon and bays 2 and 3 of the lower saloon nearside; in bays 1, 3 and 4 of the upper saloon and bays 2 and 3 of the lower saloon offside,

10–11 in bays 2 of the upper saloon and bays 2 of the lower saloon nearside; in bay 2 of the upper saloon and bay 3 of the lower saloon offside;

12–13 in bays 1, 3 and 5 of the upper saloon and bays 2 and 3 of the lower saloon nearside; in bays 1, 3 and 4 of the upper saloon and bays 2 and 3 of the lower saloon offside,

14–15 in bays 1, 3, 5 on both sides of the upper saloon and bays 2 and 4 of the lower saloon.

The upper pane dropped outside the fixed lower pane. All window glass was fixed direct to the framing using "U" section rubber.

Brackets or extensions were bolted to the roof rail immediately above the upper-deck body pillars between bays 1 and 2, and bays 2 and 3 to support the two girders of the exposed trolley gantry which was mounted above bay 2, and not in direct contact with the roof. The Park Royal and Roe bodied vehicles had noticeably wider (than their Weymann counterparts) upper-deck body pillars between the front side windows and bay 1 which on the nearside accommodated the main traction power cables from the roof. The cables entered the body through a hood positioned immediately in front of the front nearside trolley gantry bracket on 8, 9, 12, 13; positioned above the nearside front body pillar (bay 1) on 10 and 11; and centrally in the roof in bay 1 on 14 and 15.

All platform handrails and stanchions were white wholly or in part although those inside the saloons and on the staircase were black. They were covered with insulating material.

There were pull-in hopper ventilators at the top of the upper saloon front windows with top-mounted central clip catch on 8–13 (14–15 had larger fixed panes). At the rear of the upper saloon there was a bottom-hinged (3 hinges) emergency exit door incorporating two square windows which also provided access to the trolley gantry and could be retained open by leather covered chains on each side. The opening handle was in the top of the door frame above the offside window. Ventilators were also fitted to the roof, above bays 1, 3 and 5 both sides.

The driver's cab was equipped with a single opening windscreen on the offside equipped with a top-mounted windscreen wiper whilst the nearside windscreen had a bottom-mounted wiper. The frame of the opening pane had

Karrier W No. 8 seen at the Park Royal factory prior to delivery. Note the livery application (to both 8 and 9) with the primrose painted area around the lower saloon windows continuing some 6 ins beneath the waistrail and with the undertaking's initials in bays 2, 3, 4 being transferred onto this primrose area. (Cy Yandell [photographer's name not recorded])

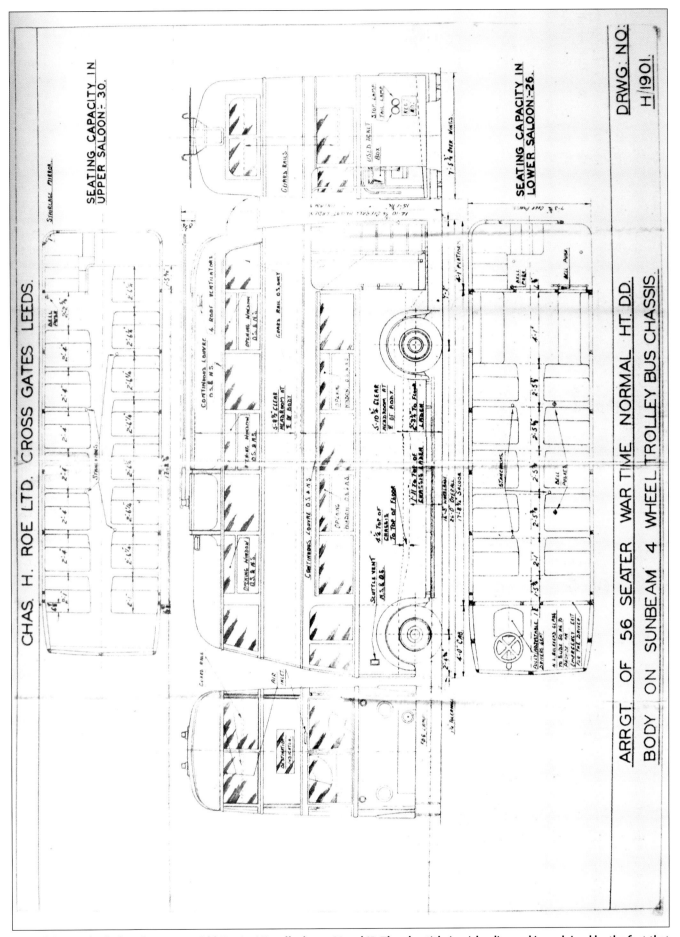

**Plan of the Roe body fitted to Pontypridd Karrier W trolleybuses 14 and 15. The plan title is misleading and is explained by the fact that the Karrier W chassis were manufactured at the Sunbeam trolleybus factory in Wolverhampton.**

radiused upper corners. There was a front hinged cab door on the offside only equipped with a sliding "signalling" window in the lower half of the pane and an inset opening handle. A vent was positioned on both sides of the cab immediately beneath the waistline, the format varying between bodybuilders. The base of the cab door was curved over the wheel arch on the Park Royal and Weymann bodies. There were two glazed panels in the bulkhead behind the driver, that on the nearside incorporating a sliding pane for easier communication with the conductor and to provide an emergency exit from the driver's cab, with a wide central pillar. Rectangular driver's rear view mirrors were mounted externally towards the top of the front cab pillars. A plain removable panel extended across the front of the cab from beneath the offside to beneath the nearside headlamp for towing purposes. A Karrier maker's badge was fitted centrally beneath the driver's windscreen, its position in relation to the lower primrose-painted band varying between the batches and body builder.

A step was let into the base of the bay 1 side panel immediately behind the front axle, on the offside, only those on 14 and 15 having any form of protection to the bodywork. The insert on 8, 9, 12, 13 had a rounded top; that on 14 and 15 was somewhat shallower also with a rounded top; and that on 10 and 11 was square, all with reinforced edges.

The staircase had 3 steps from the platform to a landing and then a 90° turn to three steps to the upper-deck.

There were also upright stanchions in both saloons although the positions may have varied between body builder:

Lower saloon: seats 2, 4 nearside; seats 1, 3 offside (confirmed in the cases of 12, 13, 14, 15)

Upper saloon: seats 3, 6 nearside; seats 2, 5 offside.

The location and number of conductor's bell pushes in the lower salon is not known. There were two bell pushes in the upper saloon located on the nearside cantrail in bays 1 and 4, and on the offside in bay 5 at the top of the stairs. On the rear platform there was a further bell push on the offside of the rear bulkhead adjacent to staircase.

There was a used ticket box below the nearside vestibule window on the rear platform. A bamboo trolley retrieval pole was carried within the lower-saloon nearside body panels at waist rail height with a tube access from the rear platform vestibule. The conductor had a locker on the rear platform under the stairs. There was a square rear registration number plate fitted on the offside of the rear platform panel. A circular conductor's mirror was fixed in the upper-deck rear offside dome at the head of the stairs.

There was a single lifeguard rail on each side extending between the front and rear axles.

There were detail differences to the bodywork between batches and body builder as follows:

10–11 Weymann

A gutter moulding ran along the base of the upper-deck side panels bays 1–5 at the joint of the upper and lower-deck structure and gave covered drainage from the floor of the upper saloon. A horizontal duct above the front cab side pillar on both sides was also provided for drainage and ventilation purposes.

The main traction power cable descended the front nearside pillar of bay 1.

Top hinged access doors were fitted at the base of the lower-deck nearside panel in bays 1–3, giving access to the shunt field resistance, and on the offside panels in bay 2, giving access to the air compressor and reservoir.

The front registration number plate was mounted centrally on the removable towing hatch.

8–9 Park Royal    12–13 Park Royal.

There were two louvres vane ventilators on each side of the front indicator box, mounted two-thirds of the distance between the outer edge of the box and the extremity of the panel, immediately above the driver's cab windscreen. Above the lower saloon windows in bay 1 on both sides in the cantrail or vent panel there were four ventilation vents slanting rearwards somewhat from the vertical at the top.

8, 9 – There were 3 horizontal ducts at the base of the upper-deck side panels fitted centrally in bay 3 and towards the rear of bay 5, and above the front cab side pillar on both sides for drainage and ventilation purposes.

12, 13 – A gutter moulding ran along the base of the upper-deck side panels bays 1–5 at the joint of the upper and lower-deck structure and gave covered drainage from the floor of the upper saloon. A horizontal duct above the front cab side pillar on both sides was also provided for drainage and ventilation purposes.

The windows in the upper saloon emergency exit door had radiused outer corners.

The driver's cab windscreen was noticeably deeper than those on the other utility bodies.

There was a horizontally mounted top-hinged outwards opening vent on both sides of the cab immediately beneath the waistrail on 8 and 9, whereas on 12 and 13 a torpedo vent was fitted on the nearside only.

Top hinged access doors were fitted at the base of the lower-deck nearside panels in bay 3, giving access to the battery cradle and shunt field resistance, and on the offside panels in bay 2, giving access to the air compressor.

The front registration number plate was mounted centrally about one-third of the way up the removable towing hatch.

14–15 Roe

The finish of these bodies was somewhat relaxed from the utility specifications approved by the MoS being a new version drawn in 1944 and introduced in 1945. The bodywork featured a number of the characteristics found in Roe's post-war deliveries including a domed roof and lower-deck waistrail at the same height along the saloon and front dash.

There were 6 horizontal ducts at the base of the upper-deck side panels fitted centrally in bays 1–5 and towards the rear of the panel above the driver's cab for drainage and ventilation purposes on both sides with a further duct towards the front of the nearside panel above the open rear platform.

There was a vertical vent on both sides of the cab immediately below the waistrail.

The windows in the upper saloon emergency exit door had radiused upper corners.

The base of the cab door was horizontal, parallel to the lower-deck waistband about 8in. below it.

Top hinged access doors were fitted at the base of the lower-deck nearside panels in bay 3, giving access to the battery cradle, and on the offside panels in bay 2, giving access to the air compressor.

**Lighting:** External lighting was 2 headlights about two-thirds towards the top of the front panel, surmounted by two front side lights.

At the rear there was a single rear light and a brake light mounted towards the bottom of the rear offside lower-deck panel or fitted behind a small access panel, immediately above the square offside registration number plate, which also illuminated the rear registration number plate immediately beneath.

A spotlight was recessed into the front panel below the nearside headlight; again there were differences between batches, 10 and 11 (Weymann) having the spotlight centred immediately beneath the headlight; 8, 9, 12 and 13 (Park Royal) having the spotlight somewhat towards the vehicle centre line; and that on 14 and 15 (Roe) being recessed into the removable towing hatch.

Internal lighting was provided by exposed tungsten bulbs arranged in groups in series and fed from the traction supply. In the lower saloon one light was mounted in the ceiling cove panels of each bay on both the nearside and the offside. In the upper saloon lights were mounted centrally in the ceiling cove panels in bays 1–4 on both sides, bay 5 on the nearside, and over the staircase above the offside rearmost window, i.e. six lights each side, with an additional light mounted centrally in the front dome. There was an additional lamp on the platform.

Internal emergency lighting was provided by means of two separate lights on each deck fed from 12-volt batteries stored in a box beneath one of the lower saloon seats. Their location varied between body builders; however, one was always located upstairs on the offside over the stairwell.

**Seating:** Wooden thinly-slatted seats and backs on both decks with wooden upper frames and diagonal cross-members, based on painted pressed steel lower frames (each body builder having its own design). The forward facing seats had cigarette stubbers affixed centrally at the rear of the wooden top rail.

The lower saloon had a three-person inwards-facing bench seat on each side over the rear axle and five rows of forwards-facing double seats. The upper saloon had seven rows of double seats on the offside and eight rows on the nearside, the eighth seat at the rear of the upper saloon above the open platform also accommodating two passengers.

The driver's seat had a pleated squab and back in leather.

**Destination equipment:** A single rectangular indicator box capable of displaying up to two lines of information in large lettering was mounted centrally at the front on the blue-painted panels above the driver's cab windscreen. The vehicles had no indicator boxes at the rear or above the platform. The box had noticeably square corners to match the design of the windows.

There were differences in the positioning of the front indicator box on the blue-painted front panels above the driver's cab windscreen between body builders:

8–9, 12–13 Park Royal placed the box at the base of the panel.

10–11 Weymann fitted a large rectangular indicator box 36½in. × 20in. centrally half way up the panel.

14–15 Roe fitted a large rectangular indicator box 36½in. × 20in. centrally half way up the panel.

**Internal Livery:** White ceilings and cove panels. The windows were surrounded by varnished wood frames with blue painted panels below. The floors were covered with lino with wooden wearing strips in the gangways. Grey platform floor. Driver's cab brown.

**Upper saloon interior of South Shields 236 showing that Pontypridd's wooden slatted seats were retained (although upholstered seat squabs may have been added at a later date) but after replacement of the original upper-deck front windows and pull-in hopper ventilators with larger rubber-mounted fixed panes. (F.W. Ivey)**

Doverite covered rods or rails protected the window panes in bay 5 and the rearmost windows on the offside of the upper saloon, the front upper saloon windows, the windows in the rear emergency door and the lower-deck rear platform window.

**External Livery:** Primrose yellow and blue (see Appendix C).

8 and 9 were delivered with the primrose painted area around the lower saloon windows continued some 6in. beneath the waistrail giving the impression of a waistband and sweeping down towards the front of the vehicle beneath the cab windows, the undertaking initials in bays 2, 3, 4 being transferred onto this primrose area. Both vehicles were subsequently repainted into the standard livery application.

8 was repainted into an all blue livery of a non-standard darker shade with aluminium painted roof shortly before withdrawal.

**Subsequent alterations:** Red reflectors were fitted at the same height as the rear light about one third of the way up the rear panel beneath the platform window, at the outer extremities of the panel, in 1954.

It is understood that the vehicles were never equipped with semaphore arm illuminated traffic indicators.

**Notes:** In 1934 Karrier Motors Ltd. had been rescued from receivership by Humber Ltd. and had thus become part of the Rootes Group, as was Sunbeam Commercial Vehicles Ltd. When the Ministry of War Transport authorised the construction of a limited number of utility trolleybuses orders were placed either with Karrier at Luton or Sunbeam at Wolverhampton. The resultant W vehicles were, however, identical, incorporating features of the pre-war Karrier E4 and Sunbeam MF2 two axle trolleybus.

The term "utility" was not an official description applied to vehicles and bodies built in the war, both "utility" and "austerity" being terms then in general use to describe any article, from furniture through to railway engines, made in this period that were not to peacetime standards. The specification for "utility bodywork" was drawn up by the National Federation of Vehicle Trades (NFVT) in conjunction with operators, the MoS and the MoWT, and was titled "General Works Specification for Standard Double-deck Bodywork (or Standard Single-deck Bodywork) of Wartime Design and Construction as approved by the Ministries of Supply and War Transport". There were written specifications, general arrangement drawings and more specific drawings, e.g. covering the "wooden slatted seat", issued at varying times during the period 1942 to 1945 by the NFVT. Pontypridd's Park Royal utility trolleybus bodies fitted to 8–9 and 12–13 most closely resembled the NFVT general arrangement drawings.

The utility bodywork suffered considerably from the use of unseasoned wood.

**Disposal:** 8, 9 sold to South Shields Corporation Transport in April 1957.
10, 11 sold to Doncaster Corporation Transport in January 1957.
12, 13 sold to South Shields Corporation Transport in April 1957.
14, 15 sold to Walsall Corporation Transport in November 1955.

## 10–11 Doncaster

Doncaster Leyland TS7 (DT7615) tow wagon made two journeys to Pontypridd to collect the trolleybuses; however, the first journey with 11 along a route having no low bridges in pre-motorway days was fraught with difficulties. Reportedly the towing gang had to remove part of the upper-deck structure en route to clear a low bridge. This led to a decision not to undertake the second journey until the top deck of 10 had been removed and the vehicle was decapitated in Pontypridd prior to departure on 1 February 1957. The remaining body of 10 and the complete body of 11 were removed by Doncaster Corporation Transport and sold to Martin (breakers), Toll Bar, Doncaster.

The chassis were renovated by Doncaster Corporation Transport and then sent to Charles Roe, Leeds for new H34/28R bodies before entering service on 1 October 1957 as Doncaster 351 (Pontypridd 10) and 352 (11), these being the only Pontypridd trolleybuses to be rebodied. It is believed that the original seat frames were reused.

In 1959/60 the original EE406/8M traction motor fitted to Doncaster 351 burnt-out and was replaced with a new Metropolitan-Vickers MV207A3 85hp motor. The vehicle was out of service for some time as parts of the wiring had to be redesigned to accommodate the change of motor. Doncaster 352 retained its English Electric traction motor until withdrawal.

After withdrawal on 30 March 1962, the chassis were sold to Bolland (breaker) Wakefield, 351 in April and 352 in May. The bodies survived to be fitted to new motorbus chassis.

Doncaster Corporation's 352 featured a new 1957 Roe H34/28R body on the overhauled Karrier W chassis of Pontypridd 11. No. 352 awaits departure time in St. Sepulchre Gate. (BTS Library [photographer R. Simpson])

Roe body ex-trolleybus 351 to Daimler CVG6 170 (170GDT) 7 July 1962 withdrawn 25 April 1972 after overturning in a crash.

Roe body ex-trolleybus 352 to Daimler CVG6 171 (171GDT) 15 August 1962 withdrawn by South Yorkshire PTE 1 April 1974

## 14–15 Walsall

The Sunbeam Trolleybus Co. Ltd., which was then in the process of supplying Walsall Corporation Transport with 22 new 30ft long Sunbeam F4A chassis, towed the Pontypridd vehicles to Walsall in December 1955. These were the first secondhand trolleybuses to be bought by Walsall.

Prior to re-entering service in April and March 1956 respectively as Walsall 301 (Pontypridd 14) and 302 (15), the vehicles were overhauled, fitted with upholstered seats and repainting into the undertaking's bright blue livery. It is known that after some weeks in service 301 was off the road until July 1956. Other than this the vehicles remained little changed during their years in Walsall.

301 was last used on 12 November 1961 and withdrawn from stock on 18 February 1962; 302 was last used on 4 October 1962 and withdrawn from stock on 6 January 1963.

301 sold to B. Jackson (dealer), Bradford in June 1962 and broken up.

302 sold to B. Jackson (dealer), Bradford in March 1963 and broken up.

## 8–9, 12–13 South Shields

Each vehicle received a major body overhaul before entering service in South Shields during which the front indicator box was reduced in size to the operator's standard format accommodating a blind displaying the final destination in a single line. A separate, square service number indicator box was built into the upper-deck front panels on the nearside of the destination indicator box and a further destination indicator box was built into the base of upper-deck nearside panels immediately above the open rear platform. The spotlight was removed. Supporting hooks were secured to the nearside cantrail or vent panel above the driver's cab rear bulkhead and above the lower saloon window pillar between bays 4 and 5 to carry the bamboo trolley retrieval pole. The vehicles were repainted into the operator's royal blue and pale primrose livery (much lighter than that in Pontypridd) with a medium grey roof and black mudguards.

At some later date in South Shields the seats in the lower saloon were replaced with utility upholstered seats and upholstered squabs (retaining slatted seat backs) were also fitted in the upper saloon. On some vehicles a roof-mounted bracket secured a transverse rod which extended across much of the width of the vehicle to avoid roof damage when pulling down the trolley poles and stowing them beneath the restraining hooks. The following subsequent alterations were made to individual vehicles:

236 the upper-deck front windows and pull-in hopper ventilators were removed and replaced by larger rubber-mounted fixed panes effectively combining the two apertures, and the metal louvres were cut back to the shape of the windows.

238, 239 the half-drop openers in the upper and lower-deck saloon side windows were removed and replaced by sliding openers fitted in bays 1, 3 of the upper saloon both sides and bays 2, 4 of the lower saloon both sides.

239 round-corner rubber-mounted panes replaced the original upper-deck front windows but the pull-in hopper ventilators were retained.

Structurally Walsall's two ex-Pontypridd trolleybuses were unchanged throughout their lives. Walsall Roe-bodied Karrier W 302 (Pontypridd 15) waits at a rather dismal suburban stop. (Photographer's name not recorded)

All ex-Pontypridd trolleybuses were withdrawn following the closure of South Shields' Marsden routes on 1 May 1963.

236 sold to J. Douglas (breaker), Newcastle upon Tyne in May 1963 and broken up.

237 sold to J. Douglas (breaker), Newcastle upon Tyne in April 1963 and broken up.

238 sold to an unknown breaker in Gilesgate, County Durham in May 1963 and broken up.

239 sold to J. Douglas (breaker), Newcastle upon Tyne in April 1963 and broken up.

Pontypridd 12 stands outside South Shields Corporation Transport's Chichester Depot prior to reconditioning. The rear of Pontypidd 8, in darker blue livery with aluminium painted roof, can be seen in front of No. 12. (BTS Library [photographer R.F. Mack])

Following a major body overhaul in which, amongst other things, the upper-deck front panels were rebuilt to incorporate the new operator's standard destination and service number displays, and the half-drop openers in the upper and lower-deck saloon side windows were removed and replaced by sliding openers, South Shields 239 (formerly Pontypridd 13) is seen at the Market terminus of service 4. Northern Counties bodied Karrier W, fleet number 259, waits behind at the service 12 stop. (BTS Library [photographer R. Simpson])

# APPENDIX B
# WARTIME LOANS

At the outbreak of the Second World War the ongoing reconstruction programme was well underway, involving one trolleybus at a time being taken into the workshops for long periods. The fleet was also depleted by regular maintenance work and by occasional accident damage. The number of passengers carried rose rapidly from 1,836,000 in 1937 to 2,698,000 in 1941 and continued to rise to 3,958,000 by 1945 whilst the operating day also became longer, both reflecting the importance of Pontypridd's staple industries to the war effort.

Between 1941 and 1946 there were two different loans of trolleybuses to Pontypridd, the first from Kingston upon Hull and the second from Portsmouth. There was a similar loan of motorbuses from London Transport.

## 1–4 Leyland TB4

| Owner's Fleet No. | Reg. No. | Chassis type | No. | Elec. Equip. | Body | No. | Into service | Delivered to Pontypridd | Departed Pontypridd | Withdrawn |
|---|---|---|---|---|---|---|---|---|---|---|
| 1 | CRH925 | Leyland TB4 | 12280 | Metrovick | Weymann | 5107 | 01.06.1937 | 19.08.1941 | 08.1942 | 02.1952 |
| 2 | CRH926 | Leyland TB4 | 12281 | Metrovick | Weymann | 5108 | 01.06.1937 | 19.08.1941 | 08.1942 | 06.1953 |
| 3 | CRH927 | Leyland TB4 | 12282 | Metrovick | Weymann | 5109 | 17.07.1937 | 26.08.1941 | 08.1942 | 07.1953 |
| 4 | CRH928 | Leyland TB4 | 12283 | Metrovick | Weymann | 5110 | 17.07.1937 | 26.08.1941 | 08.1942 | 07.1952 |

The details below refer to the vehicles as supplied on loan to Pontypridd – not as originally delivered to Kingston upon Hull Corporation Transport Department.

Chassis: Two-axle type Leyland TB4 manufactured by Leyland Motors Ltd., Leyland, Lancashire. Leyland drawing 19280 of 1936.
Motor: Metropolitan-Vickers Ltd., Type MV 201 EV (80hp at 550 volts) regulated field.
Electrical equipment: Metropolitan-Vickers Co. Ltd., Trafford Park, Manchester, augmented field regenerative contactor control.
Dewirement indicator: Assumed to have been equipped with line-lights.
Brakes: Westinghouse compressed air, hand and rheostatic brakes.
Body: Weymann H28/26R. (Body numbers 5107–5110) MCW Drawing number 1352/1.
Length: 25ft 10³⁄₁₆in. (KHCT drawing A.1018) Width 7ft 6in. over wings, 7ft 3½in. over body pillars. Height: 15ft 5³⁄₁₆in. unladen
Wheelbase: 16ft 3in. giving a turning circle on either lock of 52ft.
Unladen weight: 6 tons 19cwt 0qtrs
Tyres: 36 × 8 on all wheels.

In the period June–August 1937 Kingston upon Hull Corporation Transport took delivery of their first trolleybuses, 26 two-axle Leyland TB4 vehicles equipped with Weymann bodies with which to commence their tram to trolleybus conversion programme. They carried Hull fleet numbers 1–26, registration numbers CRH925–950. Trolleybus operations in Hull began on 23 July 1937 when service 61 King Edward Street – Chanterlands Avenue North was introduced, to be followed by an ongoing expansion. By early 1940 there were 66 vehicles in stock but as a result of a reduced local population following heavy air raids, evacuation and conscription, these were more than the undertaking reasonably required and surplus trolleybuses were offered on loan. Understandably Pontypridd was offered some of the earliest deliveries.

Hull trolleybuses 1 and 2 reached Pontypridd on 19 August 1941 followed by 3 and 4 on 26 August 1941. Two vehicles returned on 10 August 1942 and the remaining two on 17 August 1942. Upon their return to Hull they were allocated to Wheeler Street Garage and used on service 69 Anlaby Road; however, by the beginning of the 1950s, as the oldest vehicles in the fleet, they were deemed surplus to requirements.

Chassis: based on the contemporary Leyland TD4 motorbus chassis and axles; indeed the initial contact with Leyland and the Hull Transport Committee Minutes dated 29 July 1936 refer to TD4 trolleybus chassis. The frame was of channel construction with tubular cross members for rigidity.

Marles steering arranged for a fore and aft drag link with a nickel-steel forged front axle. Full-floating rear axle with underslung worm drive. The worm centre was 8in. in diameter

Two axle Leyland TB4 chassis for Kingston upon Hull Corporation Transport Department photographed at the Leyland Motors works, Leyland, Lancashire. (Malcolm Wells collection)

and the ratio was 9.33 to 1. The axle shafts had round splines and a diameter of 1¾in. There were four oil seals, one on each shaft and one on each hub, to prevent grease from reaching the brake shoes.

Semi-elliptic pattern springs, all shackles being adjustable for end play. Rubber bumper blocks were provided on the front and rear spring assemblies.

The chassis cost £989 each.

**Electrics:** The trolley collector gear was equipped with trolley wheel heads (Hull commenced replacing these with slipper heads from 1942). The 18ft 9in. long trolley booms, when restrained by the retaining hooks, extended 3 ft beyond the rear-most part of the bodywork.

In 1928 Metropolitan-Vickers (Metrovick) merged with British Thomson-Houston (BTH) and in January 1929 both companies were amalgamated into Associated Electrical Industries Limited (AEI). This resulted in a history of commercial rivalry between the two firms which even Sir Felix Pole, formerly the successful General Manager of the Great Western Railway and AEI Chairman from 1931, failed to bring under control.

The main control gear was of unit construction and featured the assembly of all electrical control items on a single insulating base, mounted in a rounded-top cabinet to the nearside of the

Kingston upon Hull Corporation Transport Leyland TB4 trolleybus no. 1 exemplifying the pre-war azure blue and white streamlined livery in which it entered service in June 1937. Some five year later it was hired to Pontypridd UDC to assist the South Wales undertaking with its growing wartime loans. Geoff O'Connell (Malcolm Wells collection)

driver's seat, rigidly attached to the chassis and backing on to the cab bulkhead. Metropolitan-Vickers controller.

The motor windings and rear axle ratio gave the vehicles a balancing speed of 35mph on the level when fully loaded.

A radio interference suppressor, to meet Ministry of Transport requirements, was mounted centrally on the roof immediately in front of the trolley bases.

A CAV-Bosch DBLR dynamo front-end mounted on the traction motor provided auxiliary low-voltage lighting.

**Brakes:** Rheostatic braking on the brake pedal was used down to 4mph, further pressure on the brake pedal at this speed bringing the compressed air brake into use. A ¾hp compressor of 5 cubic ft capacity controlled by an automatic governor supplied the Westinghouse air brakes.

RP automatic brake adjuster thereby taking up wear on the brake linings to ensure that they were kept at a predetermined distance from the drums.

The handbrake lever was to the offside of the driver's steering column.

**Bodywork:** Composite five-bay highbridge double-deck construction, enclosed forwards-ascending half-turn (90°) staircase with conventional semi-vestibuled open platform entrance and exit at the rear, and integral trolley gantry built by Weymann Motor Bodies Ltd., Addlestone, Surrey (marketed by Metropolitan Cammell-Weymann Motor Bodies Ltd.). The body cost £955.

Beclawat "Typhoon" half-drop openers having "pinch fasteners" mounted centrally at the top of each pane were fitted to the tops of the side windows in bays 1, 3 and 5 (both sides) of the upper-deck and bays 2–4 (both sides) of the lower-deck.

The front upper-deck windows were fixed. The side windows of the upper and lower-deck saloon windows had radiused bottom corners and were surmounted by metal louvres. Above the lower saloon windows in bays 1, 3, 5 on both sides in the cantrail or centre vent panel there were a series of 10 ventilation vents slanting rearwards somewhat from the vertical at the top. A gutter moulding ran along the top of the centre vent panel on both sides from above the foremost driver's cab side window to the rear of bay 5 shielding the gap along the edge of the top deck floor which provided a drain for water from wet clothing and footwear. The front upper-saloon windows were surmounted by two horizontal ventilator slats, a Weymann feature of the period, positioned towards the centre line of the vehicle and surrounded by a curved moulding. The rear upper-deck emergency exit was bottom hinged and divided vertically into two almost square windows having radiused corners, the radii at the top being greater than those at the bottom.

The roof was fitted with a gutter moulding across the top of the upper saloon front and side windows at cantrail level, following the curve of the rearmost side windows to pass beneath the rear upper saloon emergency exit at upper-deck waistrail level. To prevent water-ingress there was a second gutter moulding across the rear dome above the rear emergency exit. There were four Ashanco extractor ventilators in the roof mounted towards the rear of the panelling above bays 3 and 5.

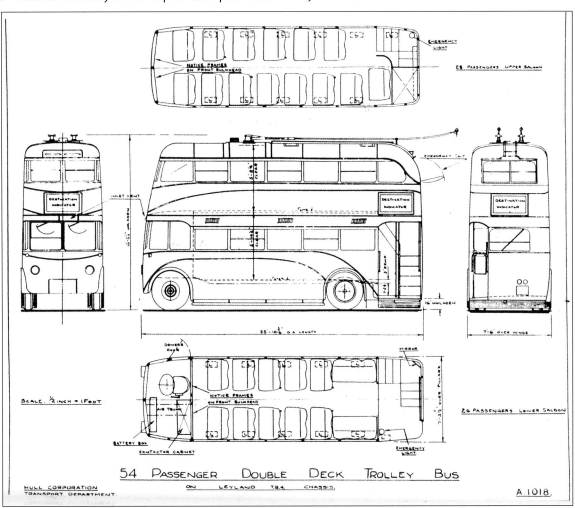

54 PASSENGER DOUBLE DECK TROLLEY BUS

HULL CORPORATION TRANSPORT DEPARTMENT. ON LEYLAND T.B.4 CHASSIS. A.1018.

There was a noticeably deep step from the open rear platform into the lower saloon. The staircase had four steps to the half-landing and then four steps to the upper-deck, all with cork tile treads and Alumalun non-slip nosings. A conductor's mirror was fixed in the upper saloon rear dome at the head of the stairs.

The driver's cab had a single, offside opening windscreen equipped with a top-mounted windscreen wiper affixed centrally above the pane. The fixed nearside windscreen was also equipped with a top-mounted windscreen wiper. There was an offside front-hinged door equipped with a sliding "signalling" window in the lower half of the pane. The waist rail beneath the cab side windows and windscreens was at the same height as the lower-saloon waist rail but the windows were deeper, the top of the rearmost side pane of the cab curving upwards to meet the top of the foremost side pane which itself gradually deepened slightly towards the front of the trolleybus.

A sheet of protective aluminium reached from the lintel of the driver's cab door to approximately the height of the top of the chromed wheel nut protector ring, immediately behind the front axle on the offside. There were two glazed panels, separated by a solid central panel about 1ft wide, in the bulkhead behind the driver. The offside glazed panel was divided vertically into two equal panes which could be slid transversely to communicate with the driver. A small rectangular driver's rear view mirror was mounted externally above the driver's cab offside side window immediately to the rear of the front pillar.

A top-hinged removable access panel which carried the rectangular pressed aluminium registration number plate at its base extended across the front of the cab from beneath the inner edge of the offside to beneath the inner edge of the nearside headlamp. Although there were variations between individual vehicles, photographic evidence suggests that whilst in Pontypridd the panel incorporated four horizontal fluted columns, the two outermost having five ventilator vanes each and the other two having four ventilator vanes each (a fifth vane would have been covered by the registration plate).

The rear platform window had all four corners radiused, the top being of greater radius than those at the bottom in the Weymann style of the period. There was a used ticket box immediately below the nearside vestibule window on the rear open platform. The rear registration number plate was mounted at the rear offside of the lower-deck rear panel.

A single lifeguard ran beneath the side panels between the front and rear axles. A bamboo trolley retrieval pole was carried in a tube mounted centrally under the chassis. Individual mud flaps hung behind each wheel with a further broad mud flap diagonally beneath the rear platform.

**Lighting:** External lighting was two protruding chromium-plated headlights with dishings behind on the front panel, two front side lights (resembling the front light of a bicycle) on stems at the side of the vehicle on the streamline lower-deck waistband in line with the front corner pillars of the driver's cab. A single rear light and brake light were fitted above the square sign written registration number plate at the base of the offside rear panel, the rear light being to the offside of the brake light.

The vehicles were delivered to Hull without a fog light. These were top-mounted to an angle arm bracket attached to the bottom edge (rather than beneath) of the front panel on the nearside just inwards of the nearside headlight.

These trolleybuses entered service in Pontypridd at the time of wartime lighting restrictions. The headlights were equipped with masks whilst the side light glasses were partially covered to emit solely a point of light.

Interior lights were equipped with rectangular diffused glass covers and chromium-plated frames, and were fitted in the cove panels on each side in each bay of both the upper and lower saloons (10 lamps on each deck), with a single fitting on the offside of the upper-deck above the staircase. In addition there was a single exposed light in the ceiling of the open rear platform above the nearside bulkhead. The interior lighting was fed from the traction power supply. Emergency lights were fitted in the upper saloon rear dome at the head of the stairs and above the nearside vestibule window on the rear open platform.

Wartime lighting restrictions meant that all the interior lights were fitted with a metal plate having a small slot in it that cast a rectangle of light onto the floor. Alternately the bulb inside the light fitting was removed.

**Seating:** Based on painted Dean's swept-top tubular steel frames with chromium-plated top shaped to a "butterfly" pattern. Squabs and backs in the lower-saloon were upholstered in Lister figured red moquette in a neo-Paisley design whilst those in the upper-saloon were upholstered with Connolly's brown leather with scratchproof brown Rexine leather cloth backs. The lower-saloon had a three-person bench seat over the rear axle on both sides and five rows of forwards-facing double seats. The upper saloon had seven rows of double seats on the nearside with a further double seat somewhat inset towards the centre line of the vehicle above the open rear platform, and six rows of double seats on the offside. The seats on the upper-deck were staggered to provide more space on the offside at the top of the staircase. The driver's seat was in quilted brown hide.

In both saloons 6ft long tubes containing heating elements were affixed to the internal side panels beneath the seats.

**Destination equipment:** Single large (36in. × 24in.) rectangular indicator boxes with square corners were mounted on the upper-deck panels somewhat lower than usual to align with the streamlined livery application at the front above the driver's cab windscreen and at the rear above the rear platform window. A further rectangular indicator box of the same size and equipped with a gutter above was fitted on the nearside immediately above the open rear platform entrance.

The boxes were equipped with Kelbus winding mechanisms for the indicator blinds but it is understood that whilst in Pontypridd the loaned vehicles ran without any destination blinds.

**Internal Livery:** Ceilings and coves were painted white with polished walnut used for all window frames and wooden ceiling mouldings. Side panels below the waist rail were covered with scratchproof brown Rexine leather cloth. The front bulkhead of the lower saloon was covered with red fluted rubber to match the upholstery. Handrails and stanchions were covered in black Doverite. The saloon floors were covered in brown linoleum.

Internal advertisement frames were mounted above the glazed panels in the bulkhead at the rear of the driver's cab and above the front windows in the upper saloon. A glass-fronted

Interior view of the lower saloon of a Weymann bodied Kingston upon Hull Corporation Transport Department Leyland TB4 trolleybus as loaned to Pontypridd UDC from August 1941 to August 1942. (Photographer's name not recorded).

panel in the rear bulkhead to the rear of the longitudinal offside seat in the lower saloon was used to display fares and timetable information.

**External Livery:** Hull's colour scheme, adopted in 1936 as standard, of azure blue with three white bands painted at the lower-deck waistband that is below the lower-deck windows, at the cantrail or centre vent panel that is above the lower-deck windows, and the upper-deck waistband that is below the upper-deck windows. The white bands at the lower and upper-deck waistband level swooped down towards the front of the vehicle in a streamlined style, popular in the period. The lower-deck waistband also swooped down and widened towards the rear reaching the base of the side panels in the rear axle area. The upper-deck waistband widened somewhat to the rear but had no streamlining effect in that area. There was no lower-deck waistband at the rear. The beading edging the white bands and streamlining were black. Mudguards were black and wheels were blue.

The City of Kingston upon Hull coat of arms was displayed on both sides of the lower-deck side panels, centred in bay 3; centrally between the headlights on the front dash and centrally at the rear beneath the rear platform window.

The upper-deck side panels were emblazoned with word HULL in large underlined gold block capital lettering shaded light blue and white, with CORPORATION TRANSPORT in much smaller blue block capital letters shaded light blue along the cantrail above the lower-deck side windows.

In May 1941 Hull started to paint the white bands and streamlining matt blue to reduce the trolleybuses visibility from the air. The beading edging to the streamlining remained black. In order to avoid applying new transfers the immediate area around CORPORATION TRANSPORT on the cantrail was left white but the coat of arms on the front dash was painted over although the fleet number was retained. The limited photographic evidence of the vehicles in Pontypridd suggests that this repainting had been carried out on 1–4 prior to their departure. The base of the front and rear panels, all mudguards and the side lifeguards were painted white to fulfil wartime "blackout" restrictions. The Hull trolleybuses thus operated in Pontypridd in their home city's full wartime livery continuing to display HULL along the upper-deck side panels.

**Disposal:**

1   Withdrawn in February 1952 and placed in store. Deleted from stock on 28.02.53 and cannibalised for spares being subsequently broken up by Kingston upon Hull Corporation Transport.

2   Withdrawn June 1953. Sold to Autowreckers, Clough Road, Hull, Yorkshire, breakers, on 11.09.53.

3   Withdrawn July 1953. Sold to Autowreckers , Clough Road, Hull, Yorkshire, breakers, on 11.09.53.

4   Withdrawn in July 1952 and placed in store. Deleted from stock on 30.09.52 and cannibalised for spares being subsequently broken up by Kingston upon Hull Corporation Transport.

## 212 AEC663T

| Owner's Fleet No. | Reg. No. | Chassis type | No. | Elec. Equip. | Body | Into service | Delivered to Pontypridd | Departed Pontypridd | Withdrawn |
|---|---|---|---|---|---|---|---|---|---|
| 212 | RV4658 | AEC663T | 074 | Eng. Electric | Eng. Electric | 14.08.1934 | 08.08.1942 | 04.1946 | 04.1946 |

The details below refer to the vehicle as supplied on loan to Pontypridd – not as originally delivered to the City of Portsmouth Passenger Transport Department (as the undertaking was known by 1942).

Chassis: Three axle type AEC 663T manufactured by the Associated Equipment Company Ltd. at the AEC works, Windmill Lane, Southall, Middlesex.
Motor: English Electric Co. Ltd., Phoenix Works, Bradford, Yorkshire, Type EE 405 (80hp at 550 volts) compound-wound, regenerative.
Electrical equipment: English Electric Co. Ltd., regenerative control.
Dewirement indicator: neon line-light.
Brakes: Westinghouse compressed air, English Electric electric rheostatic and hand brakes.
Body: English Electric Co. Ltd., Dick, Kerr Works, Preston, Lancashire, composite H32/28R.Drawing PB33/1226 dated 2 October 1933.
Length: Not known, recommended body length in 1933–34 was 26ft. Width 7ft 4in. over pillars.
Height laden 14ft 1in.
Wheelbase: 16ft 6in.
Bogie wheelbase: 4ft.
Wheel track: front 6ft 5⅜in., rear 6ft 2¾in.
Unladen weight: 8 tons 6cwt 2qtrs.
Tyres: 36 × 8 high-pressure pneumatic singles on all wheels.
Frame overall length 26ft 9in.
Height of frame laden 22½in.
Turning circle diameter: 59ft.
Chassis weight: 4 tons 4cwt.

**Chassis:** Conventional cranked chassis frame over rear bogie based on the AEC Regent 663 motorbus chassis and axles.

The side members were pressed out of ⁵⁄₁₆in. steel with a maximum depth of 11⅛in. and 3in. wide flanges swept over the front and rear axles to permit the mounting of a low floor level body. The arches over the rear bogie were reinforced by inserted channels of the same thickness. The frame was held rigid by tubular cross-members; however, there were no dumb irons, the ends of the frame channels being left open and protruding about 10in. in front of the foremost cross-member.

The axles were made from 100-ton steel 3in. in diameter and mounted on adjustable taper roller bearings. Chrome vanadium spring steel torque blade permitting freedom of motion of each axle. The socket attachments of this cross-member formed a rigid assembly with the front end of the front axle spring anchorages and, on the offside, the steering box. The rear ends of the 50in. long front axle spring are shackled by a similar arrangement to the second chassis cross-member. The 57in. long cantilever springs of the rear axles were centrally pivoted upon needle-roller trunnion bearings carried by cast-steel brackets mounted beneath the wheel arches, to which they were riveted and joined by a large cross-tube. The ends of the springs had solid eyes and were anchored to brackets under the axle tubes.

The rear axles were one-piece nickel steel forgings with fully floating shafts, the drive being from underslung worms with 7in. centres (ratio 10.3 to 1). Forged alloy steel hubs.

There was a short tubular propeller shaft, fitted with a Hardy-Spicer needle-roller self-aligning bearing universal joint at each end, connecting the traction motor with the foremost rear axle where there was a third differential to ensure an

AEC663T/English Electric 12 in London Road, Hilsea, outside the 'Coach & Horses' public house on 16 September 1934. (D.A.P. Janes [photographer G.A. Tucker])

even distribution of the driving torque between the two rear axles.

AEC Marles worm and nut steering.

The chassis including electrical equipment cost £1,230.

**Electrics:** The series-wound box frame self-ventilated inter-polar traction motor was mounted amidships and offset to the nearside between the chassis frame members. There was a single armature mounted in roller bearings. Carbon brushes were carried in four holders provided with radial adjustment, and inspection of the commutator and brush gear was facilitated by two large removable covers. The armature bearings were packed with grease, requiring replenishment by grease gun every 3 months. The armature could be easily removed. The ventilator fan was fitted at the rear end of the armature shaft. Maximum temperature rise 35°C under service conditions, well below the maximum of BESA requirements. At the rear end of the armature shaft there was a speedometer drive.

All electrical equipment, including the contactor panel, was mounted in an insulated unit on the nearside chassis frame member. There were two groups of cables carried under the frame channel sheathed in rubber ply tubing. Radio interference coils were mounted on the roof in front of the trolley gantry.

The upper-deck body pillars slotted into the wooden rail of the framework above the upper saloon windows, i.e. the cantrail. There were curved steel brackets bolted to the metal roof (inside the roof there was a steel strengthening plate on each side) and each end of the three transverse pressed steel girders, between bays 1 and 2, bays 2 and 3, and bays 3 and 4, supporting the exposed trolley gantry, which was not in direct contact with the roof, rested on these brackets, each foot being secured by four metal bolts.

The main power cable made its way forward from the trolley gantry along the centre line of the roof before it entered the front dome about 1ft 6in. to the rear of the metal louvres above the front upper-deck windows. The vehicle was equipped with Brecknell, Willis & Co. Ltd., Bristol, lightweight trolley equipment and trolley bases. The booms were 18ft 6in. long, equipped with dewirement buffers and allowed for up to 13ft deviation from the centre line of the overhead. A radio interference suppressor was mounted centrally in front of the trolley gantry. The access catwalk on the roof had two steps above the rear dome beneath the trolley boom retaining hooks.

Traction batteries for manoeuvring purposes were not fitted.

**Brakes:** A Westinghouse two-cylinder reciprocating compressor with 5 cubic ft capacity and driven by an EEC 500-volt motor was carried on the offside of the chassis frame, from which it was electrically and mechanically insulated. The compressor was equipped with an anti-freezer, the intake to which was connected by a short rubber tube (for insulation) to one of the chassis cross members, which was utilised as an intake silencer, the air being admitted at the farther end through a filter. The air reservoir and governor were attached forward of the compressor on insulated mountings with a buffer chamber on the compressor side of the valve. The governor was set to maintain a reservoir pressure of 85 lb per sq.in. and the control valve was operated by an organ type pedal mounted on the bracket carrying both the valve and power pedal. Reservoir and brake cylinder pressures were shown on gauges on the dashboard attached to the driver's steering column.

The front brake drums were 17in. diameter castings with 3in. wide facings ¾in. thick. The track rods were adjustable by means of screwed and clipped ends. All four wheels of the rear bogie were fitted with 17in. diameter brake drums having 6in. wide facings ¾in. thick. The total effective brake area was 825 sq.in.

Apart from a single flexible pipe connection, all air piping was solid drawn steel. Air cylinders were mounted on the cross tube in front of the rear bogie, whence rod connections were taken to double-armed levers on a cross-shaft carried behind the central bogie cross-member. The lower arms of the levers were coupled by pull rods to the cam levers on the leading axle and by tubular push-rods to the rear axle levers. The same mechanism was used by the handbrake. The front wheel brake cylinders were mounted on top of the king pins, the piston rods passing through the borings in the latter and operating directly on the camshaft.

Regenerative braking was obtained by the driver relieving pressure on the master controller (power) pedal so that the controller returned towards the full field position. Braking was increased as the pedal rose and strengthened the shunt field in stages. In the first notch positions rheostatic braking was obtained. Regeneration was effective down to a speed of ca. 12mph and rheostatic braking down to ca. 4mph.

Pull-on handbrakes linked by a cross-shaft, and pull and push rods to the camshaft levers and expanding in the bogie wheel brake drums to operate on the same pairs of shoes as those operated by the air brake system. The handbrake lever was to the offside of the driver's steering column.

**Bodywork:** Highbridge double-deck composite six-bay construction with conventional, enclosed forwards-ascending half-turn (90°) staircase with semi-vestibuled open platform entrance and exit at the rear, and roof ribbing. The body cost £838.

There was a slight "tumble-under" to the lower-deck side and rear panels with a shallow roof. The front elevation rose in a convex rake to the upper-deck waistline. Above the upper-deck waistline the front panel adopted a shallow "V" in plan which was retained for the slightly raked upper saloon front windows. There was a pronounced overhang, incorporating a ventilator above each pane, to the front dome. A double fold at the base of the upper-deck side panels around the vehicle provided a gutter. The trolley poles were fitted on an exposed roof-mounted gantry above bays 2 and 3. A conventional quarter-turn staircase rose from the open rear platform.

Metal louvres were fitted above the upper and lower saloon side windows. Half-drop openers equipped with a single "pinch fastener" mounted centrally at the top of each pane were fitted to the top rail of the side windows in bays 1, 3, 5 on both sides of the upper-deck, and bays 2, 3, 4 on both sides of the lower-deck. The upper saloon front windows were fixed. The upper pane dropped outside the fixed lower pane. Additional ventilation to the upper saloon was provided by two ventilators in the roof overhang above the front windows located somewhat closer to the corner pillars than to the central pillar, and four roof mounted ventilators (with circular chromed covers inside) positioned midway along bays 1 and 5 on each side. Top hinged access doors were fitted at the base of the lower-deck off-side panel bay 1, 2, 3 and part of bay 4 providing access to the air brake compressor unit. Access doors were also fitted on the nearside from approximately midway across bay 2 to midway across bay 3 providing access to the contactors which were in an insulated unit mounted on the nearside chassis member.

A bamboo trolley retrieval pole was carried externally along the cant rail or ventilator panel on the nearside with three supporting hooks fixed centrally above the pillars between bays 1 and 2, 3 and 4, and 5 and 6.

The top corners of the rear platform window and the top outer corners of the windows of the upper-deck emergency exit were radiused, the gutter around the edge of the roof curving down the upper-deck rear corner panel to end beneath the emergency exit windows (that on the nearside reaching the beading at the base of the upper-deck waistband). There was a rail across the panes at two thirds depth. The rear upper-deck emergency door was retained by four hinges at its base and had a central opening handle at the top; it could be retained open by leather-covered chains on each side to provide access to the trolley gantry.

The emergency door could be opened by an external handle mounted on the rear dome immediately above the rain strip and centrally above the door, or from inside by a comparable handle attached to a horizontal locking bar mounted on the cantrail immediately above the door. The horizontal bar was equipped with three prongs that engaged with brackets on the top of the door.

Small rubber bumpers on the nearside and offside of the emergency exit door aligned with similar bumpers on the nearside and offside top corners of the rear indicator boxes. Handrails were covered in black Doverite.

The staircase had three steps from the platform to the landing and then a further three steps to the upper-deck, each riser having aluminium kicking panels. The platform entrance was 4ft wide. An oblong conductor's mirror was fitted in the upper saloon rear dome above the stairs.

The fleet number was displayed inside the vehicle by a small white Bakelite oval disc screwed at cantrail height above the central front pillar in the upper saloon and on the front bulkhead in the lower saloon upon which the numbers were painted in black.

The driver's cab was equipped with a single opening windscreen on the off-side, the upper pane being approximately double the depth of the lower pane, equipped with a central top-mounted windscreen wiper and painted frame. There was a single nearside fixed windscreen. The shallow windscreen provided the driver with a restricted view of the overhead line above. A small recessed window in the white-painted central band or cantrail above but not as wide as the offside windscreen was added by Portsmouth at an early date to improve the line of vision.

There was a front hinged (three hinges) cab door on the offside only, with a square top. Two rubber bumpers at waistrail height, one on the door and the other on the side panel forward of the door, prevented body damage by a swinging door. The window of the offside cab door was divided horizontally into two panes, the upper portion being slightly deeper than the lower and an inset opening handle. The lower pane was equipped with a sliding "signalling" window, the rear portion sliding forwards behind the front portion. There was a large fixed side window between the cab door and the front offside corner pillar. There was a matching panel and two windows on the nearside, the rear of the two windows being vertically divided and enabling the rear pane to slide forwards outside the fixed front pane. A pronounced, square vent was positioned on both sides of the cab beneath the foremost windows on each side. The driver's cab side windows were the same depth as, and aligned with, the lower saloon

side windows although this was not immediately evident due to the encroachment of the louvres above the saloon windows.

The base of the cab door was curved over the wheel arch to a position about 4 ins from the rear of the door thereafter the base was horizontal, parallel to the white-painted waistband and about 2ft below it. A rectangular step was let into the upper part of the bay 1 side panel access door, but without any form of protection to the bodywork, immediately behind the front axle, on the offside. Individual mud flaps hung behind each wheel with a further mud flap extending the width of the vehicle diagonally beneath the rear platform.

There were two glazed panels in the bulkhead behind the driver, separated by a wide central pillar. A small rectangular driver's rear view mirror was mounted externally towards the top of the offside front cab pillar.

A large removable panel with three columns of eight louvres ventilation vanes extended across the base of the front panel between the two low-mounted headlights (the top of the panel aligned with the top of the headlight rim) with the front registration number plate centred immediately above. A chassis and equipment maker's badge, AEC in an inverted triangle surmounted by the winged EE symbol, was fitted centrally beneath the driver's windscreen on the waistband. The rear registration number plate, encompassing a single red rear light to the offside of the upper row of letters, was affixed to the white-painted panel immediately above the rear platform window on the offside.

A single tubular lifeguard, held by attachments beneath the body panels, ran beneath the side panels between the front and rear axles.

**Lighting:** External lighting was two chrome-rimmed headlights on wooden plinths mounted at the base of the front panel with two front chrome-rimmed side lights also on wooden plinths immediately above mounted slightly more towards the extremity of the panel and aligned with the outer edges of the headlights. A spotlight was mounted beneath the nearside end of the nearside column of ventilation louvres in the removable front panel. A single red rear light was incorporated into the rear registration number plate, immediately above the rear platform window on the offside.

Semaphore arm illuminated traffic indicators accommodated in a black moulding were fitted in the lower half of the driver's cab corner pillars on both sides; however, photographic evidence shows that during its time on loan to Pontypridd UDC there was solely a traffic indicator on the offside. At the rear, an inset panel mounted centrally beneath the rear platform window illuminated to show STOP when the brakes were applied.

There were square diffused light fittings in the ceiling cove panels in the lower saloon mounted centrally in bays 1–6 each side (12); and in the upper saloon in bays 1–6 on each side (12), the position in bay 1 being immediately to the rear of the body pillar but then progressively a little further towards the rear in each bay so that by bay 6 the fitting was in the centre of the bay, and one in the offside of the rear dome above the staircase. There was a further fitting in th rear dome above the staircase and above the rear platform.

This trolleybus entered service in Pontypridd at the time of wartime lighting restrictions. The headlights were equipped with masks whilst the side light glasses were partially covered to emit solely a point of light.

Wartime lighting restrictions meant that all the interior lights were fitted with dulled lamp bulbs equipped with BTCC-style shades.

**Seating:** The lower saloon had a four-person inwards-facing bench seat with 5ft 6in. cushion on each side over the rear axle and five rows of forwards-facing double seats at 2ft 5½in. pitch. The upper saloon had seven rows of double seats at 2ft 7in. pitch on the off-side and 9 rows at 2ft 6in. on the nearside, i.e. the bench seat at the rear of the upper saloon above the open platform also accommodated two passengers. The seat cushions were covered in moquette and all seat fittings painted black. Vertical handrails rose up behind the third and fifth seat on the nearside and the second and fourth seat on the offside of the lower saloon and the third and fifth seat on the nearside and second and fourth seat on the offside of the upper saloon. There were black Doverite coated ceiling mounted handrails equipped with short leather straps above the lower saloon gangway parallel with the longitudinal seats.

The driver's seat was in brown leather.

**Destination equipment:** A large rectangular indicator box 36in. × 14in. capable of displaying up to three lines of information (final destination and two lines of intermediate points) with a square service number indicator box 14in. × 14in. alongside were mounted centrally at the front and rear in the lower two-thirds of the upper-deck panels. At the front the destination and intermediate points indicator box was on the nearside above the driver's cab windscreen (but encroaching a quarter of the way above the offside windscreen) and at the rear on the offside above the rear platform window. At the front the service number indicator box was on the offside and at the rear on the nearside.

In Pontypridd the destination box displayed simply Treforest Cilfynydd in two rows of lettering, the upper row of lettering getting progressively smaller to the right (nearside) and the lower getting progressively larger to the right, whilst the service number box was officially not used although a variety of numbers seems to have been indiscriminately displayed.

There was a narrow box 24in. × 6in. capable of displaying the final destination or the final destination and an intermediate point (two lines) located inside the lower saloon at the top of the bay 6 window both sides. These were not used in Pontypridd.

**Internal Livery:** The interior panels and rear corner panels were lined with scratchproof Rexine with window mouldings and finishings in French-polished walnut. Ceilings cream. The floors were covered in brown linoleum and grey waterproof paint was applied to the rear platform.

**External Livery:** This vehicle operated in Pontypridd in the 1934 Portsmouth livery in which it had been delivered from the manufacturers slightly modified to comply with wartime restrictions but apparently with few of the minor changes introduced during the pre-war years of trolleybus operation in the city. The vehicle had not been used regularly after November 1937 and is unlikely to have ever benefited from a repaint.

The lower-deck and upper-deck window surrounds, upper and lower-deck waistbands, and cantrail or vent panel area above the lower-deck windows were white. On the outbreak of war the roof, which had previously been white, was repainted matt grey extending down the upper-deck rear corner panels on both sides of the rear emergency exit and on the emergency exit door itself. The main upper and lower-deck body panels were painted crimson. Both the lower and upper-deck waistband beadings were picked out in black as were the cantrail beadings.

The crimson panels were lined in tramcar-style double lining, comprising an outer yellow line ³⁄₈in. broad and an inner white line ¹⁄₈in. broad, the yellow line having ornate Greek corner pattern inset square designs and the white line having matching indents. The lining was applied to divide the crimson panels into separate front, side, rear corner, lower saloon platform bulkhead and rear portions. Mudguards and lifeguard rails were black, wheels were maroon. There is no photographic evidence to suggest that the vehicle's extremities, e.g. mudguards and side lifeguard rails were painted white to fulfil wartime "blackout" restrictions. Trolley gear and related equipment, and trolley boom restraining hooks were black.

The City of Portsmouth coat of arms was displayed on both sides of the lower-deck side panels, centred in bay 3.

Ownership details with the General Manager's name and title beneath were applied in small white script typeface at the base of the nearside lower-deck panels, bay 1, immediately to the rear of the front axle. The unladen weight was shown in upper case white typeface at the base of the offside lower-deck panels immediately in front of the (leading) rear axle with the maximum permitted speed in white script typeface behind the rear axle. The seating capacity was indicated in lower case left justified white typeface at the nearside base of the rear platform panel.

Large gold numerals, shaded in two tones of blue and in white, were applied on the upper half of the front panel centrally beneath the driver's cab windscreen and centrally in the lower half of the lower-deck rear platform panels, i.e. allowing space for an advertisement above. In April 1938 the Portsmouth trolleybus fleet was renumbered by the addition of 200 to the original fleet numbers. An additional figure was transferred in advance of the existing fleet number on the front and rear panels, causing the number to be offset, this situation being evident on 212 during its stay in Pontypridd.

Although Portsmouth had commenced adding additional white numerals beneath the lower-deck waistrail and lining on both sides to the rear of the driver's cab rear bulkhead from June 1938 it appears that these had not been added to 212 prior to its departure for Pontypridd.

**Notes:** 212 was withdrawn from service and placed in open storage on waste ground in Northern Parade, Hilsea, Portsmouth in late 1940. In August 1942 it was prepared for loan to Pontypridd UDC and towed to South Wales reaching Pontypridd on 8 August 1942.

At 9.20pm on 25 April 1944 whilst operating in service in Pontypridd, 212 ran away down Corn Stores Hill owing to a braking defect and only due to the driver's skill and reactions was it finally eventually brought to a stop half way across Victoria Bridge thereby preventing a serious accident.

The trolleybus was returned to Portsmouth in April 1946 and stored in Eastney Depot Yard. It was never reinstated into service.

**Disposal:**

212 Withdrawn on 21 April 1953. Sold January 1954 to Kingsway Coachworks (dealer), Emsworth, Hampshire, for £40, but considered unsafe to be moved and broken up in situ January 1954 in Eastney Depot Yard.

# 213 Sunbeam MS3

| Owner's Fleet No. | Reg. No. | Chassis type | No. | Elec. Equip. | Body | Into service | Delivered to Pontypridd | Departed Pontypridd | Withdrawn |
|---|---|---|---|---|---|---|---|---|---|
| 213 | RV4659 | Sunbeam MS3 | 12042S | BTH | Eng. Electric | 06.08.1934 | 14.08.1942 | 03.11.1945 | 21.04.1953 |

The details below refer to the vehicle as supplied on loan to Pontypridd – not as originally delivered to the City of Portsmouth Passenger Transport Department (as the undertaking was known by 1942).

Chassis: Three axle type Sunbeam MS3 manufactured by Sunbeam Motor Car Ltd., Moorfield Road, Wolverhampton.
Motor: British Thomson-Houston Co. Ltd., Rugby, Warwickshire, Type 201BXY (80hp at 550 volts) with overwound series field for regulated field control.
Electrical equipment: British Thomson-Houston Co. Ltd., Rugby, Warwickshire, Regulated Field Control (No. 201 Form DK).
Dewirement indicator: Assumed to have been fitted with line-lights.
Brakes: Lockheed vacuum assisted hydraulic, BTH electric rheostatic and hand brakes.
Body: English Electric Co. Ltd., Dick, Kerr Works, Preston, Lancashire, composite H32/28R. Drawing PB33/1226 dated 2 October 1933.
Length: Not known. Width 7ft 4in. over pillars
Height laden 14ft 1in.
Wheelbase: 16ft 8in. from front axle to centre of bogie.
Bogie wheelbase: 3ft 11¼in.
Unladen weight: 8 tons 13cwt 2qtrs
Tyres: single, 36 × 8in. high pressure all round, giving a turning circle of less than 60ft.
Track: front axle 6ft 6⅜in., rear axle 6ft 6in.

Only in November 1934 did Sunbeam separate its trolleybus activities from its private car business renaming it as Sunbeam Commercial Vehicles Ltd., which from July 1935 became part of the Rootes Group.

The Sunbeam MS3 chassis was designed to take a low-loading double-deck body, the low-loading line being achieved by offsetting the motor and transmission.

All but three of the Sunbeam MS3 chassis built were bought by Wolverhampton Corporation Transport, the exceptions beings Portsmouth 13 and 14, and Huddersfield 4.

**Chassis:** The main frame was constructed from high tensile steel with a depth of 11in. in the most heavily loaded portions and 3in. wide flanges.

Marles cam and roller type steering, requiring 4¼ turns of the wheel from lock to lock. The side steering connection was made from weldless steel tube, the ball sockets being formed solid with the tube.

The front axle was of the reversed Elliott type with an "I" section beam 4in. deep and 3in. wide. The thrust on the king pin was taken on a taper roller bearing. Underslung worm type rear axles, the main axle casing made from a steel drop forging. The differential was made up of four planet wheels and two sun wheels, contained in a steel cage to which was also mounted the worm and wheel (ratio 9.33 to 1). The worms were of hardened and ground steel meshing with phosphor bronze wheel, mounted on ball bearings. A short propeller

On its way south to Southsea South Parade Pier Sunbeam MS3 / English Electric 13 is seen on the Portsmouth system in Kingston Road at New Road on 17 August 1935. The driving position of this trolleybus and other experimental vehicles was rather high and a small recessed window has already been added to improve the driver's view of the overhead line above. (D.A.P. Janes [photographer G.A. Tucker])

shaft, fitted with a universal joint at each end, connected the traction motor with the foremost rear axle where there was a third differential to ensure an even distribution of the driving torque between the two rear axles.

All wheels were fitted with cast steel hubs mounted on taper roller bearings. The front brake drums were 16¾in. diameter Walloy castings with 3⅜in. wide shoes. The track rods were adjustable by means of screwed and clipped ends. All four wheels of the rear bogie were fitted with brake drums of 19¾in. diameter with 4in. wide shoes. The brake shoes on all six drums were suitable for ⅜in. linings.

Chassis length: 27ft 5½in.

Frame height (laden): 2ft

Frame height at platform end (laden): 1ft 11in.

The chassis including electrical equipment cost £1,187.

**Electrics:** The traction motor was mounted on a separate sub-frame amidships but on the offside of the vehicle within the chassis frame. It was attached to the main chassis frame at four points and insulated from the main frame and the transmission to permit the use of all-metal bodies by shock-absorbing and noise-reducing Silentbloc rubber bushes on the steel fixing bolts. The motor protruded a few inches above the top of the frame but as it was located beneath the lower saloon seats it did not encroach on the gangway floor space.

The resistances were also placed amidships mounted on the nearside within the chassis frame with a steel shield and stone guard beneath to protect the grids. The contactor panels were in the driver's cab. The contactors which short-circuited sections of the shunt field resistance were mounted on a panel secured to the dashboard in front of the driver, while those which made and broke the line circuit and short-circuit the starting resistance section were secured to the dashboard and the cab bulkhead. The full field speed was kept at a low figure to reduce rheostatic losses on starting. The master controller was operated by an organ type pedal beneath the driver's right foot.

Choke capacity filters were provided in the contactor circuits and radio interference coils were mounted centrally on the roof in front of the trolley gantry in an effort to eliminate radio interference. The main cable runs carried within the frame channel were encased in flexible metallic tubing.

The upper-deck body pillars slotted into the wooden rail of the framework above the upper saloon windows, i.e. the cantrail. There were curved steel brackets bolted to the metal roof (inside the roof there was a steel strengthening plate on each side) and each end of the three transverse pressed steel girders, between bays 1 and 2, bays 2 and 3, and bays 3 and 4, supporting the exposed trolley gantry, which was not in direct contact with the roof, rested on these brackets, each foot being secured by four metal bolts.

The main power cable made its way forward from the trolley gantry along the centre line of the roof before it entered the front dome about 1ft 6in. to the rear of the metal louvres above the front upper-deck windows. The vehicle was equipped with Brecknell, Willis & Co. Ltd., Bristol, lightweight trolley equipment and trolley bases. These permitted a reduced spring pressure of less than 30lb. The booms were 18ft long and equipped with dewirement buffers. The access catwalk on the roof had two steps above the rear dome beneath the utilitarian trolley boom retaining hooks.

A Sunbeam motor generator set provided low voltage (24-volt) power for lighting and auxiliary equipment. The battery was only used to supply the small demands of the side and rear lights, and regularly-used accessories such as the screen wiper, horn, bells, etc. The main current load was supplied direct from the motor generator. When the saloon lights were switched on the motor generator started and then supplied all lights and accessories whilst the battery was charged.

Traction batteries for manoeuvring purposes were not fitted.

**Brakes:** Lockheed vacuum assisted hydraulic, activated by the brake pedal and operating on all wheels. Movement of the brake pedal was transmitted by push-rod to the master cylinder bolted to the chassis frame. Three 1½in. diameter master cylinders in a single casting were operated by a single pivoted lever formed with three ball-ended arms. Each cylinder operated applied the brakes on an axle; the outer casing of the master cylinder unit formed a reservoir to maintain the system full of fluid. A compensating and sealing unit was secured to a machined face on the front of the main casting housing three rubber cups and needle valves. When the brake pedal was depressed, pressure was created in the master cylinders making the rubber cups lift and unseating the needle valves thereby compensating for any discrepancies between the cylinders and ensuring equal braking effort on all axles. In the case of any leakage in one of three braking systems, the rubber cup of the affected system did not lift but the other two systems were unaffected.

All brake shoes were expanded hydraulically by 2in. diameter application cylinders operating short push-rods and connected to the master cylinders by copper tubing and flexible hoses. A 4in. wide pair of brake shoes was applied within each drum and expanded independently by the hydraulic system or the handbrake lever.

Pull-on handbrake linked mechanically by rods to act on all the rear wheels and operating on the same pairs of shoes as those operated by the hydraulic system. The handbrake lever was to the offside of the driver's steering column.

**Bodywork:** The bodywork was basically identical to that fitted to 1934 AEC663T 212 and cost £838.

It is believed that the semaphore arm illuminated traffic indicators had been removed by the time of the vehicle's loan to Pontypridd UDC.

**Lighting:** See 212.

**Seating:** See 212.

**Destination equipment:** See 212.

**Internal Livery:** See 212.

**External Livery:** See 212.

**Notes:** In April 1938 the Portsmouth trolleybus fleet was renumbered by the addition of 200 to the original fleet numbers, i.e. trolleybus 213 had originally been numbered 13.

213 was withdrawn from service and placed in open storage on waste ground in Northern Parade, Hilsea, Portsmouth in late 1940. In August 1942 it was prepared for loan to Pontypridd UDC and towed to South Wales reaching Pontypridd on 14 August 1942.

The trolleybus was returned to Portsmouth on 3 November 1945 and stored in Eastney Depot before being reinstated to service on 1 March 1949.

**Disposal:**

213  Withdrawn on 21 April 1953, it remained at North End until sold on 23 January 1954 for £40 to Kingsway Coachworks, Emsworth, Hampshire and broken up.

## 214 Sunbeam MS3

| Owner's Fleet No. | Reg. No. | Chassis type | No. | Elec. Equip. | Body | Into service | Delivered to Pontypridd | Departed Pontypridd | Withdrawn |
|---|---|---|---|---|---|---|---|---|---|
| 214 | RV4662 | Sunbeam MS3 | 12026S | BTH | MCCW | 11.07.1934 | 14.08.1942 | 10.04.1945 | 21.04.1953 |

The details below refer to the vehicle as supplied on loan to Pontypridd – not as originally delivered to the City of Portsmouth Passenger Transport Department (as the undertaking was known by 1942).

Chassis: Three-axle type Sunbeam MS3 manufactured by Sunbeam Motor Car Ltd., Moorfield Road, Wolverhampton.
Motor: British Thomson-Houston Co. Ltd., Rugby, Warwickshire, Type 202BXY (80hp at 550 volts) compound-wound main field for regenerative control.
Electrical equipment: British Thomson-Houston Co. Ltd., Rugby, Warwickshire, Regenerative Control (No. 201 Form DK).
Brakes: Lockheed vacuum assisted hydraulic, BTH regenerative electric, BTH electric rheostatic and hand brakes.
Body: Metropolitan-Cammell Weymann Motor Bodies Ltd., Midland Works, Saltley, Birmingham, all metal H32/28R.
Length: Not known. Width 7ft 6in.
Wheelbase: 16ft 8in. from front axle to centre of bogie.
Bogie wheelbase: 3ft 11¼in.
Unladen weight: 8 tons 13cwt 2qrtr.
Tyres: single, 36 × 8in. high pressure all round.
Track: front axle 6ft 6⅜in., rear axle 6ft 6in.

Only in November 1934 did Sunbeam separate its trolleybus activities from its private car business renaming it as Sunbeam Commercial Vehicles Ltd., which from July 1935 became part of the Rootes Group.

The Sunbeam MS3 chassis was designed to take a low-loading double-deck body, the low-loading line being achieved by offsetting the motor and transmission.

All but three of the Sunbeam MS3 chassis built were bought by Wolverhampton Corporation Transport, the exceptions beings Portsmouth 13 and 14, and Huddersfield 4.

**Chassis:** Conventional cranked chassis frame over rear bogie with special insulation points for all-metal bodies.

The chassis including electrical equipment cost £1,208.
All other details see 213

**Electrics:** The exposed trolley gantry was constructed of pressed steel Welsh hat and channel sections framed together and mounted on the upper-deck cantrail structure. The Brecknell Willis lightweight trolley base was mounted as follows: a steel plate, to both sides of which insulating rubber was moulded through holes in the plate, was mounted between the channel members of the gantry. The moulded rubber and plate were of similar construction to that then used for railway carriage buffers and draw-gear springs by Messrs Spencer Moulton. The bolts securing the trolley base passed entirely through the rubber and could not come into contact with any portion of the steel structure providing a resilient mounting, insulated electrically from the vehicle's body and reducing the transmission of trolley noises to the interior. A rubber covered plate with its front and rear edges bent upwards to ensure that rain water ran off at the sides, provided dry-spot insulation between the trolley base and its rubber mounting.

The full field speed was kept at a low figure to reduce rheostatic losses on starting and to ensure that regeneration was obtained over the widest possible range of speeds.

All other details see 213

**Brakes:** See 213.

Regenerative braking was obtained by the driver relieving pressure on the master controller (power) pedal so that the controller returned towards the full field position. Braking was increased as the pedal rose and strengthened the shunt field. The starting resistance was held out of circuit until the controller reached the "off" position, providing full regeneration down to a speed of ca. 10mph. A relay was mounted on the shunt field resistance contactor panel to insert resistance in the lamp circuit should a dangerous rise in voltage occur, for example due to an interruption of the main

City of Portsmouth Passenger Transport Department 1934 Sunbeam MS3/MCCW seen at Portsmouth's Cosham Railway Station terminus after its repaint into pre-war livery but for the matt grey roof, front and rear domes, and upper-deck rear corner panels, following its return to Portsmouth. No. 214 was on loan to Pontypridd from August 1942 until November 1945. (Online Transport Archive [James Joyce]) This and a number of other images were kindly provided by OnlineTransport Archive, a UK-registered charity dedicated to the preservation of transport-related films and images. For further information see www. onlinetransportarchive.org circuit during generation, which would otherwise burn out the lamps. Rheostatic braking came into operation when the braking effort due to regeneration fell to a low value.

**Bodywork:** All metal (patented) six-bay highbridge double-deck construction, forwards-ascending half-turn (90°) staircase with conventional semi-vestibuled open platform entrance and exit at the rear, marketed by Metropolitan-Cammell Weymann Motor Bodies Ltd., and built by The Metropolitan-Cammell Carriage, Wagon and Finance Company Company Ltd., Midland Works, Saltley, Birmingham. The design was based on that of contemporary Birmingham Tramway and Omnibus Department (trading as Birmingham City Transport) motorbus and trolleybuses. The body cost £887.

In profile, the front of the body featured a "swept-back" styling between the bulbous nose surmounting the less raked front panel of the driver's cab and the upper-deck roof, the front line of the roof being in line with the front axle. The front of the upper-deck curved gently beneath the "V" shaped fixed front windows; the shallow driver's cab windscreen had a more pronounced "V-shaped" cross-section set-back beneath the upper-deck front panels and with a bulbous top to the front panel beneath. There was an upright rear profile, the base of the rear panel curving gently in to match the concave side panels. The trolley poles were fitted on an exposed roof-mounted gantry above bay 2. Platform handrails and stanchions were covered with black Doverite.

Brackets were bolted to the roof rail immediately above the upper-deck body pillars between bays 1 and 2, and bays 2 and 3, to support the two girders of the exposed trolley gantry which was mounted above bay 2, and not in direct contact with the roof.

Metal louvres were fitted above the upper and lower-deck saloon side windows. Chromium plated half-drop openers with a clip-operated gripper at the top on each side of the upper pane were fitted to the side windows in bays 1, 3, 5 of both sides of the upper-deck, bays 1, 3, 4 of the lower-deck nearside and bays 1, 2, 3 of the lower-deck offside. The upper pane dropped outside the fixed lower pane. Immediately above the lower-deck side windows in bays 1, 3 and 5, nine-vane ventilation vents slanting rearwards somewhat from the vertical at the top were fitted. There were six roof ventilators, one on each side above and towards the front of bays 1, 4, 6. At the rear of the upper-saloon there was an emergency door having three hinges at its base and two oblong fixed window panes having slightly rounded upper and lower outer corners and a horizontal rail across both panes. There was an upright opening handle mounted centrally immediately above the gutter in the rear dome above the emergency door and two protective rubber bumpers on the outer frame matching two further bumpers above the indicator screens. The rearmost offside panel behind the staircase was also glazed.

The fleet number was displayed inside the vehicle by a small white Bakelite oval disc screwed at cantrail height above the central front pillar in the upper saloon and on the front bulkhead in the lower saloon upon which the numbers were painted in black.

The driver's steering wheel was noticeably raked back. The top two thirds of the offside driver's windscreen was chromium plated and opened outwards. It carried a top-mounted windscreen wiper. There was a front-hinged door on the offside provided with a square sliding "signalling" window in the lower one-third of the pane and an inset, opening handle. There was a large fixed quarter light window between the offside cab door and the cab front corner pillar. On the nearside there was a matching panel and a single window, the window being divided vertically to enable the rear pane to slide forwards outside the fixed front pane. The base of the cab door was curved over the wheel arch to a position about 5in. from the rear of the door thereafter the base, beneath the cab door handle, was horizontal. Two large hooded inlet ducts were installed on each side above the driver's cab door and side windows; one rose gently upwards from the cab front pillar and one fell gently downwards towards the cab rear bulkhead.

A small "reverse L-shape" protruding step was let into the base of the offside side panel towards the rear of the mudguard, but without any form of protection to the bodywork, immediately behind the front axle, slightly above the height of the wheel hub to aid access to the driver's cab.

There were two glazed panels in the bulkhead behind the driver. A rectangular driver's rear view mirror was mounted externally towards the top of the offside front cab pillar.

There was a step up into the lower saloon. The staircase had three steps from the platform to the half-landing and then three steps to the upper-deck. An oblong conductor's mirror was fitted in the upper saloon rear dome above the stairs. There was a single lifeguard rail on each side extending between the flared rear of the front wheel mudguard to the leading rear axle.

There were separate mudguards to the rear wheels. A mud flap hung between the second and third axle.

There were top-hinged valance panels on both the nearside and offside in bays 1–3 and 4 (part) to access contactor equipment, resistances and other equipment.

The flat front panel incorporated a single fluted column of three horizontal louvres vanes placed centrally aligned vertically with the centre of the headlamps with the fleet number transferred immediately above. The triangular Sunbeam chassis maker's badge was fitted centrally beneath the driver's windscreen with its base on the beading separating the red and white coloured paint application. There was no removable front panel for towing purposes. The registration number plate was affixed at the base of the front panel. The rear registration number plate, encompassing a single red rear light to the offside of the upper row of letters, was affixed to the white-painted panel immediately above the rear platform window on the offside. The registration number plate was affixed at the base of the front panel. A bamboo trolley retrieval pole was carried within the lower-saloon nearside body panels at waist rail height with a tube access from the rear platform vestibule.

**Lighting:** External lighting was two headlights mounted half-way up the front panel, two circular front side lights exactly on the beading between the maroon lower panels and the white window area, and a single red rear light was incorporated into the rear registration number plate, immediately above the rear platform window on the offside.

At the rear, an inset panel somewhat to the offside of the centre line of the rear panels and aligned with the lower beading of the white-painted waistband beneath the rear platform window illuminated to show STOP when the brakes were applied.

A spotlight was fitted beneath the flat front panel its nearside frame aligned with the nearside frame of the nearside headlight.

Semaphore arm illuminated traffic indicators accommodated in a black moulding were fitted in the lower half of the driver's cab corner pillars on both sides.

There were square diffused light fittings in the ceiling cove panels in the lower saloon mounted centrally in bays 1–6 each side (12); and in the upper saloon in bays 1–6 on each side (12), the position in bay 1 being immediately to the rear of the body pillar but then progressively a little further towards the rear in each bay so that by bay 6 the fitting was in the centre of the bay, and one in the offside of the rear dome above the staircase. There was a further fitting in the rear dome above the staircase and above the rear platform.

This trolleybus entered service in Pontypridd at the time of wartime lighting restrictions. The headlights were equipped with masks whilst the side light glasses were partially covered to emit solely a point of light.

Wartime lighting restrictions meant that all the interior lights were fitted with a metal plate having a small slot in it that cast a rectangle of light onto the floor. Alternately the bulb inside the light fitting was removed.

Seating: The lower saloon had a 4-person inwards-facing bench seat on each side over the rear axles and five rows of forwards-facing double seats. The upper saloon had seven rows of double seats on the offside and nine rows on the nearside.

**Destination equipment:** A large rectangular indicator box 36in. × 14in. for displaying the final destination and intermediate points, with a square service number indicator box 14in. × 14in. alongside were mounted centrally at the front and rear in the lower half of the upper-deck panels. At the front the destination and intermediate points indicator box was on the nearside above the driver's cab windscreen (but encroaching a quarter of the way above the offside windscreen) and at the rear on the offside above the rear platform window. At the front the service number indicator box was on the offside and at the rear on the nearside.

In Pontypridd the destination box displayed simply Treforest Cilfynydd in two rows of lettering, the upper row of lettering getting progressively smaller to the right (nearside) and the lower getting progressively larger to the right, whilst the service number box was officially not used although a variety of numbers seems to have been indiscriminately displayed.

There was a narrow box 24in. × 6in. capable of displaying the final destination or the final destination and an intermediate point (two lines) built into the white-painted vent panel above the rearmost lower saloon window (bay 6) on both sides. These were not used in Pontypridd.

**Internal Livery:** The interior panels and rear corner panels were lined with scratchproof Rexine with window mouldings and finishings in French-polished walnut. Ceilings cream. The floors were covered in brown linoleum and grey waterproof paint was applied to the rear platform.

**External Livery:** This vehicle operated in Pontypridd in the 1934 Portsmouth livery in which it had been delivered from the manufacturers slightly modified to comply with wartime restrictions but apparently with few of the minor changes introduced during the pre-war years of trolleybus operation in the city. The vehicle had been little used in the late 1930s and is unlikely to have ever benefited from a repaint.

The lower-deck and upper-deck window surrounds, upper and lower-deck waistbands, and cantrail or vent panel area above the lower-deck windows were white. On the outbreak of war the roof, which had previously been white was repainted matt grey extending down the upper-deck rear corner panels on both sides of the rear emergency exit. The emergency exit door itself remained white. The main upper and lower-deck body panels were painted crimson. The beadings were not picked out in black in the livery originally applied to the Metro-Cammell bodied trolleybuses.

The crimson panels were lined in tramcar-style double lining, comprising an outer yellow line ⅜in. broad and an inner white line ⅛in. broad, the yellow line having ornate Greek corner pattern inset square designs and the white line having matching indentations. The lining was applied to divide the crimson panels into separate front, side, rear corner, lower saloon platform bulkhead and rear portions. Mudguards and lifeguard rails were black, wheels were maroon. Apart from the front mudguards, there is no photographic evidence to suggest that the vehicle's extremities, e.g. side mudguards, lifeguard rails and platform edge, were painted white to fulfil wartime "blackout" restrictions. Trolley gear and related equipment, and trolley boom restraining hooks were black.

The City of Portsmouth coat of arms was displayed on both sides of the lower-deck side panels, centred in bay 3 (on delivery in 1934 these had been applied to bay 2).

Ownership details with the General Manager's name and title beneath were applied in small white script typeface at the base of the nearside lower-deck panels, bay 1, immediately to the rear of the front axle. The unladen weight was shown in upper case white typeface at the base of the offside lower-deck panels immediately in front of the (leading) rear axle with the maximum permitted speed in white script typeface behind the rear axle. The seating capacity was indicated in lower case left justified white typeface at the nearside base of the rear platform panel.

Large gold fleet numerals, shaded in two tones of blue and in white, were applied on the front panel centrally beneath the driver's cab windscreen and centrally on the lower-deck rear platform panels. In April 1938 the Portsmouth trolleybus fleet was renumbered by the addition of 200 to the original fleet numbers. Unlike those on 212, the numbers were reapplied and centred to reflect the additional figure.

Although Portsmouth had commenced adding additional white numerals beneath the lower-deck waistrail and lining on both sides to the rear of the driver's cab rear bulkhead from June 1938 it appears that these had not been added to 214 prior to its departure for Pontypridd.

**Notes:** In April 1938 the Portsmouth trolleybus fleet was renumbered by the addition of 200 to the original fleet numbers, i.e. trolleybus 214 had originally been numbered 14 and was the first trolleybus to arrive in Portsmouth on 10 July 1934.

214 was withdrawn from service and placed in open storage on waste ground in Northern Parade, Hilsea, Portsmouth in late 1940. In August 1942 it was prepared for loan to Pontypridd UDC and towed to South Wales reaching Pontypridd on 8 August 1942. The trolleybus arrived back in Portsmouth on 10 April 1945 and was reinstated to service in November 1945.

**Disposal:**
214 Withdrawn 21 April 1953 and stored at North End Depot until sold in January 1954 to Kingsway Coachworks, Emsworth, Hampshire, for £50 and broken up.

## 215 AEC663T

| Owner's Fleet No. | Reg. No. | Chassis type | No. | Elec. Equip. | Body | Into service | Delivered to Pontypridd | Departed Pontypridd | Withdrawn |
|---|---|---|---|---|---|---|---|---|---|
| 215 | RV4663 | AEC663T | 075 | Eng. Electric | MCCW | 17.07.1934 | 08.08.1942 | 04.1946 | 21.06.1955 |

The details below refer to the vehicle as supplied on loan to Pontypridd – not as originally delivered to the City of Portsmouth Passenger Transport Department (as the undertaking was known by 1942).

Chassis: Three-axle type AEC 663T manufactured by the Associated Equipment Company Ltd. at the AEC works, Windmill Lane, Southall, Middlesex.
Motor: English Electric EE405 (80hp at 550 volts) series-wound, augmented field, manufactured by English English Electric Co. Ltd. at the Phoenix Works, Bradford, Yorkshire.
Dewirement indicator: neon line-light.
Brakes: Westinghouse compressed air and hand brakes.
Body: Metropolitan-Cammell Weymann Motor Bodies Ltd., Midland Works, Saltley, Birmingham, all metal H32/28R.
Length: Not known, recommended body length in 1933–34 was 26ft. Width 7ft 6in.
Wheelbase: 16ft 6in.
Bogie wheelbase: 4ft
Wheel track: front 6 ft 5⅜in., rear 6ft 2¾in.
Unladen weight: 8 tons 3cwt 0qrtrs
Tyres: 36 x 8 high-pressure pneumatic singles on all wheels
Frame overall length 26ft 9in.
Height of frame laden 22½in.
Turning circle diameter: 59ft
Chassis weight: 4 tons 4cwt.

Chassis: Conventional cranked chassis frame over rear bogie based on the AEC Regent 663 motorbus chassis and axles, with special insulation points for all-metal bodies.
The chassis including electrical equipment cost £1,230.
All other details see 212.

Electrics: See 212.

Brakes: A Westinghouse two-cylinder reciprocating compressor with 5 cubic ft capacity and driven by an EEC 500-volt motor was carried on the offside of the chassis frame, from which it was electrically and mechanically insulated. The compressor was equipped with an anti-freezer, the intake to which was connected by a short rubber tube (for insulation) to one of the chassis cross members, which was utilised as an intake silencer, the air being admitted at the farther end through a filter. The air reservoir and governor were attached forward of the compressor on insulated mountings with a buffer chamber on the compressor side of the valve. The governor was set to maintain a reservoir pressure of 85 lb per sq.in. and the control valve was operated by an organ type pedal mounted on the bracket carrying both the valve and power pedal. Reservoir and brake cylinder pressures were shown on gauges on the dashboard attached to the driver's steering column.
The front brake drums were 17in. diameter castings with 3in. wide facings ¾in. thick. The track rods were adjustable

AEC663T / English Electric 15 in London Road, North End, Portsmouth on 9 September 1934. (D.A.P. Janes [photographer G.A. Tucker])

by means of screwed and clipped ends. All four wheels of the rear bogie were fitted with 17in. diameter brake drums having 6in. wide facings ¾in. thick. The total effective brake area was 825 sq.in.

Apart from a single flexible pipe connection, all air piping was solid drawn steel. Air cylinders were mounted on the cross tube in front of the rear bogie, whence rod connections were taken to double-armed levers on a cross-shaft carried behind the central bogie cross-member. The lower arms of the levers were coupled by pull rods to the cam levers on the leading axle and by tubular push-rods to the rear axle levers. The same mechanism was used by the handbrake. The front wheel brake cylinders were mounted on top of the king pins, the piston rods passing through the borings in the latter and operating directly on the camshaft.

Pull-on handbrakes linked by a cross-shaft, and pull and push rods to the camshaft levers expanded in the bogie wheel brake drums to operate on the same pairs of shoes as those operated by the air brake system. The handbrake lever was to the offside of the driver's steering column.

**Bodywork:** The bodywork was basically identical to that fitted to 1934 Sunbeam MS3 214 and also cost £838.

The chassis and equipment maker's badge, AEC in an inverted triangle surmounted by the winged EE symbol, was fitted centrally beneath the driver's windscreen on the waistband.

**Lighting:** See 214.

**Seating:** See 214.

**Destination equipment:** See 214.

**Internal Livery:** See 214.

**External Livery:** See 214.

**Notes:** In April 1938 the Portsmouth trolleybus fleet was renumbered by the addition of 200 to the original fleet numbers, i.e. trolleybus 215 had originally been numbered 15 and was the fifth trolleybus to arrive in Portsmouth on 16 July 1934.

215 was withdrawn from service and placed in open storage on waste ground in Northern Parade, Hilsea, Portsmouth in late 1940. In August 1942 it was prepared for loan to Pontypridd UDC and towed to South Wales reaching Pontypridd on 8 August 1942. The trolleybus was returned to Portsmouth in April 1946 and subsequently reinstated to service.

**Disposal:**

215 Withdrawn 21 June 1955 and stored at North End Depot until sold to J. Strudwick (dealer), Horndean, 14 March 1956 for £40 and believed broken up at Eastney Depot in May 1956.

## MILEAGE RUN: PUDC TROLLEYBUSES COMPARED TO HIRED HULL & PORTSMOUTH VEHICLES

| Month/ year | Pontypridd | Hull | Portsmouth | Total | Month/ year | Pontypridd | Hull | Portsmouth | Total |
|---|---|---|---|---|---|---|---|---|---|
| 08.41 | 23,457 | 1,360 | | 24,817 | 01.44 | 14,467 | | 9,220 | 23,687 |
| 09.41 | 12,294 | 12,418 | | 24,712 | 02.44 | 12,510 | | 9,940 | 22,450 |
| 10.41 | 12,327 | 12,694 | | 25,021 | 03.44 | 13,930 | | 10,051 | 23,981 |
| 11.41 | 10,655 | 12,683 | | 23,338 | 04.44 | 14,299 | | 6,618 | 20,917 |
| 12.41 | 11,283 | 13,125 | | 24,408 | 05.44 | 15,547 | | 8,096 | 23,643 |
| 01.42 | 11,274 | 13,869 | | 25,143 | 06.44 | 16,110 | | 4,986 | 21,096 |
| 02.42 | 10,230 | 12,212 | | 22,442 | 07.44 | 13,847 | | 5,871 | 19,718 |
| 03.42 | 11,517 | 12,809 | | 24,326 | 08.44 | 12,614 | | 9,609 | 22,223 |
| 04.42 | 10,350 | 13,969 | | 24,319 | 09.44 | 12,907 | | 9,199 | 22,106 |
| 05.42 | 9,965 | 14,605 | | 24,570 | 10.44 | 12,517 | | 10,055 | 22,572 |
| 06.42 | 10,614 | 13,738 | | 24,352 | 11.44 | 12,351 | | 9,380 | 21,731 |
| 07.42 | 11,088 | 14,368 | | 25,456 | 12.44 | 10,180 | | 9,829 | 20,009 |
| 08.42 | 9,285 | 5,385 | 5,388 | 20,058 | 01.45 | 10,115 | | 8,545 | 18,660 |
| 09.42 | 11,799 | | 12,157 | 23,956 | 02.45 | 11,174 | | 8,410 | 19,584 |
| 10.42 | 10,579 | | 14,038 | 24,617 | 03.45 | 16,604 | | 5,111 | 21,715 |
| 11.42 | 9,199 | | 14,264 | 23,463 | 04.45 | 12,928 | | 6,049 | 18,977 |
| 12.42 | 13,710 | | 10,197 | 23,907 | 05.45 | 12,280 | | 6,308 | 18,588 |
| 01.43 | 13,000 | | 10,839 | 23,839 | 06.45 | 15,928 | | 6,670 | 22,598 |
| 02.43 | 9,645 | | 12,209 | 21,854 | 07.45 | 16,090 | | 6,492 | 22,582 |
| 03.43 | 11,009 | | 13,167 | 24,176 | 08.45 | 13,380 | | 9,198 | 22,578 |
| 04.43 | 10,499 | | 12,929 | 23,428 | 09.45 | 17,683 | | 5,013 | 22,696 |
| 05.43 | 11,797 | | 12,083 | 23,880 | 10.45 | 17,272 | | 6,109 | 23,381 |
| 06.43 | 10,958 | | 12,613 | 23,571 | 11.45 | 14,899 | | 6,578 | 21,477 |
| 07.43 | 11,681 | | 12,709 | 24,390 | 12.45 | 15,442 | | 5,883 | 21,325 |
| 08.43 | Not known | | Not known | Not known | 01.46 | 17,265 | | 6,221 | 23,486 |
| 09.43 | 12,044 | | 11,194 | 23,238 | 02.46 | 16,167 | | 4,945 | 21,112 |
| 10.43 | 12,509 | | 11,234 | 23,743 | 03.46 | 24,467 | | | 24,467 |
| 11.43 | 11,590 | | 11,804 | 23,394 | | | | | |
| 12.43 | 10,589 | | 12,535 | 23,124 | | | | | |

# LIVERY

Although Pontypridd UDC tramcars carried a livery of maroon and cream, confusingly similar to the maroon and yellow Rhondda Tramways Company livery, the trolley vehicles, as they were originally known, and trolleybuses introduced a new colour scheme of cobalt blue and primrose to the streets. During the trolleybus era the style of application differed minimally and related primarily to the lining detail and the application of transferred lettering.

It is important to note that the vehicles circulating on the streets did not necessarily all appear in the then current livery application: several variations could be seen at the same time.

## 1–7 English Electric WTB

These vehicles were delivered in the following Pontypridd UDC livery: the main body panels beneath the waistrail were painted cobalt blue. The window surrounds were primrose.

The blue panels above and below the waist panel were lined separately in tramcar-style double lining comprising a broader outer line in gold and a thinner inner line in white, with a complex rounded corner pattern. The beading along the waistrail, the vertical beading on the front corner panels, driver's cab doors and passenger entrance/exit, and the rear drains were finished in stock black as was the edge of the roof from approximately half the length of the driver's cab to the rear, i.e. the canvassed portion of the roof.

The entire roof area, including the roof canvas and trolley gantry, was painted white. The trolley base, trolley booms and trolley boom retaining hooks were stock black.

Mudguards, lifeguard rails, headlamp surrounds and wheels were stock black.

The gartered Pontypridd UDC coat of arms was displayed on both sides of the body, centred beneath the nearside bay 6 window and the offside bay 4 window.

The Engineer and Manager's name and title beneath was transferred in small pale blue lettering shaded in gold in two lines at the base of the bay 1 nearside panel immediately to the rear of the front axle viz. "J.E. TEASDEL M.I.E.E." with "ENGINEER & MANAGER." beneath. A small metal plate displaying the maximum permitted speed "SPEED. 20. M.P.H", in white was affixed to the upper lifeguard rail immediately below. At a later date the maximum permitted speed was shown on the offside at the base of the side panels immediately forwards of the leading rear axle. By the late 1930s both of these items of information were painted onto the base of the side panels in white.

Large gold numerals, shaded in light, mid and royal blue and black, were mounted on the front panel centrally beneath the driver's cab windscreen, the top of the number aligned with the centre of the headlamps, and at the rear centrally beneath the waist panel.

No external advertising was initially carried. From 1940 advertisements were carried across the rear waist panel beneath the saloon windows.

At the first repaint the gartered coat of arms were flanked by the initials of the undertaking's title, the "P" and "U" forward of the coat of arms, and the "D" and "C" to the rear of coat of arms, being separated by square full-stops. The ornate style letters and punctuation were in gold, shaded in light, mid and royal blue and black. Certain vehicles at subsequent repaints lost the full stop after the "U" and "C", e.g. 4 and 7.

It was soon recognised that white was an impractical colour for the roof and the entire roof area including the front dome was repainted in a khaki colour which progressively darkened with use.

The black painted beading was discontinued and there is some evidence that the lining out was simplified on certain vehicles latterly.

Wartime white edging was applied to the edges of the mudguards and the lifeguards; this was rapidly removed once hostilities came to an end.

**An English Electric single-decker seen in wartime livery next to the former tram depot building at Glyntaff. (Peter Smith collection)**

MATERIALS REQUIRED TO PAINT A SINGLE-DECK TROLLEY BUS.

BODY

| | |
|---|---|
| Yellow Work: | 1 quart Undercoating Yellow. |
| | 2 quarts Finishing Yellow. |
| | 1 lb White stopper. |
| Blue Work: | 1 quart Undercoating Blue |
| | 2 quarts Finishing Blue. |
| | 1 lb Grey Stopper. |
| | 7 books Gold Leaf. |
| | ½ gallon Finishing Varnish. |
| | ¼ pint Gold Size. |
| | 1 gallon Lead Colour. |
| | Filler |
| Wings: | ¼ pint Undercoat Black. |
| | ½ pint Finishing Black. |
| Roof Outside: | 10 yards of Canvas. |
| | 3 gallons Lead Colour. |
| | ½ gallon Camouflage paint (khaki). |
| | ¼ pint Oxide Red. |
| Roof Inside: | ½ gallon Undercoating White. |
| | ¾ gallon Finishing White. |
| Saloons: | ½ gallon Brown Undercoating. |
| | ¾ gallon Brown Finishing. (seats, etc). |
| Polish Work | 1 pint Walnut Stain. |
| | ½ gallon Polish. |
| Transfers: | 8 P.U.D.C. letters. |
| | 2 Figure transfers. |
| | 2 Coat of Arms Transfers. |

CHASSIS

| | |
|---|---|
| | ¼ gallon Chassis Black |
| | ¼ gallon Aluminium Paint. |

## 8 Guy BTX

This vehicle, although supplied as a demonstrator, was delivered in the following Pontypridd UDC livery: the main upper and lower-deck body panels beneath the window ledge, and the lower-deck waistband were painted cobalt blue. The lower-deck and upper-deck window surrounds were primrose, and the roof was painted aluminium.

The lower-deck side panels had a single gold line encompassing the entire side but following the waist rail beading at the top. A single gold line also followed the extremities of the bulbous front panel, curving inwards around the headlight mountings, and the lower-deck rear panel. Somewhat broader single gold lining was applied to the base of the upper-deck panels immediately above the side gutter moulding and thus about 4in. above the upper-deck floor line. The edge of the roof was finished in stock black.

The protective panel carrying the front registration number plate immediately beneath the front panel was painted silver.

Mudguards, lifeguard rails, headlamp surrounds and wheels were stock black.

The trolley base, trolley booms and trolley boom retaining hooks were stock black.

The gartered Pontypridd UDC coat of arms was displayed on both sides of the lower-deck, centred in bay 3. The initials of the undertaking's title were not carried.

The Engineer and Manager's name and title beneath was transferred in small white plain lettering at the base of the bay 1 nearside panel immediately to the rear of the front axle.

Beneath the title but above the single gold lining at the base of the panel the maximum permitted speed of 20mph was applied in somewhat large white plain transfers.

External advertising was carried on the upper-deck side panel bays (banners) in the form of sign-written advertisements painted directly on to the panels due to the long duration of the contracts. Sign-written advertisements were also applied to the platform rear panel.

Wartime white edging was applied to the edges of the mudguards, lifeguards and the rear platform edge; this was rapidly removed once hostilities came to an end.

The seating capacity was indicated on the nearside base of the lower-deck rear platform panels.

## 9 Bristol E

This vehicle was delivered in Bristol Tramways & Carriage Co. Ltd. livery.

The lower-deck and upper-deck window surrounds, the cantrail or vent panel area above the lower-deck windows, and the roof were painted ivory white. The main upper and lower-deck body panels were painted ultramarine blue. When repainted in the 1930s Pontypridd UDC cobalt blue and primrose livery replaced the ultramarine blue and white colour scheme.

Mudguards and lifeguard rails were black and wheels bright red. The entire upper-deck roof area was pale grey.

The main upper and lower-deck body sides, and front and rear panels had double lining comprising a broader outer gold line and a thinner inner blue line with imperceptibly rounded corners. The lower-deck waistband was separately lined with a matching gold line.

No manufacturer's name, ownership details or legal lettering, e.g. weight, whatsoever seems to have been originally applied to the vehicle.

Subsequently the gartered Pontypridd UDC coat of arms was displayed on both sides of the lower-deck waist panels, centred beneath the bay 3 window. The initials of the undertaking's title, "P", "U", "D", "C" separated by square full-stops were transferred onto the lower-deck waistband on both sides in bays 2, 3, 4. The ornate style letters and punctuation were in gold, shaded in light, mid and royal blue and black, somewhat smaller than those used on the English Electric single-deck trolleybuses due to their application within the waistband.

The Manager's name and title beneath was transferred in small white lettering in two lines at the base of the bay 1 nearside and offside panels immediately to the rear of the front axle viz. "A. ARMSTRONG A.M. INST. T" with "TRANSPORT MANAGER." beneath.

The seating capacity was indicated on the nearside base of the lower-deck rear platform panels.

Large gold numerals, shaded in light, mid and royal blue and black, were mounted on the bulbous front panel centrally beneath the driver's cab windscreen, the top of the number somewhat below the lower rim of the headlamps, and at the rear centrally beneath the waist panel.

External advertising was carried on the upper-deck side panel bays (banners) in the form of sign-written advertisements painted directly on to the panels due to the long duration of the contracts. Sign-written advertisements were also applied to the rear upper-deck panels and the platform rear panel.

Wartime white edging was applied to the edges of the mudguards, lifeguards and the base of the rear panels, whilst the wheel arch over the rear bogie and the "V"-shaped panel hanging between the wheels were painted white. This was rapidly removed once hostilities came to an end.

## 8–15 Karrier W

The lower-deck and upper-deck window surrounds, the cantrail or vent panel area above the lower-deck windows, and the roof were painted primrose. The main upper and lower-deck body panels were painted cobalt blue.

The gartered Pontypridd UDC coat of arms was displayed on the lower-deck side panels, centred in bay 3 and aligned with the top of the mudguards. The coat of arms were surmounted by the initials of the undertaking's title, the "P", "U", "D", "C", each letter being separated by a square full-stop (the full-stop between the "U" and "D" being immediately above the coat of arms), the whole being in ornate gold transfers shaded in light, mid and royal blue and black.

Mudguards, lifeguard rails and wheels were stock black.

At a later date the roofs were repainted light or silver grey.

The Manager's name and title beneath was transferred in small gold lettering in two lines at the base of the bay 1 nearside panels immediately to the rear of the front axle. The maximum permitted speed "SPEED 30 MPH" and the unladen weight were shown in small white letters and number in two

lines at the base of the bay 5 nearside panel between the rear axle and the platform.

The seating capacity was indicated on the nearside base of the lower-deck rear platform panels.

Gold numerals, shaded in light, mid and royal blue and black, were mounted in the centre of the front panel beneath the driver's cab windscreen (the actual depth varied between vehicles from between the headlights to immediately above the registration number plate) and centrally mounted at the base of the lower-deck panels, i.e. beneath the advertisement position, below the rear platform window.

Although no conclusive photographic evidence has been found, it is believed that the customary "EMERGENCY EXIT" and "TO OPEN" lettering was applied across the top of the door frame.

External paper posters or painted advertising was carried on the upper-deck side panel bays. In the case of paper banner advertisements, these were produced in a single length, in bays 1–5 only; however, in some cases sign-written painted advertisements extended the entire length of the upper-deck side panels, i.e. over the driver's cab and rear platform, and behind the staircase.

Advertisements were also displayed across the width of the vehicle on the upper-deck panels above the rear platform window, on the lower-deck panels beneath the rear platform

Weymann-bodied Karrier W 11 stands at Cilfynydd Common terminus in front of the War Memorial to the 67 men of the small mining village of Cilfynydd who were killed between 1914–1918. (Online Transport Archive [photographer RLW]. This and a number of other images were kindly provided by Online Transport Archive, a UK-registered charity dedicated to the preservation of transport-related films and images. For further information see www.onlinetransportarchive.org)

A nearside view of Karrier W 11 at John Street terminus Treforest exemplifying the livery detail and displaying a large hand-painted side advertisement. (BTS Library [photographer R. Simpson])

window and on the offside rear platform staircase panel (circular "spot").

As the war in Europe was over and lighting restrictions had come to an end at the time of their delivery, none of the Karrier Ws received white painted mudguards, lifeguard rail or front and rear panels.

**Detail differences:**
8 and 9 were delivered with the primrose painted area around the lower saloon windows extended some 6 ins beneath the waistrail giving the impression of a waistband and sweeping down towards the front of the vehicle beneath the cab windows. The initials of the undertaking's title, the "P", "U", "D", "C", each letter being separated by a full-stop, the whole being in gold transfers shaded in light, mid and royal blue and black, which were applied higher than usual on this additional area of primrose in bays 2, 3, 4. The gartered coat of arms was retained in the standard location. The roof was painted blue. Both vehicles were subsequently repainted into the standard livery application.

8 – Shortly before withdrawal this vehicle was repainted omitting the primrose painted areas completely, the entire body appearing in a darker blue but for an aluminium painted roof. A different style of un-shaded fleet number transfers was applied.

Legal lettering: maximum permitted speed "SPEED 30 M.P.H" and unladen weight e.g. "U.W 7.7.3" were shown in two lines on the nearside at the base of the lower-deck panels between the rear axle and the open platform. The manager's name and title viz. "J.M. POWELL, A.M. Inst. T., TRANPORT MANAGER, PONTYPRIDD" were shown in 3 lines on the nearside at the base of the lower-deck panels in bay 1 immediately to the rear of the front axle.

## Internal Livery, Lettering and Numerals

Throughout the trolleybus era lower and upper saloons, platform and staircase, and the driver's cab were painted in varying applications of brown and white, accompanied by Walnut stain varnished woodwork.

All metal seat fittings were painted green. The floors were normally finished in grey-painted slatting, grey waterproof paint being applied to the open rear platform area. There is no evidence that the Second World War "black-out" led to increased use of white paint to aid visibility, e.g. handrails.

As delivered, the English Electric single-deck trolley vehicles 1– 7 carried the following exhortations on the front bulkhead of the front compartment: "SPITTING STRICTLY PROHIBITED" on the upper framework of the bulkhead windows and "NO SMOKING IN THIS COMPARTMENT" applied immediately beneath the arched ceiling with gold letters having two-tone blue shading.

The fleet number was shown in black (on trolleybus 9) above the windows on the lower saloon front bulkhead behind the driver's position and on the ceiling of the upper-deck front dome above the windows.

Paper advertisements applied to the lower saloon windows.

# APPENDIX D
# POWER GENERATION & SUPPLY

One of the claimed economies of converting life-expired electric tramways to trolley vehicle operation was the continued use of the existing traction power supply system with limited additional investment and Pontypridd UDC was no exception, the current supply arrangements being exactly those installed for the tramways in 1904. The trolleybuses like the trams before them received Direct Current (DC) electric power through overhead wires suspended above the route and supplied by underground cables from the generating station and town centre substation. A trolleybus system required two overhead wires, one of positive potential carrying current to the vehicle, and the other of negative potential returning the current and completing the connection. The trolley wire closest to the centre of the road was the positive wire. A tramway uses the running rails for its return connection.

Legislation required that the positive wire was interrupted every half mile, the sections each side of the insulating break being entirely separate from each other but connectable through switchgear placed in a cast-iron roadside section pillar often referred to simply as a "box". Identical feeder pillars housed the cables from which the mains power supply was connected to the overhead wiring. Equipment in either type of pillar could be used to cut off power entirely in an emergency. The negative trolley wire was continuous but at points where negative feeder cables were connected the positive and negative feeds came either from the same pillar or there was a separate negative feeder pillar, which to the onlooker, was identical to a positive feeder pillar.

Peak traction power requirements usually occurred on a Saturday, then still a working or half working day in most industries, not least the coal mines, and a market day; the greatest demand being from around lunchtime until mid-evening encompassing the rush from work to home, shopping trips, sporting fixtures, and finally evening entertainments.

## Generating Station

The Pontypridd UDC generating station, fuelled primarily by a refuse destructor (an incinerator) was built in 1904 on rising ground between the Glamorganshire Canal and the ADR railway line to Caerphilly, immediately to the north of the Council's gas works, at Glyntaff. The new electric tramways and street lighting system were foreseen as its main customers and the tramways car shed was constructed concurrently, the rear wall abutting on the generating station.

The buildings were erected by Messrs Hughes & Stirling, Liverpool, and equipped with three vertical cross-compound Corliss engines, with reheaters (one of 500hp and two of 200hp with speeds of 125 and 150rpm respectively) supplied by Coombe, Barbour & Co., Belfast. The engines were coupled to Greenwood & Batley dynamos, arranged for supplying either lighting or traction power through a Ferranti switchboard with British Westinghouse balancers for the lighting system. Initially there were two Babcock & Wilcox boilers fitted with superheaters and having a working pressure of 200 lb per sq

ins in the boiler house. R.W. Blackwell & Co. supplied and fixed the pipe work and feed-pumps, together with a Boby water softener and Green economiser. At a later date triple expansion engines and two further boilers were installed in the destructor house. Traction power was distributed at 500 volts DC.

In 1919 the first rotary converter – a large, rotating electromechanical device and basically a hybrid of a single winding Alternating Current (AC) motor and a DC generator (dynamo) – was installed at Glyntaff. This enabled the Electricity Department to take an AC supply from the South Wales Electric Power Distribution Co. and convert it to DC for local distribution to domestic and industrial customers as well as the tramways. In 1935 a 1,000kW turbine generator was installed and the refuse destructor modernised by the installation of conveyors at a cost of £6,000.

During the 1928–29 financial year the tramways consumed 766,627 units at a cost of 1.29d per unit and with a peak load of 350kW. In July 1929 the price fell to 1.25d per unit (it had been 1.4d per unit until November 1927) resulting in the traction load forming some 23% of the tramways undertaking's standing charges and 27% of the running costs.

As a result of the Electricity Act 1947 the electricity supply industry was nationalised with effect from 1 April 1948. The British Electricity Authority took over responsibility for operating the nation's power stations and the "Grid", and the supply of electrical energy to the Area Boards. The Pontypridd UDC Electricity Department became one of the 31 local authority undertakings and 11 private companies making up the South Wales Electricity Board (SWALEB) which took over the responsibility for power supplies in Brecknockshire, Carmarthenshire, Glamorganshire, Monmouthshire, Pembrokeshire, Radnorshire and part of Cardiganshire. By 1948 the Pontypridd UDC Electricity Department had expanded considerably although the trunk DC feeders for the domestic, industrial and traction supply were still those laid in 1903–09. Various extensions and additions to the non-traction part of the undertaking had been made, notably the laying of additional main feeders between the Glyntaff Generating Station and the Gas Yard substation in the town centre. The mains network comprised more than 50 miles of local aerial and underground cables whilst a distribution network spread out from Gas Yard substation where a transforming rectifier and rotary plant were installed. In the financial year 1946–47 the Electricity Department had sold almost 8 million units of which 638,106 units were for traction purposes, with a revenue of £68,066 2s 6d, had capital assets of £280,764 and served 8,500 consumers.

Glyntaff Generating Station consumed some 14,000 tons of refuse annually which not only provided sufficient fuel to obtain the steam to generate all the power needed but also solved the town's refuse problems. In 1951 use of the destructor and power generators ceased in order to reduce costs: henceforth Pontypridd's refuse was disposed of as landfill. The British Electricity Authority through SWALEB continued to operate the rectifiers at Glyntaff taking bulk power from the grid until the changeover of the domestic and industrial supply from DC to AC, which started on 4 January 1951, was completed. The changeover was completed on Thursday 8 September 1955 making the Glyntaff plant redundant, the staff having been progressively absorbed into other power stations in Upper Boat and further afield.

## Gas Yard Substation

In 1894 Pontypridd UDC opened new gas works at Glyntaff and vacated their original premises at the north end of Gas Road which ran from Taff Street opposite its junction with Market Street in a north northeasterly direction parallel to the River Taff in the town centre. Although a large gasometer remained on the site throughout the tramway and trolleybus era the disused buildings provided an ideal site for a central traction power substation. Around the end of the 19th century Direct Current (DC) was preferred for electric traction purposes because the speed of direct current motors and thus that of the vehicle could be simply controlled by varying the voltage applied to them. The original tramway traction power feeder network was accordingly DC and Gas Yard Substation was supplied with DC from Glyntaff Generating Station through the No. 2 Feeder Cable.

Alternating Current (AC), however, was preferable to DC for power distribution and generation because power loss in transmission lines decreases significantly with higher voltages. In order to benefit from the advantages of both forms of current AC energy had to be converted or transformed into DC for use by DC traction motors.

Following its connection to the South Wales Electric Power Distribution Co.'s bulk AC supply the Electricity Department laid an additional feeder between Glyntaff Generating Station and Gas Yard Substation providing 11,000 volts AC for traction use. Two 500kW rotary converters were installed in the former gas works buildings for this purpose. Here the current was stepped down by transformers before passing to the rotary converters which converted the current from AC to DC for distribution through underground cables and cast iron feeder pillars along the trolleybus route. By 1941 the Electricity Department noted that the single 500kW rotary converter in the Generating Station retained for traction power was rarely used.

The complexity and size of rotary converters required regular attention and maintenance by skilled staff, and any loss of the incoming supply would cause protective switchgear to "drop out" requiring a manual restart. Thus from the late

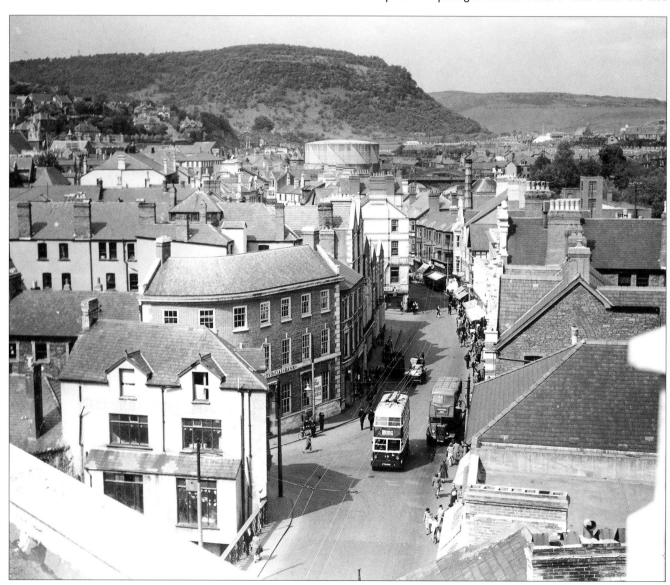

**High Street with Taff Street beyond photographed from the roof of the County Cinema. Roe-bodied Karrier W 15 is in the process of overtaking Rhondda Transport 1940 AEC Regent 8.8, fleet number 166, equipped with Weymann H54R bodywork. The absence of other traffic is noteworthy. Coed Craig-yr-hesg rises behind the gasometer. (Cy Yandell Collection)**

1920s the needs for additional or replacement equipment was met by the new technology of the mercury arc rectifier. Additionally the Electricity Department began the process of changing their transmission network, not only that for traction power, from DC to AC.

In a rectifier substation, the incoming high voltage AC supply was first reduced by transforming to the correct input voltage of approximately 11,000 volts AC, and thence converted to a nominal 500 volts DC for the overhead line, whereas a rotary converter was an AC motor driving a DC generator that produced a DC current. A mercury arc rectifier had an efficiency of about 93–95%, dependent on load, compared to a rotary converter's efficiency of just over 90%. The Electricity Department replaced the rotary converters at Gas Street Substation used for the traction supply with mercury arc rectifiers at some date prior to nationalisation of the electricity supply industry.

The operation of mercury arc rectifiers was based on the discovery that an electric spark (arc) vaporises mercury contained in a steel tank into a vapour that can only conduct electric current in a single direction between the pool of mercury and a metal anode. AC was fed to the anodes of the octopus-like glass bulbs and an arc was set up between the anodes and a pool of mercury in the bottom of the bulb. Incoming current, alternating at a frequency of 50 cycles a second (the standard frequency of the National Grid supply) flashed 50 times per second between the anodes and the mercury-covered cathodes forming a virtually continuous arc. Multiple anodes were used, fed from a multiple-phase transformer, the arc jumping from the cathode pool to each anode in sequence. The mercury bubbled constantly in the bulbs which were kept cool by an external fan.

The substation was filled with a ghostly blue light, wavering slightly and changing in intensity as the number of trolleybuses moving increased or reduced, or even changed speed.

The traction current was taken from the rectifiers to the switchboard busbars (bars of solid copper running the length of the rear of the board, their heavy rectangular section offering virtually no resistance to the current and enabling connections to the various switches to be solidly bolted to them). From the busbars, feeder cables went out to the feeder pillars, each being connected to the busbars through a heavy-duty circuit breaker and isolating switch.

If the current exceeded a set value, its magnetic effect opened the automatic circuit breaker preventing excessive current from entering a cable and damaging it. A broken positive trolley wire would cut off current if the live ends made a good contact with earth; a dewired trolley head might create a short circuit across the insulators of a frog or crossover, etc. The circuit breakers were equipped with time relays that automatically restored current after a pre-set period. If the fault was still present they reopened. If this cycle of events occurred three times, on the fourth occasion the circuit breakers stayed open and an alarm sounded. It was then necessary to locate the fault and isolate the feeder concerned until it was safe to restore current.

The rectifiers at Gas Street Substation were retained for traction power supplies after the 1955 conversion of the town supply from DC to AC and remained in use – despite recurring discussions with SWALEB about additional charges – until trolleybus abandonment.

"A dazzling blue light was flashing from these eight feet mercury arc rectifiers running from their own special transformer nearby, and the vibrant hum from the apparatus echoed through the room. The two feeders for the trolleys reflected their progress in the swinging pointers on the dials, contrasting with the motionless pointers on the feeders which previously supplied the Park, Old Bridge, Graig and every district with direct current".

*Pontypridd Observer*, 10 September 1955

PONTYPRIDD UDC ELECTRICITY DEPARTMENT
Electricity sold to the Transport Department.

| Year ending | Units | Cost per unit | Total cost | Effective date | Note |
|---|---|---|---|---|---|
| 31.03.1931 | 253,680 | 1.25d | £1,321 10s 6d | 1 July 1929 | |
| 31.03.1932 | 609,519 | 1.25d | £3,174 11s 9d | | |
| 31.03.1933 | 587,208 | 1.125d | £2,752 10s 8d | July 1932 | |
| 31.03.1934 | 583.028 | 1.07d | £2,604 1s 5d | October 1933 | |
| 31.03.1935 | 598,520 | 1.00d | £2,493 16s 8d | | |
| 31.03.1936 | 610,964 | 1.00d | £2,545 13s 8d | | |
| 31.03.1937 | 601,900 | 0.75d | £1,880 18s 9d | 1 July 1936 | |
| 31.03.1938 | 614,033 | 0.75d | £1,918 17s 1d | | |
| 31.03.1939 | 597,240 | 0.75d | £1,866 7s 6d | | |
| 31.03.1940 | 610,177 | 0.75d | £1,906 16s 1d | | |
| 31.03.1941 | 650,484 | 0.75d | £2,032 15s 3d | | |
| 31.03.1942 | 669,840 | 0.75d | £2,093 5s 0d | | |
| 31.03.1943 | 650,220 | 0.75d | £2,031 18s 9d | | |
| 31.03.1944 | 675,210 | 0.75d | £2,110 0s 8d | | |
| 31.03.1945 | 628,994 | 0.75d | £1,965 12s 2d | | 1 |
| 31.03.1946 | 667,603 | 0.75d | £2,086 5s 2d | | 1 |
| 31.03.1947 | 638,106 | 0.75d | £1,994 1s 8d | | 1 |
| 31.03.1948 | 652,060 | 0.75d | £2,037 15s 5d | | 1 |

Note 1: Plus a 10% surcharge per unit to cover the conversion losses incurred by the use of a rotary converter with effect from 1 January 1945.

## Feeder Cables

The tramway traction feeder cables were supplied and laid by W.T. Henley's Telegraph Works Co. in 1903–1905. The narrow streets meant that the existing gas and water pipes, and the domestic and industrial electricity mains belonging to the South Wales Electrical Power Distribution Co. were close to each other. Henleys had the task of adding the traction power feeders to this limited space in a manner that the respective parties could easily access their own mains. This was to prove a challenge in the later trolleybus years when it proved increasingly difficult to locate faults and make short replacements.

As far as can be ascertained no change was made to the traction power generating capacity or to the distribution network when the tramways were converted to trolleybus operation, the increased load of the trolleybuses being balanced out by the reduced size of the electrically-powered transport undertaking, i.e. the closure of the Mill Street – Trehafod route. There were thus four feeder cables:

No. 1 – Glyntaff Generating Station to *Crown Hotel*, Fothergill Street, Treforest (0.25 ins section approx. 1 mile long) feeding Taff House Junction – John Street

No. 2 – Glyntaff Generating Station to Gas Yard Substation via Broadway (0.31 ins section, approx. 2 miles long) feeding the town centre and formerly the Mill Street – Trehafod tram route.

No. 3 – Glyntaff Generating Station to Cilfynydd via Ynysangharad Road (0.31 ins section, approx. 2 miles long) feeding all section feeders north of Corn Stores Hill
Negative – Gas Yard Substation to Glyntaff Generating Station via Pentrebach Road. (0.31 ins section, approx. 2 miles long)

The majority of the original tramway feeder cable was laid in bitumen compound which made them difficult to access, however, later additions and replacements were laid in conduits. Accessibility was an expensive and time consuming challenge as the number of breakdowns and faults in the ageing feeder system increased.

At nationalisation the Transport Department retained responsibility for the DC traction power distribution network whereas Gas Yard Substation and Glyntaff Generating Station, the connection between the two and independent connections to the grid passed to the SWALEB. Maintenance of the feeder cables perforce passed to the Board as successors to the UDC Electricity Department and prior to that the combined Electricity and Transport Department.

In late 1951 the SWALEB estimated that it would cost £3,000 to carry out the substantial repairs now necessary and correcting the accumulated arrears in maintenance. This was based on retaining the traction supply through both the Glyntaff Generating Station and Gas Yard Substation. Although the Transport Manager was eager to discontinue trolleybus operation it was evident to him that this was not the right moment to do so. It was decided to limit cable repairs to faulty sections and to rely solely on Gas Yard Substation henceforth at a total cost of less than £2,000.

## Section Feeder points

In addition to the roadside cast iron pillars, section feeder points, located exactly half a mile apart, could be identified by a white band about 12 ins in depth painted on the traction posts at these locations.

| | |
|---|---|
| Cilfynydd | Cilfynydd Road, on a single bracket arm (also known as Burtons) opposite Burton's shop at 89 Cilfynydd Road, supplying Cilfynydd terminus – Norton Bridge. |
| Norton Bridge (Pontshonnorton) | Coedpenmaen Road just south of the Glamorganshire Canal bridge, supplying Norton Bridge to Church Row. |
| Corn Stores Hill (positive and negative) | Bottom of Corn Stores Hill. |
| Old Bridge (positive) (also known as Tabernacle) | Bridge Street, on west side of the River Taff outside the chapel. |
| YMCA (negative) (also known as Palladium Cinema) | North end of Taff Street, close to Gas Yard substation. |
| *New Inn* (positive and negative) (the negative feeder was also known as Brewery Lane) | Hung from wall rosettes outside the *New Inn*, Taff Street (just north of Mill Street). |
| Abbatoirs (also known as Slaughter House or Broadway) | Broadway just west of the ADR bridge opposite the railway junctions leading into the east end of Pontypridd Station. |

No. 13 pulls onto Victoria Bridge beneath the Tabernacle positive feeder heading for Cilfynydd. Note the white painted band around the traction pole on the pavement to the left of the black car intended as a warning to trolleybus drivers not to take power when passing beneath the feeder in the overhead line. (National Tramway Museum [photographer W.A. Camwell])

Having crossed Victoria Bridge over the River Taff Karrier W / Weymann 10 (FNY983) prepares to turn left into Taff Street beneath the Old Bridge positive traction feeder. (Cy Yandell [photographer Derek Lewis])

| | |
|---|---|
| *Crown Hotel*, Fothergill Street (positive and negative) (also known as Treforest) | First span in Fothergill Street south of Taff House junction, Treforest, supplying Taff House Junction – John Street |
| *Crown Hotel*, St. Dubritius Church (positive and negative) | First span in Broadway east of Taff House junction on the corner of Lawn Terrace (west side). |
| Glyntaff Generating Station (positive and negative) | Supplying the Depot area and the hill past the *Llanbradach Arms Hotel* (A470 Cardiff – Merthyr Tydfil trunk road). |

At some stage the 'New Inn' positive and negative feeders were attached to separate span wires. Until around 1949 the tramway bracket arms supporting two widely separated overhead wires remained intact from the junction with Taff Street along Mill Street to serve the Pwllgwaun Colliery with DC power from Gas Yard substation. As the tram rails had been removed it is assumed that one overhead wire was at positive potential and the other at negative.

The 1947 Bedford tower wagon heading north along Taff Street at the junction with Mill Street photographed from the roof of the County Cinema.
(Cy Yandell collection [photographer's name not known])

# APPENDIX E
# OVERHEAD EQUIPMENT

Pontypridd's overhead line layout was of the simplest nature with a turning circle at the northern end of the route in front of the War Memorial at Cilfynydd Common and a reversing triangle at John Street in Treforest. There were no intermediate turning points whatsoever although there is no evidence that this proved an operational hindrance, not least because the Estler trolley bases, featuring one trolley boom superimposed upon the other on a single central pivot, enabled the initial single-deck vehicles (1–7) to reverse without removing the trolley booms from the conductor wires until the vehicle had been completely turned (as demonstrated near the Cilfynydd terminus during the opening ceremony). It is known that in the early days of operation at least, vehicles were cut short at various intermediate points to cope with passenger demands or road closures.

Span wire construction was employed wherever possible, the MoT requiring such construction on all carriageways over 24ft wide, however, there were several narrow parts such as Cilfynydd Road, Fothergill Street and Taff Street where side bracket arms supporting both pairs of wires were necessary or deemed appropriate. Another exception was the two intersecting ornamental steel arches on Victoria Bridge over the River Taff, supplied by Johnson & Phillips at a cost of £120 and erected in 1904 to carry the tram wires, which continued to support the trolleybus overhead wiring for the life of the system.

Except for the alterations to the special work at Taff House and Glyntaff Depot referred to below, ongoing maintenance and the replacement of worn conductor wires or equipment, there was but one alteration to the overhead wiring layout during the lifetime of the system. In September 1935 a traffic island was constructed at Station Square requiring a minor deviation of the northbound line and the planting of two additional traction poles.

## General

One of the arguments in favour of replacing trams with railless electric traction was that they could continue to use much of the electrical infrastructure, including many items of tramway overhead equipment. The Pontypridd conversion, however, employed entirely new overhead wiring and fittings, although the existing feeder cables and wherever possible traction poles were retained. The initial cost of trolleybus overhead equipment, excluding special work such as junctions, varied considerably according to the geography of the route, a heavily curved or graded section such as found in Pontypridd town centre, on Corn Stores Hill and between Machine Bridge and Glyntaff Depot, requiring proportionately more traction poles and bridles or pull-off span wires.

The overhead wiring construction was carried out by Clough, Smith & Co. Ltd., Victoria Street, London, using round gauge 3/0 SWG cadmium copper trolley wire. The entire overhead wiring layout, including the Taff House crossings and junctions, was constructed on an individual basis from single line hangers and tramway-style components. Clinch ears were hammered tight around the trolley wire to grip and support

No. 14 waits on the east side of the turning circle at the northern end of the route in front of the War Memorial at Cilfynydd Common terminus. A Morris Z 5cwt van, produced from 1940 until 1953, pulls out of the lane from Trefychan. (BTS Library [photographer F.W. Ivey])

165

it. The under-running trolley wheel was inevitably pushed down from the trolley wire at each ear which led to ears being burned and radio interference, problems reduced elsewhere by the use of grooved wire employing non-fouling mechanical ears. Some operators, e.g. Rotherham, used round wire but grooved it *in situ* at the point where the ear supported the wire. Although Pontypridd used round gauge wire throughout the trolleybus era it is not known if they employed this grooving procedure.

On straight portions of trolleybus overhead the ears were 12in. long but for special work 6in. ears and for curved sections ears up to 24in. long, which tended to conform to the curvature under line tension thus avoiding acute changes in direction, were available.

A supporting boss located midway along the length of the ear retained a screw-in moulded compound insulator, widely known as an "insulated bolt", which was itself retained in the hanger or an end fitting. Pontypridd's overhead work employed a separate tramway-style hanger to support each trolley wire (a single line hanger) with a strain insulator inserted into the span wire between the positive and negative trolley wires. Although single units supporting both trolley wires (twin line hangers) became available in the mid-1930s there is no evidence that these were ever introduced in Pontypridd. Strain insulators were placed in span wires and catenaries to ensure triple insulation between positive and earth, and double insulation between negative and earth.

Although no supporting documentary evidence has been found, photographs suggest that the two conductor wires were initially hung 18in. apart, the customary gauge at this relatively early stage in trolley bus development. The trolley vehicles were equipped with under-running swivel head wheel collectors. The separation between the conductor wires appears to have been increased at a later date to 2ft (24in.), which had become the acknowledged British standard during the late 1930s, on an *ad hoc* basis, e.g. Broadway, although 18in. gauge overhead survived in some parts until closure.

The simple span wire suspension inevitably sagged towards the centre of the road and thus the negative trolley wire nearest the kerb hung at a slightly higher level than the positive one. In extreme cases this could provoke dewirements.

In a number of locations along the trolleybus route a second span wire some 3ft above that supporting the trolley wires was hung where telephone wires crossed the road between the tops of the traction poles on each side of the road (the minimum clearance laid down by the MoT was 2ft). These thin guard wires were to prevent a broken or sagging telephone wire coming into contact with the trolley wires. The guard wires were earthed through a connection to the negative trolley wire. Examples of these guard wires could be found in Cilfynydd Road, Machine Bridge, and Pontshonnorton Bridge.

Protective netting hanging vertically between the traction poles some 15–20 ft above the ground and parallel to the trolley wires immediately above the footpath was installed at points where dewirements were more frequent and where a swinging trolley pole could cause damage to nearby buildings and windows. Installations could be found until the end of trolleybus operation in High Street and Taff Street.

Trolley wire breakages at the outgoing end of rigid overhead fittings such as section insulators, negative sections and insulated crossings were a common feature of trolley vehicle operation until the early 1930s. They usually occurred close to the outgoing end of the rigid fitting and were caused either by crystallisation due to the lateral sway of the trolley wire provoked by the passage of the vehicle beneath or by the jolt of the trolley wheel, which had been rolling along the underside of the fitting or hanger, returning to the wire. Clough, Smith designed their own section insulators, negative sections and insulated crossings for use in Pontypridd and these were fitted with non-hammering ends, to avoid crystallisation at the points where the trolley wire ended. However, trolley wire breakages at these points were a feature of the Pontypridd system for the first 3–4 years of operation until those fittings of Clough, Smith's design had all been replaced with British Insulated Cables' "rampend" fittings. The company had correctly identified that the underside of the fitting was wider than the bottom of the "V" shaped groove of the trolley wheel and that at these points the wheel was forced down from the trolley wire itself. The repeated blow on the trolley wire at the end of the fitting when the wheel, forced upwards by the sprung trolley boom, returned to the wire caused the breakages. The "rampend" fittings included a gradual transition onto and off the fitting thereby eliminating the jolt.

## Traction Poles

All tramway traction poles at curves and termini were replaced by solid drawn seamless tubular steel stepped poles manufactured by British Mannesmann Co. Ltd., Newport, although many of the traction poles still in acceptable condition on straight portions of the road and capable of supporting the weight of four conductor wires were retained. An undefined number of these poles were reinforced internally with steel rods and concrete or externally with an angle welded to the back of the top section whilst some 94 poles which were simply in the wrong location to support trolleybus overhead equipment had to be moved.

A variety of pole diameters and lengths were used to provide greater strength at locations such as curves, junctions or other special work, where the increased weight of the overhead wiring placed additional strains on its supports. The lower 6ft of the traction pole was sunk into the ground, with a backwards rake to compensate for the weight of the overhead equipment, and embedded in concrete. Once the pole was supporting the overhead wiring it was pulled into the vertical. In total, the contractor Clough, Smith installed 32 light, 111 medium and 77 heavy poles. As an illustration a 31-foot heavy steel pole was 9½in. in diameter at the base, tapering initially to 8½in. and then again to 7½in. at the top. Each new traction pole was surmounted with a simple ball finial, those surviving from the tramway era sometimes retaining their original ball and spike finials. Many finials disappeared entirely during the trolleybus era, promoting water ingress and thus rust.

There was a considerable weight of equipment aloft. The two pairs of trolley wires on a straight section between two traction poles, together with the supporting hangers and span wires, weighed about 235 lb. The total installed weight of conductor wire and fittings on the system was some 8 tons. Statutory regulations stipulated a maximum longitudinal span of 120ft as for tramways, however, the virtual doubling of suspended weight meant that this was not always desirable whilst it could only be achieved on straight sections of road. Above curved sections of road where the trolley wire had to be pulled into a series of straights approximating to the desired curves these were more frequent.

Poles and bracket arms were painted at infrequent intervals with green paint which weathered down to a paler, almost olive green, shade over the years. No evidence has been found of a traction pole numbering system and it is believed that a specific location was identified by the name or number of the nearest building.

Many of the traction poles supported power supply cables and street lighting installations in addition to the trolleybus overhead equipment. In latter days this legacy of the joint UDC Electricity and Tramways Department led to the uppermost few feet of such traction poles being either painted in a different shade of green to the remainder of the pole or indeed not being painted at all due to the painter being concerned that the lines, i.e. the power supply and street lighting wires carried at the tops of the traction posts, were "live". Rusty areas at the top of the poles are clearly visible on photographs taken in the last few years of operation.

In the case of span wire overhead construction, the galvanised steel supporting wire ran between traction poles planted, normally at the kerb, on each side of the road, and attached to the upper section of the pole by a galvanised mild steel pole strap. MoT regulations required that the height of the trolley wire should not be less than 20ft above the surface of the road. Double insulation between the positive and negative trolley wires was provided by the hangers supporting the trolley wire and between the trolley wire and earth by the hanger and an insulator either in the span wire or between the span wire and the retaining bracket. Triple insulation

between the positive trolley wire and the pole was required on those bracket arm poles which also carried street lamps. Wall-mounted rosettes, anchored in roadside buildings, could replace one or both traction poles. Span wire construction provided a flexible support to the trolley wire. In January 1957 when the system was abandoned the Transport Department was paying 23 easements for wall rosettes for overhead wiring.

Where side bracket traction poles were employed the insulators supporting the trolley wire were carried by short lengths of span wire thus providing the required double insulation between the positive trolley wire and earth, and also providing a degree of elasticity to the trolley wire support thereby increasing trolley wire life (rigid suspension inevitably caused wire fractures). Further insulation was provided by a section of rubber sheet between the traction pole mounted clamp and the steel tube of the side bracket arm. Part of the weight of the arm, which in Pontypridd reached a maximum of 18ft in length, was taken by two strengthening tie-rods.

The sole railway bridge across the trolleybus route on the Broadway carrying the GWR ex-ADR Pontypridd-Caerphilly line, was too high above the road for overhead wiring bridge hangers in the usual wooden toughing but too low to permit the wires to remain unsupported. Four wooden supports hung down, two on each side of the steel girder bridge, supporting a transverse beam with bridge type hangers on the underside to hold the trolley wires and act as a buffer should the sprung trolley booms force the running wires up towards the underside of the bridge.

**Karrier W 8 (GNY301) heads west along Broadway towards the town centre and Cilfynydd. The sole railway bridge across the trolleybus route carrying the GWR ex-ADR Pontypridd-Caerphilly line can be seen behind the vehicle whilst the retaining wall to the right of the trolleybus supported the ex-TVR mainline from Merthyr Tydfil to Cardiff. The railway bridge was too high above the road for overhead wiring bridge hangers in the usual wooden toughing but too low to permit the wires to remain unsupported, and thus four wooden beams supported the trolley wires well clear of the underside of the bridge. (BTS Library [photographer's name not recorded])**

# Frogs

There were just two locations on the system where special work was installed, namely Taff House junction and in the Glyntaff Depot area, but these layouts changed more than once during the trolleybus era and the following information, gleaned from diagrams, photographs and recollections may not be accurate or complete. Again, construction was on an individual basis from single line hangers and tramway-style components, e.g. a right hand 25° facing junction would be made up of two single line 25° right hand frogs and a 25° right hand insulated crossing. There were two examples of sprung trail or shunt frogs in Pontypridd, namely at the John Street, Treforest reversing triangle and, probably, from the early 1940s in the entrance to the trolleybus depot building at Glyntaff. A reversing vehicle was able to open the "tongue" which then sprung back to its normal position permitting egress onto the main route in the opposite direction.

## Taff House

Less than 100 yards before the southern end of Broadway at St. Dubritius' Church (now known by its Welsh language equivalent, St. Dyfrig's) and Machine Bridge, the service trolleybus route branched off to head south along Fothergill Street (B4272) towards Treforest Station and ultimately John Street terminus. At this point a double junction was installed to provide depot access whereby trolleybuses could travel from town across Machine Bridge and vice versa. A hand-operated pull frog (a point or switch in the overhead wiring) was installed in the southbound Broadway wiring enabling a vehicle to turn off the main route to cross Machine Bridge. A second pull frog was installed in the northbound Broadway wiring enabling vehicles entering service over Machine Bridge to turn south around the traffic island into Fothergill Street.

A late 1930s view of St. Dubritius Church just to the east of the junction of Broadway with Fothergill Street. The westbound overhead wiring from Glyntaff Depot curves around in the foreground towards Fothergill Street and the Treforest terminus. The eastbound wiring continues past the church and over Machine Bridge across the River Taff. In the background above the road, the oxide-red painted Glyntaff depot buildings can be seen. Two pedestrian crossings, both equipped with Belisha beacons named after the then Minister of Transport, Leslie Hore-Belisha, are evident. They began to appear in mid-1935. (Cy Yandell collection)

As a result of operating difficulties the double junction and crossing at Taff House were taken out in early December 1932 and both the up and down lines were made straight through from Broadway into Fothergill Street. It now became impossible to reach the depot from the town without manually de-poling from the southbound pair of wires and transferring the booms on to a section of parallel wiring which was added above the side of the road in Broadway. Wiring from Machine Bridge into Broadway heading towards the town was removed, however, the trailing junction into the southbound Fothergill Street wiring remained. This

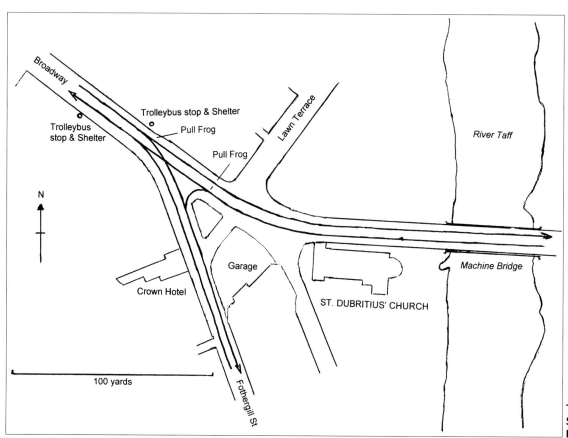

**Taff House Junction September 1930 – December 1932.**

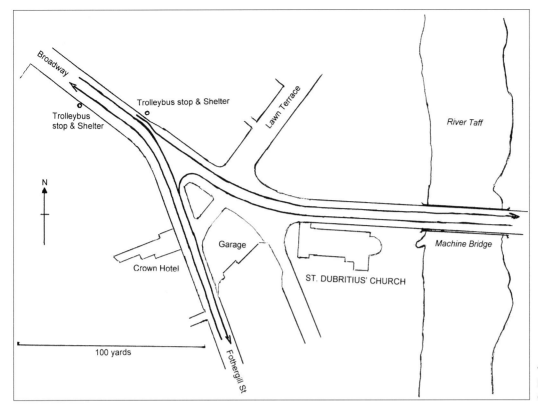

**Taff House Junction
December 1932 – July 1940
or later.**

layout is known to have remained in place until at least July 1940.

There was a return to virtually the original layout, probably to ease operations in the "black-out" and thought to have taken place in late 1940 or early 1941 although this is not corroborated by the abbreviated official records of wartime.

A hand-operated pull frog was again installed in the southbound Broadway wiring in place of the section of parallel wiring enabling a vehicle to turn off the main route

to cross Machine Bridge. A second pull frog enabled depot-bound trolleybuses from Fothergill Street to turn east from the northbound wiring towards Machine Bridge. It remained impossible, having crossed Machine Bridge, to continue along Broadway towards the town centre.

It is not known if any form of "repeater" indicator light to confirm to the trolleybus driver that the frog switch frogs had moved to the required position was installed at the Taff House junction but in view of the utilitarian nature of the installation this is considered unlikely.

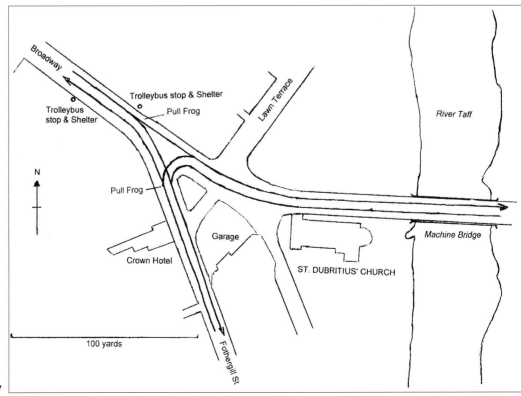

**July 1940 or later – 1957**

**Taff House junction. Karrier W No. 9 joins Broadway from Fothergill Street on its way north from Treforest to the town centre and beyond. This view well shows the post-war overhead wiring layout. It will be particularly noticed that it was impossible for a trolleybus entering service from Glyntaff Depot, having crossed Machine Bridge, to continue along Broadway. (Stephen Lockwood [photographer W.A. Camwell])**

### Glyntaff Depot

Access to and from the Transport Department's sole depot and workshops, located on the same site as the power station, refuse destructor and gasworks on the hillside above the River Taff between the Glamorganshire Canal and the railway, was by way of Machine Bridge, the steep and winding Glyntaff Road over the canal bridge and Cemetery Road. The inbound and outbound pair of wires entered the UDC property 100 yards after the right-angle turn into Cemetery Road and then passed behind a former private house fronting onto Cemetery Road followed by the undertaking's Head Office.

Photographs show that initially both pairs of wires continued past the corrugated iron trolleybus depot, motorbus garage, the tram car sheds (soon to become the departmental workshops), electricity power station and refuse destructor to terminate in front of the entrance to the gas works site. There would have been just sufficient space here for a trolleybus to carry out a 3-point turn but there is no evidence that a reverser was installed. In 1908 a triangle of track to turn tramcars, thereby equalising wear and tear, had been laid between the power station and the rear of the car sheds, however, construction in the intervening 20 years of additional outhouses at the north end of the power station ruled out the installation of a trolley vehicle reversing triangle at this point. In any case the wide lateral deviation provided by the Estler trolley base enabled the English Electric single-deck vehicles to turn without de-poling by shunting backwards and forwards several times.

Access to the open-fronted galvanised corrugated iron trolleybus depot was by means of a physically-isolated single

pair of wires at 90° to the access wiring and electrically fed through jumper cables from the northbound wiring heading out of the depot area towards the town. A second physically-isolated pair of wires, again electrically fed through jumper cables from the northbound wiring, were hung above road 1 of the easternmost bay (1) of the 3-bay tram car shed building (each bay having space for two roads) to provide access to the workshops. There were no frogs whatsoever in the depot area and a trolleybus could only reach the trolleybus depot or (tram) car shed and workshops by de-poling and rewiring.

Although the car shed had been deemed unsuitable for housing trolley vehicles, in May 1931 the physically-isolated trolley wires leading into bay 1 were slewed to hang over road 2 instead of road 1 in such a manner that they could run into both roads thereby offering additional covered accommodation for trolley vehicles likely to be displaced by the arrival of 7 new motorbuses.

The trolley wires were supported by hangers fixed to the entrance lintel and continued to the rear of the car shed building. This would have eased access to the erstwhile car shed, which with the end of tramway operation on 30 August 1931, was converted into maintenance workshops for the Department's entire fleet. This layout is known to have remained in place until at least July 1940.

The next and probable final alteration to the overhead wiring layout in the depot area took place in the early 1940s, possibly in connection with the arrival of Hull vehicles on loan. The southbound or entry wires running beyond the trolleybus depot building past the car shed and electricity works were

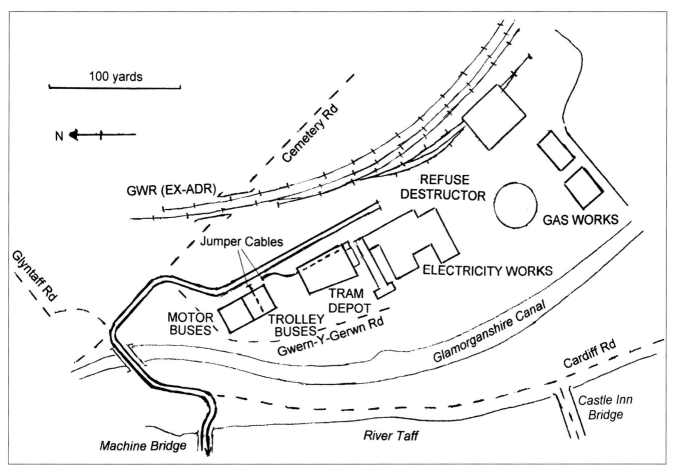

**Glyntaff Depot September 1930 – May 1931**

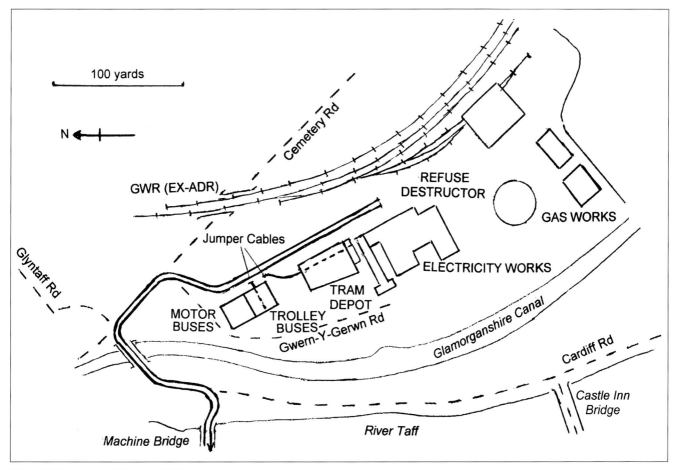

**Glyntaff Depot May 1931 – July 1940.**

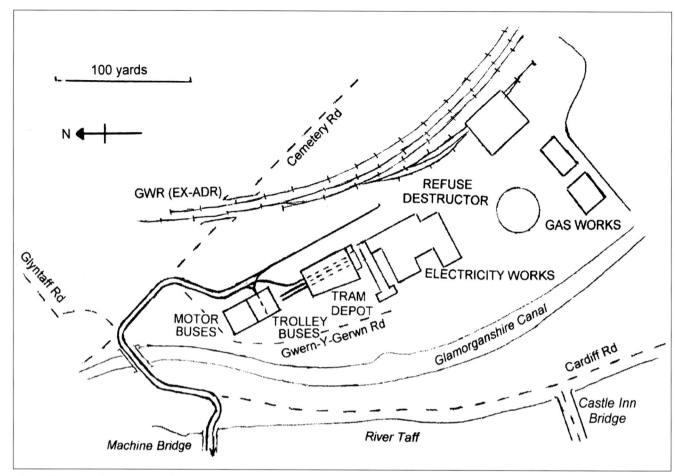

**Glyntaff Depot July 1940 – March 1957.**

removed, together with their supporting attachments on the side bracket arm. The northbound or exit wires were joined to the southbound wires just past the trolleybus depot building and a sprung trail or shunt frog, set for reversing into the building, installed at this point. A sprung junction frog, set for leaving the building, was installed immediately in front of the depot entrance creating a reversing triangle.

Probably at the same time the previously physically-isolated trolley wires leading into bay 1 of the erstwhile car shed were extended through a crossing to a second trail frog outside the trolleybus depot building where they joined the northbound or exit wires. Both roads of bay 2 of the car shed were also equipped with overhead wiring. Photographs show that two pairs of wires, supported by hangers fixed to the bay 2 entrance lintel, were installed above roads 1 and 2. It is likely that the trolley wires entering bay 2 were supported by a single traction pole on the opposite side of the yard next to the southern side wall of the trolleybus depot and that they were fed by jumper cables from those entering bay 1.

These alterations provided access to or from the depot and car shed building, and enabled both single and double-deck trolleybuses to reverse, without it being necessary to de-pole and rewire the vehicle.

It has been suggested that there may have been a second pair of wires inside the depot building at a later date, possibly as the reversing stub from the northbound wires with the sprung trail or shunt frog removed, or accessed through a hand-operated frog inside the depot building or even as a disconnected stub, but no corroborative evidence of any such layout has been found.

## Vehicle Equipment

The current collectors on the roof of each trolleybus consisted of three main parts, the trolley base carrying the trolley boom and allowing it to swing in a horizontal plane and to rise under spring tension, the boom itself and, at the extreme end of the boom, the wheel collector swivel trolley head which made contact with the under surface of the power conducting trolley wire. All three parts were insulated from each other. The current was carried from the trolley head by a flexible cable running through the hollow trolley boom which narrowed to 1 ins diameter at the trolley head end. The boom, a tapering steel tube was wrapped in black bitumen impregnated insulating tape to minimise the chance of it shorting the trolley wires in the event of a dewirement.

The English Electric SD6WTB single-deck vehicles were equipped with Estler Bros. patent pattern trolley bases which featured two superimposed trolley booms concentrically mounted on a substantial single pivot. Two springs forward of the pivot on each boom held it aloft with a vertical pressure of 30–35 lb. The negative boom was the lower and longer. All subsequent deliveries were equipped with a conventional trolley base for each boom. The springs of Guy BTX60 8 and Bristol E 9 were mounted behind each pivot and lay parallel to the vehicles' roof, whereas those on the Karrier Ws lay along the trolley boom (as did those of the wartime loans from Portsmouth and Hull). The vertical upward pressure of the trolley heads on the wire could be measured by hanging a scale from each boom and adjusted at the springs on the trolley base.

Although the majority of British trolleybus operators followed a policy of replacing wheel collectors with slider

It appears that, having used the reversing triangle at the entrance of the open-fronted trolleybus depot building, the driver of No. 8 wanted to manoeuvre the vehicle backwards into a specific part of the building. The driver is seen climbing out of his cab presumably to check that there is sufficient space to pass Guy Arab LUF motorbus 68 (STX104) delivered in 1956. (Peter Smith collection [photographer's name not recorded])

heads from the mid-1930s Pontypridd UDC continued to use wheel collector swivel trolley heads until the abandonment of the system. Indeed Pontypridd was the last British trolleybus operator to use wheel collectors. The grooved trolley wheels, 4in. in diameter, ran along the undersurface of the trolley wire and tended to make a "hissing" or "whistling" sound as they rotated at high speed above the vehicle. A change to slider heads could have doubled the life of the conductor wire and reduced the risk of dewirements but this option was never discussed. At least pre-war trolley wheels and other trolley equipment were supplied by J. Stone & Co. Ltd., Deptford, London SE14. Post-war the Transport Manager reported that trolley wheels were difficult to source and increasingly expensive.

Hoar frost effectively left a layer of insulation along the trolley wire interrupting the power supply and leading to both jerky, potentially dangerous, running and causing intense arcing which soon damaged and wore the trolley wheel.

## Maintenance

Routine overhead maintenance was carried out by a two-man gang on Sunday mornings but emergency coverage in case of breakdown or damage was available 24 hours a day, 7 days a week. A group of men specialised in trolleybus overhead wiring matters was retained by the UDC Electricity Department when this came under separate management from the Transport Department in 1940. This arrangement continued within the South Wales Electricity Board following nationalisation.

It is interesting to note that under Pontypridd UDC in the 1939 telephone directory, the home telephone number was given for the trolleybus overhead linesman. The 1946 issue listed two home telephone numbers for trolleybus overhead linesmen.

In August 1916 an Edison accumulator electric tower wagon, registration L1185, had been purchased for two six monthly

payments of £418 10s 0d and a battery charging room was set up at the depot which was also used for the Council's electric dust carts. Prior to this a horse-drawn tower wagon had been used. The Edison wagon ran in an Indian Red livery and weighed 2ton 9cwt, including the batteries. Clough Smith hired the tower wagon for the overhead erection. Despite several overhauls by the mid-1930s it had become unreliable and the battery was life expired, the horse drawn wagon of 1905 vintage being pressed into service on a number of occasions.

The Edison was replaced in 1935 with a purpose-built vehicle made up of a second-hand Bristol 2-ton lorry chassis, intended as a "sweetener" for a prospective double-deck motorbus order, equipped with a Rawlinson wind-up 3-stage tower and lorry body. On 9 July 1946 the Electricity Committee, having considered the condition of the Bristol tower wagon and the estimated cost of repairs and replacement parts which approached the cost of a new one, decided that a new tower wagon should be bought. In the meantime Cardiff Corporation Transport Department loaned their Dennis-Stevens Petrol Electric Tower Wagon BO3639 (ex-motorbus 49 of 1920) until the new tower wagon arrived. The Electricity Department took delivery of a new Bedford Tower Wagon and Workshop in early November 1947; the Pontypridd Bristol lorry was withdrawn and the Cardiff tower wagon returned. The tower wagons were officially vested in the Electricity Department and passed to the South Wales Electricity Board upon nationalisation together with responsibility for maintenance of the UDC's trolleybus overhead equipment.

In October 2009, more than half a century after trolleybuses ceased to operate in Pontypridd, the author noted that rosettes are still in place on buildings in Taff Street whilst a number of traction poles still remain on the west side of Cilfynydd Road between the 'Albion Hotel' and Richard Street with a single example in Taff Street (eight in total).

Edison accumulator tower wagon parked on the east side of Victoria Bridge in front of Ceridwen Terrace opposite the 'The Maltsters' public house in tramway days. (Peter Smith collection)

Old Bridge, Pontypridd. 1.

# APPENDIX F

# FARES, FARE TABLES AND TICKETS

## Fares

The electric tramways introduced a system of overlapping penny stages, averaging just under one mile in length, however, this simple structure was soon supplemented by a range of reduced workmen's and discounted return fares. Declining passenger numbers through the 1920s brought on by a combination of the industrial recession, miners' strikes and increasing bus or railway competition saw considerable fare discounting, e.g. a system of tokens giving a 20% reduction. In May 1929 workers' single tickets were withdrawn, to be replaced by returns costing less than double the single fare.

The trolleybuses adopted a similar stage structure with a minimum fare of 1½d, followed by ½d stages, being charged for a stage or portion of a stage. In principle the trolleybus fares were the same as those on the tram services they replaced. The first proper fare tables only appeared in the May 1933 public timetable. Thereafter detailed fare tables were included in each issue of the combined fare and timetable, separate sheets and notices on the vehicles being used for intermediate amendments. As far as fare levels on the trolleybuses were concerned, the Act of Parliament lay down a maximum charge of 1½d per mile with a 2d minimum fare for ordinary traffic and 1d per mile with 1½d minimum for workmen.

There had been some 34 stops (17 compulsory) between Treforest and Cilfynydd prior to conversion but this was reduced to 28 stops (5 compulsory) by doing away with those at the Observer Office, Motor Station, Post Office, 'Maltsters Arms', Church Road and Burton's Cilfynydd Road.

| | |
|---|---|
| F | Treforest terminus |
| R | Treforest Station Entrance |
| C | *Bush Hotel* |
| F C | Taff House |
| R | Rock House |
| F R | Taff Vale Park (Main Entrance) |
| F R | Archway |
| R | Office Office Loop |
| R | Slaughterhouse |
| F C | Station Square |
| C | Rhondda Bridge (into Town) |
| R | *New Inn Hotel* |
| F C | Fountain |
| R | YMCA |
| F R | Berw Road |
| F R | West Street |
| F R | Common Road (on down only) |
| R | Newbridge |
| F R | Baptist Chapel |
| R | *Bonvilston Hotel* |
| F R | Bonvilston Road |
| R | Taff Vale |
| F R | Norton Bridge |
| R | Police Row (top end) |
| F R | Quarry Siding |
| R | *Albion Hotel* |
| R | Workmen's Hall |
| R | Richard Street |
| F | Cilfynydd Terminus |

| | |
|---|---|
| F | fare stage |
| R | request stop |
| C | compulsory stop |

In 1934 there were 13 fare stages between Treforest and Cilfynydd, but this had been reduced to just 8 by 1952.

**Ordinary Fare.** **TREFOREST—CILFYNYDD** (S—Single. R—Return). 25

| Stage No. | | Terminus Treforest | Taff House | Taff Vale Park | Archway | Station Square | Mill Street | Fountain | Berw Road | Common Road | Baptist Chapel | Bon. Road | Norton Bridge | Quarry Siding | Cilfynydd |
|---|---|---|---|---|---|---|---|---|---|---|---|---|---|---|---|
| 1 | TREFOREST TERMINUS | ... | ... | ... | ... | ... | ... | ... | ... | ... | ... | ... | ... | ... | ... |
| 2 | TAFF HOUSE | 1½d. | ... | ... | ... | ... | ... | ... | ... | ... | ... | ... | ... | ... | ... |
| 3 | TAFF VALE PARK (Main Entrance). | 1½d. | 1½d. | ... | ... | ... | ... | ... | ... | ... | ... | ... | ... | ... | ... |
| 4 | ARCHWAY | 1½d. | 1½d. | 1d. | ... | ... | ... | ... | ... | ... | ... | ... | ... | ... | ... |
| 5 | STATION SQUARE | 1½d. | 1½d. | 1d. | 1d. | ... | ... | ... | ... | ... | ... | ... | ... | ... | ... |
| — | MILL STREET | 2d. | 1½d. | 1½d. | 1½d. | 1d. | ... | ... | ... | ... | ... | ... | ... | ... | ... |
| 6 | FOUNTAIN | 2d. | 1½d. | 1½d. | 1½d. | 1d. | 1d. | ... | ... | ... | ... | ... | ... | ... | ... |
| 7 | BERW ROAD | 2½d. | 2d. | 1½d. | 1½d. | 1d. | 1d. | 1d. | ... | ... | ... | ... | ... | ... | ... |
| 8 | COMMON ROAD | 2½d. | 2½d. | 2d. | 2d. | 1½d | 1½d. | 1½d. | 1½d. | ... | ... | ... | ... | ... | ... |
| 9 | BAPTIST CHAPEL | 2½d. | 2½d. | 2d. | 2d. | 1½d. | 1½d. | 1½d. | 1½d. | 1½d. | ... | ... | ... | ... | ... |
| 10 | BONVILSTON ROAD | 3d. | 2½d. | 2½d. | 2½d. | 2d. | 2d. | 1½d. | 1½d. | 1½d. | 1½d. | ... | ... | ... | ... |
| 11 | NORTON BRIDGE | 3d. | 2½d. | 2½d. | 2½d. | 2d. | 2d. | 2d. | 2d. | 1½d. | 1½d. | 1½d. | ... | ... | ... |
| 12 | QUARRY SIDING | 3½d. | 3½d. | 2½d. | 2½d. | 2½d. | 2½d. | 2½d. | 2d. | 2d. | 1½d. | 1½d. | 1½d. | ... | ... |
| 13 | CILFYNYDD | 3½d. | 3½d. | 3d. | 3d. | 2½d. | 2½d. | 2½d. | 2d. | 2d. | 2d. | 1½d. | 1½d. | 1½d. | ... |
| | **Workmen's Fares.** | | | | | | | | | | | | | | |
| 1 | TREFOREST TERMINUS | ... | 1½d.S 2d.R | 1½d.S 2d.R | 1½d.S 2d.R | 1½d.S 2d.R | 1½d.S 2d.R | 2d.S 3d.R | 2d.S 3d.R | 2d.S 3d.R | 2d.S 3d.R | 3d.S 4d.R | 3d.S 4d.R | 3d.S 4d.R | 3d.S 4d.R |
| 2 | TAFF HOUSE | ... | ... | 1½d.S 2d.R | 1½d.S 2d.R | 1½d.S 2d.R | 1½d.S 2d.R | 2d.S 3d.R | 2d.S 3d.R | 2d.S 3d.R | 2d.S 3d.R | 3d.S 4d.R | 3d.S 4d.R | 3d.S 4d.R | 3d.S 4d.R |
| 3 | TAFF VALE PARK (Main Entrance) | ... | ... | ... | 1d. | 1d. | 1½d.S 2d.R | 2d.S 3d.R | 2d.S 3d.R | 2d.S 3d.R | 2d.S 3d.R | 3d.S 4d.R | 3d.S 4d.R | 3d.S 4d.R | 3d.S 4d.R |
| 4 | ARCHWAY | ... | ... | ... | ... | 1d. | 1½d.S 2d.R | 2d.S 3d.R | 2d.S 3d.R | 2d.S 3d.R | 2d.S 3d.R | 3d.S 4d.R | 3d.S 4d.R | 3d.S 4d.R | 3d.S 4d.R |
| 5 | STATION SQUARE | ... | ... | ... | ... | ... | 1d. | 1d. | 1d. | 1½d.S 2d.R | 1½d.S 2d.R | 1½d.S 2d.R | 2d.S 3d.R | 2d.S 3d.R | 2d.S 3d.R |
| — | MILL STREET | ... | ... | ... | ... | ... | ... | 1d. | 1d. | 1½d.S 2d.R | 1½d.S 2d.R | 1½d.S 2d.R | 2d.S 3d.R | 2d.S 3d.R | 2d.S 3d.R |
| 6 | FOUNTAIN | ... | ... | ... | ... | ... | ... | ... | 1d. | 1½d.S 2d.R | 1½d.S 2d.R | 1½d.S 2d.R | 2d.S 3d.R | 2d.S 3d.R | 2d.S 3d.R |
| 7 | BERW ROAD | ... | ... | ... | ... | ... | ... | ... | ... | 1½d.S 2d.R | 1½d.S 2d.R | 1½d.S 2d.R | 2d.S 3d.R | 2d.S 3d.R | 2d.S 3d.R |
| 8 | COMMON ROAD | ... | ... | ... | ... | ... | ... | ... | ... | ... | 1½d.S 2d.S | 1½d.S 2d.R | 1½d.S 2d.R | 2d.S 3d.R | 2d.S 3d.R |
| 9 | BAPTIST CHAPEL | ... | ... | ... | ... | ... | ... | ... | ... | ... | ... | 1½d.S 2d.R | 1½d.S 2d.R | 2d.S 3d.R | 2d.S 3d.R |
| 10 | BONVILSTON ROAD | ... | ... | ... | ... | ... | ... | ... | ... | ... | ... | ... | 1½d.S 2d.R | 1½d.S 2d.R | 1½d.S 2d.R |
| 11 | NORTON BRIDGE | ... | ... | ... | ... | ... | ... | — | ... | ... | ... | ... | ... | 1½d.S 2d.R | 1½d.S 2d.R |
| 12 | QUARRY SIDING | ... | ... | ... | ... | ... | ... | ... | ... | ... | ... | ... | ... | ... | 1½d.S 2d.R |
| 13 | CILFYNYDD | ... | ... | ... | ... | ... | ... | ... | ... | ... | ... | ... | ... | ... | ... |

**Faretable 1934.**

**T.G.R. 513/19. TREFOREST — CILFYNYDD.**

| Stage Number | | | | | | | | |
|---|---|---|---|---|---|---|---|---|
| 1 | **Treforest Terminus** | | | | | | | |
| 2 | 1d. | **Taff House** | | | | | | |
| 3 | 2d. | 1d. | **Archway** | | | | | |
| 4 | 3d. | 2s. | 2d. | **Station Square** | | | | |
| 5 | 3d. | 3d. | 2d. | 1d. | **Old Bridge** | | | |
| 6 | 4d. | 3d. | 3d. | 2d. | 1d. | **Baptist Chapel** | | |
| 7 | 5d. S. / 9d. R. | 4d. | 4d. | 3d. | 2d. | 2d. | **Norton Bridge** | |
| 8 | 6d. S. / 10d. R. | 6d. S. / 10d. R. | 6d. S. / 10d. R. | 5d. S. / 9d. R. | 4d. | 3d. | 2d. | **Cilfynydd Terminus** |

WEEKLY TICKETS (*See Page 21 for Conditions*) :

| | Single Fare. | | Weekly Ticket. |
|---|---|---|---|
| | 5d. | ... | 3s. 4d. |
| | 6d. | ... | 4s. 0d. |

WEEKLY TRANSFER TICKETS (*See page 21 for conditions*) :

| | |
|---|---|
| Bonvilston Road — Gt. Western Colliery | 3s. 4d. |
| Treforest Terminus — Gt. Western Colliery | 3s. 4d. |
| Cilfynydd — Gt. Western Colliery | 4s. 8d. |
| Treforest Terminus — Trehafod | 4s. 0d. |
| Cilfynydd Terminus — Trehafod | 5s. 4d. |
| Treforest Terminus — Coedcae Colliery | 4s. 8d. |
| Bonvilston Road — Coedcae Colliery | 4s. 0d. |
| Cilfynydd Terminus — Coedcae Colliery | 6s. 0d. |
| Sycamore Street, Rhydyfelin/Cilfynydd (via. Town centre) | 5s. 4d. |
| Dynea, Rhydyfelin — Cilfynydd (via. Town) | 6s. 0d. |

**SPECIAL FARE** : Cilfynydd Terminus — Quarry Siding ... 1d.

**FOUR JOURNEY TICKETS** ... 1s. 0d.

Faretable July 1954.

## TREFOREST–CILFYNYDD: DISTANCES (MILES) FROM EACH STOPPING PLACES

**Stopping place**     **Distance from**

| Stopping place | | | | | | | | | | | | | | | | | | | | | | | |
|---|---|---|---|---|---|---|---|---|---|---|---|---|---|---|---|---|---|---|---|---|---|---|---|
| Treforest Terminus | | | | | | | | | | | | | | | | | | | | | | | |
| Treforest Station | 0.1 | | | | | | | | | | | | | | | | | | | | | | |
| Bush Hotel | 0.2 | 0.1 | | | | | | | | | | | | | | | | | | | | | |
| Taff House | 0.4 | 0.3 | 0.2 | | | | | | | | | | | | | | | | | | | | |
| Rock House | 0.5 | 0.4 | 0.3 | 0.1 | | | | | | | | | | | | | | | | | | | |
| Taff Vale Park | 0.5 | 0.4 | 0.3 | 0.1 | | | | | | | | | | | | | | | | | | | |
| Archway | 0.6 | 0.5 | 0.4 | 0.2 | 0.1 | | | | | | | | | | | | | | | | | | |
| Old Observer Office | 0.6 | 0.5 | 0.4 | 0.2 | 0.1 | 0.1 | | | | | | | | | | | | | | | | | |
| Station Square | 1.2 | 1.1 | 0.9 | 0.7 | 0.7 | 0.7 | 0.6 | 0.6 | | | | | | | | | | | | | | | |
| New Inn | 1.3 | 1.2 | 1.0 | 0.8 | 0.8 | 0.8 | 0.7 | 0.7 | 0.1 | | | | | | | | | | | | | | |
| Fountain | 1.5 | 1.4 | 1.2 | 1.0 | 1.0 | 1.0 | 0.9 | 0.9 | 0.3 | 0.2 | | | | | | | | | | | | | |
| Old Bridge | 1.6 | 1.5 | 1.3 | 1.1 | 1.1 | 1.1 | 1.0 | 1.0 | 0.4 | 0.3 | 0.1 | | | | | | | | | | | | |
| West Street | 1.7 | 1.6 | 1.4 | 1.2 | 1.2 | 1.2 | 1.1 | 1.1 | 0.5 | 0.4 | 0.2 | 0.1 | | | | | | | | | | | |
| Corn Stores | 1.8 | 1.7 | 1.5 | 1.3 | 1.3 | 1.3 | 1.2 | 1.2 | 0.6 | 0.5 | 0.3 | 0.2 | 0.1 | | | | | | | | | | |
| Baptist Chapel | 2.0 | 1.9 | 1.7 | 1.5 | 1.5 | 1.5 | 1.4 | 1.4 | 0.8 | 0.7 | 0.5 | 0.4 | 0.3 | 0.2 | | | | | | | | | |
| Bonvilston Hotel | 2.1 | 2.0 | 1.8 | 1.6 | 1.6 | 1.6 | 1.5 | 1.5 | 0.9 | 0.8 | 0.6 | 0.5 | 0.4 | 0.3 | 0.1 | | | | | | | | |
| Bonvilston Road | 2.2 | 2.1 | 1.9 | 1.7 | 1.7 | 1.7 | 1.6 | 1.6 | 1.0 | 0.9 | 0.7 | 0.6 | 0.5 | 0.4 | 0.2 | 0.1 | | | | | | | |
| Lower Taff View | 2.5 | 2.4 | 2.2 | 2.0 | 2.0 | 2.0 | 1.9 | 1.9 | 1.3 | 1.2 | 1.0 | 0.9 | 0.8 | 0.7 | 0.5 | 0.4 | 0.3 | | | | | | |
| Norton Bridge | 2.6 | 2.5 | 2.3 | 2.1 | 2.1 | 2.1 | 2.0 | 2.0 | 1.4 | 1.3 | 1.1 | 1.0 | 0.9 | 0.8 | 0.6 | 0.5 | 0.4 | 0.1 | | | | | |
| Quarry Siding | 2.9 | 2.8 | 2.6 | 2.4 | 2.4 | 2.4 | 2.3 | 2.3 | 1.7 | 1.6 | 1.4 | 1.3 | 1.2 | 1.1 | 0.9 | 0.8 | 0.7 | 0.4 | 0.3 | | | | |
| Albion Hotel | 3.1 | 3.0 | 2.8 | 2.6 | 2.6 | 2.6 | 2.5 | 2.5 | 1.9 | 1.8 | 1.6 | 1.5 | 1.4 | 1.3 | 1.1 | 1.0 | 0.9 | 0.6 | 0.5 | 0.2 | | | |
| Workmen's Hall | 3.3 | 3.2 | 3.0 | 2.8 | 2.8 | 2.8 | 2.7 | 2.7 | 2.1 | 2.0 | 1.8 | 1.7 | 1.6 | 1.5 | 1.3 | 1.2 | 1.1 | 0.8 | 0.7 | 0.4 | 0.2 | | |
| Richard Street | 3.4 | 3.3 | 3.1 | 2.9 | 2.9 | 2.9 | 2.8 | 2.8 | 2.2 | 2.1 | 1.9 | 1.8 | 1.7 | 1.6 | 1.4 | 1.3 | 1.2 | 0.9 | 0.8 | 0.5 | 0.3 | 0.1 | |
| Cilfynydd Terminus | 3.5 | 3.4 | 3.2 | 3.0 | 3.0 | 3.0 | 2.9 | 2.9 | 2.3 | 2.2 | 2.0 | 1.9 | 1.8 | 1.7 | 1.5 | 1.4 | 1.3 | 1.0 | 0.9 | 0.6 | 0.4 | 0.2 | 0.1 |

## Special fares

Workmen's tickets (single and returns) were issued to *bona fide* workpeople travelling to work before 8am on weekdays and to shift workers only, going to commence a shift and travelling between 12.30 and 3pm or between 8.30 and 11.30pm (the latter period did not apply on Saturdays). In the case of workmen's return fares, the return journey could be made on the day of issue after 12 noon Monday to Fridays, or after 11 am on Saturdays. Return tickets issued to night workers were available until 8am on the morning following issue. Workmen's Transfer Return tickets were also available involving a change of service *en route*. During the 1930s unemployed colliers could travel at workmen's fares to/from the collieries at which they received their compensation payments whilst all categories of the unemployed were permitted to travel to and from the Labour Exchange on their "attendance days" at the workmen's rate on production of an unemployment card. On Sundays workmen's tickets were not issued or accepted before 8.30pm. From January 1941 the increased amount of shift working and starting times led to workmen's fares being made available on Sundays from the first journey until 3pm in addition to the period after 8.30pm.

Workmen's Weekly Tickets, valid for six return journeys, were also available, it being practice to accept them for a seventh return journey on Sundays and on Fridays for night workers travelling to the colliery to collect their pay. Workmen's transfer weekly tickets were also available. In May 1942 it was decided that weekly tickets would only be issued on Mondays and would expire on the following Saturday, Sunday travel only being permitted if another day of the week was sacrificed. The additional return journey for colliers was retained as the weekly tickets had a special punch mark for night workers and only the holders of tickets so punched were granted this facility.

It was decided to abolish workmen's fares entirely in October 1952. This change was granted by the Traffic Commissioners in respect of the motorbus routes, however, the decision was queried by the MoT in respect of the trolleybuses, the solution being to make the Order under the Defence Regulation 56. Workmen's fares were finally discontinued on 5 July 1953. However, a range of return, weekly return and weekly transfer return tickets available to all passengers were introduced from the next day.

Transfer fares for all categories of passengers including workmen could be between points on the trolleybus route and any other point on the UDC's motorbus network, and it is assumed could involve the use of another operator's service where joint operation existed.

Four Journey tickets were introduced for an experimental 6-week period on 4 September 1939 at a fare of 6d. The ticket entitled a passenger to make two return journeys on the day of issue between any two points on the trolleybus route and could be issued on any vehicle up to 9am although only one journey was permitted after 3pm. It proved successful; however, plans to introduce the fare on motorbus services were prevented by the outbreak of the Second World War. Post-war the fare increased progressively to 8d, 10d in 1952, 1s from 5 July 1953 and 1s 4d from March 1956 by which time its application had been extended to all the local motorbus services and included transfer facilities.

In August 1940 a summer holiday fare was introduced allowing school children to travel from anywhere in the UDC area to Ynysangharad Park during their August holiday period on Monday, Tuesday, Thursday and Fridays at 1d return. Tickets had to be issued between 9.30am and 12.30pm, and between 3.00pm and 4.30pm, and were available for return at any time on the day of issue. This concession reappeared with minor changes to the conditions each summer until at least 1951.

In March 1950 old age pensioners' fares were introduced enabling OAPs resident in Pontypridd to travel at half ordinary fare on the Department's services within the UDC boundaries. The concession fares were only issued to those receiving the state pension but no other pension or income and confirmed by an authorisation card issued by the Transport Office. The OAP fares were not available between 8.00am and 9.00am, 12.45 and 2.15pm, or 4.30 and 6pm on Mondays to Fridays, nor on Saturdays.

## Prepaid fares

Various Council departments and other official organisations, e.g. the GPO, the South Wales Electricity Board and during the Second World War, the Air Training Corps and Home Guard, purchased stocks of prepaid or service tickets for the use of their employees or members when travelling on duty. The prepaid or service ticket was exchanged by the conductor for a normal ticket of the same value.

## Free travel

Blind persons were issued with free travel passes.

## Tickets

The broad range of fares sold were receipted with tickets printed on coloured paper, the colour varying according to the value of the ticket, category of passenger and period during the trolleybus era. The two ticket systems employed by Pontypridd UDC Transport Department on the trolleybuses are reviewed below, however, it must be stressed that this is not an exhaustive study of a complex topic and that the details of ticket colour and denomination are incomplete. The undertaking changed these details frequently whilst only incomplete, un-catalogued records survive.

### Bell Punch

Until December 1948 trolleybus tickets were of the same Bell Punch numerical fare stage colour-coded type as used on the trams. The conductor was equipped with a wooden rack holding pre-printed paper tickets, divided by value, under a spring and a cancelling punch. The cancelling punches were hired from Bell Punch. The stage numbers were printed along the edges of the ticket with the undertaking's title or abbreviated title, both of which varied during the 20 years the Bell Punch system was used on the trolleybuses, and other information in a central column. The operator's title "Pontypridd Council Transport" was displayed with "Pontypridd U.D.C. Transport" on some prepaid tickets. The conductor used a cancelling punch to make a small round hole against the fare stage, indicated by geographical name or number, where the passenger had started the journey whilst the fare paid indicated how far the passenger could travel. The cancelling punch recorded the number of holes punched on a secure register inside the machine whilst the small coloured circle of paper punched out of the ticket was retained in the machine (for accounting purposes if required). It also made an audible ring thus ensuring that a fraudulent conductor was

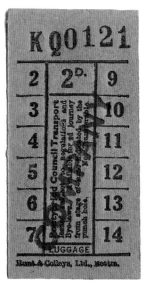

**Bell Punch style "Company" Luggage & Passenger Tickets. A selection of Bell Punch numerical fare stage colour-coded uncancelled luggage tickets for UDC employee use and a single uncancelled 3d passenger fare ticket, all printed by Hunt & Colleys, Nottingham, indicating the 1940s early 1950s period. (Enlarged) (Colin Page)**

not selling a used ticket. At the terminus or crew changeover point the conductor would record the serial number of the first ticket of each denomination on the rack and enter this on the waybill. This would be checked by inspectors, who would board vehicles at random, to ensure that the conductor was issuing tickets correctly and that passengers had paid the appropriate fare.

It is believed that from 1 April 1931 the use of geographical names for stages on the more commonly used ticket denominations progressively ceased and that new stocks

showed solely the fare stage numbers. The style was identical for ordinary and workmen's fares whether single or return. It was argued that these could be used on any service and that they were more easily adapted to fare changes whilst any passenger in doubt could always refer to the fare table displayed on each vehicle. At this time the undertaking was using 24 different types of ticket.

Ticket stocks were used indiscriminately on trolley vehicles, motorbuses and trams, and carried no special denotation "TROLLEYBUS".

**A selection of weekly Bell Punch geographical fare stage tickets including transfers. A0036 is valid for travel on both Pontypridd UDC and Rhondda Transport Co. services. (Full size) (Colin Page)**

The frequent fare increases after the Second World War led to the ingenious use of rubber stamps or stickers to amend the fare denomination shown on old ticket stocks, particularly in respect of special fares, e.g. Weekly and Weekly Transfer tickets.

Although efficient and successful, the ticketing system was "administration-heavy", slow, required considerable manual dexterity and labour intensive. Experiments with TIM machines were first broached in February 1934 but no action was taken due to the necessity of conductors working on 3 or 4 routes in a day's duty and providing ticket records giving an analysis of their takings on each. In the course of 1938 Cardiff's experiences with TIM machines were investigated but in spring 1939 it was decided that pre-printed tickets and the Bell Punch were still the best solution for Pontypridd. The undertaking continued to employ the Bell Punch, despite the use of Bellgraphic "write-in" ticket machines on certain of the longer motorbus services, until January 1949 when, after a one month trial with four machines, the Ultimate system was adopted as the undertaking's standard for short distance urban services and thus the trolleybus route.

**Ticket colours and styles**

The title "PONTYPRIDD COUNCIL TRAMWAYS" was replaced on new ticket stocks with "PONTYPRIDD COUNCIL TRANSPORT", this appearing variously during the trolleybus era in both upper and lower case printing. Geographical or numerical fare stages. All printing in black.

Single tickets were generally 1¼in. × 2½in. in size (although some issues were narrower and longer) and had the following colours (several with red value overprints, e.g. 1d and 2d):

| Colour | Denomination | Period | Comment |
|---|---|---|---|
| Cerise | ½d | Not known | |
| Mauve | 1d | Not known | |
| Brown | 1d | Not known | |
| White | 1½d | Not known | |
| Deep blue | 2d | Not known | |
| Cream | 2½d | Not known | |
| Light green | 3d | Not known | |
| Not known | 3½d | Not known | |
| Buff | 4d | Not known | |
| Pink | 5d | Not known | |
| Not known | 6d | Not known | |

Workmen's return tickets were generally 1¼in. × 2¾in., in size (although some were 2½in. long) and had the following colours:

| Colour | Denomination | Period | Comment |
|---|---|---|---|
| Orange | 2d | –1953 | |
| Light green | 3d | –1953 | |
| Not known | 4d | –1953 | |
| Cerise | 5d | –1953 | |
| Not known | 6d | –1953 | |
| Not known | 7d | –1953 | |
| Not known | 8d | –1953 | |

Workmen's weekly return ticket and the unrestricted weekly return tickets which replaced them from 1953 were generally 1¼in. × 3½ (3⁴⁄₇)in., in size (although some were narrower and others 4¼in. long) and had the following colours:

| Colour | Denomination | Period | Comment |
|---|---|---|---|
| Not known | 2s 9d | Not known | |
| White | 3s 4d | 1953– | |
| Not known | 4s | 1953– | |
| Not known | 4s 8d | 1956– | |
| Not known | 5s | 1950s | |
| Not known | 5s 4d | 1950s | |
| Cream | 6s 6d | 1956– | |

The tickets issued for unrestricted weekly transfer return fares had a red overprint "Weekly Transfer".

Workmen's weekly tickets showed the points between which the fare denomination was valid, i.e. "full geographical", together with the day of the week on each longest edge (in order that the individual journey could be punched) at the front with a grid of 31 possible starting dates at the rear. The full geographical nature of the ticket meant that new tickets were required on each occasion that there was a fare increase, evidenced by the overstamping of 2s 9d tickets with 5s.

This meant that when purchased the starting point of the outbound journey was punched, e.g. on the Weekly 3s 4d (non-workmen) example at say Cilfynydd – Station, stage 5; then on the day of the week, e.g. MON on the left hand side; and also the day of the month cancelled with a mark at the rear.

The range of return tickets introduced in July 1953 with the abolition of all workmen's fares were generally 1¼in. × 2½in., in size and included the following colours:

| Colour | Denomination | Period | Comment |
|---|---|---|---|
| Off-white | 2½d | 1953 – | |
| Deep purple | 3d | 1953 – | |
| Light pink | 3½d | 1953 – | |
| Yellow | 4d | 1953 – | |
| Light green | 6d | 1953 – | |
| Grey | 7d | 1953 – | |
| Yellow | 9d | 1953 – | |
| Not known | 10d | 1953 – | |
| Not known | 1s | 1953 – | |
| Not known | 1s 2d | 1953 – | |

Prepaid tickets showed their value on the front whilst on the rear the following spaces were printed for completion by the user: date, name, time. The following colours were in use:

| Colour | Denomination | Period | Comment |
|---|---|---|---|
| Not known | 1d | Not known | |
| Not known | 1½d | Not known | |
| Pink | 2d | | square card |
| Blue | 4d | Not known | |

Luggage, in all cases for any distance on the same route, the following colours were in use:

| Colour | Denomination | Period | Comment |
|---|---|---|---|
| Salmon | 1d | | |
| White | 1½d | 1950s | |
| Blue | 2d | 1950s | Red overprint |
| Not known | 2d | 1953– | up to 28 lb |
| Not known | 3d | 1953– | up to 48 lb |
| White | 4d | 1953– | up to 56 lb |

The undertaking purchased tickets for its Bell Punch machines from specialist printers which during the trolleybus era included the Glasgow Numerical Ticket and Check Book Printing Co. Ltd. (initially); H. Hunt & Co., Hucknall Road, Nottingham (who merged later to become Hunt & Colleys) in the 1930s; Hunt & Colleys, Nottingham in the 1940s and early 1950s, and the Bell Punch Co. Ltd., London progressively for various types of ticket from 1953–54.

### Ultimate

An experiment with four Bell Punch "Ultimate" ticket machines, which basically offered an automated version of the manufacture's traditional pre-printed ticket system, started in December 1948. Within just one month their speed of operation and the continued colour coding of tickets according to their value was deemed ideal for the short-stage, urban route of the trolleybuses. Ticket office administration was so reduced that it was anticipated that the night shift in the ticket office could be given up. It was decided to replace the Bell Punch system and standardise on the Ultimate machine for all the Council's urban routes but to retain the Bellgraphic "written-in" machines, which were still known locally by their earlier name ATM, i.e. Automatic Ticket Machines, for the rural and interurban routes requiring a wide range of different denominations of tickets.

It was decided in June 1949 to hire the Ultimate machines from the Bell Punch Co. Ltd. at £20 per machine pa; however, use of the traditional Bell Punch system continued for a variety of special purposes which, on the trolleybuses, included Weekly, Transfer and Prepaid tickets.

Although larger operators tended to change their ticketing system by depot or route if not throughout their network, it is assumed that in Pontypridd they were progressively introduced on the trolleybuses and that thus one crew may have being using an Ultimate ticket machine whilst the next was still using a traditional Bell Punch. The Ultimate machines were not issued to individual conductors or conductresses but were issued on a "common user" basis.

The Ultimate machines used in Pontypridd originally accommodated five compartments each containing a separate fare denomination, pre-printed on to colour coded rolls of 500 numbered paper tickets 1¼in. square. The blank tickets were printed in black with three "fare type" boxes or squares headed "SINGLE" on the left, "ORD.RET" (Ordinary Return) in the centre, and either "W.RET." (Workmen's Return) or from late 1952 "C.RTN" (Child Return) on a 1d issue, at the base, with a herringbone background grid effect, and titled "Pontypridd U.D.C. Trans.". Each pre-printed ticket had a unique alpha numeric identification also printed in black and made up of two serial letters (upper case followed by lower case, progressing in BaCa sequence) prefixed by a 5-digit serial number. Each new ticket roll had a piece of gummed tape to join it to the end of the old one thus avoiding the conductor having to change rolls mid-journey.

In July 1951 Bell Punch increased the cost of Ultimate machine tickets from 6⅝d to 1s 1d per thousand due to increases in the prices of paper and wages.

In order to accommodate increased fares approved in December 1955 the Ultimate ticket machines were replaced by six compartments machines.

The number of the fare stage at which a passenger had boarded the vehicle was set by turning a knurled wheel on the right hand side of the Ultimate machine. Each ticket compartment had its own operating lever which, when depressed, printed the fare stage boarded number from 00 to 99 in one of three possible "fare type" squares, in purple ink across the base of the ticket. When the lever was released, the ticket was ejected, torn off against a serrated cutter by the conductor and given to the passenger as a receipt for the fare paid. The number of tickets of each value issued was recorded from the printed serial numbers on the ticket roll and visible through a transparent "window" on the top of the machine. When a black button below the operating lever was depressed in the same issuing operation a double length ticket of the required denomination was ejected, in which case the fare

Two 1d tickets (Mg63503 & 04) were double issued 1d tickets used to achieve a 2d single fare as shown by the fare type entry only in the first ticket and the "struck through" ticket number on the second ticket. A 1d ticket He93332 and a 2d ticket Df 83351 both issued for single travel. Front (Li56498) and rear of 3d ticket, apparently uncancelled. 4d ticket (BC32094) issued for return travel. Two 5d tickets (Cd47859 & 60 ) are simply two 5d return tickets, the cancellation hole indicating that it/they was/were used on the return journey. If the two tickets had been issued for a 10d return the second ticket would have been simultaneously issued with the first but with its ticket serial number struck through (the numerator on the machine would have shown just one increment which would be shown on the conductor's waybill, one machine operation but 2 tickets were issued (evident from the ticket serial numbers)). (Enlarged) Colin Page.

(Left) Two Bell Punch Ultimate 7d tickets (65175 & 76Pb) issued for a 1s 2d return fare, the cancellation hole indicating that it/ they was/were used on the return journey. (Right) Bellgraphic "write in" ticket issued for a 3½d single fare on a motorbus service (Bellgraphics were not used on the trolleybus route). (Reverse side of each ticket shown in the next image) (Enlarged) (Colin Page)

Ultimate and Bellgraphic "write in" ticket reverse sides (reverse sides of the tickets shown in the image above). (Enlarged) (Colin Page)

stage number was printed in the appropriate square of the first ticket only whilst a cancellation was made across the serial number of the second ticket. A return ticket requiring a double length ticket to reach the required denomination was issued by pulling out the knurled wheel entirely allowing the first ticket to be imprinted with the stage number in the "W. RET." box whilst a cancellation was made across the serial number of the second ticket. As before, the conductor continued to record the number of tickets of each denomination that had been issued and entered this on the waybill at the journey's outer terminus or changeover point (Taff House during the day).

A cancellation grid featuring days of the month (1–9, 10, 20, 30) and days of the week (plus an Ex. meaning "Exchange") was printed on the rear of each ticket from the early 1950s as the last Bell Punch machines were phased out. It is believed that this grid was used solely for Ordinary Returns.

## Ticket colours and styles

Title "Pontypridd U.D.C. Trans.".

Tickets were 1³⁄₁₆in. wide × 1¼in. long, i.e. not quite square, in size.

The following Ultimate ticket colours and denominations (at least), limited to a maximum of 5 at any one time until December 1955 and 6 thereafter, were used from 1948 to 1957 on Pontypridd's trolleybuses:

| Colour | Denomination | Period | Comment |
|---|---|---|---|
| White | 1d | 1948–49 | No cancellation grid on reverse |
| White | 1d | 1950– | Some with cancellation grid on reverse |
| Salmon | 1½d | 1950– | Some with cancellation grid on reverse |
| Blue | 2d | 1948–49 | No cancellation grid on reverse |
| Blue | 2d | 1950– | Some with cancellation grid on reverse |
| Beige | 2½d | 1950– | Cancellation grid on reverse |
| Pink | 3d | 1948–49 | No cancellation grid on reverse |
| Pink | 3d | 1950– | Cancellation grid on reverse |
| Green | 4d | 1948–49 | No cancellation grid on reverse |
| Green | 4d | 1950– | Cancellation grid on reverse |
| Orange | 5d | 1948–49 | No cancellation grid on reverse |
| Orange | 5d | 1950– | Some with cancellation grid on reverse |
| Yellow | 7d | 1950– | Cancellation grid on reverse |
| Buff | 11d | 1950– | Cancellation grid on reverse |

In order to make up additional fare values, double issues of the selected denomination were made in a defined combination. The combinations varied over the years due to fare increases and the number of compartments available on the Ultimate machine.

Following the fares increase of 4 March 1956 and the introduction of 6 compartment machines, 1d, 1½d, 3d, 4d, 5d and 7d tickets were loaded and the following combinations issued:

| 1d | single | one 1d ticket |
|---|---|---|
| 1½d | single | one 1½d ticket |
| 2d | single | two 1d tickets |
| 2½ d | single | one 1d ticket plus one 1½d ticket |
| 3d | single | one 3d ticket |
| 4d | single | one 4d ticket |
| 5d | single | one 5d ticket |
| 6d | two | one 3d tickets |
| 7d | single | one 7d ticket |
| 8d | single | two 4d tickets |
| 9d | return | three 3d tickets |
| 10d | return | two 5d tickets |
| 1s | return | three 4d tickets |
| 1s 2d | return | two 7d tickets |
| 1s 4d | four journey | four 4d tickets |
| 5d | child return | one 5d ticket |
| 6d | child return | two 3d tickets |
| 7d | child return | one 7d ticket |

The reason for a defined combination was purely statistical. A counter, known as a "numerator" and recording only the number of double length issues made, was fitted beneath each ticket compartment. As a double 4d ticket was only issued when an 8d fare was taken, the number of double 4d tickets issued represented the number of passengers travelling at that fare. The number of tickets shown on the "numerator" was also recorded on the conductor's waybill. The "numerator" beneath the right hand end ticket compartment, as worn by the conductor (that beneath the 5d ticket compartment), recorded the total number of tickets sold (the "total numerator") and double issue tickets could not be issued from this compartment. This effectively meant that Pontypridd's

Ultimate machines initially could issue tickets to cover a maximum of nine (eleven from 1956) different fares during any one period of time.

Throughout the trolleybus era, the undertaking purchased tickets for its Ultimate machines solely from Bell Punch; however, from 1950 the printer's name "Bell Punch Co. London" was replaced with "Bell Punch Co. Ltd. London".

Karrier W 12 with Park Royal body is seen at Glyntaff Depot. (Peter Smith Collection [photographer Norr])

The pattern of trolleybus services varied little from the tramcar services they replaced and was heavily dependent on workmen's traffic and thus the economic vagaries of the mining industry. Initially, the first workmen's trams left Glyntaff Depot at about 4.15am and the final car ran in again between 11.30pm and midnight Monday – Saturday, however, within a few years the first tram had been cut back to just after 5.00am. Trams operated every nine minutes between Cilfynydd and Treforest throughout the day with additional workmen's cars, some of which only ran to and from the Bonvilston Road passing loop. In 1906 the normal service was reduced from a nine-minute to a 10-minute headway with additional cars at busy times. A further change took place in 1911 when the service beyond Bonvilston Road was reduced to every 20 minutes although the 10-minute service continued between Bonvilston Road and Treforest.

The service interval on the busy Mill Street – Trehafod route varied according to the time of day to offer a seven, six or five-minute service. In February 1926 Sunday afternoon and evening services were introduced on both tram routes.

The change to railless electric traction on the Cilfynydd – Treforest route brought with it a more frequent service to compensate for the reduced passenger capacity of the single-deck trolleybuses (32) in comparison to the double-deck trams (52). During much of the day trolleybuses were scheduled to run every 7½ minutes compared to a tram every 10 minutes. However, the initial vehicle shortage made this unattainable. Soon after the conversion, trolleybuses were running a 10-minute service 5.00am – 7.30am; a 7-minute service 8.00am –10am and 12.30 – 6.30pm; and from 10.00am – 12.30pm and 6.30pm – finish every eight minutes.

As can be seen from the various extracts with the arrival of more vehicles the basic schedule settled down as a 10 minute service morning and evening with a 7½-minute service in the afternoons, and a slightly more frequent service during peak times. Interestingly Saturday evenings benefited from a five-minute service, well-illustrating how people went out to entertainments during the trolleybus era. It is known that extra workmen's journeys which did not appear in the public timetables were operated and that these included short-workings, presumably to Bonvilston Road.

During the Second World War at least, the collieries were working three eight-hour shifts every 24 hours requiring trolleybuses to operate between 4am and 12.30am daily. Shift working at many factories in the area, not least the munitions factories on the Treforest Estate ensured heavy loadings throughout the day. The curtailment of motorbus services in 1939 led to increased trolleybus use. Later, where the trolley vehicles and motorbuses operated over common fare stages, a minimum fare was imposed on the motorbuses running out of the town. Town stopping places were segregated for the two kinds of vehicle so that the load was diverted to the trolleybuses to the greatest possible extent.

In contrast to the irregular rural services, the trolleybus route accommodated up to 1,000 passengers an hour from the busiest stops. Fare collection was expedited by the use of "jumper" conductors. Queue posts, segregating passengers according to destinations, were set up at various busy stops with a regulator in control.

## Fare and Timetables

It appears that the undertaking did not publish its own timetables during the first 25 years of its existence and that solely details of the first and last car, together with service intervals, were shown in local directories. The expansion of activities from a two-route tramway system with a regular-interval timetable to a motorbus and trolley vehicle operator serving a number of rural and urban routes required a timetable booklet. The General Manager first proposed issuing such a booklet, to be subsidised by advertisements, in March 1933 and it is likely that this appeared in June 1933; however, the first issue that has come to light is that of April 1934.

Throughout the trolleybus era public *Time Tables, Fare Lists, Luggage Charges, Extracts from Bye-Laws, etc.* in the form of a 7⅜ × 4⅞in. booklet, were issued quarterly, except during the Second World War and some two years thereafter. The booklets were supplied without charge by Percy S. Phillips, a local printer, his costs being recovered by a number of advertisements contained therein. The print-run was initially some 5,000 copies but by 1936 had reached 15,000 copies. Each issue also included a potted history of Pontypridd and details of places of local interest for visitors. The booklets were sold for a nominal fee (in 1934 one halfpenny). Prior to any timetable change detailed information was published in the local newspapers a few days beforehand and traffic notices appeared on the vehicles.

No fare and timetable booklets were published from 1939 until October 1947 and information about service changes seems to have been limited to announcements in the local newspapers and notices in the vehicles. When in September 1947 Mr Powell suggested a similar form of subsidised publication but involving the undertaking's advertising contractor to reach a wider and more lucrative source of advertisements, and thus increase advertising revenue, he was instructed to continue to make arrangements locally.

An interesting feature of the trolleybus timetables which continued throughout the lifetime of the system was the manner in which Cilfynydd to Treforest timings were only shown as far as Berw Road, Pontypridd (in principle the west side of the Old Bridge) with no information shown as to the onward journey through the town centre to Treforest, John Street. Similarly the Treforest to Cilfynydd timings were only shown as far as Station Square, Pontypridd, with no information shown for the onward journey through the town centre to Norton Bridge and Cilfynydd. Presumably local residents were well aware of the schedule and did not need to refer to a timetable. There is no evidence that passengers were carried on the depot access line between Taff House and Glyntaff.

Each issue of the booklet also contained the applicable fare tables.

## MONDAYS TO FRIDAYS.  TREFOREST TO CILFYNYDD.

| | | | | | | | | | | | | | | |
|---|---|---|---|---|---|---|---|---|---|---|---|---|---|---|
| Treforest Terminus | a.m. 5.20 | 5.40 | 5.50 | 6.0 | 6.10 | 6.20 | 6.30 | 6.45 | 7.0 | 7.15 | 7.30 | 7.45 | 7.52 | 8.0 |
| Station Sq., Pontypridd | 5.25 | 5.45 | 5.55 | 6.5 | 6.15 | 6.25 | 6.35 | 6.50 | 7.5 | 7.20 | 7.35 | 7.50 | 7.57 | 8.5 |
| Treforest Terminus | a.m. 8.7½ | 8.15 | 8.22½ | 8.30 | 8.37½ | 8.45 | 8.52½ | 9.0 | 9.7 | 9.17 | 9.27 | 9.37 | 9.47 | 9.57 |
| Station Sq., Pontypridd | 8.12½ | 8.20 | 8.27½ | 8.35 | 8.42½ | 8.50 | 8.57½ | 9.5 | 9.12 | 9.22 | 9.32 | 9.42 | 9.52 | 10.2 |
| Treforest Terminus | and at similar 10 mins. in each hour until | | | 12.7 | 12.15 | 12.20 | 12.30 | 12.37½ | 12.45 | 12.52 | 1.0 | 1.7½ | 1.15 | 1.22½ |
| Station Sq., Pontypridd | | | | 12.12 | 12.20 | 12.25 | 12.35 | 12.42½ | 12.50 | 12.57½ | 1.5 | 1.12½ | 1.20 | 1.27½ |
| Treforest Terminus | p.m. 1.30 | 1.37½ | 1.45 | 1.52½ | 2.0 | and at similar 7½ mins. in each hour until | | 6.30 | 6.37 | 6.47 | 6.57 | 7.7 | 7.17 |
| Station Sq., Pontypridd | 1.35 | 1.42½ | 1.50 | 1.57½ | 2.5 | | | 6.35 | 6.42 | 6.52 | 7.2 | 7.12 | 7.22 | |
| Treforest Terminus | p.m. 7.27 | 7.37 | 7.42 | 7.57 | and at similar 10 mins. in each hour until | | 9.57 | 10.5 | 10.13 | 10.21 | 10.29 | 10.37 | 10.47 |
| Station Sq., Pontypridd | 7.32 | 7.42 | 7.52 | 8.2 | | | 10.2 | 10.10 | 10.18 | 10.26 | 10.34 | 10.42 | 10.52 | |
| Treforest Terminus | p.m. 10.58 | 11.10 | | | | | | | | | | | | |
| Station Sq., Pontypridd | 11.3 | 11.15 | | | | | | | | | | | | |

## SATURDAYS.

| | | | | | | | | | | | | | | |
|---|---|---|---|---|---|---|---|---|---|---|---|---|---|---|
| Treforest Terminus | As above until | p.m. 5.0 | 5.5½ | 5.11 | 5.16½ | 5.22 | 5.28 | 5.33½ | 5.39 | 5.45 | 5.50½ | 5.56 | 6.1½ | |
| Station Sq., Pontypridd | | 5.5 | 5.10½ | 5.16 | 5.21½ | 5.27 | 5.33 | 5.38½ | 5.44 | 5.49 | 5.55½ | 6.1 | 6.6½ | |
| Treforest Terminus | p.m. 6.7 | 6.13 | 6.18½ | 6.24 | 6.30 | 6.35½ | 6.41 | 6.46½ | 6.52 | 6.58 | 7.3½ | 7.9 | 7.15 | 7.20½ |
| Station Sq., Pontypridd | 6.12 | 6.18 | 6.23½ | 6.29 | 6.35 | 6.40½ | 6.45 | 6.51½ | 6.57 | 7.3 | 7.8½ | 7.14 | 7.20 | 7.25½ |
| Treforest Terminus | p.m. 7.25 | 7.31½ | 7.37 | 7.43 | 7.48½ | 7.54 | 8.0 | 8.5½ | 8.11 | 8.16½ | 8.22 | 8.28 | 8.33½ | 8.39 |
| Station Sq., Pontypridd | 7.31 | 7.36½ | 7.42 | 7.48 | 7.53½ | 7.59 | 8.5 | 8.10½ | 8.16 | 8.21½ | 8.27 | 8.33 | 8.38½ | 8.44 |
| Treforest Terminus | p.m. 8.45 | 8.50½ | 8.55 | 9.1½ | 9.7 | 9.13 | 9.18½ | 9.24 | 9.30 | 9.35½ | 9.41 | 9.46½ | 9.52 | 9.58 |
| Station Sq., Pontypridd | 8.50 | 8.55½ | 9.1 | 9.6½ | 9.12 | 9.18 | 9.23½ | 9.29 | 9.35 | 9.40½ | 9.46 | 9.51½ | 9.57 | 10.3 |
| Treforest Terminus | p.m. 10.3½ | 10.9 | 10.15 | 10.20½ | 10.26 | 10.31½ | 10.37 | 10.43 | 10.48½ | 10.54 | 11.0 | 11.8 | 11.16 | 11.24 |
| Station Sq., Pontypridd | 10.8½ | 10.14 | 10.20 | 10.25½ | 10.31 | 10.36½ | 10.42 | 10.48 | 10.53½ | 10.59 | 11.5 | 11.13 | 11.21 | 11.29 |

## SUNDAYS.

| | | | | | | | | | | | | | |
|---|---|---|---|---|---|---|---|---|---|---|---|---|---|
| Treforest Terminus | p.m. 1.30 | 1.50 | 2.10 | and at similar 20 mins. in each hour until | | 5.10 | 5.20 | 5.30 | 5.50 | 6.0 | 6.15 | 6.30 | 6.45 |
| Station Sq., Pontypridd | 1.35 | 1.55 | 2.15 | | | 5.15 | 5.25 | 5.35 | 5.55 | 6.5 | 6.20 | 6.35 | 6.50 |
| Treforest Terminus | and at similar 15 mins. in each hour until | | p.m. 9.45 | 9.55 | 10.5 | 10.15 | 10.25 | 10.35 | 10.50 | | | | |
| Station Sq., Pontypridd | | | 9.50 | 10.0 | 10.10 | 10.20 | 10.30 | 10.40 | 10.55 | | | | |

An Extra Workmen's Bus leaves Treforest (Taff House) at 2.40 p.m., returning from Cilfynydd 3.7 p.m., when required.

## MONDAYS TO FRIDAYS.  CILFYNYDD TO TREFOREST.

| | | | | | | | | | | | | | | |
|---|---|---|---|---|---|---|---|---|---|---|---|---|---|---|
| Cilfynydd Terminus | a.m. 5.40 | 6.0 | 6.10 | 6.20 | 6.30 | 6.40 | 6.55 | 7.7 | 7.22 | 7.37 | 7.52 | 8.7 | 8.17 | 8.22 | 8.29½ |
| Berw Road, Pontypridd | 5.50 | 6.10 | 6.20 | 6.30 | 6.40 | 6.50 | 7.5 | 7.17 | 7.32 | 7.47 | 8.2 | 8.17 | 8.27 | 8.32 | 8.39½ |
| Cilfynydd Terminus | a.m. 8.37 | 8.44½ | 8.52 | 8.59 | 9.7 | 9.14½ | 9.22 | 9.27 | 9.37 | 9.47 | 9.57 | 10.7 | 10.17 | 10.27 |
| Berw Road, Pontypridd | 8.47 | 8.54½ | 9.2 | 9.9 | 9.17 | 9.24½ | 9.32 | 9.37 | 9.47 | 9.57 | 10.7 | 10.17 | 10.27 | 10.37 |
| Cilfynydd Terminus | a.m. 10.37 | 10.47 | 10.57 | 11.7 | and at similar 10 minutes in each hour until | | 12.37 | 12.44½ | 12.52 | 12.59½ | p.m. 1.7 | 1.14½ | 1.22 |
| Berw Road, Pontypridd | 10.47 | 10.57 | 11.7 | 11.17 | | | 12.47 | 12.54½ | 1.2 | 1.9½ | 1.17 | 1.24½ | 1.32 | |
| Cilfynydd Terminus | p.m. 1.29½ | 1.37 | 1.44½ | 1.52 | 1.59½ | and at similar 7½ minutes in each hour until | | 6.52 | 6.57 | 7.7 | 7.17 | 7.27 | 7.37 |
| Berw Road, Pontypridd | 1.39½ | 1.47 | 1.54½ | 2.2 | 2.9½ | | | 7.2 | 7.7 | 7.17 | 7.27 | 7.37 | 7.47 | |
| Cilfynydd Terminus | p.m. 7.47 | 7.57 | and at similar 10 minutes in each hour until | | 10.17 | 10.25 | 10.33 | 10.41 | 10.49 | 10.57 | 11.7 | 11.18 | 11.30 |
| Berw Road, Pontypridd | 7.57 | 8.7 | | | 10.27 | 10.35 | 10.43 | 10.51 | 10.59 | 11.7 | 11.17 | 11.28 | 11.40 | |

## SATURDAYS.

| | | | | | | | | | | | | | | |
|---|---|---|---|---|---|---|---|---|---|---|---|---|---|---|
| Cilfynydd Terminus | As above until | p.m. 4.59½ | 5.7 | 5.14½ | 5.22 | 5.27½ | 5.33 | 5.38½ | 5.44 | 5.50 | 5.55½ | 6.1 | 6.7 | |
| Berw Road, Pontypridd | | 5.9½ | 5.17 | 5.24½ | 5.32 | 5.37½ | 5.43 | 5.48½ | 5.44 | 6.0 | 6.5½ | 6.11 | 7.17 | |
| Cilfynydd Terminus | p.m. 6.12½ | 6.18 | 6.23½ | 6.29 | 6.35 | 6.40½ | 6.46 | 6.52 | 6.57½ | 7.3 | 7.8½ | 7.14 | 7.20 | 7.25½ |
| Berw Road, Pontypridd | 6.22½ | 6.28 | 6.33½ | 6.39 | 6.45 | 6.50½ | 6.56 | 7.2 | 7.7½ | 7.13 | 7.18½ | 7.24 | 7.30 | 7.35½ |
| Cilfynydd Terminus | p.m. 7.31 | 7.37 | 7.42½ | 7.48 | 7.53½ | 7.59 | 8.5 | 8.10½ | 8.16 | 8.22 | 8.27½ | 8.33 | 8.38½ | 8.44 |
| Berw Road, Pontypridd | 7.41 | 7.47 | 7.52½ | 7.58 | 8.3½ | 8.9 | 8.15 | 8.20½ | 8.26 | 8.32 | 8.37½ | 8.43 | 8.48½ | 8.54 |
| Cilfynydd Terminus | p.m. 8.50 | 8.55½ | 9.1 | 9.7 | 9.12½ | 9.18 | 9.23½ | 9.29 | 9.35 | 9.40½ | 9.46 | 9.52 | 9.57½ | 10.3 |
| Berw Road, Pontypridd | 9.0 | 9.5½ | 9.11 | 9.17 | 9.22½ | 9.28 | 9.33½ | 9.39 | 9.45 | 9.50½ | 9.56 | 10.2 | 10.7½ | 10.13 |
| Cilfynydd Terminus | p.m. 10.8½ | 10.14½ | 10.20 | 10.25½ | 10.31 | 10.37 | 10.42½ | 10.48 | 10.53½ | 10.59 | 11.5 | 11.10½ | 11.17 | 11.22 |
| Berw Road, Pontypridd | 10.18½ | 10.24½ | 10.30 | 10.35½ | 10.41 | 10.47 | 10.52½ | 10.58 | 11.3½ | 11.9 | 11.15 | 11.20½ | 11.27 | 11.32 |
| Cilfynydd Terminus | p.m. 11.30 | 11.33 | 11.46 | | | | | | | | | | | |
| Berw Road, Pontypridd | 11.40 | 11.43 | 11.56 | | | | | | | | | | | |

## SUNDAYS.

| | | | | | | | | | | | | | |
|---|---|---|---|---|---|---|---|---|---|---|---|---|---|
| Cilfynydd Terminus | p.m. 1.50 | 2.10 | 2.30 | and at similar 20 minutes in each hour until | | 5.30 | 5.40 | 5.50 | 6.10 | 6.23 | 6.38 | 6.53 | 7.8 |
| Berw Road, Pontypridd | 2.0 | 2.20 | 2.40 | | | 5.40 | 5.50 | 6.0 | 6.20 | 6.33 | 6.48 | 7.3 | 7.18 |
| Cilfynydd Terminus | p.m. 7.23 | 7.38 | 7.53 | and at similar 15 minutes in each hour until | | 9.53 | 10.5 | 10.15 | 10.25 | 10.35 | 10.45 | 10.55 | 11.10 |
| Berw Road, Pontypridd | 7.33 | 7.48 | 8.3 | | | 10.3 | 10.15 | 10.25 | 10.35 | 10.45 | 10.55 | 11.5 | 11.15 |

1934 trolleybus timetable.

## (6) MONDAYS TO FRIDAYS. TREFOREST TO CILFYNYDD.

| | a.m. | | | | | | | | | | | | | | |
|---|---|---|---|---|---|---|---|---|---|---|---|---|---|---|---|
| Treforest Terminus | 5.20 | 5.40 | 5.50 | 6.0 | 6.7½ | 6.15 | 6.22½ | 6.30 | 6.45 | 7.0 | 7.15 | 7.30 | 7.45 | 7.52 | 8.0 |
| Station Sq., Pontypridd | 5.25 | 5.45 | 5.55 | 6.5 | 6.12½ | 6.20 | 6.27½ | 6.35 | 6.50 | 7.5 | 7.20 | 7.35 | 7.50 | 7.57 | 8.5 |

| | a.m. | | | | | | | x | | | | | | |
|---|---|---|---|---|---|---|---|---|---|---|---|---|---|---|
| Treforest Terminus | 8.7½ | 8.15 | 8.22½ | 8.30 | 8.37½ | 8.45 | 8.52½ | 9.0 | 9.7 | 9.17 | 9.27 | 9.37 | 9.47 | 9.57 |
| Station Sq., Pontypridd | 8.12½ | 8.20 | 8.27½ | 8.35 | 8.42½ | 8.50 | 8.57½ | 9.5 | 9.12 | 9.22 | 9.32 | 9.42 | 9.52 | 10.2 |

| | | p.m. | | | | | | | | | | |
|---|---|---|---|---|---|---|---|---|---|---|---|---|
| Treforest Terminus | and at similar 10 mins. in each hour until | 12.7 | 12.15 | 12.20 | 12.30 | 12.37½ | 12.45 | 12.52½ | 1.0 | 1.7½ | 1.15 | 1.22½ |
| Station Sq., Pontypridd | | 12.12 | 12.20 | 12.25 | 12.35 | 12.42½ | 12.50 | 12.57½ | 1.5 | 1.12½ | 1.20 | 1.27½ |

| | p.m. | | | | | | | | | | | | |
|---|---|---|---|---|---|---|---|---|---|---|---|---|---|
| Treforest Terminus | 1.30 | 1.37½ | 1.45 | 1.52½ | 2.0 | and at similar 7½ mins. in each hour until | 6.30 | 6.37 | 6.47 | 6.55½ | 7.0 | 7.7½ | 7.17 |
| Station Sq., Pontypridd | 1.35 | 1.42½ | 1.50 | 1.57½ | 2.5 | | 6.35 | 6.42 | 6.52 | 7.0½ | 7.5 | 7.12½ | 7.22 |

| | p.m. | | | | | | | | | | | | |
|---|---|---|---|---|---|---|---|---|---|---|---|---|---|
| Treforest Terminus | 7.27 | 7.37 | 7.47 | 7.57 | and at similar 10 mins. in each hour until | 9.57 | 10.5 | 10.10 | 10.15 | 10.20 | 10.29 | 10.37 | 10.47 |
| Station Sq., Pontypridd | 7.32 | 7.42 | 7.52 | 8.2 | | 10.2 | 10.10 | 10.15 | 10.20 | 10.25 | 10.34 | 10.42 | 10.52 |

x WEDNESDAY, FRIDAY and SATURDAY MORNINGS.---The service is increased as follows : 9.0 a.m. and every 8 minutes to 9.56 ; 10.4 and every 8 minutes to 10.52 ; 11.0 a.m. and every 8 minutes to 11.56 ; 12.4 p.m. and every 8 minutes to 12.20, then as above.

| | p.m. | |
|---|---|---|
| Treforest Terminus | 11.0 | 11.10 |
| Station Sq., Pontypridd | 11.5 | 11.15 |

### SATURDAYS (after 5 p.m.).

| | | p.m. | | | | | | | | | | | |
|---|---|---|---|---|---|---|---|---|---|---|---|---|---|
| Treforest Terminus | As above until | 5.0 | 5.5½ | 5.11 | 5.16½ | 5.22 | 5.28 | 5.33½ | 5.39 | 5.45 | 5.50½ | 5.56 | 6.1½ |
| Station Sq., Pontypridd | | 5.5 | 5.10½ | 5.16 | 5.21½ | 5.27 | 5.33 | 5.38½ | 5.44 | 5.49 | 5.55½ | 6.1 | 6.6½ |

| | p.m. | | | | | | | | | | | | | | |
|---|---|---|---|---|---|---|---|---|---|---|---|---|---|---|---|
| Treforest Terminus | 6.7 | 6.13 | 6.18½ | 6.24 | 6.30 | 6.35½ | 6.41 | 6.46½ | 6.52 | 6.58 | 7.3½ | 7.9 | 7.15 | 7.20½ | 7.26 |
| Station Sq., Pontypridd | 6.12 | 6.18 | 6.23½ | 6.29 | 6.35 | 6.40½ | 6.46 | 6.51½ | 6.57 | 7.3 | 7.8½ | 7.14 | 7.20 | 7.25½ | 7.31 |

| | p.m. | | | | | | | | | | | | | | p.m. |
|---|---|---|---|---|---|---|---|---|---|---|---|---|---|---|---|
| Treforest Terminus | 7.31½ | 7.37 | 7.43 | 7.48½ | 7.54 | 8.0 | 8.5½ | 8.11 | 8.16½ | 8.22 | 8.28 | 8.33½ | 8.39 | 8.45 | 8.50½ |
| Station Sq., Pontypridd | 7.36½ | 7.42 | 7.48 | 7.53½ | 7.59 | 8.5 | 8.10½ | 8.16 | 8.21½ | 8.27 | 8.33 | 8.38½ | 8.44 | 8.50 | 9.0½ |

| | p.m. | | | | | | | | | | | | | | |
|---|---|---|---|---|---|---|---|---|---|---|---|---|---|---|---|
| Treforest Terminus | 8.56 | 9.1½ | 9.7 | 9.13 | 9.18½ | 9.24 | 9.30 | 9.35½ | 9.41 | 9.46½ | 9.52 | 9.58 | 10.3½ | 10.9 | 10.15 |
| Station Sq., Pontypridd | 9.1 | 9.6½ | 9.12 | 9.18 | 9.23½ | 9.29 | 9.35 | 9.40½ | 9.46 | 9.51½ | 9.57 | 10.3 | 10.8½ | 10.14 | 10.20 |

| | p.m. | | | | | | | | | | |
|---|---|---|---|---|---|---|---|---|---|---|---|
| Treforest Terminus | 10.20½ | 10.26 | 10.31½ | 10.37 | 10.43 | 10.48½ | 10.54 | 11.0 | 11.8 | 11.16 | 11.24 |
| Station Sq., Pontypridd | 10.25½ | 10.31 | 10.36½ | 10.42 | 10.48 | 10.53½ | 10.59 | 11.5 | 11.13 | 11.21 | 11.29 |

### SUNDAYS.

| | p.m. | | | | | | | | | | | |
|---|---|---|---|---|---|---|---|---|---|---|---|---|
| Treforest Terminus | 1.30 | 1.50 | 2.10 | and at similar 20 mins. in each hour until | 5.10 | 5.20 | 5.30 | 5.50 | 6.0 | 6.15 | 6.30 | 6.45 |
| Station Sq., Pontypridd | 1.35 | 1.55 | 2.15 | | 5.15 | 5.25 | 5.35 | 5.55 | 6.5 | 6.20 | 6.35 | 6.50 |

| | p.m. | | | | | | | | | |
|---|---|---|---|---|---|---|---|---|---|---|
| Treforest Terminus | 7.0 | 7.10 | 7.20 | 7.30 | 7.40 | 7.50 | 8.0 | and every 10 mins. to | 10.40 | 10.50 |
| Station Sq., Pontypridd | 7.5 | 7.15 | 7.25 | 7.35 | 7.45 | 7.55 | 8.5 | | 10.45 | 10.55 |

6.22½ a.m. ex Treforest connects a Mill Street with 6.18 a.m. ex Porth.

## MONDAYS TO FRIDAYS. CILFYNYDD TO TREFOREST. (7)

| | a.m. | | | | | | | | | | | | | | | |
|---|---|---|---|---|---|---|---|---|---|---|---|---|---|---|---|---|
| Cilfynydd Terminus | 5.40 | 6.0 | 6.10 | 6.20 | 6.35 | 6.40 | 6.45 | 6.55 | 7.7 | 7.22 | 7.37 | 7.52 | 8.7 | 8.17 | 8.22 | 8.29½ |
| Berw Road, Pontypridd | 5.50 | 6.10 | 6.20 | 6.30 | 6.45 | 6.50 | 6.55 | 7.5 | 7.17 | 7.32 | 7.47 | 8.2 | 8.17 | 8.27 | 8.32 | 8.39½ |

| | a.m. | | | | | | | | | | | | | |
|---|---|---|---|---|---|---|---|---|---|---|---|---|---|---|
| Cilfynydd Terminus | 8.37 | 8.44 | 8.50 | 8.57 | 9.7 | x9.14½ | 9.22 | 9.27 | 9.37 | 9.47 | 9.57 | 10.7 | 10.17 | 10.27 |
| Berw Road, Pontypridd | 8.47 | 8.54 | 9.0 | 9.7 | 9.17 | 9.24½ | 9.32 | 9.37 | 9.47 | 9.57 | 10.7 | 10.17 | 10.27 | 10.37 |

| | a.m. | | | | | | | | | p.m. | | |
|---|---|---|---|---|---|---|---|---|---|---|---|---|
| Cilfynydd Terminus | 10.37 | 10.47 | 10.57 | 11.7 | and at similar 10 minutes in each hour until | 12.37 | 12.44½ | 12.52 | 12.59½ | 1.7 | 1.14½ | 1.22 |
| Berw Road, Pontypridd | 10.47 | 10.57 | 11.7 | 11.17 | | 12.47 | 12.54½ | 1.2 | 1.9½ | 1.17 | 1.24½ | 1.32 |

| | p.m. | | | | | | | | | | | | | | |
|---|---|---|---|---|---|---|---|---|---|---|---|---|---|---|---|
| Cilfynydd Terminus | 1.29½ | 1.37 | 1.44½ | 1.52 | 1.59½ | and at similar 7½ minutes in each hour until | 6.52 | 6.57 | 7.7 | 7.14½ | 7.22 | 7.30 | 7.37 | 7.47 | 7.57 |
| Berw Road, Pontypridd | 1.39½ | 1.47 | 1.54½ | 2.2 | 2.9½ | | 7.2 | 7.7 | 7.17 | 7.24½ | 7.32 | 7.40 | 7.47 | 7.57 | 8.7 |

| | p.m | | | | | | | | | | | | | | |
|---|---|---|---|---|---|---|---|---|---|---|---|---|---|---|---|
| Cilfynydd Terminus | 8.7 | 8.17 | 8.27 | 8.37 | and at similar 10 mins. in each hour until | 10.17 | 10.25 | 10.35 | 10.40 | 10.45 | 10.50 | 10.57 | 11.7 | 11.20 | 11.30 |
| Berw Rd., Pontypridd | 8.17 | 8.27 | 8.37 | 8.47 | | 10.27 | 10.35 | 10.45 | 10.50 | 10.55 | 11.0 | 11.7 | 11.17 | 11.30 | 11.40 |

### SATURDAYS. (after 5 p.m.).

xWED., FRI, and SAT. MORNINGS; As above to 9.14½ a.m. then 9.20 a.m., and every 8 minutes to 9.52 a.m., 10.0 a.m., and every 8 minutes to 10.56, 11.4, and every 8 minutes to 11.52, 12.2, 12.12, 12.22, 12.30, 12.37, then as above.

| | | p.m. | | | | | | | | | | | |
|---|---|---|---|---|---|---|---|---|---|---|---|---|---|
| Cilfynydd Terminus | As above until | 4.59½ | 5.7 | 5.14½ | 5.22 | 5.27½ | 5.33 | 5.38½ | 5.44 | 5.50 | 5.55½ | 6.1 | 6.7 |
| Berw Road, Pontypridd | | 5.9½ | 5.17 | 5.24½ | 5.32 | 5.37½ | 5.43 | 5.48½ | 5.54 | 6.0 | 6.5½ | 6.11 | 6.17 |

| | p.m. | | | | | | | | | | | | | | |
|---|---|---|---|---|---|---|---|---|---|---|---|---|---|---|---|
| Cilfynydd Terminus | 6.12½ | 6.18 | 6.23½ | 6.29 | 6.35 | 6.40½ | 6.46 | 6.52 | 6.57½ | 7.3 | 7.8½ | 7.14 | 7.20 | 7.25½ | 7.31 |
| Berw Road, Pontypridd | 6.22½ | 6.28 | 6.33½ | 6.39 | 6.45 | 6.50½ | 6.56 | 7.2 | 7.7½ | 7.13 | 7.18½ | 7.24 | 7.30 | 7.35½ | 7.41 |

| | p.m. | | | | | | | | | | | | | | |
|---|---|---|---|---|---|---|---|---|---|---|---|---|---|---|---|
| Cilfynydd Terminus | 7.37 | 7.42½ | 7.48 | 7.53½ | 7.59 | 8.5 | 8.10½ | 8.16 | 8.22 | 8.27½ | 8.33 | 8.38½ | 8.44 | 8.50 | 8.55½ |
| Berw Road, Pontypridd | 7.47 | 7.52½ | 7.58 | 8.3½ | 8.9 | 8.15 | 8.20½ | 8.26 | 8.32 | 8.37½ | 8.43 | 8.48½ | 8.54 | 9.0 | 9.5½ |

| | p.m. | | | | | | | | | | | | | | |
|---|---|---|---|---|---|---|---|---|---|---|---|---|---|---|---|
| Cilfynydd Terminus | 9.1 | 9.7 | 9.12½ | 9.18 | 9.23½ | 9.29 | 9.35 | 9.40½ | 9.46 | 9.52 | 9.57½ | 10.3 | 10.8½ | 10.14 | 10.20 |
| Berw Road, Pontypridd | 9.11 | 9.17 | 9.22½ | 9.28 | 9.33½ | 9.39 | 9.45 | 9.50½ | 9.56 | 10.2 | 10.7½ | 10.13 | 10.18½ | 10.24 | 10.30 |

| | p.m. | | | | | | | | | | | | | |
|---|---|---|---|---|---|---|---|---|---|---|---|---|---|---|
| Cilfynydd Terminus | 10.25½ | 10.31 | 10.37 | 10.42½ | 10.48 | 10.53½ | 10.59 | 11.5 | 11.10½ | 11.17 | 11.22 | 11.30 | 11.33 | 11.46 |
| Berw Road, Pontypridd | 10.35½ | 10.41 | 10.47 | 10.52½ | 10.58 | 11.3½ | 11.9 | 11.15 | 11.20½ | 11.27 | 11.32 | 11.40 | 11.43 | 11.56 |

### SUNDAYS.

| | p.m. | | | | | | | | | | | |
|---|---|---|---|---|---|---|---|---|---|---|---|---|
| Cilfynydd Terminus | 1.50 | 2.10 | 2.30 | and at similar 20 minutes in each hour until | 5.30 | 5.40 | 5.50 | 6.10 | 6.23 | 6.38 | 6.53 | 7.8 |
| Berw Road, Pontypridd | 2.0 | 2.20 | 2.40 | | 5.40 | 5.50 | 6.0 | 6.20 | 6.33 | 6.48 | 7.3 | 7.18 |

| | p.m. | | | | | | | | | |
|---|---|---|---|---|---|---|---|---|---|---|
| Cilfynydd Terminus | 7.20 | 7.30 | 7.40 | 7.50 | 8.0 | 8.10 | 8.20 | and every 10 minutes to | 11.0 | 11.10 |
| Berw Road, Pontypridd | 7.30 | 7.40 | 7.50 | 8.0 | 8.10 | 8.20 | 8.30 | | 11.10 | 11.20 |

6.10 a.m. trolley bus x Cilfynydd connects at Station Square with the 6.24 to Rhydyfelin, and the 6.35 a.m. ex Cilfynydd with the 6.48 ex Mill Street for Porth.
SUNDAYS—10.45 p.m. ex Cilfynydd connects at Berw Road with the 10.55 to Rhydyfelin.

**March 1937 trolleybus timetable. Note the 5½-minute service interval on Saturday evenings until 11.30pm!**

## Recorder Clocks

The conductor carried a recorder card, which was inserted into the clock and stamped at the correct departure time (according to the running card) to provide a permanent record of a timely departure or a delay incurred *en route*. It is known that a recorder clock used by trolleybuses was situated at Ynysangharad Park entrance, down a lane or passageway, opposite Mill Street (set in a green case on a shop wall). No others, e.g. at the outer termini, are known.

Good time-keeping was considered to be of the greatest importance and the Transport Department made bulk purchases of watches for its crews from time to time. These were offered for sale with payment through staged wage deductions. Those who joined the Department when such watches were not available were left to their own devices.

Trolleybus Driver David Morgan bought a watch on Pontypridd Market for 1s 11d when he started as a tram conductor in 1926. He claimed that it kept perfect time with the Bundy clock until his retirement. He rose to be one of two trolleybus driving instructors.

## Stop Signs

It will be noticed from this book's illustrations that there is no evidence of any stop flags or other markings to indicate the stopping places of either trolleybuses or motor buses.

Having descended Corn Stores Hill, Karrier W 12 crosses Victoria Bridge over the River Taff on its way to Treforest. The 'Maltsers Arms' public house is the stone building on the right behind the trolleybus. (Hugh Taylor collection [photographer C.Carter])

# LEGISLATION

Trolleybuses in the UK were essentially regulated in the same manner as their predecessors, the trams, and treated as light railways. This necessitated that a Bill be promoted in Parliament and an Act secured for the construction of a new trolleybus system or the conversion of an existing tramway to trolleybus operation.

Note: the grammar, language, punctuation and spelling in the following extracts are those of the original documents.

Sections of the 1929 Act not directly related to the trolleybus network and its operation have been omitted for brevity. The Regulations and Byelaws are quoted in their entirety.

---

**CHAPTER xciv**

An Act to empower the Pontypridd Urban District Council to provide and work trolley vehicles and omnibuses and for other purposes.

[10th May 1929.]

WHEREAS the district of Pontypridd in the county of Glamorgan (in this Act called "the district") is an urban district and is under the management of the Pontypridd Urban District Council (in this Act called "the Council"):

And whereas the Council are the owners of and are working a system of tramways within the district and it is expedient to empower them to provide and work vehicles adapted for use upon roads without rails and moved by electrical power transmitted thereto from some external source (in this Act called "trolley vehicles") along the routes described in this Act along some of which routes tramways have been constructed and to confer upon the Council all necessary and convenient powers in regard thereto:

And whereas it is expedient to confer powers upon the Council for the running of omnibuses:

And whereas it is expedient to make further provision with regard to the finances of the Council and the application of revenue derived from their several undertakings:

And whereas it is expedient that the other provisions contained in this Act be enacted

And whereas the purposes of this Act cannot be effected without the authority of Parliament:

And whereas estimates have been prepared by the Council for the purposes hereinafter mentioned and such estimates are as follows:–

| | |
|---|---:|
| The provision of trolley vehicles | 19,500 |
| The provision of electrical equipment and the construction of other works necessary for working trolley vehicles | 5,972 |
| The reconstruction of the roads upon which the tramways to be removed or discontinued under the provisions of this Act are situate | 21,900 |
| The adaptation or erection of buildings for the purposes of the trolley vehicles and omnibuses of the Council | 5,000 |
| The provision of omnibuses | 15,000 |

And whereas the several works included in such estimates are permanent works and it is expedient that the cost thereof should be spread over a term of years:

And whereas in relation to the promotion of the Bill for this Act the requirements of the Borough Funds Acts 1872 and 1903 have been observed:

May it therefore please Your Majesty that it may be enacted and be it enacted by the King's most Excellent Majesty by and with the advice and consent of the Lords Spiritual and Temporal and Commons in this present Parliament assembled and by the authority of the same as follows (that is to say):—

PRELIMINARY.

1. This Act may be cited as the Pontypridd Urban District Council Act 1929.

2. The Lands Clauses Acts (so far as the same are applicable for the purposes and are not inconsistent with the provisions of this Act) are hereby incorporated with this Act but with the following exceptions (namely):—

*(a)* The provisions of the Lands Clauses Consolidation Act 1845 with respect to the purchase and taking of lands otherwise than by agreement;

*(b)* Section 127 of the Lands Clauses Consolidation Act 1845 (relating to the sale of superfluous lands).

3. In this Act the several words and expressions to which meanings are assigned by the Acts wholly or partially incorporated herewith or by the Public Health Acts have the same respective meanings unless there be something in the subject or context repugnant to such construction And in this Act unless the subject or context otherwise requires—

"The Council" means the Pontypridd Urban District Council;

"The district" means the urban district of Pontypridd;

"The clerk" and "the treasurer" mean respectively the clerk, and the treasurer of the Council and respectively include any person duly authorised to discharge temporarily the duties of those offices;

"The general rate fund" and "the general rate" mean respectively the general rate fund and the general rate of the district;

"Trolley vehicle" means a mechanically propelled vehicle adapted for use upon roads without rails and moved by electrical power transmitted thereto from some external source;

"Trolley vehicle routes" means the routes upon which the Council are by this Act authorised to work and use trolley vehicles:

"Omnibus" means any stage carriage moved by animal power or by mechanical power (including in that expression steam electrical and every other motive power not being animal power) obtained from some internal source;

"Road authority" means with reference to any road or part of a road over which any proposed omnibus or trolley vehicle service will pass the authority company or person charged with or liable to contribute to the maintenance of such road or part of a road;

"Statutory borrowing power" "statutory security" and "revenues of the Council" have the meanings assigned to them respectively by section 3 (Interpretation) of the Act of 1903;

"The Act of 1893" "the Order of 1901" "The Order of 1902" "the Act of 1903" "the Act of 1907" and "the Act of 1920" mean respectively the Pontypridd Local Board (Gas) Act 1893 the Pontypridd Urban District Council Tramways Order 1901 the Pontypridd Urban District Council Tramways Order 1902 the Pontypridd Urban District Council Act 1903 the Pontypridd Urban District Council Act 1907 and the Pontypridd Urban District Council Act 1920.

TROLLEY VEHICLES OMNIBUSES AND TRAMWAYS.

4.—(1) Subject to the provisions of this Act the Council may provide maintain and equip (but shall not manufacture) trolley vehicles and may use the same upon all or any of the following trolley vehicle routes in the district (that is to say):—

Route No. 1 Commencing in the Cardiff-Merthyr main road at the point opposite the entrance to the Albion Colliery at Cilfynydd passing in a southerly direction along that road to Norton Bridge along Coedpenmaen Road Corn Stores Hill Bridge Street Taff Street High Street Broadway Fothergill Street and Park Street and terminating in that road at a point opposite John Street;

Route No. 1a Commencing in Park Street Treforest at its junction with John Street passing along John Street and Long Row to and terminating by a junction with Route No. 1b in Forest Road;

Route No. 1b Commencing in Park Street Treforest at its junction with Forest Road passing Forest Road across Castle Bridge along the Cardiff-Merthyr main road across the Glyn Taff Bridge over the Glamorganshire Canal and along Cemetery Road to and terminating at the car depot of the Council;

Route No. 1C Commencing in Broadway at its junction with Fothergill Street proceeding thence across Machine Bridge to and terminating by a junction with Route No. 1b in the Cardiff-Merthyr main road;

Route No. 1d Commencing by a junction with Route No. 1 at the northern junction of Market Street with Taff Street proceeding along Market Street to and terminating by a junction with Route No. 1 at the southern junction of Market Street with Taff Street;

Route No. 2 Commencing in Mill Street at its junction with Taff Street passing in a westerly direction along that road the Viaduct Rhondda Road Hopkinstown Road Gyfeillon Road and Trehafod Road to and terminating at the boundary of the district;

Route No. 2a Commencing in Trehafod Road at its junction with the unnamed road between Nos. 113 and 114 Trehafod Road passing along such unnamed road in a southerly direction to its junction with Ivor Street at its westerly end thence in a westerly direction to a junction with and proceeding along the unnamed road between the Trehafod Hotel and No. 117 Trehafod Road to and terminating by a junction of such last mentioned unnamed road with Route No. 2 in Trehafod Road; and with the consent of the Minister of Transport along any other street or road in the district which the Council think it necessary or convenient to use for the purpose of providing a turning point of or connecting trolley vehicle routes or of obtaining access thereto from any depôt garage building or work of the Council.

(2) Before equipping any trolley vehicle route to include a turning point or before arranging for a new turning point on any route the Council shall submit plans of the turning point to the Minister of Transport for approval. No turning point shall be fixed upon any road or street belonging to or maintained by a railway company without the consent in writing of such company.

*Paragraphs 5–9 omitted*

10.—(1) The trolley vehicles and the electrical equipment thereof used under the authority of this Act shall be of such form construction weight and dimensions ; as the Minister of Transport may approve and no trolley vehicle shall be used by the Council which does not comply with the requirements of the Minister of Transport.

(2) Before applying to the Minister for his approval of the weight of any trolley vehicle to be used upon any road which crosses a bridge belonging to or repairable by a railway company the Council shall give to the railway company notice of the weight of the trolley vehicles proposed to be used by them upon such road and the Minister shall consider and determine after such inquiry as he may think fit any objections which may be submitted by the railway company to him on the ground that the strength of the bridge is insufficient to carry trolley vehicles of such weight. Provided that a copy of the objections shall be sent by the railway company to the Council at the same time as they are sent to the Minister

11. No trolley vehicle route shall be opened for public traffic until it has been inspected and certified to be fit for traffic by an officer appointed by the Minister of Transport.

*Paragraph 12 omitted*

13.—(1) Subject to the provisions of this Act the following provisions of the Order of 1901 the Order of 1902 the Act of 1903 and the Act of 1920 (as amended by this Act) shall extend and apply to the trolley vehicles authorised by this Act as if those provisions were with all necessary modifications re-enacted in this Act (that is to say):—

The Order of 1901-

Section 18 (Additional cross-over roads &c. may be made where necessary);

Section 19 (Temporary tramways may be made when necessary);

Section 20 (Application of road materials excavated in construction of works);

Section 22 (Provisions as to motive power);

Section 23 (Mechanical power works);

Section 25 (Byelaws);

Section 27 (Special provisions as to use of electrical power);

Section 30 (Promoters' lessees not bound to carry animals goods &c);

Section 31 (Passengers' fares);

Section 32 (As to fares on Sundays and holidays);

Section 33 (Passengers' luggage);

Section 34 (Cheap fares for labouring classes);

Section 35 (Rates and charges for animals goods &c.);

Section 37 (Periodical revision of rates and charges);

The schedule.

The Order of 1902—

Section 5 (Notice of alterations of tramways &c.);

Section 6 (For protection of Postmaster-General).

The Act of 1903—
Section 27 (Attachment of brackets to buildings);
Section 36 (Supply of electrical energy for traction purposes).

The Act of 1920—
Section 11 (Use of tramway posts by Postmaster-General);
Section 14 (Shelters or waiting-rooms);
Section 15 (Cloakrooms &c);
Section 16 (Power to reserve cars for special purposes);
Section 17 (Penalty for malicious damage);
Section 18 (Lost property);
Section 19 (Payment of fares rates and charges);
Section 21 (For protection of railway companies as to tramways);
Section 22 (Through cars);
Section 23 (Attachment of signs indicating stopping-places to lamp-posts &c.);
Section 25 (Use of tramways for sanitary purposes);
Section 27 (Power to acquire patent rights).

(2) Provided that in the application of the provisions referred to in subsection (1) of this section—

(a) the same shall be read and have effect as if the working equipment for trolley vehicles were tramways within the meaning of the said provisions and as if trolley vehicles were carriages used on the tramways of the Council and as if the trolley vehicle undertaking authorised by this Act formed part of the tramway undertaking authorised by the Orders of 1901 and 1902 and the Acts of 1903 and 1920;

(b) sections 31 and 34 of the Order of 1901 shall be read and have effect as amended by the section of this Act of which the marginal note is "Increase of rates for passengers on tramways";

(c) for the purposes of section 27 of the Act of 1903 the word "building" where used therein shall include any bridge or other structure belonging to a railway company.

(3) Provided also that the trolley vehicles shall only be used for the purpose of conveying—

(a) passengers and their luggage;

(b) dogs in the care of passengers the maximum charge for any such dog to be a sum not exceeding the fare payable by the passenger;

(c) mails;

(d) parcels not exceeding fifty-six pounds in weight;

(e) materials required by the Council in the exercise of the powers conferred upon them by section 25 of the Act of 1920; and

(f) materials required for the purposes of the Council or for or in connection with the several undertakings of the Council; and save as aforesaid shall not be used for the carriage of animals minerals or goods.

*Paragraph 14 omitted*

15.—(1) If at any time hereafter the Council desire to provide maintain equip and use trolley vehicles upon any road as defined by the Tramways Act 1870 within the district (other than the streets and roads in this Act hereinbefore referred to) they may make application to the Minister of Transport and the Minister of Transport is hereby empowered to make a Provisional Order authorising the use by the Council of trolley vehicles subject to such conditions and restrictions (if any) as he may think fit upon any road or roads to which such application relates and containing such incidental provisions as the said Minister may

deem expedient and subject to the terms of the Provisional Order the provisions of this Act shall apply as if the use of trolley vehicles upon such road were authorised by this Act.

(2) No such application shall be entertained by the Minister of Transport unless the Council shall—

(a) have published once in each of two successive weeks in the months of October or November notice of their intention to make such application in some newspaper or newspapers circulating in the district;

(b) have also published such notice once in the months of October or November in the *London Gazette*;

(c) have posted for fourteen consecutive days in the months of October or November in conspicuous positions in each of the roads to which such application relates a notice of their intention to make such application;

and each such notice shall state the time and method for bringing before the Minister of Transport any objections to the grant of such application.

(3) The Minister of Transport may and he is hereby empowered to prescribe the procedure with respect to any application for a Provisional Order under this section.

(4) The Minister of Transport shall consider any such application and may if he thinks fit direct an inquiry to be held in relation thereto or may otherwise inquire as to the propriety of proceeding upon such application and he shall consider any objection to such application that may be lodged with him in accordance with the prescribed procedure and shall determine whether or not it is expedient and proper that the application be granted either with or without addition or modification or subject or not to any restriction or condition.

(5) In any case where it shall appear to the Minister of Transport expedient that the application be granted he may settle and make a Provisional Order authorising the same and shall as soon as conveniently may be thereafter procure a Bill to be introduced into either House of Parliament for an Act to confirm the Provisional Order which shall be set out at length in the schedule to the Bill and until confirmation with or without amendment by such Act of Parliament a Provisional Order under this Act shall not have any operation.

(6) If while any such Bill is pending in either House of Parliament a petition is presented against any Provisional Order comprised therein the Bill so far as it relates to the Order petitioned against may be referred to a select committee and the petitioner shall be allowed to appear and oppose as in the case of a Bill for a special Act.

(7) The Act of Parliament confirming a Provisional Order under this Act shall be deemed a public general Act.

(8) The making of a Provisional Order under this section shall be prima facie evidence that all the requirements of this section in respect of proceedings required to be taken previously to the making of such Provisional Order have been complied with.

(9) Any expenses incurred by the Minister of Transport in connection with the preparation and making of any such Provisional Order and any expenses incurred by the Minister of Transport in connection with any inquiry under this section shall be paid by the Council.

16. All subsisting regulations and byelaws relating to the tramways of the Council made in pursuance of the Tramways Act 1870 or of any other statutory enactment so far as the same are applicable shall with the necessary Modifications apply to the trolley vehicles provided by the Council in pursuance of this Act.

*Paragraphs 17–21 omitted*

22. Notwithstanding anything contained in this Act the Council shall not except with the consent of the Pontypridd Markets Fairs and Town Hall Company —

*(a)* use any trolley vehicles in Market Street within the district on any market or fair day; or

*(b)* run omnibuses in that street on any market or fair day if such running of omnibuses interferes with the market or fair then being carried on in such street; but nothing in this section shall take away or prejudice any rights of the Council in over or affecting the said street.

23.—(1) The Council and any company body or person may enter into and carry into effect agreements, for the working user management and maintenance subject to the provisions of this Act of any trolley vehicle and omnibus services which the Council are for the time being empowered to run or which the Rhondda Tramways Company Limited are for the time being empowered, to run from the boundary of the district at Trehafod to Porth.

(2) Any agreement made under subsection (1) of this section may provide for all or any of the following purposes (that is to say):—

*(a)* The formation of junctions between the trolley vehicle systems of the contracting parties;

*(b)* The working user management and maintenance of any trolley vehicles omnibuses lands depots buildings sheds and property provided in connection with any such trolley vehicle and omnibus services as aforesaid by either of the contracting parties and the right to provide and use the same and to demand and take the fares and charges, authorised in respect of such services provided that the omnibuses of the Council shall not be worked used or managed outside the district except within that part of the urban district of Rhondda which is referred to in subsection (1) of this section;

*(c)* The supply by any of the contracting parties under and during the continuance of any such agreement under this section of trolley vehicles and omnibuses and conveniences in connection therewith respectively necessary for the purposes of such agreement and the employment of officers and servants;

*(d)* The interchange accommodation conveyance transmission and delivery of traffic arising on or coming from or destined for any trolley vehicle or omnibus service of the contracting parties;

*(e)* The payment collection and apportionment of the fares and charges and other receipts arising from any such trolley vehicle or omnibus service as aforesaid.

(3) During the continuance of any agreement under this section for the working running over or user by one of the contracting parties of the trolley vehicle or omnibus systems of the other the trolley vehicle or omnibus systems of the parties so contracting shall for the purposes of calculating maximum fares and charges in respect of conveyance partly over the trolley vehicle or omnibus systems of the one party and partly over those of the other be considered as one trolley vehicle or omnibus system as the case may be and the maximum charge for each portion of the entire distance shall be calculated at the maximum rate which according to the scale applicable to such portion would be chargeable for the entire distance.

(4) The Council shall not enter into or carry into effect any agreement under the provisions of this section in relation to any omnibus service lands depots buildings sheds or property in the urban district of Rhondda otherwise than with the consent of the Rhondda Urban District Council Provided that on complaint being made to the Minister of Transport that such consent is unreasonably withheld the said Minister may if he think fit by order dispense with such consent.

*Paragraphs 24–25 omitted*

26. The Council may appoint the stations and places from which their trolley vehicles and their omnibuses shall start or at which they may stop for the purposes of taking up or setting down passengers and may fix the time during which such trolley vehicles and omnibuses shall be allowed to remain at any such place.

27. Any byelaws and regulations made by the Council under the provisions contained in this Act shall be made subject and according to the provisions of the Tramways Act 1870 with respect to the making of byelaws.

*Paragraphs 28–31 omitted*

FINANCIAL PROVISIONS

32.—(1) The Council may from time to time independently of any other borrowing power borrow at interest for and in connection with the purposes mentioned in the first column of the following table the respective sums mentioned in the second column thereof and in order to secure the repayment of the said sums and the payment of interest thereon they may mortgage or charge the revenues of the Council and they shall pay off all moneys so borrowed within the respective periods (which for the purposes of this Act and of any enactment incorporated therewith or applied thereby shall respectively be "the prescribed period") mentioned in the third column of the said table (namely) :—

| 1 | 2 | 3 |
| --- | --- | --- |
| Purpose. | Amount. | Period of Repayment. |
| *(a)* The provision of trolley vehicles – | 19,500 | Ten years from the date or dates of borrowing. |
| *(b)* The provision of electrical equipment construction of other works necessary for working trolley vehicles. | 5,972 | Twenty years from the date or dates of borrowing. |
| *(c)* The reconstruction of the roads upon which the tramways to be removed or discontinued under this Act are situate. | 21,900 | Twenty years from the date or dates of borrowing. |
| *(d)* The adaptation or erection of buildings for the purposes of the trolley vehicles and omnibuses of the Council. | 5,000 | Twenty-five years from the date of borrowing. |
| *(e)* The provision of omnibuses – | 15,000 | Eight years from the date or dates of borrowing. |
| *(f)* The payment of the costs charges and expenses of this Act. | The sum requisite. | Five years from the passing of this Act. |

(2) *(a)* The Council may also borrow with the consent of the Minister of Transport such further moneys as may be necessary for any of the purposes of the foregoing provisions of this Act.

*(b)* The Council may also borrow such further moneys as may be necessary for the purpose of providing a fund for working capital—

(i) as respects the tramway undertaking of the Council or the trolley vehicle or omnibus undertakings authorised by this Act with the consent of the Minister of Transport;

(ii) as respects the electricity undertaking with the consent of the Electricity Commissioners;

(iii) as respects any undertaking of the Council other than the tramway trolley vehicle omnibus and electricity undertakings with the consent of the Minister of Health.

*(c)* Any money borrowed under this subsection shall be repaid within such period as may be prescribed by the Minister or Commissioners with whose consent it is borrowed and that period shall be the prescribed period for the purposes of this Act and the enactments incorporated therewith or applied thereby.

*(d)* In order to secure the repayment of any money borrowed under this subsection and the payment of interest thereon the Council may mortgage or charge the revenues of the Council.

*Paragraphs 33–46 omitted*

### STATUTORY RULES AND ORDERS
### 1930, No.1080.

### TROLLEY VEHICLE.
### Pontypridd Urban District Council System.

REGULATIONS AND BYELAWS, DATED DECEMBER 19, 1930, MADE BY THE MINISTER OF TRANSPORT AS REGARDS ELECTRICAL POWER ON THE PONTYPRIDD URBAN DISTRICT COUNCIL TROLLEY VEHICLE SYSTEM.

The Minister of Transport under and by virtue of the powers conferred upon him in this behalf, does hereby, make the following regulations for securing to the public, reasonable protection against danger in the exercise of the powers conferred by Parliament with respect to the use of electrical power on the trolley vehicle system on the routes on which the use of such power has been authorised by the provisions, of the Pontypridd Urban District Council Act, 1929, (a) and the applied provisions of the Pontypridd Urban District Council Tramways Order, 1901(b) (hereinafter called "the routes"):

And the Minister of Transport does also hereby make the following byelaws with regard to the use of electrical power on the routes.

### REGULATIONS

I. Every trolley vehicle used on the routes shall comply with the following requirements that is to say:—

*(a)* It shall be fitted, if and when required by the Minister of Transport, with an apparatus to indicate to the driver the speed at which it is running.

*(b)* It shall be fitted with at least two independent brakes each capable of stopping and holding the vehicle on any gradient on the routes. One of the brakes at least must be applied by pedal.

*(c)* It shall be conspicuously numbered inside and outside.

*(d)* It shall be fitted with a bell, horn, gong or other approved means for giving warning when necessary.

*(e)* It shall be so constructed as to enable the driver to command the fullest possible view of the road.

II. No trailer vehicle shall be used on the routes except in the case of the removal of a disabled trolley vehicle.

III. No passenger shall be allowed to travel standing on the steps, platform, staircase or upper-deck of a trolley vehicle.

IV. During the hours of darkness, which expression means in summer time the time between one hour after sunset and one hour before sunrise and during the remainder of the year the time between half-an-hour after sunset and half-an-hour before sunrise, and at any time during fog, every trolley vehicle on the routes shall carry a lamp on each side so constructed and placed as to exhibit white lights visible within a reasonable distance to the front and every such vehicle shall carry a lamp so constructed and placed as to exhibit a red light visible within a reasonable distance to the rear. The front lamps shall be fixed on opposite sides of the vehicle, be as nearly as possible of the same power and be fixed at the same height from the ground in such position that no part of the vehicle or its equipment extends laterally on the same side as the lamp more than 12 ins beyond the centre of the lamp. The rear lamp shall be fixed either on the centre line or on the off-side of the vehicle.

V. The speed at which the trolley vehicles fitted with pneumatic tyres on all wheels shall be driven or propelled along the routes shall not exceed the rate of—

*Twelve* miles an hour—

*(a)* Between Coedpenmaen Post Office and the top of Cornstores Hill.

*(b)* In Taff Street and High Street.

*(c)* In Broadway, between High Street and the Great Western (Newport Branch) Railway Bridge.

*(d)* In Fothergill Street and Park Street.

*Eight* miles an hour—

*(a)* When approaching and traversing Pont-Shon-Norton Canal Bridge.

*(b)* Between the top of Cornstores Hill and the junction of Bridge Street with Taff Street.

*Four* miles an hour—

*(a)* When passing round all turning circles.

*(b)* When passing through all trolley wire junctions and crossings.

*(c* When passing under the Great Western (Newport Branch) Railway Bridge.

*(d)* When entering and leaving John Street.

At all other places not specifically mentioned the speed shall not exceed the rate of *Sixteen* miles an hour.

VI. The electrical pressure or difference of potential between the two overhead conductors used in connection with the working of the routes shall in no case exceed 600 volts. The electrical energy supplied through feeders shall not be generated at or transformed to a pressure higher than 650 volts, except with the written consent of the Minister of Transport, and subject to such regulations and conditions as he may prescribe.

VII. The interval between the supports to which the overhead conductors used in connection with the working of the routes are attached shall not, except with the approval of the Minister of Transport, exceed 120 ft, and as a general rule the overhead conductors shall in no part be at a less height than 20 ft from the surface of the street except where they pass under railway or other bridges or at curves.

VIII. Each positive overhead conductor shall be divided up into sections not exceeding (except with the special approval of the Minister of Transport) one-half of a mile in length, between every two of which shall be inserted an emergency switch so enclosed as to be inaccessible to pedestrians.

IX. Each separate insulator on the overhead conductors shall be tested not less frequently than once in a month, and any insulator found to be defective shall at once be removed and an efficient insulator substituted.

X. All electrical conductors fixed upon the trolley vehicles in connection with the trolley wheels shall be formed of flexible cables protected by india-rubber insulation of the highest quality, and additionally protected wherever they are adjacent to any metal so as to avoid risk of the metal becoming charged.

XI. The insulation of the electrical conductors from the metal work of each trolley vehicle shall be tested and recorded daily before the vehicle is used for passenger traffic with a testing pressure not less than 500 volts. No trolley vehicle shall be taken out for use if the leakage current exceeds 3 milliamperes.

XII. The hand-rails used by passengers on entering or leaving a trolley vehicle shall either be constructed of some non-conducting substance or be covered with a suitable insulating material.

XIII. An emergency cut-off switch shall be provided and fixed so as to be conveniently reached by the driver in case of any failure of action of the controller switch.

XIV. If and whenever telegraph, telephone, or other wires, unprotected with a permanent insulating covering, cross above, or are liable to fall upon, or to be blown on to, the overhead conductors of the routes, efficient guard wires shall be erected and maintained at all such places.

Provided that this regulation shall not apply to Post Office over-road stay wires or other uncovered wires which are not electrical conductors where they are connected at each end to the negative conductor.

XV. The guard wires shall be connected to the negative overhead conductor at intervals of not more than two spans.

X.VI. The poles carrying section switch boxes shall be efficiently connected with earth.

XVII. Where on the routes there are two negative trolley wires these shall be cross-connected at intervals of not more than half a mile.

XVIII. No gas or electric lamp bracket shall be attached to any pole unless triple insulation is provided between the pole and the positive overhead conductors.

In the case of any lamp suspended from the span wire carrying the overhead conductors that portion of the span wire from which the lamp is suspended shall be separated from that portion or portions on which the trolley wire or wires are carried by a suitable insulator.

[Note.—This regulation will not apply to lamps or brackets erected before the 18th day of December, 1926.]

*Penalty.*

Note.—The Pontypridd Urban District Council, or any company or person using electrical power on the routes contrary to any of the above regulations is, for every such offence, subject to a penalty not exceeding £10; and also in the case of a continuing offence, to a further penalty not exceeding £5 for every day during which such offence continues after conviction thereof.

Byelaws.

I. The bell, horn, gong or other approved apparatus shall be sounded by the driver of the trolley vehicle whenever necessary as a warning.

II. The trolley vehicles on the routes shall be brought to a standstill as soon as possible whenever it is necessary to avoid impending danger and on all occasions at the following points:—

(a) Before crossing Pont-Shon-Norton Canal Bridge on the southbound journey.

(b) At the top of Cornstores Hill on the southbound journey.

(c) At the junction of Bridge Street and Taff Street.

(d) In High Street before crossing the bridge over the River Rhondda on the northbound journey.

(e) In Station Square, Pontypridd Station.

(f) At the junction of Fothergill Street and Broadway.

III. A printed copy of these regulations and bye laws shall be kept in a conspicuous position inside of each trolley vehicle in use on the routes.

*Penalty.*

Note.—Any person offending against or committing a breach of any of these byelaws is liable to a penalty not exceeding forty shillings.

The provisions of the Summary Jurisdiction Acts, with respect to the recovery of penalties, are applicable *to* the penalties for the breach of these regulations or byelaws.

Signed this 19th day of December, 1930.

*E.W. Rowntree,*
Assistant Secretary, Ministry of Transport.

# PERSONALITIES

### Adam A. Armstrong A.M. Inst. T.

Adam Armstrong was born on 8 February 1871 in Langholm, Scotland. Little is known about his younger years but he was living and working in Edinburgh until after 1906. On the certificate of his first marriage his stated profession was Tramways Conductor whilst on the birth certificate of one of his children it is shown as Cable Car Inspector (Edinburgh having the fourth largest cable tramway system in the world). At some date thereafter he moved to Gateshead.

In 1918 Mr Armstrong of the Gateshead & District Tramways Co. was appointed Traffic Superintendent at £150 pa with responsibility for the commercial and traffic activities of Pontypridd UDC tramways. He reported to Mr Teasdel, the Electrical Engineer and Tramways Manager.

By the early 1930s the Council were eager to divide the management of their electrical and transport undertakings. Upon the death of Mr Teasdel, in April 1931, the commercial management of the transport undertaking passed to Mr Armstrong initially with the title Acting Traffic Manager and from April 1932 as Transport Manager. Responsibilities for engineering and technical aspects remained with Mr Evans. He retired on 5 July 1938 after 40 years' service in public transport and at a complimentary dinner at the 'Llanbradach Arms', Treforest he was presented with an ebony walking stick and illuminated clock on behalf of the department.

Outside his professional activities Mr Armstrong taught the local police self-defence whilst he was known for playing the bagpipes around the town on New Year's Eve.

He died in Pontypridd on 7 July 1943 aged 72 years.

### Gwilym J. Evans A.M.I.E.E.

Gwilym John Evans was born in St. Davids, Pembrokeshire on 3 August 1875, the eldest son of Rev. Benjamin Evans, Baptist Minister of St. Davids and from 1876 Gadlys, Aberdare. Following his training as an electrical engineer he was initially employed running the Gadlys colliery electricity generating station on the Bute Estate.

By 1901 he was a Shift Engineer with the Cardiff Corporation Electric Lighting and Tramways Department, where he probably met John Teasdel, from whence he successfully applied in 1905 for the position of Deputy Electrical Engineer and Tramways Manager to the Pontypridd UDC in the newly created Electricity and Tramways Department. This involved supervision of the Council's electric power and lighting, power generation including the refuse destructor and tramway activities, reporting to John Teasdel.

On the death of Mr Teasdel, Mr Evans was appointed Acting Electrical Engineer and Transport Manager but following the division of managerial responsibilities for the commercial and engineering activities of the transport undertaking in April 1932 he was given the title of Electrical and Transport Engineer.

Gwilym Evans married Lily Arnold of Aberdare in 1901 and they had two children. He was deeply involved in the Baptist Church and in his earlier years at Pontypridd gave evening classes on electrical engineering at Mountain Ash. Upon his retirement in September 1940 the commercial and engineering

Gwilym J. Evans, Pontypridd UDC Electrical and Transport Engineer 1932–1940. (Dr. Alun Hughes)

management of the transport undertaking were entrusted to Mr Powell whereas management of the electricity undertaking passed to Charles Bancroft then Pontypridd UDC Mains and Technical Assistant. Mr Evans was the Council's chosen technical consultant in the difficult discussions with the SWEB about the trolleybus traction feeder cables in the early 1950s.

Gwilym Evans died on 6 June 1957.

### Jack John

Mr John joined the Pontypridd UDC Tramways in April 1906 as a tram cleaner. He then rose through the ranks to become a fitter, assistant inspector and then in 1916 car shed superintendent responsible for the engineering in the transport department. Upon the conversion of the tramways to trolleybus operation he was designated Rolling Stock Superintendent and with the division of the Electricity and Transport Department into separate organisations in 1941 he became responsible for the rebuilding and reconstruction of the careworn and overworked motor and trolleybuses.

His home, at "Wainsworth", 11 John Street, Treforest, by the reverser, gave him a unique opportunity to supervise operations!

He retired on 2 October 1953 after 47 years service and devoted his time to his interest in local history.

## Herbert G. Ludlow

A native of Aberdare, Herbert George Ludlow was the son of a saddler at the Albion Colliery Cilfynydd and was educated at Pontypridd Grammar School.

He joined the undertaking as a tram conductor in 1931. In 1936 he became a trolleybus and motorbus driver being promoted to Temporary Inspector and Relief Ticket Office Clerk in 1941. He was called-up for military service in the Pay Corps in May 1944.

Upon his return to the Department in early 1947 he took up the post of Traffic Superintendent replacing Mr J. Freeman on his retirement, and was promoted upon Mr Powell's death to become Transport Manager. Ill-health forced his early retirement in 1973 and he died on 1 April 1976.

George Ludlow photographed at an early stage of his employment with Pontypridd UDC Transport Department. (Dr Stuart Burrows)

## John M. Powell A.M. Inst. T.

John Morgan Powell was born at Upper Boat in 1903, the son of a farmer who latterly worked on the Glamorganshire Canal. His formal education took place at Hawthorn and Mill Street Schools in Pontypridd; however, as a young man further studies led to him obtaining professional transport qualifications.

He joined the Pontypridd UDC Electrical and Tramways Department in May 1916 as an office boy in the general office. Over the next 15 years he acquired Institute of Transport qualifications and was promoted to Traffic Clerk. On the promotion of Mr Armstrong and death of Mr Teasdel in 1931, he took over the administration and control of the traffic side of the undertaking. In 1930 he received an MPTA medal for his essay on "The Case for a Controlled Monopoly of Passenger Transport within a Statutory Area" and while he was a Graduate of the Institute of Transport he received a medal for a paper entitled " Some Considerations of Propaganda Applied to Road Passenger Transport." Before the war Mr Powell lectured on transport subjects at Cardiff Technical College.

When Mr Armstrong retired, he was appointed Transport Manager effective 1 July 1938. In 1941 the UDC's Transport and Electricity Departments were formally separated with John Powell as Transport Manager. Upon his appointment as Chairman of the South Wales & Monmouthshire Section of the Institute of Transport in 1956 he became a member of the Institute's Executive Council.

Mr Powell was considered a humane manager by the standards of the time. His busy professional life was accompanied by an equally full private life. As a life long member of Carmel Welsh Presbyterian Church, Upper Boat, he was a deacon for 21 years and an organist for 40 years; Secretary of the Pontypridd Rotary Club; Officer of the Hen Bont Masonic Lodge, and a prolific writer and dramatist.

Until the outbreak of World War Two he was the producer of the Carmel Dramatic Society and wrote three full-length plays that were performed throughout the area. His father's work no doubt influenced his lifetime interest in canals and inland waterways indeed for much of his life he lived in a small canal-side cottage, Lock House in Rhydyfelin.

He was taken ill after arriving at the Masonic Lodge, Courthouse Street, Pontypridd, on the evening of Monday 10 February 1958 and died the next day at Graig Hospital Pontypridd.

## John Edwin Teasdel M.I.E.E.

John Teasdel was born in Yarmouth in 1868. He was educated at Ford's Grammar School, Sheffield and the Cardiff Technical College. After an apprenticeship with Messrs. Sydney F. Walker & Olliver Co., Cardiff, electrical engineers, he became one of the firm's departmental managers and carried out several installations for them in the North of England and elsewhere. He joined the Cardiff Corporation electricity undertaking at its inception in 1894 and rose to become Chief Assistant and Deputy to the Engineer. In November 1904 he was appointed Pontypridd UDC's Electrical Engineer and Tramways Manager at a salary of £300 pa.

He rapidly became popular with the men under his employment and members of the Council, however, the enthusiasm of both waned somewhat over the years as he was confronted with the growth of trade unionism, the General Strike and the heavy responsibility of managing both the UDC's entire power generation and supply (domestic, industrial and traction), and tramways activities.

A charming, well-dressed man he was a churchwarden and superintendent of the Sunday school at St. Matthews Church, Coedpenmaen, for many years. He was a member of the Merlin Lodge of Freemasons.

His health deteriorated in the mid-1920s and from 1926 onwards the Council began to consider dividing the management of the Electricity and Tramways Departments but nothing was done until 13 February 1931 when the Tramways Committee instructed Mr Teasdel to prepare a report on the advisability or otherwise of separate management. Whilst stressing that Mr Teasdel had done a competent job it was decided to entrust the tramways management to Mr Armstrong, the Traffic Superintendent, however, this was not implemented until after Mr Teasdel's death.

Mr Teasdel died in post on 11 April 1931 after a short illness and was buried at Glyntaff Cemetery. He was survived by a widow and four adult children. His tramways responsibilities passed to Mr Armstrong and his power supply responsibilities passed to Mr G.J. Evans.

# The personalities who ran the trolleybuses

An incomplete list of some of the individuals who kept the trolleybuses running in peace and in war, in the depression and the post-war boom:

## PLATFORM STAFF
*Inspectors* who had obviously worked through the ranks of conductors and drivers:
Tudor Dork (depot inspector), Jack Evans, Brinley Jones, George Ludlow (subsequently General Manager), Bill Owen, Bill Rowlands, Bert Thomas

*Drivers* who started their careers as conductors
Bill Banwell, Arthur Barnes (later an inspector), Bill Bevan, Evan Boulin, Ernie Bull, Eddie Cummings (later a motorbus driving instructor), Harold Davies, Henry Davies, Les Davies, George Emery, David Evans (started as a tram conductor in 1926, later trolleybus driving instructor), R. Greening (late 1940s), Mal Hughes, H.L. Jones (late 1940s), Ernie Kerslake, Horace Lambert, Jack Lambert (brother of Horace Lambert), Charles Lethbridge, Tudor Lewis, Wyndam Lewis, W. Leyshon (late 1940s), Dick Lucas, William Marsh (a "slow-coach" driver and part time fireman "Fireman Bill"), Bill Masson, George Minty, David Morgan (later trolleybus driving instructor), D.C. Nichols (late 1940s, later an inspector and depot inspector), Albert Nicholls (who drove the last tram, father of Harry), Harry Nicholls (who drove the last trolleybus, son of Albert), Henry Penwill, Noah Rees, Jack Rowsell, Ernie Scaplehorn, Alf Smith, Griff Stephens (later trolleybus driving instructor), Bill Thomas, John Thomas (killed in a motorbus accident driving motorbus 34 which was in collision with a Red & White bus on Cilfynydd Common on 7 October 1949), Bob Waites, Charles Venn, Fred Workman.

Conductress Olive Hunt, one of the great characters of Pontypridd's trolleybuses. (Cy Yandell collection)

*Conductors and Conductresses*
Ken Ash, Stanley Barnes, Charles Beer, Roy Bull, Ronald Copp, Ruby David, Rees Davies, Mrs (Annie?) Devereux (variously Senior Conductress, Inspector & Staff Canteen Supervisor), Nal Edwards, George Emery, Beryl Evans, Gwilym Evans, Jack Evans, Eddie Harrigan (late 1940s), Olive Hunt, R. Hughes, Roy Hunt, Harry Jacobs, Phyllis James, Mabel Jones, Mamie Jones (wife of Brinley Jones), Mel Jones, Gwyneth Jones, Kate Mahones, Rose Mantle, Fred Masson (jumper conductor),

A group of PUDCTD Conductresses. (Cy Yandell collection)

Mamie Jones in her PUDCTD conductress' uniform. Mamie became the wife of Inspector Brinley Jones who was the uncle of local enthusiast Cy Yandell. (Cy Yandell collection)

Pontypridd UDC Transport Department uniform cap badge. (Cy Yandell Collection)

Haydn Morgan, Ivy Moore, Tom Murphy, Albert Nicholls, Ray Passmore, Reg Perrott, Glyn Pritchard, Ivor Pugh, Archie Purnell, Charles Purnell (jumper conductor), Viv Roberts, Myrtle Smith, Fred Standard, Thelma Stephens (wife of Griff Stephens), Bernard Stogden, Bill Thomas (second of two of same name), Doreen Thomas, Nobby Thomas, Phyllis Trembarth, Jack Trevor, Phyllis Voicey, Cliff Walker, R. Watkins, Ernie Webb.

There were married couples working in the platform staff:

Mr & Mrs Pullen who were always driver and conductress on the same bus; Mr Brinley & Mrs Mamie Jones; Griff & Thelma Stephens; Gywneth Nicholls (née Boulin) was related to Driver Evan Boulin and the wife of Harry Nicholls

From left to right, 1931 Bristol B motorbus no. 13 with Eastwood & Kenning B32R body, another unidentifiable Bristol B motorbus, Guy BTX trolleybus 8 and another Bristol B motorbus in the shed entrance; 1932 Morris RP motorbuses nos. 16 & 17 with Petty B20F bodies and Bristol E trolleybus no. 9 standing outside by the entrance to the Glyntaff Depot area. Jack John stands in the middle (in suit) of the photograph. Driver Ernie Bull stands at the front on the left. (Photographer's name not recorded)

Bristol E no. 9 decorated for the Coronation of King George VI in 1936. The young man on the right, immediately beneath the driver's steering wheel, is 18 year old George Glaves who joined the Portsmouth UDC Transport Department in 1934 and rose to be shed foreman. The man wearing a suit and with receding hair, sixth from the left in the back row, is Jack John. Jack John's daughter became Mrs. Glaves just before the Second World War. It really was a family concern! (Mrs. J.M. Watkins (daughter of George Glaves))

## MAINTENANCE STAFF

*Fitters*
George Glaves, Omar Easterbrook, Arthur James, Ken Escott, Cyril Morgan, Haydn Boyle, Wally Jeans, Walter Benjamin, Alan Jones, Dilwyn Legg, Wayne Johnson, Ben Jenkins (originally a driver), Peter Clayton.

*Blacksmith*
Ned Johnston, Arthur Wells (assistant).

*Coachbuilders*
Reg Smith, George Yeo, Dilwyn Evans, Dick Osman, Owen Jenkins (glazier), Stan Evans (seat materials trimmer).

*Electrician*
Idris Richards, Garry Price, Ken John.

*Welder*
Arthur Williams

*Tyre Fitter*
William Morris

*Shiftmen*
Trevor Price, Bill Case, George David, Stanley Ware.

*Store Keeper*
Sam Morgan

*Paint Shop*
Charles Saunders, Glyn Flood, George Morgan, Emlyn Jones, ? Jeffries.

*Cleaners*
Harry Burt, Ivor Rankin.

Edgar Daniel (Shedmaster), Trevor Williams

## TRANSPORT OFFICE STAFF

The clerical staff were based in the house at the entrance to the depot:

*Ticket Office*
Hector Jacobs, Marina Jones, Gwyneth Parrish, Rhone Tricket, Molly ?

*Clerk's Office:*
Mrs Betty Ward
Edryd Evans, Chief Clerk

*(Clerical Staff)*
Carol Warner, Paul Williams, Herbert Rees (successor to Mr Ludlow as manager)

*Transport Clerks Department: Mileage Office*
Idris Knott, Roy Skuse, Trevor Williams.

*Transport Manager's Secretary*
Mrs Gulliford, then Mrs Margaret Williams (née Jones), then Mrs Betty Ward (née Selway)

*Canteen*
Mrs James, Mrs Rankin (wife of Ivor James).

# Employment Conditions

The changeover from trams to trolley vehicles brought few advantages for the employees although the drivers benefited from a seat to sit on and protection from the weather rather than standing on the open front platform of a tramcar. In theory all employees had a 48-hour week, guaranteed except for circumstances beyond the control of the department; however, such circumstances had existed since 1921 and nobody was regularly working this number of hours in 1930. Although Clough, Smith employed as many PUDCTD workmen as possible during the conversion, the economic depression and short-time working in the coal industry meant that the undertaking had no alternative but to constantly look for economies. The end of tramway operation on 30 August 1931 made 7–8 men surplus to requirements, 3 being dismissed and two drivers reduced to conductors. In respect of the maintenance employees, short-time working was introduced at the end of 1931: 3 men having to take one day off per week in lieu of Sunday duty with 4 having to work 39½ hours instead of 47 per week. Every effort was made to retain established employees on the pay-roll by a reduced working week which fell to as little as a guaranteed 32 hours, including every Saturday, in 1932.

Commencing on 4 April 1932 wages were reduced nationally by ½d per hour for drivers and 1s per week for conductors less than 21 years of age. As an indication of the challenges facing the undertaking's management in May 1932 the Maritime Colliery closed down and other mines in the town lost 77 shifts. In the preceding five years the resident population had fallen by some 14% (to 42,950) due to emigration. In an effort to cut costs the number of platform staff fell from 73 in 1932 to 70 in 1933, including the virtual elimination of all conductresses, and 4 inspectors.

The unpredictability of traffic meant that overtime was still required from those fortunate enough to have a job. New duties providing for the guaranteed 48-hour week put into effect on 24 October 1934 for a trial 3 month period resulting in 32½ hours shed work for platform staff compared to 14 hours in the past, the previous schedules being based on a 51-hour week. This allowed a margin for loss of hours at collieries and with a weekly basis varying between 52 and 44 hours this averaged 48 hours over a period of 13 weeks in the case of trolleybus crews. Even then one Sunday evening duty was covered by shed hands.

Wage comparisons are somewhat meaningless without full consideration of their purchasing power and the rates paid in comparable industries, however, as an indication from August 1934 the highest rate of pay for a conductor, over 21 years old with 5 years of service, was £2 11s 6d per week. In comparison the Transport Manager received a salary of £375 pa which equates to £7 4s 2d per week. Throughout the 1930s it was more important to remain in regular paid employment than to seek higher wages or improved conditions and thus when in spring 1937 the TGWU suggested that the Pontypridd rates be aligned with maximum prevailing in the South Wales area, Pontypridd UDC granted a lower increase and that only to conductors (2s 6d).

In autumn 1937 the NJIC for the Road Passenger Transport Industry applied for a 4s wage increase for a 48-hour week and improved conditions of service, although only 2s was subsequently granted in December 1937, subject to there being no further wage claim or request for improved conditions for at least 2 years. The new conditions of service provided for a minimum of 8 hours pay for spreadover duties exceeding 11 hours, and payment at time and a quarter for every hour or part thereof exceeding 11 hours. Unchanged was the guarantee of a 48-hour week to at least 90% of the employees, however, for the remaining 10% of the platform staff only a 40-hour week was guaranteed (previously 36 hours). Normal duty schedule continued to average 48 hours per week of six days again calculated over a period of several months with no weekly schedule less than 46 hours and no daily schedule less than 7 hours.

The employment situation began to change as industry geared-up for war. In spring 1939 there were a previously unheard-of 7 resignations and 5 temporary conductors were taken on from the waiting list for the summer. The majority of staff was working until 10 or 11 pm and plans were made in anticipation of a call-up of employees for military service, 22 conductors being less than 26 years of age. Pontypridd's strategic location in the coalfield ensured that there was no reduction in trolleybus services. The trolleybus fleet grew in size and, as in most of the UK, traffic figures soared. The additional vehicles led to a shortage of drivers. It is believed that towards the end of 1942 new duty schedules were introduced whereby the facility of working drivers and conductors on a 6-day week and giving a day off in a week during which this involved a Sunday duty, ceased. This resulted in a 7-day week once in every 4 weeks.

By early 1944 the shortage of drivers was critical, making it difficult to give traffic staff their annual holidays. It was agreed with the TGWU that the work normally covered by 22 duties would be shared over 20 duties with all time over 48 hours paid. On 18 May 1944 an NJIC Wage Award came into effect granting 5s on the war wage and 12 days holiday with pay for all employees after 12 months service in place of 8 days after 12 months, 10 days after 2 years, and 12 days after 3 years service. The guaranteed 48-hour week was extended to all employees.

In July 1946, in agreement with the TGWU, PUDCT was regraded as a Group 1 undertaking resulting in new maximum pay rates of £5 per week for drivers and £4 16s for conductors, with appropriate increase for depot employees. Soon afterwards the commencing rates were increased to £4 17s and £4 13s per week respectively, increasing by 1s per week after 12 months' service to the maximum shown above. Effective 1 April 1947, the working week was reduced to 44 hours in six days without reduction in the weekly rate of pay and with a minimum daily duty tour of 7 hours and a maximum of 8½ hours. Sundays were in future paid at time and a half (instead of time and a quarter).

Many of the men who had returned from the forces began to seek more remunerative work and less unattractive working hours. This was a national phenomenon. The early 1950s were marked by a series of small improvements aimed at raising the attractiveness of working in the transport industry. Uniformed staff were permitted to travel free of charge to and from duty, however, off-duty concession travel was only introduced in March 1953 subject to the purchase of an annual pass costing 5s. In January 1954 the Industrial Court awarded a fifth Bank Holiday with pay at time and a half (Good Friday) in conjunction with an increase of 4s per week. This was followed by a further increase of 8s in December 1954 with all work by drivers and conductors after 1 pm Saturday paid at time and a quarter.

The absence of designated break times remained firmly entrenched when Bernard Stogden joined the undertaking as a trolleybus conductor in 1954 at the age of seventeen.

"We took sandwiches to work and managed to get a jug of tea from one of the cafes at Taff House. I had to hold it until we got to the terminus at John Street; I dared not spill a drop! Then we would eat and drink as the passengers were getting on the trolleybus. You could virtually guarantee that there would be someone waiting at the terminus, tapping their feet waiting for us to go!

We dare not be a minute late. We had to fill in our way board at each end of the run, the first thing that the inspector would do when he got on the bus was get our way board from the rack underneath the stairs and start going around the passengers checking tickets. They didn't trust us at all but I would fool them and keep the board in my uniform pocket and then they would have to wait for me, they didn't like that at all, I would act dull and pretend that I didn't know what they were looking for. We had one inspector called Jack Evans. If I knew he was on duty I would never leave it in the rack. He would hide in a shop doorway until we were at the stop and then jump out on us. I used to laugh to myself because I had seen him hiding before we got there.

We had split shifts (spreadovers): We would start at about 5 am and work until the schools had started about 9–9.30 am then we would re-start at about 1.30 pm and work until 5.30–6.00 pm Monday to Friday, then on Saturday we would either have an early shift or start at midday. My wages when I got married was about £6 for a basic 44-hour working week".

Throughout the trolleybus era new entrants had to start as a conductor first before being selected for driver training. Trolleybus conductors could be employed from 17 years of age as they did not require a PSV licence for which the minimum age was 18 years. A large proportion of the work force were ex-miners who had given up employment in the collieries for health reasons (coal dust on the lungs) and some of them found driving hard work, pulling on the wheel in the days before power steering.

Crews synchronised their watches at the Transport Department's Bundy clock set in its green case on a shop wall in the Ynysangharad Park entrance opposite Mill Street.

A notorious spot for trolleybuses to be stranded was at the foot of Fothergill Street in Treforest where buses turning towards Machine Bridge for the depot had to make a wide and exact sweep (beneath a frog and crossing).

During the day trolleybus shift-changes took place at Taff House and the crews walked back to Glyntaff Depot to sign out.

**258**
No. of Licence.

*58*

# Electric Car Driver's Licence

We, the Urban District Council of Pontypridd,

pursuant to the powers and authorities enabling us in this behalf, and upon the application of _____ Mr. H. y. Carvill _____

residing at _____ c/o. Guage Transport Dept _____

do hereby license him to act as a Driver of an Electric Trolley Vehicle plying for hire within the Urban District of Pontypridd; this licence to continue in force until the 31st December, 19 54, unless the same be sooner revoked or suspended.

Given under the Seal of the Urban District Council of Pontypridd this _____ 13th _____ day of _____ December _____ One thousand nine hundred and _____ fifty three _____

*John Hilton*

CLERK.

SEAL

1946 Karrier W No. 8 seen at the Park Royal factory prior to delivery.
(Peter Smith collection [photographer's name not recorded])

# BIBLIOGRAPHY

| Title | Author | Publisher | Date | ISBN number |
|---|---|---|---|---|
| **Books, Brochures and Pamphlets** | | | | |
| *The Bristol Story Part One 1908–1951* | Alan Townsin | Venture Publications Limited | 1996 | 1 898432252 |
| *Bristol's Trams Remembered* | John B. Appleby | John B. Appleby | 1969 | – |
| *British Trolleybuses 1911–1972* | Geoff Lumb | Ian Allan Publishing | 1995 | 0 7110 2347 6 |
| *The Cardiff Trolleybus (1942 to 1970)* | D.G. Bowen & John Callow | National Trolleybus Association | 1969 | 0 850240026 |
| *Great British Tramway Networks* | W.H. Bett & J.C. Gillham | Light Railway Transport League | 1962 | – |
| *History of the British Trolleybus* | Nicholas Owen | David & Charles | 1974 | 0 7153 6370 0 |
| *Kingston upon Hull Trolleybuses* | Malcolm Wells | Trolleybooks | 1996 | 0 904235 16 5 |
| *Llanelly Trolleybuses* | Geoff L. Griffiths | Trolleybooks | 1992 | 0 904235 15 7 |
| *Nottingham Trolleybuses* | David R.H. Bowler | Trolleybooks | 2006 | 0 904235 20 3 |
| *Passenger Tramways of Pontypridd* | Robert Large | Oakwood Press | 1977 | – |
| *The People's Carriage* | | Bristol Omnibus Co. | 1974 | – |
| *Pontypridd Tickets 1953–1957* | Roger Atkinson | Transport Ticket Society | 1957 | – |
| *Portsmouth Trolleybuses* | David R.H. Bowler | Adam Gordon | 2014 | 978-1-874422-96-9 |
| *The Trolleybuses of South Shields* | Geoff Burrows | Trolleybooks | 1976 | 0 904235 04 1 |
| *Tramways of South Wales* | W.H. Bett & J.C. Gillham | Light Railway Transport League | 1993 | 0 948106 14 X |
| *Trackless to Trolleybus* | Stephen Lockwood | Adam Gordon | 2011 | 978-1-874422-86-0 |
| *Trolleybus Trails* | J. Joyce | Ian Allan Ltd. | 1963 | – |
| *The Ultimate Review* | | Transport Ticket Society | 1967 | – |
| *Under Two Liveries* | H. Brearley & D.T. Beach | West Riding Transport Society | 1970 | – |

**Newspapers**

*Pontypridd Observer* — Various issues 1929–1957. Copies held at the Pontypridd Library.
*Rhondda Free Press* — Various issues 1929–1943 weekly

**Professional Periodicals**

*Bus & Coach* — In particular April 1945 edition.
*Electric Railway, Bus and Tram Journal* — In particular 10 October 1930 edition.
*Tramway and Railway World* — In particular 16 October 1930 edition.
*The Transport World*

**Enthusiasts' Magazines and Periodicals**

*Buses* — Ian Allan Ltd.
*(In particular the February 1978 edition containing an article on Pontypridd by A.G. Newman, and the April 1982 edition containing an article on the Rhondda trackless trolleys by A.G. Newman and C.J. Taylor.)*

| Title | | Publisher | Date |
|---|---|---|---|
| *Buses Illustrated* | | Ian Allan Ltd. | 1949–67 |
| *National Trolleybus Association Newsletter* | | National Trolleybus Association | 1963–67 |
| *Reading Transport Society Newsletter* | | Reading Transport Society | 1961–71 |
| *Trolleybus (Journal/Magazine of the British Trolleybus Society)* | | British Trolleybus Society | 1971–date |
| *Trolleybus Society Newsletter* | | Trolleybus Society | 1954–55 |
| *Trolleybus Magazine* | | National Trolleybus Association | 1963–date |

**Others**

Acts of Parliament
Minutes of the Pontypridd Electricity Committee — Copies held at the Glamorgan Record Office
Minutes of the Pontypridd Tramways Committee — Copies held at the Glamorgan Record Office
Minutes of the Pontypridd Passenger Transport Committee — Copies held at the Glamorgan Record Office
Pontypridd Urban District Council Minutes — Copies held at the Glamorgan Record Office

The first Karrier W to enter service in Pontypridd, Weymann bodied no. 10 disgorges part of its load and takes queuing passengers on board at the Tumble, outside the 'The Greyhound Inn' opposite Station Square. (Hugh Taylor collection [photographer D.A. Jones])

# STATISTICS

Surviving records suggest that there was no consistency in the way that monthly reports were prepared for the Transport Committee. These normally included full details of expenditure, income and mileage operated; however, this information is partially or completely absent for many individual months in the 1930s. Where copies of the undertaking's annual report covering the months in question are also missing it has proved impossible to calculate complete statistics or even approximates.

As an illustration, in the financial year 1932–33 detailed reports were prepared for the months of April, May, June, October, November and December 1932 and January 1933 indicating cumulative trolleybus mileage of 157,240 and traffic receipts £7,547 with 990,342 passengers carried; cumulative motorbus mileage 232,068 and traffic receipts £9,861 with 1,878,846 carried. Other documents show that the total trolleybus mileage operated for the year was 267,510 but no motorbus figure is available for comparison.

Monthly and annual results were not published during the Second World War to avoid compromising national security as required by Defence Regulations. Abbreviated summaries for this period have survived but these contain no details of the mileage run by the greatly expanded motorbus fleet.

## TROLLEYBUS SERVICE STATISTICS

|  | 1930–31 | 1931–32 | 1932–33 | 1933–34 | 1934–35 | 1935–36 | 1936–37 | 1937–38 | 1938–39 |
|---|---|---|---|---|---|---|---|---|---|
| Revenue miles run |  | 295,460 | 267,510 | 265,935 | 266,657 | 269,654 |  | 276,260 | 267,994 |
| Passengers carried |  | 2,068,841 | 1,682,820 | 1,815,410 | 1,832,674 | 1,820,834 | 1,835,809 | 1,935,859 | 2,015,940 |
| Passengers per mile |  | 7.002102 | 6.290681 | 6.826518 | 6.872777 | 6.752483 |  | 7.007381 | 7.522333 |

|  | 1939–40 | 1940–41 | 1941–42 | 1942–43 | 1943–44 | 1944–45 | 1945–46 | 1946–47 | 1947–48 |
|---|---|---|---|---|---|---|---|---|---|
| Revenue miles run | 274,208 |  | 293,444 | 284,432 | 282,534 | 255,933 | 263,650 | 271,215 | 282,873 |
| Passengers carried | 2,246,211 | 2,697,863 | 3,454,628 | 3,882,909 | 3,912,432 | 3,958,000 | 3,894,000 | 4,361,073 | 4,657,827 |
| Passengers per mile | 8.191632 |  | 11.772699 | 13.651449 | 13.847650 | 15.464985 | 14.769581 | 16.079763 | 16.466142 |

|  | 1948–49 | 1949–50 | 1950–51 | 1951–52 | 1952–53 | 1953–54 | 1954–55 | 1955–56 | 1956–57 |
|---|---|---|---|---|---|---|---|---|---|
| Revenue miles run | 285,374 | 280,613 | 277,954 | 274,724 | 267,124 | 259,537 | 262,592 | 243,838 | 190,427 |
| Passengers carried | 4,630,354 | 4,786,141 | 5,046,399 | 5,115,487 | 4,795,813 | 4,232,060 | 3,884,206 | *3,437,000 | **3,163,000 |
| Passengers per mile | 16.225564 | 17.056020 | 18.155519 | 18.620459 | 17.953508 | 16.306191 | 14.791791 | 14.095424 | 16.610039 |

* Excludes January & February 1956 – power workers strike.
** 1 April 1956–31 December 1956 only.

## MILEAGE & PASSENGERS

| Year Ending March | Mileage | | Hours in service | Passengers (thousands) |
|---|---|---|---|---|
|  | Revenue | Non-Revenue |  |  |
| 1932 | 295,460 | 89 | – | 2,069 |
| 33 | 267,510 | 70 | 32,606 | 1,683 |
| 34 | 265,935 | 0 | 31,014 | 1,815 |
| 35 | 266,657 | 15 | 31,150 | 1,833 |
| 36 | 269,654 | 117 | 31,260 | 1,821 |
| 37 | – | – | – | 1,836 |
| 38 | 276,260 | 79 | 32,410 | 1,936 |
| 39 | 267,994 | 38 | 31,104 | 2,016 |
| 40 | 274,208 | 141 | 32,060 | 2,246 |
| 41 | – | – | – | 2,698 |
| 42 | 293,444 | 340 | 35,540 | 3,455 |
| 43 | 284,432 | 144 | 36,018 | 3,883 |
| 44 | 282,534 | 217 | 35,424 | 3,912 |
| 45 | 255,933 | 0 | 31,991 | 3,958 |
| 46 | 263,650 | 19 | 32,896 | 3,894 |
| 47 | 271,215 | 351 | 33,903 | 4,360 |
| 48 | 282,873 | 780 | 35,320 | 4,658 |
| 49 | 285,374 | 527 | 35,666 | 4,630 |
| 50 | 280,613 | 1,203 | 35,075 | 4,784 |
| 51 | 277,954 | 1,980 | 34,744 | 5,046 |
| 52 | 274,724 | 313 | 34,340 | 5,115 |
| 53 | 267,124 | 0 | 33,390 | 4,796 |
| 54 | 259,537 | 1,212 | 32,442 | 4,232 |
| 55 | 262,592 | 352 | 32,823 | 3,884 |
| 56 | 243,838 | 0 | 30,481 | *3,437 |
| 57 | 190,429 | 0 | 23,866 | **3,163 |

*Excludes January & February 1956 – power workers strike.
**1 April 1956–31 December 1956 only.

## TROLLEYBUS & MOTORBUS COMPARATIVE STATEMENT

| | 1930–31 TRAMS Amount | Per Mile | 1930–31 TROLLEYBUSES Amount | Per Mile | 1930–31 MOTORBUSES Amount | Per Mile | 1931–32 TRAMS Amount | Per Mile | 1931–32 TROLLEYBUSES Amount | Per Mile | 1931–32 MOTORBUSES Amount | Per Mile | 1932–33 TROLLEYBUSES Amount | Per Mile | 1932–33 MOTORBUSES Amount | Per Mile |
|---|---|---|---|---|---|---|---|---|---|---|---|---|---|---|---|---|
| Traffic Expenses | 8,253 | | 3,313 | | 2,464 | | 1,938 | | 6,375 | 5.18 | 6,218 | | | | | |
| General Expenses | 1,552 | | 593 | | 520 | | 487 | | 1,220 | 0.99 | 1,437 | | | | | |
| Licences | | | | | | | - | | 503 | 0.41 | 828 | | | | | |
| Maintenance & Repairs | 4,547 | | 1,434 | | 677 | | 2,429 | | 2,887 | 2.35 | 1,747 | | | | | |
| Power | 2,603 | | 1,321 | | 955 | | 625 | | 3,174 | 2.58 | 2,746 | | | | | |
| Rates | 593 | | 196 | | 171 | | 228 | | 175 | 0.14 | 175 | | | | | |
| Total Revenue Expenses | 17,549 | | 6,857 | | 4,787 | | 5,707 | | 14,334 | 11.64 | 13,151 | | | | | |
| Passengers | 19,204 | | 6,997 | | 3,445 | | 4,250 | | 15,123 | 12.28 | 13,888 | | | | | |
| Advertising | 440 | | 15 | | 9 | | 96 | | 81 | 0.07 | 65 | | | | | |
| Miscellaneous | 2 | | 1 | | | | | | 2 | 0 | 1 | | | | | |
| Total Income | 19,646 | | 7,013 | | 3,454 | | 4,346 | | 15,206 | 12.35 | 13,955 | | | | | |
| Through Running Adjust. | -28 | | | | | | -13 | | - | - | +16 | | | | | |
| GROSS SURPLUS (+) or DEFICIT (-) | +2,069 | | +156 | | -1,332 | | -1,374 | | +872 | 0.71 | +819 | | | | | |
| Discounts & Interest rcvd | +60 | | | | | | +200 | | +35 | 0.03 | +25 | | | | | |
| Interest on Debt | -2,850 | | - | | - | | -1,823 | | -748 | -0.61 | -455 | | | | | |
| Loan Repayment | -1,909 | | - | | - | | -1,954 | | - | - | - | | | | | |
| NET SURPLUS (+) or DEFICIT (-) | -2,630 | | +156 | | -1,332 | | -4,951 | | +159 | 0.13 | +389 | | | | | |

| | 1933–34 | | | | 1934–35 | | | | 1935–36 | | | |
| | TROLLEYBUSES | | MOTORBUSES | | TROLLEYBUSES | | MOTORBUSES | | TROLLEYBUSES | | MOTORBUSES | |
| | Amount | Per Mile | Amount | Per Mile | Amount | Per Mile | Amount | Per Mile | Amount | Per Mile | Amount | Per Mile |
|---|---|---|---|---|---|---|---|---|---|---|---|---|
| Traffic Expenses | 4,963 | 4.48 | 8,853 | 4.24 | 5,110 | 4.60 | 9,513 | 4.40 | 5,033 | 4.48 | 9,793 | |
| General Expenses | 1,198 | 1.08 | 2,348 | 1.12 | 1,027 | 0.92 | 2,188 | 1.01 | 1,043 | 0.93 | 2,288 | |
| Licences | 596 | 0.54 | 934 | 0.45 | 595 | 0.54 | 1,109 | 0.51 | 595 | 0.53 | 1,159 | |
| Maintenance & Repairs | 1,808 | 1.63 | 2,791 | 1.34 | 2,240 | 2.02 | 2,951 | 1.36 | 2,138 | 1.9 | 2,946 | |
| Power | 2,604 | 2.35 | 4,453 | 2.13 | 2,494 | 2.24 | 4,053 | 1.87 | 2,546 | 2.27 | 4,267 | |
| Total Revenue Expenses | 11,169 | 10.08 | 19,379 | 9.28 | 11,466 | 10.32 | 19,814 | 9.15 | 11,355 | 10.11 | 20,453 | |
| Through Running Adjust. | - | - | -11 | -0.01 | - | - | - | - | - | | 11 | |
| Total Income | 13,518 | 12.20 | 22,553 | 10.80 | 13,402 | 12.06 | 23,654 | 10.93 | 13,341 | 11.87 | 24,049 | |
| GROSS SURPLUS (+) or DEFICIT (-) | +2,349 | +2.12 | +3,163 | +1.51 | +1,936 | +1.74 | +3,840 | +1.78 | +1,986 | 1.77 | +3,585 | |
| Discounts & Interest rcvd | +77 | +0.07 | +8 | - | +69 | +0.06 | +26 | +0.01 | +5 | | +35 | |
| Loan Repayment | -1,894 | -1.71 | -2,345 | -1.12 | -1,792 | -1.61 | -2,324 | -1.08 | -2,514 | -2.24 | -3,522 | |
| Interest on Debt | -935 | -0.84 | -678 | -0.32 | -937 | -0.84 | -698 | -0.32 | | | | |
| NET SURPLUS (+) or DEFICIT (-) | -403 | -0.36 | +148 | +0.07 | -724 | -0.71 | +844 | +0.39 | -523 | -0.47 | +98 | |

| | 1936–37 | | | | 1937–38 | | | | 1938–39 | | | |
| | TROLLEYBUSES | | MOTORBUSES | | TROLLEYBUSES | | MOTORBUSES | | TROLLEYBUSES | | MOTORBUSES | |
| | Amount | Per Mile | Amount | Per Mile | Amount | Per Mile | Amount | Per Mile | Amount | Per Mile | Amount | Per Mile |
|---|---|---|---|---|---|---|---|---|---|---|---|---|
| Traffic Expenses | | | | | | | | | 5,819 | 5.21 | 12,237 | |
| General Expenses | | | | | | | | | 927 | 0.83 | 2,193 | |
| Licences | | | | | | | | | 538 | 0.48 | 1,533 | |
| Maintenance & Repairs | | | | | | | | | 2,599 | 2.33 | 4,397 | |
| Power | | | | | | | | | 1,866 | 1.67 | 5,819 | |
| Superannuation | | | | | | | | | 514 | 0.46 | 1,120 | |
| Total Revenue Expenses | | | | | | | | | 12,263 | 10.98 | 27,299 | |
| Through Running Adjust. | | | | | | | | | - | - | -47 | - |
| Total Income | | | | | | | | | 14,268 | 12.78 | 30,025 | |
| GROSS SURPLUS (+) or DEFICIT (-) | | | | | | | | | +2,005 | 1.8 | +2,773 | |
| Loan Repayment / Interest on Debt | | | | | | | | | 2,366 | 2.12 | 3,624 | |
| NET SURPLUS (+) or DEFICIT (-) | | | | | | | | | -361 | -0.32 | -851 | |

207

| | 1939–40 | | | | 1940–41 | | | | 1941–42 | | | |
|---|---|---|---|---|---|---|---|---|---|---|---|---|
| | TROLLEYBUSES | | MOTORBUSES | | TROLLEYBUSES | | MOTORBUSES | | TROLLEYBUSES | | MOTORBUSES | |
| | Amount | Per Mile | Amount | Per Mile | Amount | Per Mile | Amount | Per Mile | Amount | Per Mile | Amount | Per Mile |
| Traffic Expenses | 6,198 | 5.42 | 11576 | | 7,094 | | 12,136 | | 7,794 | 6.37 | 14,854 | |
| Vehicle Hire | | | | | | | | | 1,086 | 0.89 | - | |
| General Expenses | 960 | 0.84 | 2122 | | 1,157 | | 2,626 | | 1,255 | 1.03 | 2,622 | |
| Licences | 535 | 0.47 | 1485 | | 520 | | 1,521 | | 652 | 0.53 | 1,619 | |
| Maintenance & Repairs | 2,771 | 2.43 | 4321 | | 3,595 | | 3,988 | | 4,624 | 3.78 | 5,502 | |
| Power | 1,907 | 1.67 | 5061 | | 2,034 | | 5,416 | | 2,093 | 1.71 | 6,362 | |
| Superannuation | 561 | 0.49 | 1109 | | 693 | | 1,317 | | 709 | 0.58 | 1,418 | |
| ARP, War Damage Ins. | 52 | 0.05 | 104 | | 104 | | 207 | | 151 | 0.12 | 618 | |
| Total Revenue Expenses | 12,984 | 11.36 | 25778 | | 15,197 | | 27,211 | | 18,364 | 15.02 | 32,995 | |
| Through Running Adjust. | | | 157 | | - | - | -92 | | - | - | -104 | |
| Total Income | 16,661 | 14.58 | 32,279 | | 20,008 | | 35,554 | | 25,148 | 20.57 | 47,916 | |
| GROSS SURPLUS (+) or DEFICIT (-) | 3,677 | 3.22 | 6344 | | +4,811 | | +8,251 | | +6,784 | 5.55 | +15,025 | |
| Discounts & Interest rcvd | | | | | | | | | +68 | 0.06 | +136 | |
| Loan Repayment / Interest on Debt | 2,329 | 2.04 | 3,714 | | 1,304 | | 2,642 | | -779 | 0.64 | -2,898 | |
| NET SURPLUS (+) or DEFICIT (-) | +1,348 | +1.18 | +2,630 | | +3,507 | | +5,609 | | +6,073 | 4.97 | +12,263 | |

| | 1942–43 TROLLEYBUSES | | 1942–43 MOTORBUSES | | 1943–44 TROLLEYBUSES | | 1943–44 MOTORBUSES | | 1944–45 TROLLEYBUSES | | 1944–45 MOTORBUSES | |
|---|---|---|---|---|---|---|---|---|---|---|---|---|
| | Amount | Per Mile | Amount | Per Mile | Amount | Per Mile | Amount | Per Mile | Amount | Per Mile | Amount | Per Mile |
| Traffic Expenses | 8,783 | 7.41 | 18,903 | | 9,463 | 8.04 | 23,014 | | 9,667 | 9.07 | 27,993 | |
| Vehicle Hire | 1,720 | 1.45 | 617 | | 1,200 | 1.02 | 1,494 | | 1,200 | 1.13 | 920 | |
| General Expenses | 1,311 | 1.11 | 2,832 | | 1,711 | 1.45 | 3,678 | | 1,334 | 1.25 | 4,251 | |
| Licences | 789 | 0.67 | 1,665 | | 735 | 0.62 | 2,309 | | 829 | 0.78 | 3,013 | |
| Maintenance & Repairs | 5,657 | 4.77 | 6,314 | | 6,480 | 5.5 | 8,096 | | 5,831 | 5.47 | 11,220 | |
| Power | 2,032 | 1.71 | 6,995 | | 2,110 | 1.79 | 7,566 | | 1,966 | 1.84 | 8,507 | |
| Superannuation | 749 | 0.63 | 1,498 | | 414 | 0.35 | 828 | | 530 | 0.5 | 1,590 | |
| ARP, War Damage Ins. | 179 | 0.15 | 519 | | 112 | 0.1 | 401 | | 51 | 0.05 | 279 | |
| Make-up of civilian pay | – | – | – | – | 1,321 | 1.12 | 2,463 | | 199 | 0.19 | 598 | |
| Total Revenue Expenses | 21,220 | 17.91 | 39,343 | | 23,546 | 20 | 49,849 | | 21,607 | 20.26 | 58,371 | |
| Through Running Adjust. | – | – | 165 | | – | – | 21 | | – | – | – | |
| Total Income | 28,468 | 24.02 | 57,267 | | 30,089 | 25.56 | 69,029 | | 30,928 | 29 | 77,302 | |
| GROSS SURPLUS (+) or DEFICIT (−) | +7,248 | 6.12 | +17,759 | | +6,543 | 5.56 | +19,159 | | +9,321 | 8.74 | +18,931 | |
| Discounts & Interest rcvd | +106 | 0.09 | +213 | | +124 | 0.11 | +245 | | +97 | 0.09 | +407 | |
| Loan Repayment / Interest on Debt | } −875 | −0.74 | } −2,955 | | } −796 | −0.68 | } −2,571 | | } −782 | −0.73 | } −2,007 | |
| NET SURPLUS (+) or DEFICIT (−) | +6,479 | 5.47 | +15,017 | | +5,747 | 4.88 | 16,588 | | +8,636 | 8.1 | +17,331 | |

| | 1945–46 | | | | 1946–47 | | | | 1947–48 | | | |
|---|---|---|---|---|---|---|---|---|---|---|---|---|
| | TROLLEYBUSES | | MOTORBUSES | | TROLLEYBUSES | | MOTORBUSES | | TROLLEYBUSES | | MOTORBUSES | |
| | Amount | Per Mile | Amount | Per Mile | Amount | Per Mile | Amount | Per Mile | Amount | Per Mile | Amount | Per Mile |
| Traffic Expenses | 10,367 | 9.44 | 32,025 | | 12,077 | 10.69 | 38,642 | 9.51 | 13,255 | 11.21 | 47,395 | 9.34 |
| Vehicle Hire | 1,084 | 0.99 | 554 | | 130 | 0.12 | - | - | - | - | - | - |
| General Expenses | 1,648 | 1.5 | 5,172 | | 2,186 | 1.93 | 6,768 | 1.67 | 2,247 | 1.90 | 7,542 | 1.49 |
| Licences | 952 | 0.87 | 3,118 | | 836 | 0.74 | 3,158 | 0.78 | 685 | 0.58 | 3,504 | 0.69 |
| Maintenance & Repairs | 6,020 | 5.48 | 14,332 | | 5,731 | 5.07 | 16,389 | 4.03 | 5,433 | 4.60 | 18,285 | 3.60 |
| Power | 2,086 | 1.9 | 8,554 | | 1,994 | 1.77 | 10,085 | 2.48 | 2,038 | 1.72 | 10,754 | 2.12 |
| Superannuation | 622 | 0.57 | 1,860 | | 716 | 0.63 | 2,134 | 0.52 | 1,525 | 1.29 | 4,559 | 0.90 |
| Make-up of civilian pay | 123 | 0.11 | 369 | | 58 | 0.05 | 175 | 0.04 | - | - | - | - |
| Total Expenditure | 22,902 | 20.85 | 65,984 | | 23,728 | 21.00 | 77,351 | 19.03 | 25,183 | 21.30 | 92,039 | 18.14 |
| Through Running Adjust. | - | - | 50 | | - | - | 99 | 0.02 | - | - | 57 | 0.01 |
| Total Income | 30,391 | 27.66 | 80,219 | | 32,550 | 28.80 | 80,753 | 19.86 | 32,251 | 27.28 | 97,343 | 19.19 |
| GROSS SURPLUS (+) or DEFICIT (-) | +7,489 | 6.82 | +14,285 | | +8,822 | +7.80 | +3,303 | +0.81 | +7,068 | +5.98 | +5,361 | +1.06 |
| Discounts & Interest rcvd | +44 | 0.04 | +377 | | +56 | +0.01 | +478 | +0.01 | +47 | +0.04 | +412 | +0.03 |
| Interest on Debt | -706 | -0.64 | -1,757 | | -205 | -0.18 | -126 | -0.03 | -237 | -0.23 | -352 | -0.08 |
| Loan Repayment | | | | | -977 | -0.94 | -666 | -0.18 | -1,721 | -1.46 | -1,782 | -0.34 |
| Others | | | | | -96 | - | -222 | -0.03 | -51 | - | -406 | -0.05 |
| NET SURPLUS (+) or DEFICIT (-) | +6,827 | 6.21 | +12,905 | | +7,600 | 6.70 | +2,767 | +0.58 | +5,106 | +4.33 | +3,233 | +0.63 |

| | 1948–49 | | | | 1949–50 | | | | 1950–51 | | | |
| | TROLLEYBUSES | | MOTORBUSES | | TROLLEYBUSES | | MOTORBUSES | | TROLLEYBUSES | | MOTORBUSES | |
| | Amount | Per Mile | Amount | Per Mile | Amount | Per Mile | Amount | Per Mile | Amount | Per Mile | Amount | Per Mile |
|---|---|---|---|---|---|---|---|---|---|---|---|---|
| Traffic Expenses | 15,110 | 12.40 | 54,218 | 10.98 | 15,909 | 13.61 | 56,839 | 10.99 | 15,866 | 13.70 | 56,347 | 11.20 |
| General Expenses | 2,578 | 2.11 | 8,348 | 1.69 | 4,460 | 3.82 | 14,673 | 2.84 | 3,579 | 3.09 | 12,074 | 2.40 |
| Licences | 691 | 0.57 | 3,381 | 0.68 | 691 | 0.59 | 3,930 | 0.76 | 691 | 0.59 | 3,845 | 0.76 |
| Maintenance & Repairs | 5,148 | 4.22 | 22,707 | 4.60 | 8,323 | 7.11 | 26,932 | 5.21 | 5,122 | 4.43 | 23,119 | 4.59 |
| Power | 2,349 | 1.93 | 11,805 | 2.39 | 2,233 | 1.91 | 12,027 | 2.33 | 2,767 | 2.39 | 16,538 | 3.28 |
| Superannuation | 1,191 | 0.98 | 3,555 | 0.72 | 1,326 | 1.13 | 3,960 | 0.76 | 1,611 | 1.39 | 4,814 | 0.97 |
| Total Expenditure | 27,067 | 22.21 | 104,014 | 21.06 | 32,942 | 28.17 | 118,361 | 22.89 | 29,636 | 25.59 | 116,737 | 23.20 |
| Through Running Adjust. | - | - | 3 | | - | - | 21 | 0.01 | - | - | - | - |
| Total Income | 33,645 | 27.61 | 105,241 | 21.31 | 34,252 | 29.29 | 112,664 | 21.79 | 35,009 | 30.23 | 109,345 | 21.73 |
| GROSS SURPLUS (+) or DEFICIT (-) | +6,578 | +5.40 | +1,230 | +0.25 | +1,310 | +1.12 | -5,676 | -1.09 | +5,373 | +4.64 | -7,392 | -1.47 |
| Discounts & Interest rcvd | +11 | 0.01 | +360 | 0.07 | +75 | +0.06 | +365 | 0.07 | +41 | 0.04 | +361 | 0.07 |
| Interest on Debt | -257 | -0.22 | -630 | -0.13 | -240 | -0.21 | 1,007 | -0.19 | -235 | -0.20 | -1,287 | -0.26 |
| Loan Repayment | -1,202 | -1.01 | -2,157 | -0.44 | -1,261 | -1.08 | 5,815 | -1.12 | -1,283 | -1.11 | -7,012 | -1.39 |
| Others | -50 | -0.04 | -359 | -0.04 | -139 | -0.12 | 807 | -0.16 | -213 | -0.18 | -1,209 | -0.24 |
| NET SURPLUS (+) or DEFICIT (-) | +5,080 | 4.27 | -1,556 | -0.29 | -255 | -0.23 | -12,940 | -2.49 | +3,683 | 3.18 | -16,539 | -3.29 |

| | 1951–52 | | | | 1952–53 | | | | 1953–54 | | | |
|---|---|---|---|---|---|---|---|---|---|---|---|---|
| | TROLLEYBUSES | | MOTORBUSES | | TROLLEYBUSES | | MOTORBUSES | | TROLLEYBUSES | | MOTORBUSES | |
| | Amount | Per Mile | Amount | Per Mile | Amount | Per Mile | Amount | Per Mile | Amount | Per Mile | Amount | Per Mile |
| Traffic Expenses | 16,506 | 14.42 | 60,492 | 11.92 | 17,511 | 15.73 | 62,723 | 12.77 | 17,279 | 15.98 | 65,911 | 13.55 |
| General Expenses | 4,652 | 4.06 | 12,007 | 2.36 | 4,672 | 4.20 | 11,990 | 2.44 | 3,607 | 3.34 | 10,251 | 2.10 |
| Licences | 691 | 0.61 | 3,725 | 0.73 | 691 | 0.62 | 3,814 | 0.78 | 671 | 0.62 | 3,756 | 0.77 |
| Maintenance & Repairs | 6,888 | 6.02 | 24,383 | 4.80 | 5,937 | 5.33 | 27,337 | 5.57 | 6,904 | 6.38 | 26,719 | 5.49 |
| Power | 3,045 | 2.66 | 20,930 | 4.12 | 2,444 | 2.20 | 24,685 | 5.03 | 2,577 | 2.38 | 22,683 | 4.66 |
| Superannuation | 1,448 | 1.26 | 4,323 | 0.86 | 1,516 | 1.36 | 4,528 | 0.92 | 2,166 | 2.00 | 8,339 | 1.71 |
| Total Expenditure | 33,230 | 29.03 | 125,860 | 24.79 | 32,771 | 29.44 | 135,077 | 27.51 | 33,204 | 30.70 | 137,659 | 28.28 |
| Through Running Adjust. | - | - | 94 | 0.02 | - | - | 113 | 0.02 | - | - | - | - |
| Total Income | 36,632 | 32.00 | 122,434 | 24.11 | 38,087 | 34.22 | 136,778 | 27.85 | 38,938 | 36.00 | 149,419 | 30.7 |
| GROSS SURPLUS (+) or DEFICIT (-) | +3,402 | +2.97 | -3,332 | -0.66 | +5,316 | 4.78 | +1,588 | +0.32 | +5,734 | +5.30 | +11,760 | 2.42 |
| Interest | 221 | 0.19 | 1,269 | 0.25 | 188 | 0.17 | 1,087 | 0.22 | 141 | 0.13 | 918 | 0.19 |
| Loan Repayment | 1,301 | 1.14 | 8,184 | 1.61 | 1,296 | 1.17 | 8,632 | 1.75 | 1,266 | 1.17 | 9,081 | 1.87 |
| Others | 191 | 0.17 | 749 | 0.15 | 167 | 0.15 | 639 | 0.13 | 192 | 0.17 | 1,003 | 0.20 |
| NET SURPLUS (+) or DEFICIT (-) | +1,689 | +1.47 | 13,534 | -2.67 | +3,665 | +3.29 | -8,770 | -1.78 | +4,135 | +3.83 | +758 | 0.16 |

| | 1954–55 TROLLEYBUSES Amount | Per Mile | 1954–55 MOTORBUSES Amount | Per Mile | 1955–56 TROLLEYBUSES Amount | Per Mile | 1955–56 MOTORBUSES Amount | Per Mile | 1956–57 TROLLEYBUSES Amount | Per Mile | 1956–57 MOTORBUSES Amount | Per Mile |
|---|---|---|---|---|---|---|---|---|---|---|---|---|
| Traffic Expenses | 18,218 | 16.65 | 68,621 | 14.55 | 19,162 | 18.86 | 74,690 | 15.49 | 17,353 | 21.90 | 79,706 | 16.12 |
| General Expenses | 3,601 | 3.29 | 10,085 | 2.14 | 3,738 | 3.68 | 11,156 | 2.31 | 2,698 | 3.40 | 13,160 | 2.66 |
| Licences | 691 | 0.63 | 3,728 | 0.79 | 648 | 0.64 | 4,011 | 0.83 | 432 | 0.54 | 4,273 | 0.86 |
| Maintenance & Repairs | 6,255 | 5.72 | 28,737 | 6.09 | 5,577 | 5.49 | 28,112 | 5.84 | 3,262 | 4.11 | 30,228 | 6.11 |
| Power | 2,658 | 2.43 | 20,692 | 4.39 | 2,635 | 2.59 | 20,933 | 4.34 | 2,401 | 3.03 | 23,433 | 4.74 |
| Superannuation | 2,358 | 2.16 | 9,418 | 1.99 | 2,439 | 2.40 | 9,779 | 2.03 | 2,158 | 2.72 | 10,383 | 2.10 |
| Total Expenditure | 33,781 | 30.88 | 141,281 | 29.95 | 34,199 | 33.66 | 148,681 | 30.84 | 28,304 | 35.70 | 161,183 | 32.59 |
| Through Running Adjust. | - | - | - | - | - | - | 99 | 0.02 | - | - | 196 | 0.04 |
| Total Income | 38,558 | 35.24 | 142,101 | 30.12 | 38,477 | 37.87 | 154,245 | 32.00 | 31,718 | 39.98 | 174,480 | 35.28 |
| GROSS SURPLUS (+) or DEFICIT (-) | +4,777 | +4.36 | +820 | +0.17 | +4,278 | 4.21 | +5,465 | 1.14 | +3,414 | +4.28 | +13,493 | +2.73 |
| Interest | 129 | 0.12 | 785 | 0.16 | 101 | 0.10 | 670 | 0.14 | 53 | 0.07 | 1,422 | 0.29 |
| Loan Repayment | 1,330 | 1.22 | 9,179 | 1.95 | 478 | 0.47 | 6,051 | 1.26 | 155 | 0.20 | 8,257 | 1.67 |
| Others | 84 | 0.07 | 558 | 0.12 | 31 | 0.03 | 397 | 0.08 | 28 | 0.03 | 390 | 0.08 |
| NET SURPLUS (+) or DEFICIT (-) | +3,234 | +2.95 | -9,702 | -2.06 | +3,668 | +3.61 | -1,653 | -0.34 | +3,178 | 3.98 | +3,424 | +0.69 |

Trolleybus figures for 10 months ending 31 January 1957.
Motorbus figures for 12 months ending 31 March 1957

213

## COMPARISON OF REVENUE MILES RUN

| Year | Trolleybus | Motorbus | Tram | Total |
|---|---|---|---|---|
| 1930–31 | Not known | Not known | Not known | |
| 1931–32 | 295,460 | Not known | Not known | |
| 1932–33 | 267,510 | Not known | - | |
| 1933–34 | 265,935 | Not known | - | |
| 1934–35 | 266,657 | Not known | - | |
| 1935–36 | 269,654 | Not known | - | |
| 1936–37 | Not known | Not known | - | |
| 1937–38 | 276,260 | Not known | - | |
| 1938–39 | 267,994 | Not known | - | |
| 1939–40 | 274,208 | Not known | - | |
| 1940–41 | Not known | Not known | - | |
| 1941–42 | 293,444 | Not known | - | |
| 1942–43 | 284,432 | Not known | - | |
| 1943–44 | 282,534 | Not known | - | |
| 1944–45 | 255,933 | Not known | - | |
| 1945–46 | 263,650 | Not known | - | |
| 1946–47 | 271,215 | 975,574 | - | 1,246,789 |
| 1947–48 | 282,873 | 1,136,808 | - | 1,419,681 |
| 1948–49 | 285,374 | 1,185,186 | - | 1,470,560 |
| 1949–50 | 280,613 | 1,241,117 | - | 1,521,730 |
| 1950–51 | 277,954 | 1,207,646 | - | 1,485,600 |
| 1951–52 | 274,724 | 1,218,734 | - | 1,493,458 |
| 1952–53 | 267,124 | 1,178,588 | - | 1,445,712 |
| 1953–54 | 259,537 | 1,168,191 | - | 1,427,728 |
| 1954–55 | 262,592 | 1,131,837 | - | 1,394,429 |
| 1955–56 | 243,838 | 1,156,809 | - | 1,400,647 |
| 1956–57 | 190,429 | 1,186,903 | - | 1,377,332 |

Trolleybus figures for 10 months ending 31 January 1957.
Motorbus figures for 12 months ending 31 March 1957.

## LUBRICATION

TROLLEY BUSES
Number of nipple positions on Trolley Buses = 95 also the Steering Column, Differentials, Compressor Cylinder, Sump, Springs and Brake Pins have to be oiled.

*Daily:*
Rear Differentials
Spring Trunnions
Carden shaft
Axle Pivots
Air Compressor Check

Steering Box
Front Brake Shafts
Brake cam shafts
Shaft Differentials when overhauling
Change oil
Universal joints when necessary

*Weekly:*
Rear Brake shafts
Steering Ball Ends
Footbrake pedals
Brake shoe pins
Spring shackles
Air Cylinders
Hand Brake levers

*Monthly:*
Wheel Bearings
Air Compressor change oil
Springs

*Three Months:*
Axle Pivot pins
Armature and Compressor.

## TURNOUT OF VEHICLES FOR MONDAY TO FRIDAYS SERVICE:

| Time Out | Time In | Hours in service | Number of vehicles in service |
|---|---|---|---|
| **TROLLEY BUSES** | | | |
| 4.35 am | 12.10 am | 19½ | |
| 4.50 am | 11.35 pm | 18¾ | |
| 5.05 am | 11.55 pm | 18¾ | } 4 |
| 5.30 am | 7.10 am | 1¾ | |
| 7.45 am | 11.25 pm | 15¾ | |
| 7.53 am | 10.33 am | 2½ | |
| 8.02 am | 11.45 pm | 15¾ | } 5 |
| 8.15 am | 10.08 am | 2 | |
| 8.20 am | 11.05 pm | 14¾ | |
| 11.58 am | 7.30 pm | 7½ | |
| 12.22 pm | 7.54 pm | 7½ | |
| **MOTORBUSES** | | | |
| 4.55 am | 7.30 am | 2½ | } 2 |
| 5.05 am | 7.00 am | 2 | |
| 7.35 am | 11.40 pm | 16 | |
| 7.50 am | 11.30 pm | 15¾ | |
| 8.12 am | 9.27 am | 1¼ | } 4 |
| 8.20 am | 11.15 pm | 15 | |
| 11.53 am | 7.25 pm | 7½ | |
| **TRAMCARS** | | | |
| 4.45 am | 7.15 am | 2½ | |
| 5.00 am | 12.10 am | 19¼ | } 3 |
| 5.15 am | 11.20 pm | 18 | |
| 7.40 am | 11.50 pm | 16¼ | |
| 1.50 pm | 3.20 pm | 2½ | |
| 2.15 pm | 11.35 pm | 9¼ | |
| 7.27 pm | 11.25 pm | 5 | |

## TURNOUT OF VEHICLES FOR SATURDAY SERVICE:

| Time Out | Time In | Hours in service | Number of vehicles in service |
|---|---|---|---|
| **TROLLEY BUSES** | | | |
| 4.35 am | 11.30 pm | 19 | |
| 4.50 am | 11.50 pm | 19 | |
| 5.05 am | 12.00 pm | 19 | } 4 |
| 5.30 am | 7.10 am | 1¾ | |
| 7.45 am | 11.30 pm | 15¾ | |
| 7.53 am | 10.33 am | 2½ | |
| 8.02 am | 12.00 pm | 16 | } 5 |
| 8.15 am | 10.08 am | 2 | |
| 8.20 am | 12.20 pm | 16 | |
| 11.58 am | 11.00 pm | 7½ | |
| 12.22 pm | 12.10 pm | 11¼ | |
| 5.00 pm | 11.10 pm | 6¾ | |
| **MOTORBUSES** | | | |
| 4.55 am | 7.30 am | 2½ | } 2 |
| 5.05 am | 7.00 am | 2 | |
| 7.35 am | 11.30 pm | 16 | |
| 7.50 am | 11.25 pm | 15¾ | |
| 8.12 am | 9.27 am | 1¼ | } 5 |
| 8.20 am | 11.30 pm | 15¼ | |
| 11.53 am | 11.40 pm | 15¾ | |
| 5.25 pm | 11.40 pm | 6¼ | } 2 |
| 5.27 pm | 11.50 pm | 6¾ | |
| **TRAMCARS** | | | |
| 4.45 am | 7.15 am | 2½ | |
| 5.00 am | 12.10 am | 19¼ | } 3 |
| 5.15 am | 11.30 pm | 18¼ | |
| 7.40 am | 11.50 pm | 16¼ | |
| 1.50 pm | 3.20 pm | 2½ | |
| 2.15 pm | 12.15 pm | 10 | |
| 5.02 pm | 11.40 pm | 6¾ | |
| 5.20 pm | 11.15 pm | 6 | |

# Municipal Trolleybus Records

## SPECIALLY COMPILED BY THE TRANSPORT WORLD

| NAME | Year Ended 1939 | Total Capital Outlay to date £ | Total Operating Income £ | Total Operating Expenses £ | Percentage of Working Expenses To Gross Receipts % | Gross Profit £ | Net Surplus or Deficit £ | Provision for Renewals £ | Total Bus Miles Run | Total Passengers Carried | Passengers per Bus Mile | Average Revenue per Bus Mile Total d. | Traffic d. | Average Fare Charged per Mile d. |
|---|---|---|---|---|---|---|---|---|---|---|---|---|---|---|
| Ashton-u-Lyne... | Mar. 31 | 54,787 | 31,667 | 22,947 | 72·46 | 8,720 | 3,391 | — | 435,457 | 6,342,849 | 14·56 | 17·453 | 17·421 | 1·19 |
| Belfast ... | Mar. 31 | 44,440 | 40,070 | 24,663 | 61·55 | 15,407 | 9,847 | — | 495,284 | 8,188,422 | 16·53 | 19·42 | 19·41 | 0·66 |
| Birmingham ... | Mar. 31 | 201,890a | 154,171 | 130,741 | 84·8 | 23,430 | 3,201 | — | 2,202,796 | 26,268,789 | 11·9 | 16·797 | 16·797 | 0·72 |
| Bournemouth ... | Mar. 31 | 1,344,943b | 182,618 | 132,629 | 72·62 | 49,989 | 8,337 | — | 2,917,087 | 27,390,558 | 9·39 | 15·02 | 14·78 | 1·15 |
| Bradford ... | Mar. 31 | 359,467 | 260,881 | 222,710 | 85·368 | 38,171 | 2,389 | — | 3,976,205 | 42,520,051 | 11·0 | — | — | — |
| Cleethorpes ... | Mar. 31 | 83,290 | 26,034 | 25,361 | 68·7 | 7,470 | 673 | — | 408.615 | 5,071,368 | 12·4 | 15·29 | 15·03 | 0·71 |
| Darlington ... | Mar. 31 | 217,298c | 77,770 | 61,589 | 79·2 | 16,245 | 4,982 | — | 1,734,537 | 18,073,397 | 10·4 | 10·7 | 10·6 | 0·57 |
| Derby ... | Mar. 31 | 323,582 | 172,564 | 134,240 | 77·79 | 38,325 | 12,308 | 8,503 | 2,599,217 | 29,684,093 | 11·420 | 15·934 | 15·777 | 0·88 |
| Doncaster ... | Mar. 31 | 172,821 | 86,106 | 53,602 | 62·25 | 32,503 | 16,863 | — | — | 14,995 102 | — | 16·039 | 15·908 | — |
| Grimsby ... | Mar. 31 | 47,798 | 41,610 | 29,028 | 69·76 | 12,582 | 8,666 | — | 627,315 | 9,501,332 | 15·1 | 15·919 | 15·891 | 1·59 |
| Huddersfield ... | Mar. 31 | 457,431 | 196,371 | 150,648 | 76·72 | 4,573 | 34,996 | 34,996 | — | 35,898.634 | — | — | — | — |
| Hull ... | Mar. 31 | 107,460 | 65,334 | 50,328 | 76·61 | 15,366 | 5,922 | — | 1,066,859 | 11,725,657 | 10·99 | 14·78 | 14·70 | 0·91 |
| Ipswich ... | Mar. 31 | 238.202 | 111,478 | 92,054 | 82·58 | 19,424 | 265 | — | 2,331,187 | 18,973,845 | 8·14 | 11·477 | 11·248 | 0·994 |
| Maidstone ... | Mar. 31 | 49,141 | 32,912 | 21,868 | 66·71 | 10,928 | 5,644 | 5,644 | 429,055 | 5,515,463 | 12·863 | 18·410 | 17·965 | 1·217 |
| Manchester ... | Mar. 31 | 279,564 | 135,155 | 100,063 | 75·0 | 35,092 | 5,857 | 7,454 | 1,866,115 | 23,708,953 | 12·70 | 17·382 | 17·150 | 0·693 |
| Newcastle ... | Mar. 31 | 287,967 | 223,273 | 137,263 | 61·48 | 86,009 | 65,318 | 24,964 | 2,866,165 | 39,281,180 | 13·71 | 18·696 | 18·656 | 0·674 |
| Nottingham ... | Mar. 31 | 457,654 | 254,510 | 212,903 | 83·652 | 41,607 | 4,837 | 4,837 | 3,786,398 | 47,779,928 | 12·619 | 16·132 | 15·923 | 0·765 |
| Pontypridd ... | Mar. 31 | 35,574 | 14,261 | 12,264 | 83·20 | 1,997 | −361 | — | 268,033 | 2,260,118 | 8·43 | 12·77 | 12·70 | 1·311 |
| Portsmouth ... | Mar. 31 | 360,543 | 166,439 | 131,845 | 79·0 | 34,594 | 4,528 | — | 2,520,907 | 27,821,366 | 11·036 | 15·845 | 15·696 | 0·988 |
| Reading... | Mar. 31 | 94,500 | 9,058 | 7,957 | 87·9 | 1,101 | 1,217 | — | 149,564 | 2,048,424 | 13·70 | 14·535 | 14·213 | 1·214 |
| Rotherham ... | Mar. 31 | 184,969 | 92,777 | 62,162 | 67·1 | 30,159 | 20,841 | 20,841 | 1,851,506 | 16,125,308 | 8·7 | 12·00 | 11·96 | — |
| St. Helens ... | Mar. 31 | 163,575 | 115,785 | 82,772 | 71·87 | 33,012 | 18,099 | 11,250 | 1,993,421 | 17,354,680 | 8·68 | 14·00 | 14·87 | 1·10 |
| Southend ... | Mar. 31 | 85,090 | 40,920 | 36,794 | 89·919 | 4,126 | 5,231 | — | 750.052 | 7,514,397 | 10·018 | 13·094 | 12·995 | 1·168 |
| South Shields ... | Mar. 31 | 135,200 | 71,399 | 54,916 | 76·91 | 16,483 | 5.842 | — | 1,238,249 | 15,390,269 | 12·0 | 13·838 | 13·804 | 0·89 |
| Tees-Side ... | Mar. 31 | | 21,087 | 16,693 | 79·1 | 4,394 | | — | 460,222 | 3,409,814 | 7·41 | 10·99 | 10·95 | 0·80 |
| Walsall ... | Mar. 31 | 100,063 | 47,741 | 32,718 | 68·532 | 14,992 | 5,558 | — | 702,753 | 7,822,842 | 11·132 | 16·303 | 16·206 | 1·023 |
| W. Hartlepool ... | Mar. 31 | 66,885 | 32,278 | 25,548 | 79·0 | 6,730 | 378 | — | 556,024 | 5,650,277 | 10·02 | 13·93 | 13·82 | 1·07 |
| Wolverhampton | Mar. 31 | 686,508 | 299,992 | 220,922 | 73·64 | 79,070 | — | — | 4,757,610 | 51,300,576 | — | 15·133 | 15·071 | 0·932 |

| NAME | Average Fare Paid per Passenger d. | Average Distance of 1d. Fare Miles | Operating Expenses per Bus Mile — Traffic d. | General d. | Licences d. | Repairs and Maintenance d. | Power d. | Miscellaneous d. | Total d. | Length of Route miles | Average Miles per Day per Bus | Average Speed per Hour miles | Trolleybuses Number In Use Daily | Number In Stock | Average Seating Capacity |
|---|---|---|---|---|---|---|---|---|---|---|---|---|---|---|---|
| Ashton-u-Lyne... | 1·19 | 0·70 | 5·366 | 2·025 | 0·454 | 2·779 | 2·024 | — | 12·648 | 3 | 190 | 9·49 | 5 | 7D | 60 |
| Belfast ... | 1·17 | 1·15 | 6·88 | 0·98 | 0·89 | 1·55 | 1·65 | — | 11·95 | 3·3 | 146·6 | 8·89 | 13 | 14D | 68 |
| Birmingham ... | 1·408 | 1·33 | 6·279 | 1·141 | 0·798 | 3·488 | 2·113 | 0·425 | 14·244 | 10·2 | 96·80 | 9·8 | 74 | 78D | 55·8 |
| Bournemouth ... | 1·58 | 0·87 | 5·36 | 1·43 | 0·60 | 1·48 | 2·04 | — | 10·91 | 33·00 | 127 | 10·40 | 61 | 1S 103D | 56 |
| Bradford ... | — | 0·97 | | | | | | | | 34·716 | 131 | 10·52 | 83 | 18S 117D | 54 |
| Cleethorpes ... | 1·21 | 0·81 | 4·70 | 1·35 | 0·63 | 1·20 | 1·56 | 1·06 | 10·50 | 2·24 | 86·12 | 9·23 | 11 | 13D | 56 |
| Darlington ... | 1·03 | 1·167 | 5·365 | 1·020 | — | 1·185 | 0·854 | — | 8·424 | 11·38 | 104·3 | 8·74 | 46 | 51S | 32 |
| Derby ... | 1·381 | 0·85 | 5·823 | 1·165 | 0·680 | 2·860 | 1·486 | 0·381 | 12·395 | 24·48 | 146 | 8·68 | 49 | 86D | 55·8 |
| Doncaster ... | | | 4·537 | 1·305 | 0·690 | 1·467 | 1·632 | 0·354 | 9·984 | 12·97 | | 9·20 | 30 | 44D | 60 |
| Grimsby ... | 1·048 | 1·05 | 5·852 | 1·991 | 0·016 | 1·706 | 1·540 | — | 11·105 | 3·47 | 123 | 9·23 | 14 | 7S 10D | 47 |
| Huddersfield ... | | | | | | | | | | 31·28 | — | 10·41 | 103 | 140D | 64 |
| Hull ... | 1·34 | 0·88 | 5·78 | 1·16 | 0·70 | 1·77 | 1·66 | 0·25 | 11·32 | 7·89 | 90 | 9·36 | 35 | 46D | 54 |
| Ipswich ... | 1·376 | 0·90 | 5·429 | 1·050 | 0·450 | 1·601 | 0·947 | — | 9·477 | 21·62 | 123·02 | 9·68 | 46 | 30S 15D | 40·3 |
| Maidstone ... | 1·394 | 0·663 | 5·093 | 2·246 | 0·733 | 2·360 | 1·801 | 0·015 | 12·248 | 5·005 | 98·16 | 8·763 | 13 | 15D | 57 |
| Manchester ... | 1·35 | 1·442 | 6·999 | 1·522 | 0·820 | 1·592 | 1·538 | 0·398 | 12·869 | 17 | 85 | 10·3 | 60 | 76 | 62 |
| Newcastle ... | 1·361 | 1·01 | 6·143 | 0·768 | 0·704 | 1·952 | 1·927 | — | 11·494 | 22·2 | 98 | 10·08 | 97 | 101D | 60 |
| Nottingham ... | 1·2467 | 1·087 | 6·532 | 2·254 | 0·751 | 1·865 | 2·093 | — | 13·495 | 23·20 | 104 | 8·550 | 100 | 125D | 62·68 |
| Pontypridd ... | 1·505 | 0·48 | 5·21 | 0·77 | 0·48 | 2·33 | 1·67 | 0·06 | 10·52 | 3·3 | 138 | 9·9 | 6 | 7S 2D | 38·1 |
| Portsmouth ... | 1·436 | 0·92 | 6·373 | 1·594 | 0·774 | 1·873 | 1·469 | 0·467 | 12·552 | 19·33 | 69 | 8·476 | 64 | 100D | 51·92 |
| Reading... | 1·04 | 0·93 | 5·876 | 1·407 | 0·722 | 1·880 | 1·572 | 1·311 | d12·768 | 1·79 | 102 | 7·4 | 4 | 6D | 51 |
| Rotherham ... | 1·38 | — | 3·62 | 1·01 | 0·44 | 1·40 | 1·53 | — | 8·00 | 20·43 | 127 | 11·21 | 40 | 55S | 36 |
| St. Helens ... | 1·59 | 0·94 | 4·921 | 1·062 | 0·505 | 1·706 | 1·642 | 0·198 | 9·965 | 19·20 | 140 | 9·80 | 39 | 5S 50D | 49 |
| Southend ... | 1·297 | 0·707 | 5·608 | 0·944 | 0·497 | 2·489 | 2·107 | 0·129 | 11·774 | 5·093 | 144·959 | | 14·176 | 20D | 53·5 |
| South Shields ... | 1·097 | 1·000 | 5·306 | 1·550 | 0·568 | 1·156 | 2·057 | 0·007 | 10·644 | 10·37 | 136 | 9·41 | 25 | 35D | 55 |
| Tees-Side ... | 1·47 | 0·75 | 4·65 | 1·08 | 0·44 | 1·45 | 1·08 | — | 8·70 | 5·1 | 97 | 10·50 | 13 | 13S | 32 |
| Walsall ... | 1·456 | 0·94 | 5·006 | 1·714 | 0·691 | 1·975 | 1·787 | — | 11·173 | 8·930 | 129 | 10·877 | 15 | 21D | 60 |
| W. Hartlepool ... | 1·36 | 0·89 | 5·23 | 1·78 | 0·70 | 1·41 | 1·90 | — | 11·02 | 6·29 | 80 | 8·19 | 19 | 7S 14D | 46 |
| Wolverhampton | 1·406 | — | 5·422 | 1·451 | 0·586 | 2·296 | 1·389 | — | 11·144 | 47·255 | 121 | 9·312 | 108 | 124 | |

(a) Includes £36,962 Assets not purchased from Loans.  (b) Including £769,975 for tramways superseded.  (c) Includes superseded tramways.
(d) Includes .728d. for driving tuition.  (e) Including Workmen's Returns.